COSMOS · CREATOR
AND
HUMAN DESTINY

*Answering Darwin,
Dawkins,* AND THE *New Atheists*

DAVE HUNT

BEND, OREGON

COSMOS, CREATOR
AND HUMAN DESTINY:

Answering Darwin, Dawkins, and the New Atheists

Published by The Berean Call
Copyright © 2010 by Dave Hunt

ISBN 978-1-928660-64-4

Library of Congress Control Number: 2010901985

Unless otherwise indicated, Scripture quotations are from
The Holy Bible, King James Version (KJV)

The Berean Call
PO Box 7019
Bend, Oregon, 97708-7019

PRINTED IN THE UNITED STATES OF AMERICA

IN APPRECIATION

Barbara Romine, my managing editor, whose enthusiasm for the subject infused the book with vitality and whose patient, faithful, and insightful suggestions as I dictated added much to *Cosmos'* readability.

Sally Oppliger, who proofread meticulously and checked the accuracy of the hundreds of footnotes.

Mark Dinsmore, whose insight and artistry captured the essence of the book's content.

Ruth, my wife, who shared the vision for this book, gave invaluable counsel, and added the final editing touches.

CONTENTS

PREFACE

Anyone who sets out with an honest heart, an inquiring mind, and a sincere desire to find answers to the most important questions one can face in life will recognize a significant few that must be given priority. Does God exist? What is the origin of the universe and of the life found in such abundance on our tiny planet? What is life and what is its purpose?

Another vital question is whether or not our vast universe of astonishing complexity and order is all the result of a giant explosion commonly called "The Big Bang." This theory is a radical departure from the conclusion that had been reached by the theistic founders of modern science. The undeniable order that they had observed caused them to look for laws that must govern the phenomena. Having discovered these laws, they concluded that the universe had been created by a "God of order."

Thus was laid the theistic foundation of modern science, but that foundation is no longer accepted. Atheists have taken over and now claim the sole right to speak for science. They cannot deny the order evident everywhere but grudgingly refer to it as the "appearance" of order. Appearance? Such an oft-repeated half-admission ought to be an embarrassment to legitimate scientists.

It was principally two men, Charles Darwin and Sigmund Freud, who attempted to quash any possibility that the God of the theists portrayed in the Bible could be the Creator. No creator was needed.

The universe, through what became known as evolution and natural selection, had appeared out of nowhere, arranged itself into order, and had mysteriously transformed dead chemicals into living entities—a thesis that has yet to be supported by observation.

Countless books have been written on both sides of what has become a hotly contested issue. Anyone who studies even a fraction of these volumes must face at least three undeniable facts: 1) the disagreements are endless; 2) they are irreconcilable, and 3) they mostly lead nowhere.

Beginning with Darwin himself, atheists have left a plethora of false promises. Darwin's first book was titled *The Origin of Species*, yet even his staunchest admirers admit that in spite of many pages filled with many words, Darwin never explained the origin of any species. Nor has any atheist yet succeeded in doing so. In spite of this undeniable fact, Darwin's admirers continue to grow in numbers as desperate minds try by some means to support his original thesis.

One of today's most highly acclaimed supporters of Darwin is Daniel Dennett. Following in the tradition established by Darwin, Dennett, too, writes books that make promises that they do not fulfill. One of his volumes is titled *Consciousness Explained*. When it was published in 1991, the *New York Times* hailed it as "one of the ten best books of the year."

Let's see how Dennett explains "consciousness." After listing "great mysteries that remain," such as "the origin of the universe, the mystery of life and reproduction, the mystery of the design found in nature, the mysteries of time, space, and gravity," Dennett admits that these remain not only "areas of scientific ignorance but of utter bafflement and wonder."

Dennett also confesses that he and his fellow atheists do not "yet have the final answers to any of the questions of cosmology and particle physics, molecular genetics, and evolutionary theory...." Nevertheless, he declares, "we do know how to think about them...." As for consciousness, instead of fulfilling his promise to explain it, Dennett admits "we are still in a terrible muddle.... [It's] a topic that often leaves even the most sophisticated thinkers tongue-tied and confused."

This "explanation of consciousness," which occurs in the first two chapters of *Consciousness Explained*, is the closest Dennett comes, in the entire 468-page volume, to living up to the promise of the title. From beginning to end, no explanation of consciousness can be found anywhere in this highly acclaimed volume.

Today's leading atheist, Richard Dawkins, has a standard response when faced by critics who point out the fact that he and his fellow atheists don't even come close to explaining the origin of energy, matter, a single cell, DNA that defines life, or life itself. Almost mantra-like, with boyish enthusiasm he repeats, "We're working on that." We have yet to see any evidence that their "working on that" has produced any substantive results.

Dawkins leads a group that calls itself "The New Atheists." They refer to themselves as "the brights," thus relegating theists to the status of "dimwits." Christopher Hitchens, looked to by the brights as one of their brightest, declared in a debate with former Oxford professor Alister McGrath, a theist, "I've just made a lot of money on a God-bashing book!"

In *Cosmos, Creator, and Human Destiny*, we intend to show that we dimwits are not intimidated by the "brights," however dramatic their present success among credulous readers might be. Read on!

But it is also possible that we are really alone in the universe. . . .

—RICHARD DAWKINS, WALL STREET JOURNAL

Certainly, the confessed faith in God even of eminent scientists does not seem to have any modulating effect on the strident tones used by [leading atheists] as they orchestrate their war against God in the name of science. . . . They are convinced . . . that the war is over and science has gained the final victory. The world simply needs to be informed that, to echo Nietzche, "God is dead, and science has buried him."

—JOHN LENNOX, IN GOD'S UNDERTAKER, 17

In Dec. 2008, an atheist organization kicked off an ad campaign in Washington, D.C., that suggests believing in humanism is a better alternative for Christmas enthusiasts than believing in God. Sponsored by the American Humanist Association (AHA), ads reading: "Why believe in a god? Just be good for goodness' sake" began appearing Tuesday on buses in the nation's capital. The ads, which will run through December, are a play on the lyrics from the famous Christmas song: "Santa Claus is Coming to Town." Earlier this year, humanist ads popped up outside New York City and Philadelphia, which read: "Don't believe in God? You are not alone" while in Europe, a similar campaign supported by the British Humanist Association and best-selling atheist author Richard Dawkins was launched by a 28-year-old comedy writer. Ads from that campaign reading: "There's probably no God. Now stop worrying and enjoy your life," will begin appearing on London buses in January.

—WWW.FOXNEWS.COM/STORY/0,2933,450445,00.HTML

Science and religion cannot be reconciled, and humanity should begin to appreciate the power of its child, and to beat off all attempts at compromise. Religion has failed, and its failure [should be] exposed. Science...should be acknowledged king.

—ATHEIST PETER ATKINS,
PROFESSOR OF CHEMISTRY, UNIVERSITY OF OXFORD

ONE

THE CHALLENGE
OF THE COSMOS

S PACE HAS BEEN CALLED "the last frontier," and its exploration the greatest challenge faced by mankind in its history. Our astronauts deserve our sincerest admiration and we should never diminish their great accomplishments to date. The simple fact, however, is that "great," with no matter what other superlatives one might add, will never be enough for physical craft (much less manned) to explore our own galaxy, the Milky Way, and certainly not to reach out to any of the other, perhaps as many as one trillion, galaxies in the universe.

It is conceivable that within a few thousand years (if they were available) man could thoroughly explore and learn everything there is to know about our own solar system. What, then, would have been achieved at great cost in time, effort, money, and, quite possibly, more lives? The obvious answer is almost *nothing* in comparison to the overall cosmos! This is not what space scientists are leading us to believe, nor is it what their supporters want to hear. It is, however, the uncomfortable truth.

The facts are simple. Estimates vary that there are from 100-500 billion other suns in our own galaxy, the Milky Way, and perhaps as many as one trillion other galaxies in the universe, many of them larger than ours. So, after learning all there is to know about our solar system, our descendants would have in their computers information from one-100-billionth of one-trillionth of a sample of the universe—statistically meaningless.

According to the cold mathematics, however, there is no way that mankind can ever "explore *space*." Space stretches from one side of the universe to the other, and we cannot tell where it begins or ends. The vastness of the cosmos mocks our most ingenious efforts, yet to admit that fact is a pill too bitter for our proud species to swallow— and especially for the "space" scientists.

In 1974, at great cost and with the prospect of even more billions of dollars being spent, we sent a series of radio messages to a globular cluster of stars known as M13. At the speed of radio waves, which is the speed of light, it will take 25,000 years for our message to reach M13 and another 25,000 years to receive a reply (if there is any intelligent life to send one).

Let me pose a simple question. Is it rational for our generation to invest large amounts of time and money in *anything* that couldn't pay off for another 50,000 years? Even writing those words seems un-American. There is a mystique surrounding our country's space program that places it in a realm approaching the sacrosanct.

WHEN WILL WE ADMIT THE TRUTH?

Without seeming to belittle our efforts, the truth is that the size of the cosmos is so far beyond our wildest imagination that our "space program" is like an ant climbing to the tip of a blade of grass. In a state of euphoria at its achievement, which is destined to be honored with headlines all over the ant world, it calls down to the other ants standing in awed admiration below, "I'm exploring the world!" The fact is, it hasn't even begun to explore the lawn, much less the town, county, state, country, and certainly not the world.

As great as our exploits have been in walking on the moon and sending robots to other planets in our solar system, they are far, far less an accomplishment relative to the cosmos than an ant's conquest of a blade of grass would be in proportion to exploring the world. This humbling reality is difficult to face, but it should become clear in the following pages, not only with regard to our space program but concerning much else now declared in the name of science and accepted as such by a trusting public.

The uncomfortable truth is that much time, effort, money, and many lives could be saved if we would face the reality of our severe limitations. Our achievements in exploring our solar system have been noteworthy, have greatly advanced our knowledge, and have brought many scientific benefits, but to imagine that we can to any purpose send manned spacecraft beyond those limits is to engage in costly self-delusion. Throughout this volume, we will not only look at scientific facts but will continually call readers back to simple common sense.

It is apparent that from presidents on down, we persist in pursuing a vain ambition. In a speech to NASA, based on the latest information he had been given and enthusiastically cheered by the space scientists and other insiders present on January 14, 2004, then-President George W. Bush declared:

> America has ventured forth into space . . . because the desire to explore is part of our character. . . . Our current programs and vehicles for exploring space have brought us far and they have served us well. . . . Robotic explorers have found evidence of water—a key ingredient for life—on Mars and on the moons of Jupiter. . . . The *Mars Exploration Rover Spirit* is searching for evidence of life beyond the Earth. . . .
>
> [We hope] to return to the moon by 2020, as the launching point for missions beyond. . . . With the experience and knowledge gained on the moon, we will then be ready to take the next steps of space exploration: human missions to Mars and to worlds beyond. (Applause)

Robotic missions will serve as trailblazers—the advanced guard to the unknown. Probes, landers and other vehicles of this kind continue to prove their worth, sending spectacular images and vast amounts of data back to Earth. Yet the human thirst for knowledge ultimately cannot be satisfied by even the most vivid pictures, or the most detailed measurements.

We need to see and examine and touch for ourselves. And only human beings are capable of adapting to the inevitable uncertainties posed by space travel.

As our knowledge improves, we'll develop new power generation propulsion, life support, and other systems that can support more distant travels. We do not know where this journey will end, yet we know this: human beings are headed into the cosmos. (Applause)

GROWING DOUBTS

Although "cosmos" is a general term with several meanings, it has never been used for our solar system alone. There is a clear distinction between space within our solar system and the cosmos, which includes it but is synonymous with all of space. That was certainly the way Carl Sagan used this term in his book *Cosmos* and his TV series of the same name. By saying that "human beings are headed into the cosmos," President Bush surely meant manned missions beyond our miniscule solar neighborhood. Yet the vastness of the cosmos that only begins far beyond our sun's gravitational pull makes this impossible—not *virtually* impossible, but *absolutely* impossible.

There are growing doubts among space scientists of the value of the planned lunar base and resistance in the Democrat-controlled administration about how to pay for the estimated $200 billion cost of building it. The highly touted International Space Station is widely considered to be "one of NASA's worst failures. The facility has not delivered on promised research benefits."[1] There are widespread fears that any lunar base would be more of the same.

As for "physically launching Mars missions from the moon, [that] would require an industrial aerospace infrastructure on the moon that would take decades or even centuries to develop. 'Sometime in (the) next 100 years we may have the construction base on the moon to do this,' said Lawrence Krauss, Case Western Reserve University physicist, who supports building a human presence on the moon over the long term."[2]

After more than thirty years of travel, *Voyager I* is just exiting our solar system. It is now in the heliosheath, the termination shock region between the solar system and interstellar space, a vast area where the Sun's influence gives way to the other bodies in the galaxy. If *Voyager I* is still functioning when it finally passes the heliopause, scientists will get their first direct measurements of conditions in the interstellar medium.

With our radio telescopes, we are sending verbal messages at the speed of light and hoping to receive a response from "somewhere" and "someone." Growing numbers of space scientists now concede that this is a pointless pursuit.

APPLAUDING MAN'S BLINDNESS

President Bush continued:

> This will be a great and unifying mission for NASA, and we know that you'll achieve it. . . . Achieving these goals requires a long-term commitment. We begin this venture knowing that space travel brings great risks. . . . Since the beginning of our space program, America has lost twenty-three astronauts, and one astronaut from an allied nation—men and women who believed in their mission and accepted the dangers. The *Columbia's* crews did not turn away from the challenge, and neither will we. (Applause)

[W]e choose to explore space because doing so improves our lives and lifts our national spirit. So let us continue the journey. May God bless. (Applause)

It was an inspiring speech delivered with conviction. A little reflection, however, reveals the simple truth, which the scientists in this audience must all have known: manned vehicles will never explore beyond our solar system. The vast distances in the cosmos that begin on that fringe present an impassable barrier to our grandest ambitions.

The president's declaration that man can never be satisfied with remote information provided by robots and cameras but that we must "see and examine and touch for ourselves" surely did not refer only to the planets and moons orbiting around our sun. His bold words could not help but inspire the general public. Although the space scientists present knew that manned missions accomplishing "hands-on" examination of anything beyond our solar system cannot and will not happen, they cheered the president (along with those ignorant of the truth). After all, "space exploration" is their profession and livelihood. To keep that going, both the public and our leaders must imagine that there are theoretically no limits to what our ingenuity can accomplish, when, in fact, there are—and serious ones.

THE UNDERLYING PURPOSE OF THE "SPACE PROGRAM"

Much, if not most, of the time, money, and effort being expended on the "space program" is driven by the speculative hope of proving that belief in "God" is an outdated hypothesis that is no longer needed to explain anything. Richard Dawkins, leading atheist and former Simonyi Professor of the Public Understanding of Science, Oxford University, has told us, "Darwin explained everything about life here on earth."

Everything about life? To put it mildly, this is a gross overstatement. In fact, Darwin didn't really explain anything about life. He didn't tell us what life is, how it originated, what its purpose is, why it ends, and whether that is all or whether there is something to follow. One of the missing elements in all of the discussions between evolutionists and creationists, which we will emphasize repeatedly in this book, is the fact that no one involved in this entire discussion—from Darwin to Dawkins, nor any of the creationists—ever talks about what is really important. What makes a human being what he or she is, and what distinguishes mankind from every other living creature? Darwin never talked about it, nor has Dawkins.

How *does* life originate? Those who, like atheists, reject the biblical claim that God created every living thing including man, have no other way of explaining how life began. All they can say is that it must have spontaneously come into existence. This is called spontaneous generation. About 150 years ago, Louis Pasteur had already proved that "spontaneous generation" was nothing but superstition. As a result, the law of biogenesis was firmly established as inviolable scientific fact. This law unequivocally declares that life comes only from life. Although atheists admit that they cannot challenge the validity of this established law, they object that unless there is at least one exception they are forced to acknowledge that life could have come about only through a supernatural act of creation. For atheists, this conclusion is of course unacceptable. They claim that there must have been millions of exceptions to this law that occurred all over the universe and that the origin of life on Earth was one of them. Of course, this is both irrational and unscientific.

Has it ever been shown that there is even one exception to the law of biogenesis anywhere in the cosmos? Never! Yet the only hope to salvage evolution would require millions, and possibly even billions, of exceptions to this law, evidenced by life appearing spontaneously all over the universe. It is, in fact, similarly irrational expectations that drive much of science. The search for extraterrestrial life certainly is a major motivation behind the space program. Likewise, the same hope provides the only rational basis for the long-standing and desperate search for a "missing link" that would bridge the unbridgeable chasm between animals and man.[3]

Could there be an exception to the law of gravity? Is not gravity a universal phenomenon? Would we dare to base our hope of eventually landing men on Mars upon the odd chance that there just might be an exception to one of the laws of physics or chemistry? Why is it legitimate to base evolution upon a supposed breach of the law of biogenesis, for which no example has ever been shown?

We are on a search for answers to what Richard Dawkins declares are man's most important questions. To anyone familiar with Dawkins or his cohorts, it comes as no surprise that the answers to such questions are all to be found in Darwinism and in Darwinism alone. For example, Dawkins declares that "Intelligent life on a planet comes of age when it first works out the reason for its own existence."[4] This is a philosophical question, not a scientific one. The consensus among scientists of all kinds is that science cannot answer the question *why* about anything. For example, why do we exist? Why do we find that question intriguing? Is this a quest that has been forced upon us by our genes? Whatever its origin, this quest has us searching the cosmos as far as we can reach to find a satisfactory answer. Stephen Hawking, Cambridge University mathematics professor and author of *A Brief History of Time*, sums it up in a single sentence: "Why does the universe go to all the bother of existing?"[5]

Dawkins himself admits that man has not reached this stage of knowledge. We will quote dozens of leading scientists who all confess that the answers to the ultimate questions are not to be found in science at all. For example, in contrast to Dawkins's frequent boast concerning the omniscience of Darwinism, consider the following realistic admission from Erwin Schrödinger, Nobel Prize-winning physicist and one of the architects of quantum mechanics. He was certainly at least as qualified to speak for today's science as Dawkins or any of his "new atheist" colleagues:

> The scientific picture of the real world around me is . . . ghastly silent about all . . . that is really near to our heart, that really matters to us. . . . It knows nothing of beautiful and ugly, good or bad, God and eternity. . . .

Whence came I and whither go I? That is the great unfathomable question, the same for every one of us. Science has no answer to it.[6]

The simple truth is that no scientist in any field has been able to improve upon the opening words of Genesis: "In the beginning God created the heaven and the earth." Of course atheists show nothing but contempt for this statement, a contempt for which they have no foundation in any scientific fact. For atheists, it is this rejection of God's existence that underlies the passion to probe space. It is likewise this same determination that compels atheistic scientists to dig feverishly all over our planet in order to disprove the biblical basis for the existence of the cosmos and the life within it. Ignoring the overwhelming evidence supporting the creation of everything by the biblical God, the atheist is determined to prove that life on Earth is not a unique event but that it has originated time and again all over the cosmos by purely natural means.

Dawkins goes on to say, "Living organisms had existed on earth without ever knowing why, for over three thousand million years before the truth finally dawned on one of them. His name was Charles Darwin . . . who first put together a coherent and tenable account of why we exist. Darwin made it possible to give a sensible answer to the curious child . . . [who asks] 'Why are people?' [i.e., What is man's purpose in life?]. . . . We no longer have to resort to superstition when faced with the deep problems: Is there a meaning to life? What are we for? What is man? After posing the last of these questions, the eminent zoologist G. G. Simpson put it thus: 'The point I want to make now is that all attempts to answer that question before 1859 are worthless and we would be better off if we ignored them completely.'"[7]

The truth is that the post-1859 attempts to answer this question are no better. Darwin didn't even claim to give us the answers we seek. The only place Dawkins knows to look is in Darwinism. In his rare attempts to provide answers from that source, Dawkins has nothing to offer and, in the process, contradicts himself repeatedly.

In spite of that fact, Darwin's followers will not confess the bankruptcy of his theories.

"AUNT MATILDA'S" CAKE

John Lennox, Professor of Mathematics at the University of Oxford, Fellow in Mathematics and Philosophy of Science, and Pastoral Advisor at Green Templeton College, has a very appealing way of explaining the question of a maker and the meaning and purpose upon which that maker alone could decide. He declares that everything that exists either grows or has been made. The purpose of anything that is made (from rocks on Earth to the farthest star or "black hole") and the use for which he designed them, resides only in the maker's mind. Without a Maker, the universe itself and everything in it, including man, is without meaning or purpose. Lennox illustrates this fact by proposing a chemical analysis by top scientists of a hypothetical cake that his Aunt Matilda has just made:

> The nutrition scientists can tell . . . the number of calories . . . and nutritional effect; the biochemists . . . the structure of the proteins, fats, etc. . . ; the chemists . . . the elements involved and their bonding; the physicists . . . the cake's . . . fundamental particles. . . ; the mathematicians . . . a set of elegant equations to describe the behavior of those particles . . . an exhaustive description of the cake. . . .
>
> Suppose I now ask the assembled group of experts . . . *why* was the cake made? All the nutrition scientists, biochemists, chemists, physicists and mathematicians in the world will not be able to answer the question . . . explaining . . . "why'" the cake was made.
>
> In fact, the only way we shall ever get an answer is if Aunt Matilda reveals it to us. But if she does not . . . no amount of scientific analysis will enlighten us.
>
> To say with Bertrand Russell that, because science cannot tell us why Aunt Matilda made the cake, we cannot

know why she made it, is patently false. All we have to do is
ask her. The claim that science is the only way to truth . . .
is unworthy of science itself.[8]

Everyone would recognize the futility of asking the cake why it exists.
But how is that any different from science trying to wring from the
universe the reason for its existence? Why not consult its Maker?

Stephen Hawking seems to agree with the point made in Lennox's
Aunt Matilda story, namely, that science cannot answer the question
of why there is a universe. As he asks of the universe, Hawking would
say, "Why does Aunt Matilda's cake go to all the bother of existing?"

What does this have to do with the space program? Many of the
scientists involved are sound Christians. The last thing they would
give up is their confidence in the God of the Bible as the Creator
of the universe. Nevertheless, Christians are partners in an endeavor
that, if successful, leads to the atheistic conclusion, so often expressed
by Dawkins and the other New Atheists, that God is not needed to
explain anything in the cosmos. Of course, what is commonly called
the "death of God" necessitates a resurrection of Darwin. Tragically,
this exaltation of Charles Darwin to almost godlike status has cost us
a great deal in time, effort, money, and lives, and continues to do so,
with disappointing results.

THE IMPOSSIBLE DREAM LIVES ON

On November 30, 2006, Stephen Hawking was honored with the
British Royal Society's highest award for scientific achievement. First
awarded in 1731, recipients have included Darwin, Einstein, and
Pasteur. Lord Rees, the society's president, said, "Stephen Hawking has
contributed as much as anyone since Einstein to our understanding
of gravity. This medal is a fitting recognition of an astonishing
research career spanning more than 40 years." As a further honor,
British astronaut Piers Sellers carried Hawking's medal on his trip in
July 2006 to the international space station. Said Sellers, "Stephen

Hawking is a definitive hero to all of us involved in exploring the Cosmos. It was an honor . . . to fly his medal into space. We think that this is particularly appropriate, as Stephen has dedicated his life to thinking about the larger universe."

In a BBC interview, Hawking said that his next ambition is to "go into space." We have already pointed out the impossibility of travel to other habitable planets ever being physically achieved. More recently, he expressed that desire again and explained the urgency behind it. He believes that populating planets scattered throughout the cosmos could offer the only hope for human survival. Here we confront two problems for Hawking, who seems at least to be a Deist, and for all other evolutionists who claim to believe in God:

1) Doesn't the belief that space has other intelligent, human-like occupants (a necessary corollary to the theory of evolution) do away with the entire idea of a supernatural act of creation and thus with the God of the Bible? If "spontaneous generation" could happen on planet Earth, why not on millions of other similar planets? The clear implication from Genesis to Revelation is that the creation of Adam and Eve was a unique event, never having occurred before nor would ever occur again, anywhere in the cosmos.

At this point, we are not arguing for acceptance of either the biblical account or of the atheistic account but simply showing their incompatibility with each other. How can any "believer" share in the search for extraterrestrial intelligence when such creatures could not exist except through a creative act of God? Yet what the Bible says from Genesis to Revelation reveals that the search for human-like creatures outside of Earth, which is a large part of the space program, of necessity denies the existence of the Creator God in whom all Christians supposedly believe.

2) Moreover, one wonders why there should be any concern for the survival of man or any other species. What does it matter whether we survive if we are what we are told we are by those who are popularly looked to as the spokespersons for today's "science"? If we are simply the accidental product of a "big bang," plus chance, plus

billions of years of something called evolution working through "natural selection" (which has supposedly brought into existence every living thing), of what importance could man's brief survival be in the billions of years of evolutionary history? The cosmos doesn't care, so why should we, a few unimportant creatures unknown to the cosmos, have any concern for our own survival? Did natural selection implant that concern within us? If so, why?

MAN, OF NO MORE WORTH THAN A FUNGUS?

In the foreword to Dawkins's first book *The Selfish Gene*, Robert L. Trivers (one of today's most influential living evolutionary theorists) wrote, "There exists no objective basis on which to elevate one species above another. Chimp and human, lizard and fungus, we have all evolved over some three billion years by a process known as natural selection."[9] Presumably, this statement expresses Dawkins's view as well.

Is Stephen Hawking equally concerned for the survival of every other species on Earth, including chimpanzees and lizards? Shouldn't he be, if Darwin was right? It will take a huge fleet of space ships, billions of "Noah's arks," to accomplish Hawking's escape from planet Earth if he is to bring all other living things with him. If not all, on what basis could he exclude any?

Every species has its instinct for self-preservation. In man, however, it is not a blind urge but a rational desire that places inestimable value on human life. Why? Science has no answer to that philosophical/religious question. Nor is the reference to Darwinism at this point out of place. It continues to motivate the space program.

Oddly enough, out of such concern came eugenics: the desire not just to preserve but to "improve" the human race—at the expense of those members considered not worth keeping. J. C. Sanford explains:

> Darwin's book, *Origin of the Species and the Survival of Favored Races,* introduced the new idea that strong and continuous selection ("survival of the fittest") might halt

this perceived degenerative trend [in the human species]. Darwin repeatedly pointed to human efforts in animal and plant breeding as a model for such man-directed selection.

In his book, *The Descent of Man*, Darwin . . . contended that there is a need for superior races (i.e., the white race) to replace the "inferior races." This ushered in the modern era of racism, which came to a head in Hitler's Germany.

Before World War II, many nations, including America, had government-directed eugenics programs [which] included forced sterilization of the "unfit," and aggressive promotion of abortion/fertility-control for the underclasses. Ever since the time of Darwin, essentially all of his followers have been eugenicists at heart, and have advocated the genetic improvement of the human race.

When I was an evolutionist, I also was, at heart, a eugenicist. The philosophers and scientists who created the modern "synthetic theory" of evolution were uniformly eugenicists. However, after the horrors of WWII, essentially all open discussions of eugenics were quietly put aside.[10]

It is difficult to imagine how evolutionists can justify anyone's concern for the survival of any kind of life on Earth or condemn attempts to "improve" the human race by eugenics programs. After all, aren't all living things merely lumps of a peculiar form of the same matter of which the universe itself is made and holds in such contempt that it consumes it as fuel to keep the stars burning? According to the second law of thermodynamics, won't it all eventually sink into oblivion, with not even a surviving memory? Then why should we, who will be gone in a mere 70, 80, 90, or perhaps even 100-plus years—why should we sacrifice our present desires to benefit future equally transient and meaningless generations?

Why should anyone care who or what lives or dies, if we are of no more value than a garden slug, as evolutionists declare? Yet the revulsion we feel for death persists not just for ourselves but for others. Most irrational of all is the concern that we have for the environment

and for "endangered species," which natural selection would exterminate if we did not interfere. Could natural selection have implanted
this ethical anxiety that is clearly peculiar to the human species? Not
according to Dawkins, who declares in all seriousness:

> Much as we might wish to believe otherwise, universal love
> and the welfare of the species as a whole are concepts that
> simply do not make evolutionary sense."[11]

Then what is the source of such sentiments, if not natural selection? Isn't a loving concern for others good? Not according to Dawkins
because, far from enhancing chances of survival, it would be a hin-
drance. This fact leaves us with the unsolved mystery of why, if we
are the product of evolution, we feel this concern. Moreover, why
might we "wish to believe otherwise," which Dawkins cannot deny
is the case? That "wish" may be a good indication that not only is the
theory of evolution by natural selection morally bankrupt, but there
is something else seriously wrong at its very foundation. Now we are
on dangerous ground, because even questioning Darwinism is as un-
American as challenging the space program.

CAN'T EVOLUTIONISTS TRUST "NATURAL SELECTION"?

Why can't we just trust the future of living things into the all-knowing
hands of "the selfish gene" that Dawkins says is our creator? If natural
selection made us what we are, as atheists insist, surely it will protect
us to whatever extent it thinks necessary. If billions die in the process
of the next upward move to a higher species, so what? Isn't that how
evolution works?

Yet here we are, worried about endangered species and our own
survival and trying to "help" nature do its job. Obviously, natural
selection did not implant this concern. What did?

Isn't it the height of presumption for us humans to imagine that we know better than the omnipotent, omniscient, and omnipresent evolutionary forces that supposedly brought us into and control our existence? Our meddling might set back the evolutionary process millions of years. Shame on us for interfering out of selfish concern for our own meaningless survival!

Wouldn't it be presumptuous and even dangerous for humans, recent arrivals on the evolutionary scene, to act as self-appointed guardians of this process? Such a desire and the capacity to interfere are either the product of natural selection and thus legitimate and neither right nor wrong—or they are sufficient proof that evolution is simply not true.

Be that as it may, Hawking seems genuinely concerned that humans could be wiped out as a species unless we speed up the colonizing of other planets widely scattered throughout the cosmos. He told the BBC that "humans will have to colonize planets in far-flung solar systems if the race is to survive." But we've already shown that it would be impossible to reach any other planets "widely scattered throughout the cosmos," much less to "colonize" them.

Hawking is considered to be one of today's most brilliant scientists, yet he apparently imagines such colonization to be possible. He says, "The long-term survival of the human race is at risk as long as it is confined to a single planet. Sooner or later, disasters such as asteroid collision or nuclear war could wipe us all out. But once we spread out into space and establish independent colonies, our future should be safe."[12]

Our future? Hawking dares to ask this present generation to sacrifice its time, money, effort, and present enjoyment to invest in the survival of hypothetical generations so far in the future that they may never exist? Could the desire to contribute to such incredible philanthropy be the result of unthinking, unfeeling evolutionary forces, which care nothing about wiping us all out in the interest of evolutionary progress? Why should we care, anyway, when human life is merely an accident and the energy that supposedly spawned us couldn't care less?

Atheism and natural selection certainly give us no basis for concern about the survival of our species any more than for that of a virus or fungus. But why should we believe the amoral opinions of any atheists? No matter what scientific credentials they possess, we have the right to reject them as meaningless. The theories of atheists tell us that our entire existence is without purpose. Why should we accept such statements, which they claim are no more than the latest motions of atoms that began with a huge explosion and after billions of years of evolution culminated in the human brain and the very thoughts we think and speak? Isn't it time that we use our common sense to object to the irrationality of some of what is being presented to us in the name of "science"?

A WILD GOOSE CHASE THROUGH "SPACE"?

Hawking claims that if the human race is to survive, we must migrate to distant star systems and then spread out onto widely scattered planets. He offers no guesses as to how many centuries it could take to reach this capability, and since the propellants we currently use can only get us there in thousands or even millions of years, Hawking says we will have to use matter/antimatter annihilation propulsion such as that described in the *Star Trek* television series. What? *Star Trek* is science fiction—yet this is the only hope that one of the smartest men alive holds out for human survival?

This desperate statement from Hawking tells us how inadequate he thinks our present "space" program is. The *Star Trek* system (could we develop it in 200 or even 300 years?) isn't even in the feasibility study stage. Even if possible, the cost would be prohibitive and its value almost nothing in relation to the size of the cosmos. That advancement would supposedly allow us to travel at or near the speed of light. But it would still take 100,000 years to cross our galaxy and 250,000 to circle it. The distances across space from one star and galaxy to another are realities that we can't change! Might this entire space exploration idea be a fantasy driven by pride and personal ambition?

What started us off on this wild goose chase through space? The answer is undeniable: it was Darwinism and its corollary, atheism. A biblical theist would never imagine that life existed anywhere outside our own planet and would therefore waste no time in bothering to pursue it. Only an atheist/evolutionist could entertain the notion that life began by chance on Earth and therefore could have begun by the same chance and might exist elsewhere in the cosmos. A major goal of the space program is to find that life—if it exists.

The struggle today between atheism and theism, though an ancient one, has reached new intensity. Atheists try to give the impression that only uneducated fools any longer believe in God. This is by no means true. Francis Collins, one of the most famous geneticists alive, at the age of 27 turned from atheism to theism.

Among the literally hundreds of examples we could give, "Fritz" Schaefer, Graham Perdue Professor of Chemistry and the director of the Center for Computational Quantum Chemistry at the University of Georgia, third most quoted chemist in the world today, has said:

> The significance and joy in my science comes in the occasional moments of discovering something new and saying to myself, "So that's how God did it!" My goal is to understand a little corner of God's plan.[13]

This quotation, of course, is no more than one scientist's opinion and is not intended as any proof of God's existence. It only shows that, in contrast to what Dawkins says, not every scientist is by any means an atheist or Darwinian. Yet those theories have risen to dominance in the scientific and academic worlds, thanks to the aggressiveness of the New Atheists. It is hardly possible to escape this issue today.

LOST IN SPACE?

Forget the fact that *Voyager I* and *II* may well have run out of power from their radioisotope thermal generators before this book's publishing date, leaving them drifting aimlessly—hardly a stone's throw from Earth, measured in cosmic distances. Let's assume that our distant descendants could one day send out similar craft that would never lose power. What then? As Hawking realizes, the effort would still be in vain. In fact, our present spacecraft are a bad joke in the face of the vastness of the cosmos! In spite of what may seem like a great accomplishment, Wernher von Braun confessed, "Our space ventures have been only the smallest of steps in the vast reaches of the universe and have introduced more mysteries than they have solved."[14]

The *Voyager I* "space probe" travels about *335 million miles* per year. At that rate, it would be 40,000 years before it would come close to another star—"close" meaning within 1.7 light years (almost 10 trillion miles), still too far away to be of any significance. It would take another 37,000 years (a total of 77,000 *years* since leaving Earth) to reach Alpha Centauri, the nearest star system in our galaxy where there might be some planets that could be checked for evidence of life.

How could any knowledge (no matter how revolutionary or valuable) that won't be discovered until that far into the future benefit anyone alive today? Is the time and money spent on any project that can't possibly pay off for *77,000 years* a wise investment for the present generation? The fact that the government eagerly spends taxpayers' money in that manner ought to be troubling to everyone with minimal intelligence.

It's true that we've made significant progress toward exploring our solar system, but it's only one of *billions* just in our own galaxy. What about the other hundreds of billions of galaxies, each presumably with its billions of solar systems as well? And we talk about a *space program*—about *launching into the cosmos*? How can such limited creatures maintain this grandiose delusion—creatures who, in relation to the incredible dimensions of this universe, are sub-microscopic egotists on a nearly invisible speck of dust called Earth? The distances involved in the cosmos are just too great for us to comprehend the impossibility we face. We find it difficult to admit this disappointing truth to ourselves.

Although President Bush's reference to the heroic exploits of Earth's early explorers may be inspiring, it is inappropriate in the present context. What Columbus dreamed of was do-able. The "space exploration" we irresponsibly boast of accomplishing one day is outrageously impossible.

This statement is not intended to reflect the hopeless pessimism that grips the atheist, whose cosmos is meaningless and, like himself as part of it, is headed for oblivion. It is simply a fact—and it is a fact with which the atheist can only concur. Richard Dawkins expresses it like this:

> Fred Hoyle's own science of astronomy puts us in our place, metaphorically as well as literally, scaling down our vanity to fit the tiny stage on which we play out our lives—our speck of debris from the cosmic explosion.[15]

Of course, attempting to satisfy our irrepressible curiosity about the cosmos can be a fascinating and even addicting pursuit—and being absorbed in it, oddly enough, can restore that "vanity" of which Dawkins says it should have cured us. The universe has been opened to amateur astronomers as never before. There is

> . . . a growing online community that sifts through mountains of data collected by professional scientists in search of other worlds.
>
> Professionals are increasingly enlisting the aid of novices with personal computers to help pore through images and data—all in pursuit of the next great breakthrough. . . .
>
> Thanks to technology, novices are effectively turning from lonely skywatchers into research assistants. . . . One of the earliest online citizen scientist projects was SETI [Search for Extraterrestrials] (at) home, which distributed software that created a virtual supercomputer by harnessing idle, Web-connected PCs to search for alien radio transmissions. . . . Since 2001, the National Science Foundation has funded a $10 million project to create a "national virtual

observatory" that compiles data from ground and space-based telescopes—including dazzling images from the Hubble Space Telescope and X-ray data from the Chandra Observatory.

The project, which is still under development is primarily used by professionals who want to go to one source to mine archival images. High school and college students are increasingly tapping into the Web site as well. . . .[16]

WHAT CAN WE REALISTICALLY DO?

It would take the *Voyager* craft about 1.3 billion years to reach the closest galaxy outside our Milky Way, the Sagittarius Dwarf elliptical galaxy (forgetting the much closer Canis Major dwarf galaxy, which is being swallowed up by the Milky Way), and more than 3 billion years to reach the next closest galaxy, the Large Magellanic Cloud galaxy. Is that exciting? Even if that feat were possible, so what? It would be meaningless to anyone alive today. Any crew aboard would have been skeletons for most of the journey.

If such distant-future dreams are by very definition without any value for Earth's present inhabitants or for those in the foreseeable future, why should we plan and pay for and work toward them? Shouldn't we rather admit the humbling truth that manned or even robotic "space probes" are impossible outside our solar system? How can we boast of a "space program" that has "human beings . . . headed into the cosmos" when our sun is only one of some 200 billion stars in our galaxy and there could be up to a trillion galaxies?

And how can we imagine that we are gaining accurate information about the cosmos with the miniscule sampling that we have already shown would be the best we could hope for? Isn't one out of 200 billion star systems in our galaxy, which is only one galaxy of a trillion in the universe, too small a sample to be of any value in any scientific test? What could one two-hundred billion trillionth mean in relation to the cosmos? A little sober reflection forces us to admit, no matter how reluctantly, that our galaxy alone (much less the cosmos) is far too immense even to begin to explore by the most fantastic space vehicles we could ever conceive.

In view of the impossibly great distances, what should we do? We could continue to probe our own solar system to the best of our ability. That would keep space scientists and astronauts busy with all the challenges they could handle for many decades to come. In spite of President Bush's enthusiasm, however, for the supposed advances in science that could be reaped by establishing bases on the moon and Mars, some scientists think that such projects might not be worth the effort and cost. One planetary geologist with the U.S. Geological Survey said:

> I wish it were not so, but I'm somewhat skeptical that we're going to learn an awful lot about Earth by looking at other planetary bodies. The more we look at the different planets, the more each one seems to be unique.[17]

Moreover, the variety in the composition of moons and planets and their distinctiveness from the sun's chemical makeup raises serious questions about the origin of the universe that does not fit the Big Bang theory. Whatever knowledge may be reaped from probing our solar system, let's face the humbling truth and forget about trying to develop "advanced craft," manned or unmanned, to go beyond these realistic limits. We cannot rationally continue to support with our tax dollars the exciting preparations but impossible ambition to "explore the cosmos"!

Abandoning this dream would save a lot of money (and probably lives) and free our minds from fantasy to focus on what is possible. Can the human ego submit to this truth? This is the question we will return to again and again as we present undeniable facts that are unpalatable to science and its devotees today.

YES, BUT AT THE SPEED OF LIGHT. . . !

Optimists point out that we have another weapon in our space arsenal—the radio messages we've been transmitting from Earth for many years. Though we can't get far enough physically to penetrate even the fringe of space, at least we can communicate with any intelligent life that might be out there. After all, radio waves travel at the speed of light—186,000 miles per second, nearly 670,000,000 miles per hour—twice as far in 60 minutes as the *Pioneer* craft go in a year. That's fast!

Yes, but it's fast only by Earth's standards—and far too slow to reach "into the cosmos" in any length of time that would be meaningful to creatures of such limited longevity as ourselves. Let's look at the facts again. At the speed of light, it would take radio waves 100,000-150,000 years to cross our galaxy, the Milky Way. It would take about 250,000 years to travel around its circumference, and many thousands to billions of years after leaving the Milky Way to reach other galaxies. Even at the speed of light, exploring the tiniest fraction of the cosmos would still be far beyond man's reach.

Radio cuts 76,995.7 years from *Voyager's* snail's-pace travel time and reaches Alpha Centauri in 4.3 years. Theoretically, then, we could have had a reply to our radio messages in less than 9 years. We've been listening for intelligent sounds for more than 50 years, however, without hearing anything that offers even the slightest possibility that it comes from an intelligent source. There are only three other star systems in addition to Alpha Centauri with the possibility of a radio reply in less than 100 years, and then the distances mount rapidly: 260 years for a reply from Aldebaran (brightest star in Taurus), 300 years for a reply from Regulus (brightest star in Leo), over 1,000 years for a reply from Spica (brightest star in Virgo), nearly 1,600 years from the Pleiades, 6,000 from Orion, 24,000 for a reply from the Crab Nebula, etc. Do these figures inspire any reasonable hope for contact? Try putting an ad in *The Wall Street Journal* that would read something like this: "Needed: Fifty Trillion Dollars to Back Fantastic

New Invention! Guaranteed Return of One Million Percent in only 6,000 Years! Investors contact (phone number and email address)."

CONTINUING THE DELUSION

Well, what about the images and messages we've placed on our Voyager spacecrafts for aliens to find? Couldn't they lead to contact? No, they are also useless for several reasons, among them the fact that there is no one out there to contact (which we will prove beyond reasonable doubt). Even if there were intelligent life on some other planets capable of repeated manned space probes, the impossible distances would be a barrier to them, just as they are to us. The chance that any space-faring beings, even traveling at the speed of light, would ever find our spacecrafts to decipher the gold records they carried, with the sounds and images supposedly representative of life on Earth, would be far less than finding the proverbial needle in the largest haystack here on Earth, or, indeed, more like finding a needle in a haystack larger than the sun.

What about our telescopes? Don't they show us distant galaxies? We can continue reaching out many thousands of light years with our telescopes—can't we? Not really. Even the most powerful telescopes are limited by the speed of light that brings the out-of-date images to us. We are not seeing distant stars as they *are now* but as they *were* when that light began its long-ago journey toward Earth. Our strongest telescopes can't show us the universe as it is today. We're looking at ancient history, for which any connection to the present can only be surmised.

When it comes to searching for life with the best telescopes that we can build in tandem with the latest technology, NASA says we are limited to "planets up to 100 light years away. . . ."[18] That means our radio messages would take 100 years to get there and another 100, minimum, for a reply to be received. That seems a great distance: nearly 587 *trillion* miles from Earth. In fact, it is hardly a stone's throw away in cosmic perspective. Even if we could analyze every star and planet within that distance surrounding us, it would represent such an infinitesimal sample of the cosmos as to be virtually meaningless.

What if we built spacecraft that could exceed the speed of light? Even if we could travel at an impossible *ten times* the speed of light, it would still take 10,000 years to cross our galaxy, 25,000 years to circle it, and from hundreds of thousands to billions of years to reach other parts of the cosmos. Moreover, the general consensus (and certainly admitted by NASA at the present) is that the speed of light (which has proved to be the maximum for particles in an accelerator) cannot be exceeded by physical objects. That well-known fact provides additional proof that does away with the notion that UFOs could be physical craft coming in from distant worlds.

PUSHING GOD OUT OF HIS UNIVERSE

Unlike the brilliant founders of science (most of whom were theists), upon whose genius science was built and still rests, modern man has been persuaded that belief in God is an unscientific hypothesis and thus unworthy of consideration in any scientific discussion. Refusing to acknowledge as even a rational possibility the God who offers instantaneous access to Him in "the prayer of faith," today's science persists in attempting to find other intelligent creatures somewhere in the impossibly vast universe that might comfort us with the realization that we are not alone. This irony was expressed succinctly by a scientist:

> Radio telescopes, linked with computers, simultaneously search millions of radio frequencies for a non-random, non-natural, extraterrestrial signal—any short sequence of information. Yet the long sequence of information in the DNA of every living thing is a signal from . . . a vast intelligence—a Creator. But if those searching for extraterrestrial life ever accepted the evidence for a Creator, the evolutionary basis for their search would disappear.[19]

In a future chapter, we'll consider how the cosmos, which certainly hasn't been here forever, began. For the moment, however, all can agree to the fact that any life existing anywhere in the universe, intelligent or not, must have begun after the so-called Big Bang. We are not endorsing this popular theory, which is opposed by increasing numbers of scientists, but mention it as the only belief concerning "origins" that is given any credence in America's public schools and major media. We will consider the Big Bang carefully in due time.

One can only wonder why the promoters of the Big Bang theory fail to note that if the universe did begin in this manner, it would have been sterilized a trillion times over, making it utterly impossible for life ever to exist thereafter, anywhere in the cosmos. The law of biogenesis, established by experiment and accepted by all scientists, declares that life comes only from life—it cannot arise from lifeless matter.

The very fact that life exists upon Earth is proof that the universe, of which our earth, teeming with life, is part, did not come into existence with a sudden burst of mindless energy. What other alternative is there but by a supernatural act of creation? Even though this is an unavoidable conclusion based upon all the evidence, the evolutionists *will not accept it* under any circumstances. Do they have any evidence for rejecting this unavoidable conclusion? Absolutely not! It is their total commitment to atheism and materialism that will not allow them to face the facts.

Atheists have succeeded in convincing many that science can explain everything without God. Dawkins declares, "Most people . . . think that you need a God to explain the existence of the world, and especially the existence of life. They are wrong. . . ."[20]

"Wrong, absolutely wrong" is the judgment pronounced upon all who disagree with atheists. The New Atheists humbly call themselves the "brights," with the implication that the rest of us are dimwits. The assertion that no educated, thinking person believes in God anymore is continually heard from the mouths of university professors. It would be safe to say that the vast majority of university students are intimidated into accepting this unsubstantiated statement and passing it on to others so that this has become a truism in academia.

That statement couldn't be more wrong, as we will prove repeatedly in this book, showing that many of the brightest scientists in history have been staunch believers in God as Creator. Among them are: Francis Collins, longtime director of the Human Genome Project; Professor Bill Phillips, winner of the Nobel Prize for Physics in 1997; Sir Brian Heap FRS, former Vice-President of the Royal Society, and Sir John Houghton FRS, former director of the Meteorological Office, co-Chair of the Intergovernmental Panel on Climate Change and currently director of the John Ray Initiative on the Environment.

In contrast to the cocksure pride of atheists, Wernher von Braun (who was at least as bright as any of the "brights"), speaking out of the humility and reality of his own experience as the founder and for many years the director of America's space program, declared:

> One cannot be exposed to the law and order of the universe without concluding that there must be a divine intent behind it. . . . Speaking for myself, I can only say that the grandeur of the cosmos serves to confirm my belief in the certainty of a Creator.[21]

Dawkins keeps forgetting, as we will repeatedly discover, what he himself admits, "Darwin didn't explain the origin of life. . . . There are still gaps in our understanding. We don't understand how the cosmos came into existence in the first place. . . ."[22] But with the same incurable human pride that drives the space program, Dawkins always adds, "but we're working on that. . . ." This is his standard escape clause when challenged with questions dealing with the most basic elements essential to a scientific understanding of the universe. Let us just call this mantra what it is—a cop-out.

TWO MESSAGES FROM SPACE

As for the atheists' claim that no intelligent, educated person any longer believes in God, one must admit that astronauts are certainly required to be intelligent, as well as to be scientists. During the first-ever manned orbiting of the moon, William Anders announced, "For all the people on Earth, the crew of Apollo 8 has a message we would like to send you . . . 'In the beginning God created the heaven and the earth. . . .'" Anders, followed by Jim Lovell and Frank Borman, broadcast back to earth the first ten verses of Genesis (though Anders inadvertently skipped verse 3).

After their return to Earth, a reporter asked Borman whether he had seen God out there. He replied, "No . . . but I saw His evidence."

In the Apollo 11 space mission, Neil Armstrong and Buzz Aldrin were the first men to walk on the moon. Michael Collins, third member of the group, was in charge of the command module, essential for their return to Earth. It circled the moon while Armstrong and Aldrin landed. The moon lander touched down at 3:17 Eastern Standard Time, Sunday, July 20, 1969.

Aldrin had brought with him a tiny communion kit, given to him by his church. It had a silver chalice and wine vial about the size of the tip of his finger. During the morning, he radioed, "Houston, this is Eagle. This is the LM pilot speaking. I would like to request a few moments of silence. I would like to invite each person listening in, whoever or wherever he may be, to contemplate for a moment the events of the last few hours, and to give thanks in his own individual way."

"In the radio blackout," he wrote later, "I opened the little plastic packages, which contained the bread and the wine. I poured the wine into the chalice our church had given me. In the one-sixth gravity of the moon, the wine slowly curled and gracefully came up the side of the cup. Then I read the Scripture, 'I am the vine, you are the branches. Whosoever abides in me will bring forth much fruit.' I had intended to read my communion passage back to Earth, but at the last minute Deke Slayton had requested that I not do this. NASA was already embroiled in a legal battle with Madalyn Murray O'Hair, the celebrated opponent of religion, over the Apollo 8 crew reading from Genesis while orbiting the moon at Christmas. I agreed reluctantly. . . .

"*Eagle*'s metal body creaked. I ate the tiny Host and swallowed the wine. I gave thanks for the intelligence and spirit that had brought two young pilots to the Sea of Tranquility. It was interesting for me to think: the very first liquid ever poured on the moon, and the very first food eaten there, were the communion elements."[23]

PROFESSOR OF RADIOLOGY SHOOTS DOWN THEORY OF SPACE TRAVEL AT SPEED OF LIGHT

"Contrary to what you see in your favorite sci-fi movie franchise, when a space ship approaches light speed, everybody dies.

"According to William Edelstein, a visiting professor of radiology at Johns Hopkins University, a spacecraft traveling on the cusp of light speed would be assaulted by a deluge of hydrogen atoms that have roughly the same energy as protons whizzing around the Large Hadron Collider [LHC—a particle accelerator at CERN in Geneva, Switzerland].

"'For the crew,' Edelstein explains, 'it would be like standing in front of the LHC beam.' That beam would expose a human in its path to nearly 2,000 times the amount of radiation that the body can withstand."

http://www.asylum.com/2010/02/18/traveling-at-light-speed-like-standing-in-large-hadron-collider/

"Edelstein's work showed that a starship traveling at just 99 percent of the speed of light would get a radiation dose from hydrogen of 61 sieverts per second, when just one tenth of that number of sieverts would deliver a fatal dose for humans. And that's not even the 99.999998 percent of light-speed necessary to make the journey to the center of the Milky Way in 10 years....

"On top of killing the crew, such powerful levels of energy would also likely destroy the starship electronics. 'Getting between stars is a huge problem unless we think of something really, really different,' Edelstein said. 'I'm not saying that we know everything and that it's impossible. I'm saying it's kind of impossible based on what we know right now.'"

http://www.space.com/businesstechnology/warp-speed-kills-100308.html

This most beautiful system [The Universe] could only proceed from the dominion of an intelligent and powerful Being.

—Sir Isaac Newton

If life comes only from life, does this mean that there was always life on the earth? It must, yet we know that the world was once without life—that life appeared later. How? We think it was by spontaneous generation.

—George Wald, in *Biological Science: An Inquiry Into Life* (Harcourt, Brace & World, Inc., 1963), 42

We owe it to [Darwin] that the world was brought to believe in evolution; . . . Here is a theory that released thinking men from the spell of a superstition, one of the most overpowering that has ever enslaved mankind.

—C. D. Darlington, "Origin of Darwinism," *Scientific American* (May 1959), 60-66

The first point to make about Darwin's theory is that it is no longer a theory, but a fact. No serious scientist would deny the fact that evolution has occurred, just as he would not deny the fact that the earth goes around the sun.

—Julian Huxley, in *Issues in Evolution*, edited by Sol Tax (Chicago: University of Chicago, 1960)

The second property of almost all living things is their complexity and, in particular, their highly organized complexity. This so impressed our forebears that they considered it inconceivable that such intricate and well-organized mechanisms would have arisen without a designer. Had I been living 150 years ago I feel sure I would have been compelled to agree with this Argument from Design.

—Francis Crick, "Lessons from Biology," *Natural History*, vol. 97 (November 1988), 32-39

I woke up and realized that all my life I had been duped into taking evolutionism as revealed truth in some way.

—Colin Patterson, "Evolution and Creationism," Speech at the American Museum of Natural History, New York (November 5, 1981)

TWO

SCIENCE THEN AND NOW

Richard Dawkins pronounces with all the authority of a Papal Bull, "Most of what we strive for in our modern life uses the apparatus of goal seeking that was originally set up [by natural selection] to seek goals in the state of nature. But now the goal-seeking apparatus has been switched to different goals, like making money, or hedonistic pleasures of one sort or another."[1]

Goal-seeking apparatus? How does Dawkins know that such an "apparatus" exists? What might that "apparatus" be? In what organ of the body or in what gene is it centered— in the ambitious part, perhaps? And where is that? And what letters in the DNA define it? Of course, he has no evidence that such an "apparatus" ever existed. This is wild speculation like most of what Dawkins pronounces so authoritatively. It is part of the shameless nonsense that has been the stock in trade of evolutionists from the very beginning, the guesses garnished with endless "perhapses . . . maybes . . . " etc.

Dawkins and the rest of the "Four Horsemen" (Christopher Hitchens, Sam Harris, and Daniel Dennett) leading the New Atheist movement deny that objective truth exists. How could truth come through random mutations, most of which are harmful? Nor is there any plan or design so that subsequent mutations build upon what has gone before. The very suggestion of design is anathema to Dawkins et al. "Goal-seeking apparatus" is odd language considering the fact that they deny that natural selection has any goal whatsoever in mind.

After God, there is nothing that Dawkins and his colleagues hate more than the idea of purpose, plan, and design. They are riding the crest of a tsunami of popularity that is making fortunes for each of them.

This apparatus is another product of Dawkins's runaway imagination to go along with "selfish genes, memes, phenotypes, Mount Improbable," etc. Why should we believe him without any supporting scientific evidence? The current aura of success doesn't mean that all of his pronouncements are scientifically valid. And once again, his theorizing doesn't meet the criteria of common sense. We have to do a little thinking of our own.

What the average person believes to be *his* or *her* inner motives, desires, or deepest thoughts, says Dawkins and other New Atheists, are really the product of evolution turning each person into a puppet of the impersonal forces of natural selection! You *think* you think, but you really don't. It's your selfish genes doing the thinking for you, and *you* are a meaningless lump of protein molecules. Here is how Francis Crick (co-discoverer of the structure of the DNA molecule, along with James D. Watson and Maurice Wilkins) seriously expressed the nonsense that he promoted:

> "You," your joys and your sorrows, your memories and your ambitions, your sense of personal identity and free will, are in fact no more than the behavior of a vast assembly of nerve cells and their associated molecules.[2]

Did Crick or Dawkins have any evidence for this state of affairs that turns one's ambitions and one's greatest and noblest accomplishments into purposeless delusion? No—none! It is all conjecture, yet it is accepted as the latest science because "men of science" declare it.

Real life, however, as it is lived by individuals all over the world and has been throughout history, refutes such a hopeless philosophy as contrary to everything we know about our own daily experiences.

Could it be that the theories we've been mentioning are the product of a strong desire to justify the atheism that certain eminent scientists espouse? Shouldn't we be aware of the fact that an atheist's rejection of God provides a powerful motive for his research to prove that God does not exist? Might that not adversely affect his scientific theories? Remember Pascal's wager? Here it is in essence: If a Christian bets his life on God's existence and eternity in bliss with Him and is wrong, he has only lost this life, which atheists claim is a meaningless delusion anyway. But if an atheist bets that there is no God and thus no eternal judgment after death and is wrong, he will suffer for it forever.

When asked to offer his "gut feeling," Carl Sagan replied, "I try not to think with my gut."[3] Dawkins gives his approval to this rejoinder. However, the physical brain (like the gut and the entire body) is merely a complex arrangement of protein molecules. Protein is not conscious and does not think, no matter in what part of the body it is located.

Doesn't the brain think? Of course, it doesn't. Does protein think? Certainly not, but physically, that's all the brain is. Whether it's in the muscles of the arms or in the brain, protein in *any form* does not think. Dawkins of course disagrees. He must, because according to most atheists, matter is all that exists. "The evolution of complex life, indeed its very existence in a universe obeying physical laws, is wonderfully surprising. . . . Surprise is an emotion that can exist only in the brain, which is the product of that very surprising process."[4]

LET'S PAUSE TO DO SOME RATIONAL THINKING ON OUR OWN

What does common sense tell us? If the brain thinks, this physical organ must decide what to think about, compose its thoughts, come to a rational conclusion, and reason about the consequences. Where do you and I come into this? Who or what are *we*? Are we waiting breathlessly to find out what our brains are going to think of and demand of us next? Apparently not, because according to Dawkins and atheistic logic, there is no "you" or "I."

Such irrational "logic" is forced upon otherwise rational scientists by the theory of atheism. Yes, atheism is a theory and it has never been proved. The atheist will counter that theism is also a theory that has never been proved. That is not true. There is irrefutable proof for the existence of God and for the Bible as God's Word. We will come to that in a later chapter.

Are we merely bags of molecules, as Crick says? Or, as Dawkins tells us, physical containers for selfish genes over which we have no control—vehicles *they* use to assure their own survival? Is this reasonable? Do you experience your life as a slave of selfish genes? Are you the victim of an illusion created by the molecules that make up your body?

Genes don't know what kind of body or what part of it they occupy, nor could they care. Carrots, garden slugs, and fungi have the same DNA that we have, but the genes don't know the difference. Sagan's reply wasn't so clever after all. One's physical brain is no more capable of thinking than is one's gut—or than a head of lettuce. The DNA alphabet is identical in all living things. The arrangement of the *words* in the DNA is what matters, but genes no more understand the meaning of the words they contain than do the paper and ink in a dictionary or encyclopedia understand the information they offer.

In fact, the brain is like a computer, very useful for a thinking person, but the computer no more thinks than do the fingers purposefully punching the keyboard. For a theist, who believes that the mind is nonphysical like the ideas it conceives and uses, Sagan's clever put-down is exposed as more meaningless gibberish.

WELCOME TO THE WORLD OF ATHEISM

The sardonic bumper sticker used to read, "One atomic bomb could ruin your whole day!" Dawkins's nihilistic nonsense could ruin your whole life. He advises, "The here and now is all we have, and that is an inspiration to make the most of it. . . . We are privileged to be alive. And we should make the most of our time on this world."[5] *Make the most of it*? Is living a life that has no meaning worthwhile or even possible? And how could any life be worthwhile if it lasts hardly a nanosecond on the cosmic time scale and then passes into oblivion? How could such a life be lived to the fullest? What rational person could be happy about that?

"Meaning" and "worthwhile" have no physical description or any other relationship to the physical world. Therefore, these thoughts cannot be held in the brain because it is a physical organ. If the brain can be said to hold thoughts, it is only in the same way a computer does. As Sir John Eccles and Wilder Penfield and other neurologists agree, thoughts are nonphysical and can only be held in the nonphysical mind. The mind exists in a dimension separate from the brain. It is in the mind that these immaterial thoughts originate and from whence they influence the physical world through one's voice, words used in anger, expressions of love, or possibly persuasive arguments. But the brain does no more than that.

No matter how many and how great one's accomplishments, when the sun eventually burns all life and matter on Earth to ashes, not even a memory will remain, nor will there be anyone left to remember. What will "worthwhile" mean then? It will mean exactly what the atheist says it means right now—nothing—unless the thinker, who lived in the body and who used the brain, survives the body's death.

The Apostle Paul explained this obvious fact in reasoning with unbelievers in his day: "If the dead rise not . . . let us eat and drink; for to morrow we die."[6] This is atheism. Christopher Hitchens, who will in death soon face the Creator he repeatedly maligns, assures us all, "When you're dead, you won't know it, and you won't feel it."

This is the nihilism underlying the thinking of Dawkins and of all atheists. Oblivion upon death is the atheist's great hope. What if it turns out that Hitchens is dead wrong, that no one can escape judgment after this life on Earth is finished and atheists lose Pascal's wager? All of the evidence, as we shall see, is on the side of those who believe that death doesn't end it all, but that the nonphysical thinker who, unlike his body, is not subject to the laws of thermodynamics, survives death. That possibility should be worth some serious consideration.

DOGMATISM WITHOUT REASON

Has there been any verification by careful and extensive experimentation to show how and when *natural selection* developed a moral and spiritual side in man? That would be impossible because natural selection can only affect man's physical being. Morality and spirituality, however, are clearly not physical. Dawkins can't acknowledge this widely accepted scientific fact without renouncing his atheism. Has there been any proof demonstrated that this spiritual side is unnecessary because ethics, morals, compassion, a love of beautiful music, reverence, and worship can all be described and explained in purely physical terms? Has any atheist demonstrated that the barrier between man and animals that, as Mortimer J. Adler declared, evolution could never cross, has in fact been, or could theoretically be, crossed?[7] No one has even tried because even atheists know there is a great gulf separating the physical, mental, and moral worlds.

Atheism and its corollary, materialism, are speechless when asked to account for the human qualities that we all value so highly and that distinguish us from all other creatures: the appreciation of music and poetry, the enjoyment of beauty in nature (in which even Dawkins exults), the ability to form conceptual ideas and express them in words, to understand mathematics in relation to the universe, to use the imagination as do architects and engineers, to feel and express a love that is so clearly unique to humans—and so many other qualities and capabilities, which we all know that animals do not share with us.

Lesser creatures possess none of these purely human characteristics that we value so highly, nor can these capabilities be explained by natural selection or evolution. We owe nothing to these allegedly scientifically proven processes for our moral, ethical, and spiritual qualities.

Evolution and natural selection can no more account for man's physical features than they can for his moral and spiritual nature. The complexity and ingenuity of design, beginning with the smallest cell, could not possibly have come about by chance. At this point, Dawkins protests loudly, as we've heard him do in a number of debates, "Of course evolution couldn't come about by chance! Natural selection is the very opposite of chance!"

Here Dawkins is guilty of denying the problem of origins. When theists say evolution and natural selection could not come about by chance, they speak the truth. Atheists forget that these theories upon which they rely require the existence of a replicating organism even to get started. This is what could only come about by chance. The mathematics undeniably proves that it is impossible, and we will deal with that fact in depth later. So, no matter how loudly Dawkins protests, it is irrefutable that evolution and natural selection cannot explain the origin of biological life.

Can Dawkins give us a physical description of the phrase "couldn't come about" or of the word "chance"? Or would he prefer to try giving a physical description of the phrase "the very opposite"? As a materialist, he insists that nothing exists but the physical world. But many of the ideas he expresses continually do not have physical qualities nor do they occupy physical space. Neither are they found anywhere in the physical universe. Where does Dawkins put them? We're waiting for him to tell us.

BACK TO THE "GOAL-SEEKING APPARATUS"

We dimwits will not let Dawkins off the hook until he explains himself and makes some sense out of this nonsense. How and when was this amazing *apparatus* first developed in the long history of evolution? What was the natural selection process that brought it about and now controls it? When, how, and why in the evolutionary process was this "goal-seeking" apparatus "switched to different goals"?

How does this physical (it *must* be physical) "apparatus," which Dawkins can neither locate nor describe, know about goal seeking? How does natural selection insert into the mind this conscious ambition and determination? Has this scientist identified the gene or genes involved? How does he know this, so that he can make these astonishing statements with such authority?

Surely these are reasonable questions that we have the right and really an obligation to ourselves and to others to ask. We must not take the pressure off Dawkins until he explains himself coherently. We are not going to let the self-proclaimed brights intimidate us no matter how high their higher education or how glittering their degrees, honors, and careers. Incredibly, much of the scientific world, now under the spell of atheism, supinely submits—and that's the difference between scientific subjects (chemistry, physics, and genetics) as they were in the early days when scientists uncovered evidence and supported established laws, and what they have become since the advent of Darwin and Freud.

Who could prove that Dawkins's declaration isn't true? No one. This theory is not science but a never-never land of unproved theories stated as truth. This is bald-faced conjecture confidently presented as if it were scientific fact. It is not falsifiable, as any truly scientific theory must be, yet it is authoritatively announced as though it were. This is deliberate deception. He gets away with it because this is Richard Dawkins speaking, Oxford University's former Simonyi Professor of the Public Understanding of Science. Surely he wouldn't betray that noble status and give the public anything but scientific facts, would he?

THE NEW ANTI-GOD CRUSADE

Leading the New Atheists as one of the Four Horsemen, Dawkins is a crusader for the rejection of the existence of God. What is the atheists' agenda? Of course they want to destroy faith in God. In the process, as John Lennox told Dawkins in their "The God Delusion" debate in October 2007, "atheism undermines science by denying its very foundation. Almost all the founders of science accepted that the universe has order because it has an intelligent Creator."

Read the atheists' books and listen to their talks. They overflow with the same evangelistic fervor for which they criticize evangelical Christians. The major goal in life for Dawkins and his fellow New Atheists is to convert the world to atheism. They consider evangelism for atheism a legitimate, even a moral, obligation, but evangelism for Christ is illegitimate and ought to be banned. No bias there, of course. In fact, Richard Dawkins goes so far as to say that "children are especially vulnerable to infection by the virus of religion. . . . It's time to question the abuse of childhood innocence with superstitious ideas of hellfire and damnation. . . . Such labeling of children with their parents' religion ('Christian' child and 'Muslim' child) is child abuse."[8]

The New Atheists' aggressiveness and organization is a recent phenomenon, light years beyond the days when Madalyn Murray O'Hair was the only well-known atheist. Never before have atheists been so belligerent as a group nor has atheism been so openly confessed and so popular among so many. Between the four of them, Dawkins, Dennett, Harris, and Hitchens have sold millions of books that are having a major impact in today's world. Dawkins said, "What I want to urge upon you is *militant atheism*. . . . My approach to attacking creationism is to attack religion as a whole."[9] They have made an impressive start toward that goal.

THE HITCHENS "CHALLENGE"

Christopher Hitchens has issued a challenge, now widely publicized, which he says no one has been able to answer. It goes like this: "Name me an ethical statement made or an action performed by a believer that could not have been made or performed by a non-believer." In fact, many people have answered his challenge on the internet, but he ignores them. Hitchens imagines that his "unanswered" challenge supports his statement that "you don't have to believe in God or be religious to do good things."

The challenge is not as clever as Hitchens imagines it to be. It is hardly worthy of the intellect he usually displays. In fact, it's rather naïve, for it actually supports theism instead of refuting it, in that it presupposes an innate moral and ethical value system. If all mankind did not share this common set of morals, the challenge would be worthless because it would mean different things to different people. In specific response to Hitchens, it could be said that although an unbeliever is capable of doing the same good deeds as a believer, he cannot do them for the same moral and rational reasons.

Natural selection did not create this common conscience. Here we come back to a major problem for the evolutionist atheist: there is no place in the philosophy of materialism for morals or even ideas. Atheists like to pretend that God is not needed and have desperately tried to support this assertion.

It is clear that our species' understanding of right and wrong did not come through natural selection because Darwinism can deal only with the physical world. Although the exhaustive instruction manual in the DNA is written in words, its instructions only involve the physical, not the realm of the mental or moral, and indeed could not, if materialism is to be accepted as a valid philosophy.

What is the source of mankind's universal moral understanding? The credit certainly cannot be given to Darwin. Hitchens, Dawkins, and most other atheists love to repeat their mantra, "You don't have to have a book to tell you what is right and what is wrong."

How did natural selection develop this "ghost" that supposedly haunts us with morals? One thing we do know: conscience hasn't "changed over the decades." In fact, it can be traced back to Moses and the Law of God that he received on Mount Sinai, and it has unquestionably come down to us intact. What *do* change are society's customs and taboos, but what has not changed are the timeless moral standards that God wrote in the conscience when our first parents ate of the forbidden fruit and "became as gods, knowing good and evil."

Notice that it doesn't say they "became like God" but "as *gods*," another name for Satan's minions, who, like mankind, are following their master's clearly stated rebellious ambition: "I will be like the most High."[10] Here we have the beginning of conscience—it was implanted in man at the moment he joined Satan's rebellion.

Hitchens's challenge is actually pointless because the Bible, the very book he hates and misrepresents, answered his challenge nearly 2,000 years ago:

> For when the Gentiles, which have not the law, do by nature the things contained in the law, these, having not the law, are a law unto themselves: which show the work of the law written in their hearts, their conscience also bearing them witness, and their thoughts the meanwhile accusing or else excusing one another.[11]

DARWIN'S AMAZING INFLUENCE ON RELIGION AND SOCIETY AS A WHOLE

A century ago, England was the major center of Christianity in the West. For many years, it had been sending out thousands of missionaries carrying the message of Christ to the world. Darwin and Freud changed all that. Dawkins explains, "Any creationist lawyer who got me on the stand could instantly win over the jury simply by asking me: 'Has your knowledge of evolution influenced you in the direction of becoming an atheist?' I would have to answer yes."[12] Dawkins confesses that Darwinism turned him from a fine "Christian" English youth into an atheist. He even says that he might still be a theist had it not been for Darwin:

> [I] lost my faith for good at about the age of 15 or 16. That was because I discovered Darwinism. I recognized that there was no good reason to believe in any kind of supernatural creator. And my final vestige of religious faith

disappeared when I finally understood the Darwinian explanation for life.[13]

He was badly mistaken. In fact, neither Darwinism nor any branch of science can explain life, its origin, or its meaning, and Darwinism doesn't even make a serious attempt to do so, but the teenage Dawkins thought it had. We can excuse him for such naiveté *then*. For making such erroneous statements *today*, however, we must charge him with deliberate misrepresentation because now he knows better. Dawkins knowingly credits and praises Darwin for what he did not and could not accomplish. This is deceitful and misleads those who ignorantly accept such misrepresentations as scientifically valid.

As every perceptive reader had known from the time of its publication, Darwin's first book, *On The Origin of Species by Means of Natural Selection, or The Preservation of Favoured Races in the Struggle for Life,* far from living up to the promise in its name, did not offer an explanation of the origin of even one species! It did, however, provide "scientific" justification for racism while convincing young Dawkins of evolution and natural selection.

Having been converted to atheism through Darwinism, Dawkins attempts to promote and defend this theory at every turn. He is not one from whom we would solicit an unbiased scientific opinion about whether evolution is true and has been proved as a fact. Rare would be any evolutionist who would admit to the gaping holes in this theory or to its glaring defects. For example, here is a typical response one would receive from Googling "evolution as fact":

> Evolution is a fact, not a theory. Scientists generally agree that Darwin's Theory of Evolution is the correct explanation of how life on earth evolved. . . .[14]

Even if that were a true statement, it tells us nothing about the origin of life, what life is, or its meaning. Hundreds of scientists disagree with evolution and are signing up on an internet site, in a list that daily grows, to express their opposition to this unscientific theory.[15] It is dishonest for Dawkins and other atheists to continue to give the impression that no credible scientists oppose evolution. Moreover, isn't it a gross misrepresentation to claim to explain "how life on earth evolved," when science admits it can't tell us what life is or how it first appeared on earth?

OPPOSITION TO EVOLUTION GROWS IN AMERICA

We will give more than sufficient scientific reasons for rejecting evolution and natural selection later, but for the moment, let us continue a simple commonsense approach. Darwin immediately ran into stiff opposition from numbers of scientists. Due to the influence of biblical Christianity, evolution was once almost unanimously rejected by the entire Western world, especially by leading scientists, a fact we have documented by citing Christians who are still looked to as the founders of modern science.

Sir Isaac Newton gave us the most important scientific book ever written: *Philosophiae Naturalis Principia Mathematica*. Yet he wrote more about the Bible than about science. Robert Boyle is known as the first modern chemist and is credited with laying the foundation of modern chemistry. His book *The Skeptical Chymist* was a cornerstone work of modern chemistry. He endowed a lecture series, "The Boyle Lectures" (ironically still carried on at Oxford University, where Dawkins held forth as professor), "for proving the Christian religion against notorious infidels."

Right here, we are forced to distinguish between *biblical* Christianity and those sects that still ostensibly use the Bible as some sort of a guide but do not believe that it is all inspired and who accept evolution as the way God created man and animals. As more and more pastors, churches, and denominations deny the infallibility and sufficiency of the Bible, the acceptance of evolution among Christians grows.

In contrast to its initial rejection in the West, evolution was taken for granted in the East as well as throughout Europe. This was largely due to the influence of Buddhism and Hinduism, where evolution (through the teaching of reincarnation) has been an intimate part of both culture and religion for thousands of years. It remains so today.

We noted some of the founders of modern science who opposed Darwin from the very start. They were nearly all Christians. In the West, the opposition to evolution can be largely attributed to the influence of Christianity. The latest polls show figures that alarm atheists, particularly the scientists among them and especially the belligerent New Atheists.

In spite of reports in the media and the fact that the teaching of Intelligent Design, even as an alternative to evolution, is still generally forbidden in public schools (especially in universities, as the documentary film *Expelled* clearly shows), here are some of the results of recent polls, which are most disturbing to atheists:

> In 2004: a Gallup poll revealed that 81 percent of American teenagers think that God controlled or influenced the origin of humans.
>
> A CBS News Poll found that 65 percent of Americans think that both creationism and evolution should be taught in schools, and that 55 percent believe that "God created humans in present form.
>
> The Gallup poll showed that 45 percent believe that the world is less than 10,000 years old; the same poll found that 35 percent say that evolution is well supported by the evidence; 35 percent say that it is not.[16]
>
> According to a National Geographic survey in 2005, only 14 percent of adults in America thought that evolution was "definitely true," while about a third firmly rejected the idea.
>
> Researchers point out that the number of Americans who are uncertain about the theory's validity has increased over the past 20 years.[17]

The figures for Europe are just the opposite. There, atheism has long dominated the scene. Understandably, Dawkins has felt the need for a special effort to persuade Americans to accept the atheist point of view, i.e., to embrace evolution. Remember, it was Darwinism that turned Dawkins into an atheist, and he is hoping to do the same for the rest of the world. For him, of course, the evidence for evolution is so persuasive that a proper presentation would convince everyone:

> The standard creationist argument is this (there is only one, they all reduce to this one): "Living creatures are too complex to have come about by chance. Therefore, they must have had a designer." This argument, of course, shoots itself in the foot. Any designer capable of designing something really complex has to be complex in himself. . . .[18]

Isn't Dawkins the one who is shooting himself in the foot? Isn't he saying that human beings, capable of conceiving complex scientific theories, must themselves have been designed? Of course he wants this sequence to continue on endlessly and not allow it to stop at God, the ultimate Designer. Otherwise, the little child is correct in endlessly asking "why, Daddy?" How is Daddy going to stop this neverending string of questions without eventually giving the ultimate answer to all questions, which indeed there must be? If God does not exist, there is no ultimate explanation. Obviously, God did not come about by chance, nor can He be explained. Part of the definition of God is that He is transcendent, beyond space, time, matter, and in a category of His own. God *must* be unique. He is the *Creator*, and rules of logic relative to His creation do not necessarily apply to Him.

We have already commented upon what seems to be an obvious fact: Dawkins treats Darwin almost as though he were God. Whatever Darwin said must be true. This superhuman status given to Darwin by evolutionists ought in itself to cast suspicion on this whole evolutionary system. It indicates a form of blindness when it comes to Darwinism. No human being is infallible. Darwin is not pronouncing natural law such as the laws of physics and chemistry, which can be verified and also falsified. He is merely giving us a theory with which many scientists disagree, scientists who were certainly at least as intelligent and competent as he, and obviously, with the advance of science since Darwin's day, now know far more than he did. Then why should we fall in line and embrace what clearly has so many contradictions, lack of evidence, and so many "missing links"?

As evidence of our evaluation of the Darwinian movement, notice the superlatives in what Dawkins goes on to reverently utter:

> Darwinian natural selection is so stunningly elegant because it solves the problem of explaining complexity in terms of nothing but simplicity. Essentially, it does it by providing a smooth ramp of gradual, step-by-step increments.[19]
>
> I could not imagine anyone being an atheist at any time before 1859, when Darwin's *Origin of Species* was published.... Although atheism might have been logically tenable before Darwin, Darwin made it possible to be an intellectually fulfilled atheist."[20]

Of course, much depends upon one's definition of God. The polls consistently show 90-95 percent of Americans, year after year, believing in some sort of "God," but a very small minority of them believe in the God of the Bible. Most of them would likely be deists of some sort, as was Einstein:

> I do not believe in a personal God and I have never denied this but have expressed it clearly. If something is in me which can be called religious then it is the unbounded admiration for the structure of the world so far as our science can reveal it.[21]

PARDON ME, YOUR BIAS IS SHOWING

Dawkins's assertion that genes (which by his own admission are not conscious, know nothing of purpose, and do not look ahead) are attempting through *psychological manipulation* to change our brains for their own purposes is incredible.[22] No less amazing is how genes learned psychological techniques—another mystery that Dawkins has not explained. This is unsupported theory, undemonstrated, unproved, and unreliable, like so much of what Dawkins dares to pronounce as scientifically established truth. In fact, it is sheer speculation used as a cover to support his atheism.

We must, however, credit Dawkins with an amazingly fertile imagination. Suddenly, without explanation, example, or scientific experimental proof, natural selection has graduated from creating visible physiological characteristics to manipulating invisible emotional and psychological behavior. Does Dawkins have any factual basis to support this unique idea? If so, he's keeping it a secret.

No one denies genetic changes of physical traits and related behavior *within a species*, such as the first example that Darwin used to illustrate his theory, that of the finches on the Galapagos Islands. Their beaks changed slightly. But when we ask for examples of natural selection creating *new species,* we hit a stone wall of evasiveness and tentative theories lacking concrete examples. After "millions of years of evolution" and more than 100 years of scouring the planet for fossils that would solidly back up Darwinism, virtually nothing of substance has been found. And yet boards of education and legislative bodies still refuse to allow evolution to be challenged, and the media resists allowing competent scientists to expose the nakedness of their new emperor.

No, *emperor* is the wrong word. *Dictator* would be far more appropriate. It is time to no longer play the part of lemmings following the brights over a cliff. We demand solid proof before we take another step on this trail that Dawkins wants us to follow to blind acceptance of evolution and Darwinism.

Natural selection *within a species* is accepted by virtually everyone, including creationists. It is, however, supposed to be the means by which *new* species evolve from other species. After millions of years of this alleged process in the formation of the 400,000 species of plants from moss to vegetables, 17,000 species of fish and other sea creatures,

950,000 species of insects, 225,000 species of animals, there ought to be tens of thousands of intermediary fossils for evolutionists to present as proof of this theory. In fact, there are *none*.

Now and then we find an evolutionist who is willing to admit the truth. The late senior paleontologist of the British Museum of Natural History, Colin Patterson, came directly to the point. Ten years before his death, in a personal letter responding to a reader's inquiry concerning the complete lack of transitional forms in his book *Evolution*, he wrote:

10th April 1979

Dear Mr Sunderland,

I fully agree with your comments on the lack of direct illustration of evolutionary transitions in my book. If I knew of any, fossil or living, I would certainly have included them. You suggest that an artist should be used to visualize such transformations, but where would he get the information? I could not, honestly, provide it, and if I were to leave it to artistic license, would that not mislead the reader. . . ?

Gradualism is a concept I believe in . . . because my understanding of genetics seems to demand it. Yet Gould and the American Museum people are hard to contradict when they say there are no transitional fossils. . . .

You say that I should at least "show a photo of the fossil from which each type of organism was derived." I will lay it on the line—there is not one such fossil for which one could make a watertight argument. The reason is that statements about ancestry and descent are not applicable in the fossil record. Is Archaeopteryx the ancestor of all birds? Perhaps yes, perhaps no: there is no way of answering the question. It is easy enough to make up stories of how one form gave rise to another, and to find reasons why the stages should be favoured by natural selection. But such stories are not part of science, for there is no way of putting them to the test.

So, much as I should like to oblige you by jumping to the defence of gradualism, and fleshing out the transitions between the major types of animals and plants, I find myself a bit short of the intellectual justification necessary for the job. Thanks again for writing.

Yours sincerely,

[signature]

Colin Patterson [23]

Like Colin Patterson, American Museum of Natural History paleontologist Stephen Jay Gould, widely quoted and respected author, acknowledged that there is *not one* reliable example of an intermediary form. Yet this unsubstantiated theory continues to be taught as *fact* in the media and in textbooks, with no challenge allowed. To do so is unconscionable.

An article written by Dawkins in the October 5, 2009, issue of *Newsweek*, titled "The Angry Evolutionist: More Americans believe in angels than in evolution," does indeed have an angry tone as Dawkins tries once again to defend his idol, Charles Darwin, and the theory of evolution. His article offers nothing new. Basically, it is an attempt to respond to what he imagines are creationists' major objections to evolution, such as gaps in the fossil record, why there are "so few fossils before the Cambrian era," etc. He makes the astonishing statement that "we don't need fossils in order to demonstrate that evolution is a fact." This seems odd, since evolutionists spend so much time offering fossils as evidence.

The problem is the "missing link" from animal to man. Evolutionists have been searching all over the world and have finally zeroed in on Africa. The chimpanzee, according to its DNA, is supposedly the closest relative to man. How could Dawkins say that no fossils are needed "to demonstrate that evolution is a fact"? Certainly, there is a *huge* gap in the fossil record from chimpanzee to man. Moreover, in this book, we show that the difference between the animal world and mankind is not a matter of physical structure, whether of the brain itself or of any other part of man's body. Something else is involved, and explaining what that is comprises much of the following pages.

There is a shameful suppression of any challenge to Darwinism and atheism in the scientific and academic world. This extends to both sides of the Atlantic. That fact is fully documented through filmed interviews with Ben Stein in Paramount Pictures' movie, *Expelled*. Numerous tenured and published professors with impeccable reputations and credentials in scientific fields testify on camera that as soon they so much as mentioned in a book, academic paper, or classroom discussion the two words, *Intelligent Design*, they were either fired or pressured into resigning.

SCIENCE "THEN" AND "NOW"

There is an important difference between science as it was *then*, in the days of Newton, Boyle, and the other theist founders, when ongoing physical observation led to theories, which, after careful verification, became established laws—and science *now*, since Darwin, when wild tales are told and automatically accepted without essential verification. Apparently, a public gullible enough to swallow the impossible dreams of the "space program" and to pay for them with tax dollars can be talked into almost anything, no matter how outrageous, if applauded by "scientists."

The theories postulated and carefully verified by science *then* became the foundational laws of science as we have it today: the laws of physics, chemistry, genetics, of motion, gasses, and so much else that today's science still relies upon. Why don't today's scientists continue to provide us with an increasing number of similar laws? It was because these laws were born of the belief that the God of the Bible exists, that He is the Creator of the physical universe and all life, and that He has established laws governing it—laws that man can discover, understand, and use to his betterment.

In stark contrast, science *now* is atheistic and built upon the con-temptuous rejection of a personal Creator. As a consequence, we have a disorder in modern science that Dawkins and his cohorts boast about—indeed, insist upon. Incredibly, they will not consent to any intelligence whatsoever being involved at any stage. Consider this statement by evolutionary biologist and geneticist Richard Lewontin, typical of what atheists declare: "We are forced by our *a priori* adher-ence to material causes to create an apparatus of investigation and a set of concepts that produce material explanations, no matter how counter-intuitive . . . materialism is an absolute, for *we cannot allow a Divine Foot in the door* (emphasis added)."[24]

Lewontin, like other atheists, is not at all reluctant to admit his unscientific bias. Nor is Dawkins hesitant to pass his atheistic preju-dices off as the only true science:

> Certainly I see the scientific view of the world as incompatible with religion, but that is not what is interesting about it. It is also incompatible with magic, but that also is not worth stressing. What is interesting about the scientific worldview is that it is true, inspiring, remarkable and that it unites a whole lot of phenomena under a single heading.[25]

Dawkins expresses his personal opinion yet dares to call it "the scientific view of the world." Tragically, what is called "science" today is actually a new brand of paganism. Paul's explanation of the roots of idolatry is insightful for today:

> When they knew God, they glorified him not as God, neither were thankful; but became vain in their imaginations, and their foolish heart was darkened. Professing themselves to be wise, they became fools, and changed the glory of the uncorruptible God into an image made like to corruptible man, and to birds, and fourfooted beasts, and creeping things.[26]

Like Dawkins, and showing the accuracy of Paul's prophecy, Victor Ferkiss, Emeritus Professor of Government at Georgetown University, approvingly claims that ecological concern "starts with the premise that the Universe is God."[27] Likewise, Carl Sagan, the deceased high priest of cosmos worship, declared with the authority of academia behind him: "If we must worship a power greater than ourselves, does it not make sense to revere the Sun and stars?"[28] No, it doesn't make sense, except to those who reject the witness of creation, conscience, and common sense.

One finds it difficult to see much difference between the ancient pagan worship of nature and the creatures inhabiting it and what Sagan and Ferkiss had to say. Has the new science, driven by atheism, taken us full circle back to our pagan roots? This seems ironic, considering the pride with which Dawkins and his fellow atheists view their "higher education" and the disdain with which they regard all those who believe in God as somehow incapable of sound reasoning.

DARWIN, DARWIN, DARWIN

True science began with discoveries that became theories and were finally established as laws by repeated experimentation. Any theory depends to a large extent upon the originator's worldview. Dawkins has made his view very clear. It is an outgrowth of his atheism and he is adamant about it. To the atheist, nothing has any purpose or meaning. Absolutely nothing. Dawkins believes that his "creator" genes have neither mind nor will, cannot foresee the future, nor plan ahead. No wonder he titled one of his books *The Blind Watchmaker*.

Dawkins really believes this stuff and pushes it with a religious fervor. He is passionately convinced that his "creator" is totally blind and *must* be, has no understanding (and must not) of anything, doesn't know what's going to happen next—in fact, doesn't know anything and isn't even conscious. Could anyone rationally live as though this were the "force" in charge of one's destiny? Perhaps Dawkins only hopes that God is *morally* blind and will exact no retribution, either in this life or in a life to come, if there happens to be one.

Obviously, if a scientist believes that his "creator" is blind, everything he discovers will tend to verify this, and it will become the foundation of the "science" for which he will then seek evidence. The worldview of the founders of modern science was basically the opposite of the atheists who today claim to speak for the science that theists founded. The impact of this fact is so staggering that it could bring the destruction of the Western world. This book will continue to sound the alarm as a warning of the destructive nature of atheism and where it could take us.

It is impossible to escape the obvious similarities between the false hopes spawned by the space program and the false promises of Darwinism and its followers today. We have already seen how nearly the entire world has been carried away with the enthusiastic promise that space beyond our solar system can be fruitfully explored, when in fact this is a popular delusion promoted by the space industry to their own advantage. Is it possible that the theory of evolution is a similar delusion, this time promoted by evolutionists in order to justify their hatred of God and to protect their jobs and their standing in the academic world?

It's long past time for a voice out of the throng of admiring onlookers to cry in alarm, "The emperor is naked!"

We do not understand the process of dying, nor can we say anything clear, for sure, about what happens to human thought after death.

—LEWIS THOMAS, M.D., "ON SCIENCE AND UNCERTAINTY,"
DISCOVER, VOL. 1 (OCTOBER 1980), 59

Since the big bang theory implies that the entire observed universe can evolve from a tiny speck, it's tempting to ask whether a universe can in principle be created in a laboratory. Given what we know of the laws of physics, would it be possible for an extraordinarily advanced civilization to create new universes at will?

—ALAN H. GUTH, "COOKING UP A COSMOS,"
ASTRONOMY, VOL. 25 (SEPTEMBER 1997), 54-57

The first, and main problem is the very existence of the big bang. One may wonder, What came before? If space-time did not exist then, how could everything appear from nothing? What arose first: the universe or the laws determining its evolution? Explaining this initial singularity—where and when it all began—still remains the most intractable problem of modern cosmology.

—ANDRÉ LINDE, "THE SELF-REPRODUCING INFLATIONARY UNIVERSE,"
SCIENTIFIC AMERICAN, VOL. 271 (NOVEMBER 1994), 48-55

The popular conception of primitive cells as the starting point for the origin of the species is really erroneous. There was nothing functionally primitive about such cells. They contained basically the same biochemical equipment as do their modern counterparts. . . . How, then, did the precursor cell arise? The only unequivocal rejoinder to this question is that we do not know.

—DAVID E. GREEN AND ROBERT F. GOLDBERGER,
MOLECULAR INSIGHTS INTO THE LIVING PROCESS
(NEW YORK: ACADEMIC PRESS, 1967), 403

It was already clear that the genetic code is not merely an abstraction but the embodiment of life's mechanisms; the consecutive triplets of nucleotides in DNA (called codons) are inherited but they also guide the construction of proteins. . . . So it is disappointing that the origin of the genetic code is still as obscure as the origin of life itself.

—JOHN MADDOX, "THE GENESIS CODE BY NUMBERS,"
NATURE, VOL. 367 (JANUARY 13, 1994), 111

THREE

THE NEW ATHEISTS' SPECULATIVE "SCIENCE"

ONE OF THE MOST HILARIOUS SHOWS on the internet stars Richard Dawkins playing himself back in the early days when he was ascending the first few rungs of the ladder to fame and fortune. With some updates, this early DVD has now become part of a series that is being offered to every secondary school in the UK. Looking surprisingly youthful, even boyish, in this early video, the star steps onto the stage and faces a rather small audience surrounded by numerous props including prehistoric creatures, a huge take-apart plastic eye, and a model of "Mount Improbable" made famous by Dawkins's book by that name. It is amazing how precisely the model shows the various hazards on this totally imaginary "mount," depicting the tortuous upward path of natural selection from a single cell to man.

How could Dawkins have known enough to *accurately* portray natural selection's alleged path in developing species? His presentation is pure speculation in its most brazen form. We're all familiar with models of the solar system or models of new houses under construction—but models that show how evolution and natural selection work? This was a new idea that Dawkins proudly pioneered, and much of the scientific world has gone along with it. Atheists love it because they think it gives them the perfect escape from God. The layman is excited because he trustingly believes it provides a clear picture of what happens in natural selection.

In explaining the models' depiction of how evolution supposedly works, Dawkins's presentation is so self-assured that the average audience of atheists and evolutionists enthusiastically accepts it all as truth instead of the elaborate fiction that it really is. A Christian audience, however, finds this scam outrageously unbelievable.

WHERE, O WHERE, HAS OUR "EVIDENCE" GONE?

Even Dawkins, in an honest moment, would not deny that his mythical "Mount Improbable" is a product of his imagination and lacks any evidence to support its precise landscape. He would protest, however, that it was never intended to be the basis of a comedy show. Its purpose was to provide an illustration of the process of natural selection as it modifies existing species and evolves new ones.

Why, however, was this make-believe Mount even necessary, and why did Dawkins think it would be helpful? Are there not sufficient real-life examples providing more proof than necessary? Wouldn't fossil evidence be preferable? What about the literally billions of fossils that ought to be littering the landscape? The simple but suppressed answer to that question is that *there are none*. How does a non-scientist like myself dare to make such a statement? One may "Google"

and "Yahoo" to the point of exhaustion asking for "Examples of evolution and natural selection." What is offered? We're faced with the
same worn-out and discredited examples that continue to show up in
evolutionists' textbooks and websites: the peppered moth, the developing human fetus with supposed gills and a tail, "Lucy," bacteria and
viruses that develop immunity to antibiotics by losing information,
not by evolving higher, *ad infinitum*.

There is not just a paucity of fossil evidence—*it doesn't exist*. Isn't it
time for us to ask the "brights" for more than just a hint of something
hoped for here and there? We demand the overwhelming evidence
that ought to exist if evolution is true. Where is it? When we ask why
we don't see evidence of natural selection in progress today, we are
told that this occurs in very tiny steps over millions of years. If that
is true, natural selection should have left in its wake *billions* of fossils
testifying both to its successful upward step-by-step progress and to
the many failures that had to be discarded along the way.

We don't ask for thousands of examples—or even hundreds—but
shouldn't there at least be a few dozen unquestionable ones? Where
are they? Isn't it pitiful that the Leakeys have devoted a lifetime in
pursuit of the missing link between man and the chimpanzee or some
other primate species and come up with nothing but very questionable specimens?

There is an embarrassing lack of fossil evidence that persists across
the entire spectrum of evolutionary theory. Here is a puzzling fact that
haunts evolutionists honest enough to face the truth. Darwin tried to
explain away the seemingly odd absence of intermediary forms as due
to "the extreme imperfection" of the fossil record. That excuse is no
longer plausible. We have uncovered millions of fossils since Darwin's
day, but there are no unquestionable "missing links" of any consequence among them.

Evolutionists continue their fruitless pursuit of some solid evidence. The latest fossil find that has raised their hopes has been named
Ardipithicus ramidus, triumphantly known as "Ardi."[1] The remains
were found in the Middle Awash region of Ethiopia over the course

of 15 years. The find has elicited much further discussion and speculation. As always, however, there is not a word about the vast chasm that separates all living creatures from man. Is there anything in the skeletal remains of this latest find that suggests it may have been developing human qualities, such as the ability to form conceptual ideas and express them in words? Of course not! These qualities are not to be found in physical remains. So what is the point of this continued search for a missing link among the widely scattered fossils?

This fact raises further questions and casts a dark shadow over the entire subject of evolution and natural selection. Dawkins's claim that no fossil evidence is needed is rationalized because, supposedly, it's all there in the DNA. That is troubling. If it's not in the fossil record, doesn't that logically raise questions concerning the confident conclusions supposedly supported by DNA analysis? It is hardly necessary to repeat the embarrassing trail of such fraudulent "missing links" as Piltdown Man, Java Man, Nebraska Man, Neanderthal Man, et al.

In the previous chapter, we saw the difference between the old science and the new, science as it was originally, when theists were making groundbreaking discoveries, and "science" as it is today under the control of atheists. In the early days, science depended upon established laws of physics, chemistry, astrophysics, biology, mathematics, etc. Tragically, however, today's "science" is founded on the unproven and unprovable assumption of atheism. It remains a "science" of speculation, unsupported by evidence, with a predetermined goal: to prove there is no God.

For those who object to this statement, though we supported it in the previous chapter, let's call back from the grave and to the witness stand for their testimony two impeccably qualified experts.

EMBARRASSING AND SUPPRESSED FACTS

On May 20, 2002, the late Stephen Jay Gould, a leading spokesperson for evolution, stated: "The extreme rarity of transitional forms in the fossil record persists as a trade secret of paleontology. The evolutionary trees that adorn our textbooks have data only at the tips and nodes of their branches; the rest is inference . . . not the evidence of fossils."[2] We have already quoted Colin Patterson declaring, "There is not one [transitional] fossil for which one could make a watertight argument." Such facts should be honestly admitted in high school and college textbooks rather than suppressed. In spite of the lack of evidence, evolutionists continue to publish and lecture as though the hopeful scenario they present is actually factual. The very "artistic license" shunned by Patterson has been, for more than 100 years, a major means of promoting evolution by natural selection as an established fact of science.

Talking about "artistic license," what about Dawkins's phony model, which he so laboriously constructed and used in his lectures? His book *Climbing Mount Improbable* has carried this avoidance of truth to new heights of imagination. On our climb up Mount Improbable, Dawkins gives the example of tigers and lions, once a single species but through geographical separation becoming so dissimilar that they had to be treated as different species. Does he call this a valid example of "evolution" from plants to humans forming new species? Are we supposed to be convinced on the basis of such examples that the highly touted theories of evolution and natural selection are established fact?

There are obvious and huge differences between breeds of dogs, but they are still dogs. No examples are given of a dog changing into a cat or a rabbit into a coyote. If, back at the beginning of life, in the first living cell, we all had one common ancestor and, in this tortuous process over millions of years, there has been much branching off, creating thousands of additional single ancestors from which diverse species descended, where are the fossils that document this trail? Why doesn't Dawkins join Gould and Patterson in admitting the truth? Atheists are still hoping for the "missing link" that will rescue them from the embarrassment of admitting they've been wrong all these years. How much longer must we wait?

One soon discovers that everything depends upon how "species" is defined and that the experts don't agree among themselves. In the

Foreword to Dawkins's *The Selfish Gene*, Robert Trivers said, "Natural selection has built us, and it is natural selection we must understand if we are to comprehend our own identities."[3] What is this identity that Trivers and Dawkins want us to understand and that has been given to us by natural selection, which, as an unthinking process, knows nothing about "identity"?

Consider just two examples: Dawkins says, "We're not just like animals, we are animals. . . . What are all of us but self-reproducing robots? We have been put together by our genes and what we do is roam the world looking for a way to sustain ourselves and ultimately produce another robot child."[4]

This is quite a revelation from Dawkins as to where the religion of atheism logically leads. I doubt that there is one person in a thousand who would be happy to know that he or she was nothing but an *animal* and a *self-reproducing robot*.

"HALF AN EYE"?

Still on stage, in his continuing fantasy, Dawkins tells his eager and trusting audience, "The creationist's favourite question is, 'What is the use of half an eye?' Actually, this is a lightweight question, a doddle to answer. Half an eye is just 1 per cent better than 49 per cent of an eye. . . ."

Dawkins speaks with such confident authority! Has he, or anyone else, ever verified in controlled experiments that 49 percent or 50 percent of an eye could exist, much less function—or that half an eye could really see one percent better than 49 percent? One may be absolutely certain that Dawkins has no experimental data to support such claims. Suppose we ask, "Instead of 50 percent of an eye, what good would 1 percent of an eye be?" It couldn't be 1 percent better than no eye. Dawkins is offering a desperate argument that common sense immediately recognizes as fallacious. Half an eye has no value at all, and natural selection would have eliminated it as worthless long before it got to that stage of "evolutionary development." This is make-believe, at which Dawkins is the unsurpassed master, all the while presenting it as fully established scientific fact. The man has built his worldwide reputation on such imaginative tales presented in book after book, all of them bestsellers that have charmed millions of eager readers.

Why doesn't Dawkins admit the truth instead of offering "scientific facts" without admitting that there is no supporting data? He's following a long tradition. That's the way it is and has been with evolution since the very beginning: very little substance but a lot of diagrams and artists' depictions, even phony fossils, some of which are still presented pictorially in textbooks in spite of having been exposed as fraudulent. Dawkins is just a whole lot more successful in telling this tale than anyone else.

Evolution is the most elaborate justification for atheism that has ever been devised, and some scientists, such as the Leakeys, have devoted their lives without significant success to digging up various parts of the world in order to support atheism "scientifically." Make no mistake—atheism is what evolution and natural selection are all about. Its effect not only on science but also on society has been far beyond anything Darwin could have imagined. Is it possible that the atheistic transformation of modern society has only begun and will be more far-reaching than we can imagine? Will it be progress to overturn the theistic foundation of western science?

AN ELABORATE HOAX

Obviously, the scenario Dawkins presents is a deception, as is the rest of Mount Improbable, where the amazing formation of thousands of different eyes allegedly occurs. In fact, no eyes are formed there. The eye could not be built in stages. An eye is of no value at all for survival unless it can see. Clearly, it must be created complete. Evolution could never take it as far as half an eye (no matter what that might mean) because anything that did not contribute to survival at any stage (1 percent, 2 percent, 3 percent, etc.) would be eliminated by natural selection, preventing this process from even getting started. Dawkins himself declared:

> Unrelentingly and unceasingly, as Darwin explained, "Natural selection is daily and hourly scrutinizing throughout the world every variation, even the slightest; rejecting that which is bad, preserving and adding up all that is good; silently and insensibly working, whenever and wherever opportunity offers at the improvement of each organic being. . . . Ruthless utilitarianism trumps, even if it doesn't always seem that way"[5]

Dawkins claims that it must be a *smooth, gradual development* from no eye to a fully developed eye. How can he make this declaration with such confidence? As he so often does, Dawkins offers no evidence to support this definitive statement. What fraction of an eye would be able to contribute to survival? Surely neither 5 percent of an eye, nor 6 percent, nor 20 percent of an eye could see. Would 80 percent aid in survival? To get to 80 percent, the developing eye would have had to get to 1 percent, 2 percent, 3 percent, etc., but none of these would escape natural selection's *hourly scrutinizing* rejection. "Gradual" simply won't work, because the process couldn't even get started.

This is all make-believe, supposedly coinciding with the slow and laborious ascent up "Mount Improbable" that has taken billions of years. This imaginary Mount is the central attraction in Dawkins's Darwinian fantasyland.

Atheists claim to have found eyes representing every stage of evolution in natural selection's alleged development process. This assertion is specious and desperate. These alleged examples of "developing eyes" are found in different species and different areas of the world with no evidence that one evolved from or into the other. Of course, this is nothing but make-believe, so Dawkins could fill it in with any fantasy. There are plenty of those available as one climbs Mount Improbable. A more rational explanation would be that these different eyes are variations produced by the same designer, whom Dawkins himself refers to as the "architect"[6] because no other word describes what the evidence demands.

And why is it that lower creatures such as lobsters or squids or eagles have lenses that are so far advanced beyond the lenses in our eyes—not only better than the lenses in our eyes but better than any lens we have been able to produce? The brittle star, for example, has a lens in each of its more than 1,000 eyes (designed to act as one eye) that focuses light ten times better than anything man has been able to manufacture. On what peak of Mount Improbable did man get stuck, leaving his eyes so inferior to those of lower creatures? Could it be that we stopped to rest somewhere on Mount Improbable and began making eyeglasses for ourselves instead of evolving further? What a shortsighted decision!

Dawkins is going to explain the origin and evolution of the eye. How does he do it? By *imagining an almost-eye* that is so close to the real eye that it only takes a small final step to complete the journey from "no eye" to the marvel of the human eye as it exists.

Let's illustrate it this way. Let me tell you how to become a multibillionaire the way Dawkins explains evolution, whether of the eye or anything else. We'll start off by assuming that you already have accumulated $999,999,000. You can see that it would be only a small step from there to becoming a billionaire. You only need $1,000 more—and it would only take a million such steps had we started off with $1,000 at the beginning.

Isn't this ingenious! Anyone could become a billionaire. This is great news! You just do it the way evolution does it—one tiny step at a time over billions of years! Well, of course we don't have billions of years, so with another stroke of Dawkins's magic, let's shrink the time scale. Now you can see that it's quite easy to become a billionaire if we just take it in small enough steps. Anyone could surely earn $1,000. Then you could earn another thousand just as easily. And taking it a tiny step at a time it would only take another $1,000 to arrive at a nest egg of $3,000, and so forth, up to $1 billion.

A child could see through this subterfuge. It's a nice fairy tale, but the problem is there aren't any fairies to make it work. There are many obvious problems. How do we get the first $1,000? Oh, well, let's not even worry about the first $1,000. Let's assume that by "punctuated equilibrium," we've already taken a giant leap up to at least $500,000,000.

LET'S PLAY A FANTASY GAME ABOUT WINGS

The "evolution" of the wing presents a serious problem for evolutionists. In the process of trying to explain it, they resort to much hopeful self-delusion and science fiction. Consider the following speculation from James H. Marden, assistant professor of biology at Pennsylvania State University in University Park:

> *Could* early aquatic insects have used the surface of a pond for their own aerodynamic *experiments*? [Who is supposed to answer this question?] *If so*, they *may well have* stepped into what ecologists call predator-free space. Trout and salmon have existed for only about *two million years*. It is harder to *estimate* when the first surface-feeding fish emerged. But the jaw structures of bony fish fossils *suggest* that, until about *300 million years ago*, most fish fed along the bottom or within the water column. In nature, not only the strongest but also the most active tend to survive. Individuals that can gather the most food or encounter the most mates pass on the most genes. . . .
>
> By rising atop the water and moving through the air—a medium fifty times less viscous than water—aquatic insects sent their lives into overdrive. Like rockets escaping the earth's atmosphere, they freed their small bodies from the exhausting effects of drag and the need to keep their shapes streamlined. Once atop the surface, they were morphologically liberated. Forms and functions that once spelled death now offered unexpected advantages. [Emphasis added][7]

Marden is spinning a yarn. His scenario raises huge questions. How would these aquatic insects even get the impulse to "experiment" with flying? Wouldn't that take wings? In fact, these are larvae hatching. They already have wings, and built into them is the instinct to fly. How long would the fish allow these "aerodynamic experiments" without eating all of these tempting morsels—unless the fish at that time had already developed "altruistic genes"?

Dawkins continues the tale: "The ease with which small animals float *suggests* that we have *only to assume* that flying evolved originally in small animals and the flying peak of Mount Improbable immediately looks less formidable. . . . Kingsolver and Koehl . . . *worked on the theory* that the first insect wings were pre-adapted. . . ." [Italicized words show the speculative nature of Dawkins's theorizing.][8]

Speculation, of course, can lead to problems. As a result, Dawkins has had admissions forced upon him by evidence that is far more rational than anything ever discovered by any explorer on Mount Improbable. Some of these admissions are damning. For example, "Biology is the study of complicated things that *give the appearance* of having been designed for a purpose."[9] Isn't it natural selection, and not *a presumably nonexistent "God,"* that is in charge of how the evolutionary process all turns out? Then why would an independent neutral observer, looking at the evidence, be led to the conclusion that natural selection is the result of *design*?

Even more damning, almost amounting to a repudiation of evolution, is Dawkins's confession that, "It is almost as if the human brain were specifically *designed* to misunderstand Darwinism, and to find it hard to believe."[10] This passage has been quoted in many a creationist tome and on many a creationist web page. We all know that Dawkins is not saying that things *are* designed; he's saying things *look* like they are designed and that humans (odd as it may seem) are *programmed* by evolution not to understand evolution!

The Blind Watchmaker (like many of his books that followed) was an attempt by Dawkins to elucidate this distinction. As he stated, "The purpose of this book is to resolve this paradox to the satisfaction of the reader [and] to impress the reader with the power of the illusion of design."[11]

Methinks thou dost protest too loudly! Dawkins is not alone in confessing that natural selection has produced this amazing illusion. No one, however, is able to explain it. Why would natural selection create an *appearance* of design that clearly contradicts everything evolution stands for? Here are two more similar confessions from Dawkins:

> As an academic scientist I am a passionate Darwinian, believing that natural selection is, if not the only driving force in evolution, certainly the only known force capable of producing the illusion of purpose which so strikes all who contemplate nature.[12]
>
> Darwinian natural selection can produce an uncanny illusion of design. An engineer would be hard put to decide whether a bird or a plane was the more aerodynamically elegant. So powerful is the illusion of design, it took humanity until the mid-19th century to realise that it is an illusion.[13]

Come again? *Evolution has developed an elaborate hoax to trick people into imagining that natural selection isn't the way it happened?* Why would evolution develop such a delusion? Consider the following from the foreword to John Maynard Smith's book *The Theory of Evolution*:

> Natural selection is the only workable explanation for the beautiful and compelling illusion of "design" that pervades every living body and every organ.[14]

Illusion of design? The eye (along with every other functional part of every living thing) falls victim to the atheists' attempts to explain away the evidence of design so clearly seen everywhere in the entire cosmos. Dawkins contributes his speculative version:

Half a wing is indeed not as good as a whole wing, but it is certainly better than no wing at all. Half a wing could save your life by easing your fall from a tree of a certain height. And 51 percent of a wing could save you if you fall from a slightly taller tree. Whatever fraction of a wing you have, there is a fall from which it will save your life where a slightly smaller winglet would not. . . . There must be a smooth gradient of advantage all the way from 1 percent of a wing to 100 percent. . . . It is easy to imagine situations in which half an eye would save the life of an animal where 49 percent of an eye would not."[15]

Dawkins is cheating. He's *starting with half an eye.* To which "half" is he referring? No one could possibly know what "half an eye" means or whether it could even exist. He doesn't tell us which half of the eye develops first or how this monstrosity could come into existence. Nor does Dawkins offer any examples of this ever occurring. In fact, it couldn't occur except in Dawkins's imagination.

"Easy to imagine situations in which half an eye would save the life of an animal, where 49 percent of an eye would not"—even if the creature could see with either freakish production of natural selection? We theists aren't that stupid. I challenge Dawkins to provide even *one* such example. It is disappointing to see a scientist writing and lecturing in this reckless manner.

Smooth gradient of advantage? Has Dawkins experimentally and scientifically demonstrated and verified that concept? Five percent of an eye would contribute slightly more to survival than 4 percent of an eye, and thus would move natural selection along? Is this absurd? Doesn't Dawkins realize how ridiculous this whole concept is? And what about the brainwashed millions who think this is brilliant?

"Smooth gradients" and tiny steps over millions of years of evolution and natural selection open up a fascinating vista. Welcome to Dawkins's fantasy worldwide graveyard. The abundant fossil record reveals a horror show of freakish cast offs, many barely recognizable skeletons of partially formed bodies in all stages of evolutionary development. Strewn about are deformed skulls with remnants of fossilized partially developed brains clinging inside. Our vision blurs as, with heads bowed in reverent admiration, we contemplate Darwin's genius and the unflinching loyalty of Dawkins.

A more basic question would be *How does evolution or natural selection get from no life to life and from no cell to a cell?* We're talking about the origin of life, a concept that atheists studiously avoid. If the eye made Darwin shudder, as we will see later, why didn't he think of this even more frightening question: *How did life begin, and what is it?* Perhaps it was so terrifying that he didn't want to admit to himself that his entire theory wasn't even worth thinking about, unless there was a living, replicating cell to start it all off.

Every scientist agrees that the law of biogenesis has been fully established. Natural selection cannot even begin to function until some living thing exists. But how did the first life begin without any preexistent life to "jump-start" it? "Spontaneous generation" is the key, say atheists, even though they know it isn't possible.

THE ATHEISTS' "EXPLANATION" FOR ELIMINATING GOD

In the first of these three comedy shows, Dawkins "explains how the eye evolved" as though it were a scientifically verified fact instead of pure speculation. Listen as he takes us on a guided tour of Mount Improbable in his video series:

> Nautilus [a mollusk that has a pinhole "for an eye"] has a pretty poor eye compared with its relatives, the squids and octopuses, because they do have a lens. So we can't help wondering, *why doesn't Nautilus have a lens?* Why didn't it evolve a lens? Well, I *suspect* that Nautilus may have got itself *stuck on a little peak* some way up *Mount Improbable.* [Emphasis added]

Dawkins talks about "Mount Improbable" as though it really exists and he has explored it from top to bottom. His invention has become so real to Dawkins that it now defines for him and his large following how evolution and natural selection supposedly work. His readers and listeners think that they, too, understand how it all works, and they love it. Come along with Richard Dawkins as he continues his fantasy journey climbing Mount Improbable:

> So we can't help wondering, why didn't Nautilus . . . evolve a lens? . . . [He gestures to the model. . . .] You see that although we've got one big peak there, there are also various other peaks on the way. There are quite a lot of them. . . . When the ancestors of Nautilus got to this point, that way up hill *looked just as inviting . . . evolutionarily*, as that way. . . .
>
> Evolution has no way of knowing that if you travel up that way, you're going to end up with a lens. . . . So . . . *perhaps* Nautilus has got itself trapped . . . and is unable to escape because . . . *the one thing you cannot do on Mount Improbable is ever go downhill.*
>
> *But let's imagine* what the ancestors of the squid and octopus did when they got to this junction here. *They just happened to go up this way* [uses his hands to illustrate walking up Mount Improbable], and they started evolving a lens. And we [humans] did at a different time in history.
>
> How might the lens have evolved? Well, *let's imagine* [And he mocks faith in the essential Creator?] that it started with just a single sheet of some transparent material. And all that this is doing—it's not a lens yet—is just protecting the eye [What eye?].
>
> [Demonstrates, using optician's lenses.] So this is the next stage in evolution. [Inserts second lens.] If an animal had an eye like that [How would it get it? Dawkins doesn't tell us!] it would have a very, very clear view of its world and could tell exactly what its predator was. [Emphasis added]

This is the child's make-believe game: "Let's imagine. . . ." Surely Dawkins can't be serious, but he is, and his entranced audience loves it! We don't know what really happened, admits Dawkins tentatively, but let's play a *fantasy game* and *imagine* it just *might* have been like this.

This is science? Spare us! But it's the best atheism has to offer, showing the bankruptcy of evolutionary theory. Incredibly, Dawkins has built a worldwide reputation as a brilliant scientist on this sort of fantasizing.

When we ask for specific examples of natural selection not merely making changes within a species but actually *creating* new species, we hear nothing but more theory: "It might have been," or "this is one possibility," or "perhaps," or it "possibly could have been," etc. None of the New Atheists' so-called "Four Horsemen" can provide specific examples of transitional forms. No wonder evolutionists are so happy with "Mount Improbable." This ingenious but ludicrous mountain-climbing tale is the best "example" that atheists can produce.

Dawkins offers great advice about remaining skeptical, but only in relation to what he calls "religion":

> Next time somebody tells you something that sounds important, think to yourself, "Is this the kind of thing that people probably know because of evidence or is it the kind of thing that people only believe because of tradition, authority or revelation?" And next time somebody tells you that something is true, why not say to them, "What kind of evidence is there for that?" And if they can't give you a good answer, I hope you'll think very carefully before you believe a word they say.[16]

This is sound advice from Dawkins, but it's astonishing that he expects his followers not to follow it when it comes to anything he and other atheists propose. Well, we dimwits are following his advice in evaluating his most popular delusion, Mount Improbable—and when we do, that mythical "mount" suffers a volcanic eruption. It's a pity that Dawkins didn't take his own advice as a 15-year-old when Darwinism converted him to the fallacious religion of atheism.

THE "IDEA OF GOD"

We saw in the last chapter that ideas are not physical, an indisputable fact that is easy to prove but ignored by atheists because of its devastating disproof of materialism. Therefore, ideas cannot be located in the physical brain and can neither originate by evolution nor be influenced by natural selection.

Dawkins's books are of necessity filled with nonphysical concepts that are impossible to avoid even for such a rabid atheist and materialist as he. Though genes are physical, they are not aware of their own existence and have no understanding of genetics. Nor do genes know anything of what Dawkins boasts about them. They certainly do not understand the concept of God, or atheism—or *anything*.

Vladimir Lenin was as rabid an atheist and materialist as Dawkins and the other "Four Horsemen." He hated God to the extent that whenever the thought arose, it threw him into an uncontrollable rage. One problem, however, plagued him all of his troubled life: how did the idea of God invade the human brain? He correctly understood that it was impossible even to think of anything that did not exist. For example, no one can conceive of a new prime color for the rainbow.

What about pink elephants? Pink exists, and so do elephants. "Pink elephants" is just a bizarre combination of two elements that already exist. What about the weird creatures on other planets shown in science fiction films such as *Star Wars* and *Avatar*? They are nothing new, but simply outrageous caricatures of creatures on Earth.

That being the case, from whence came this idea of "God," if God does not exist? Of course, in Lenin's mind, "God" was an *opiate of the people*, an insidious lie sown in fertile imaginations by religious leaders in order to control lesser mortals. But where did the preachers get this idea of "God"? Lenin was unable to answer that question, and it bothered him. Dawkins, of course, has a "scientific" answer to the problem. It is quite ingenious. For their own deceptive purposes, the genes imposed this belief in God through evolution and natural selection.

"We do not know how . . . the idea of God . . . arose in the meme pool," writes Dawkins, but he's willing to play the same guessing game and pass it off as established science:

> Probably it originated many times by independent "mutation." In any case, it is very old indeed. How does it replicate itself? By the written and spoken word, aided by great music and great art. . . . What is it about the idea of a god that gives it its stability and penetrance?[17]

A SCIENCE OF "ONCE UPON A TIME"

Everyone intuitively recognizes that if God exists, He must be a spirit that does not have physical qualities or occupy any physical spatial location in the physical universe. In excluding God, the Creator, we are left with a physical universe that must be explained on its own. Here is the way Dawkins attempts to do it:

> *Once upon a time*, natural selection consisted of the differential survival of replicators floating free in the *primeval soup*. Now, natural selection favors replicators that are good at building survival machines, genes that are skilled in the *art of controlling embryonic development*. In this, the replicators are no more conscious or purposeful than they ever were. The same old processes of automatic selection between rival molecules by reason of their longevity, fecundity, and copying-fidelity, still go on as blindly and inevitably as they did in the *far-off days*. . . .
>
> In recent years—the last 600 million or so—the replicators *have achieved* notable triumphs of *survival-machine technology* such as the muscle, the heart, and the eye (evolved several times independently). Before that, they radically altered fundamental features of their way of life as replicators [How does he know this?], which must be understood if we are to proceed with the argument.[18]

Once upon a time . . . far-off days? Isn't that the way fairy tales begin? Dawkins has absolutely *no factual basis* for telling us what happened in the "primeval soup" billions of years ago or that 600 million years ago a huge advance in evolution took place.

Evolution has been a fairy tale from the beginning. Instead of gathering momentum with facts and finding that digging holes in the ground for fossils didn't produce the desired evidence, evolutionists decided to take all the dirt they'd dug up and turn it into a mountain. Dawkins brilliantly called it Mount Improbable. There's no real factual support for anything that allegedly occurs on this magic mountain, so atheists hide behind, "Given enough time anything could happen." Isn't that the ultimate cop-out?

The evolutionist is saying, "More than 100 years of searching has left us with no substantive proof, but we know what happened back then, and given enough time even *this* or probably *that* might have happened, so let's continue our speculation." The most essential ingredient in Darwinism is billions and billions of years. Given enough time, evolution can do miracles. Dawkins declares:

> Darwin's big idea *explains all of life and its consequences*, and that means everything that possesses more than minimal complexity.
>
> *You can pare Darwin's big idea down to a single sentence . . . :* "Given sufficient time, the non-random survival of hereditary entities (which occasionally miscopy) will generate complexity, diversity, beauty, and *an illusion of design* so persuasive that it is almost impossible to distinguish from deliberate intelligent design.". . .
>
> "Given sufficient time" is not a problem . . . except for human minds struggling to take on board the terrifying magnitude of geological time. [Emphasis added][19]

The truth is, as Dawkins very well knows, Darwinism explains nothing of life. It cannot tell us what life is, how it began, or what is its meaning. So why does he make these statements?

"JUST LET US HAVE ONE TINY EXCEPTION"

Again we are confronted with the disturbing difference between science as founded and advanced by theists, and "science" as it has become today under the control of atheists. Imagine Pasteur saying, "The evidence certainly indicates that if something is sterilized, no life can survive. But there *could* be an exception, you can *never be sure.*" Instead of "The Law of Biogenesis," we would have "The *Perhaps* of Biogenesis." Or how about "The Law of Maybe"?

Atheists have done something unconscionable. They have undermined our confidence in the laws of nature. Why? *Because evolution can't be made to work within the framework of established laws.* Nobelist Harvard Professor George Wald admits that according to the law of biogenesis, spontaneous generation has been forever consigned to the trash heap of "myths once part of science." But because that law implies that life could only begin by a supernatural act of creation, and "we atheists know that couldn't happen," one exception must be allowed.

Instead of establishing and confirming laws that can be relied upon, evolution is founded upon a denial of established law. What new laws of nature have come out of 150 years of Darwinism? None. In effect, this is what Wald is saying: "All we need to get evolution started is one tiny exception to this one law. Look the other way for a moment and we'll be off and running with the new science of evolution"—or is it "revolution"!

Atheists mock any belief in the resurrection of Jesus Christ as folk superstition yet are not embarrassed to declare in the name of science that all the life on Earth sprang spontaneously from dead matter, even after it had been sterilized a trillion times over by a so-called Big Bang. Consider the following from George Wald:

> The reasonable view was to believe in spontaneous generation; the only alternative, to believe in a single primary act of supernatural creation. There is no third position. . . . One [must] concede that the spontaneous generation of a

living organism is impossible. Yet here we are—as a result, I believe, of spontaneous generation.[20]

Scientists are expected to search for the facts and follow them without prejudice wherever they lead. But when it comes to facing the evidence that God the Creator exists, too many scientists today, for the first time in history, are abandoning all the rules of logic and scientific inquiry in favor of atheism. Sir Julian Huxley, atheist and humanist, is reported to have said (rather prematurely, it would seem), "There is no longer either need or room for the supernatural." That was a statement of *faith*, what he *believed*, but without any evidence.

In fact, the law of biogenesis is clear: life comes only from life. Pasteur's proof has never been challenged on scientific grounds. No amount of waffling will allow atheists to escape the unpalatable conclusion that spontaneous generation of life does not and cannot occur. The *only* possible answer to the inevitable question, "Where did the first life come from?" is a supernatural one.

How can it be the "reasonable view" to believe that an event occurred that science declares and Wald admits is *impossible*? Atheism creates an irrational disconnect from truth and reality in order to maintain the rejection of God. That fact ought to be reason enough to call for a re-examination of atheism on rational grounds. Yet Wald, in spite of his intellectual brilliance, clung to "spontaneous generation" his entire life—an irrational belief that was forced upon him by his refusal to accept the existence of God. In the old science, belief in God was assumed by the order of the universe. Now atheism must be proved by disorder.

THOSE DEVILISHLY CLEVER GENES!

In addition to claiming an exception to the law of biogenesis, one thing more was needed: a plausible way to explain away design! How to do that was the problem, since evolution and natural selection unmistakably seemed to point to design. Evolutionists needed a good cover.

To whom did Dawkins turn for help? It was to his closest friends and confidants, the genes themselves, of course! That wouldn't be easy, because Dawkins himself admits, "Genes have no foresight. They do not plan ahead. Genes just *are*."[21]

But Dawkins needed genes to do a whole lot more than just *be*. And he didn't even need to train them. They are devilishly clever on their own. Not only did they agree to go along with natural selection in support of that theory; they devised a clever scheme to cover the whole thing up by *making it look like design* to confuse theists. Of course, they let their friend Dawkins in on the plot, and he was so ecstatic that he couldn't keep the secret. He is so proud to tell us that these tricky genes have created *"an illusion of design* so persuasive that it is almost impossible to distinguish from deliberate intelligent design."[22] Now *that* is ingenious!

Listen to Dawkins again. He claims to know what the genes are up to, but he is also a bit confused, falling prey to some contradictions:

> Natural selection . . . has lifted life from primeval simplicity to the dizzy heights of complexity, beauty, and *apparent design* that dazzle us today.[23] After Darwin, we all should feel, deep in our bones, suspicious of the very idea of design. The *illusion of design* is a trap that has caught us before, and Darwin should have immunized us by raising our consciousness.[24]

Is Dawkins just confused, or is this part of another cover-up that he hasn't told the genes about? He credits natural selection with giving us the illusion of apparent design. Then he tells us that the illusion of design is a trap from which Darwin intended to rescue us.

Why is it that not only multitudes of ordinary Americans reject evolution, but it runs into so much opposition among scientists as well? Dawkins is the man to tell us, and the revelation is rather astonishing:

It is almost as if the human brain were specifically *designed* to misunderstand Darwinism, and to find it hard to believe.[25]

No wonder Dawkins seems to run around in circles when it comes to "design." Does he believe that the human brain was designed, or doesn't he? And how could evolution itself create two contradictory effects at the same time: the illusion of design and also program into the brain a rejection of it? Those "selfish genes" are so devilishly clever at cover-up that they've even confused their patron, Richard Dawkins.

In the science, evolution is a theory about changes; in the Myth it is a fact about improvements. To those brought up on Myth, nothing seems more normal, more natural, more plausible, than that chaos should turn into order, death into life, ignorance into knowledge.

—C. S. Lewis

Paleontologists have paid an exorbitant price for Darwin's argument. We fancy ourselves as the only true students of life's history, yet to preserve our favored account of evolution by natural selection we view our data as so bad that we never see the very process we profess to study.

—Stephen Jay Gould, "Evolution's Erratic Pace,"
Natural History, vol. 86 (May 1977), 12-16

To translate our suggestion into that form of speech, we think that the chimp is descended from man, that the common ancestor of the two was much more man-like than ape-like.

—John Gribbon and Jeremy Cherfas,
"Descent of Man—or Ascent of Ape?"
New Scientist, vol. 91 (September 3, 1981), 592-95

Human Language appears to be a unique phenomenon, without significant analogue in the animal world.

—Noam Chomsky, Language of Mind
(New York: Harcourt Brace Jovanovich, Inc., 1972)

Language is perhaps the most important single characteristic that distinguishes humans from other animal species.

—Stephen Matthews, Bernard Comrie, and Marcia Polinsky, eds.,
Atlas of Languages: The Origin and Development of Languages
Throughout the World (New York: Facts on File, Inc., 1996), 10

FOUR

IMPASSABLE CHASMS, IMPOSSIBLE CLIFFS

WHEN RICHARD DAWKINS SPEAKS, the world listens. He's the expert, the one-time Simonyi Professor of the Public Understanding of Science at the University of Oxford. We are charging Dawkins with betraying that trust by giving the public misinformation about science. He does so in a number of his books, speeches, and debates, a fact that we will continue to document in the following pages. He is the *de facto* leader of the New Atheists, who gave themselves this name to call attention to the fact that the "old atheism," once headed by Madalyn Murray O'Hair, was far too mild. As we've already mentioned, the New Atheists call themselves "the brights" and the implication is that anyone stupid enough to believe in God is a dimwit.

By Dawkins's own confession, natural selection is impersonal and cannot think of or plan the future. However, it has, Dawkins insists, determined our personal identities! Isn't this irrational?

As we've already seen, atheism confuses facts with fantasy. The latter is upheld by make-believe tales carried on the whispering, seductive wind that at times becomes a gale of wild delusion howling across the slopes of Mount Improbable. The following is a brief excerpt from a speech given by George Wald at MIT:

> I tell my students, with a feeling of pride that I hope they will share, that the carbon, nitrogen, and oxygen that make up ninety-nine percent of our living substance were cooked in the deep interiors of earlier generations of dying stars. Gathered up from the ends of the universe, over billions of years, eventually they came to form, in part, the substance of our sun, its planets, and ourselves.[1]

How does he know this? It's a fantasy tale that he as an atheist hopes might be true. *Feeling of pride?* Even if what Wald says were true, what basis would there be for pride on the part of humans? We had nothing to do with gathering "from the ends of the universe, over billions of years," the materials that supposedly make up our bodies. So what is this *pride* about? Would it somehow generate pride to know that no personal God played any role in the mindless process of bringing us into existence? Atheists seem to take a twisted pleasure in declaring their independence from the Creator and from any purpose or meaning that He would have brought into this universe and into our lives. This sense of exhilaration is hard to understand considering the fact that it comes from embracing the religion of atheism, which says we are nothing more than the chemicals making up our bodies.

SHAKING OUR PUNY FISTS IN DEFIANCE

As we previously noted, Mount Improbable is the chief attraction in Dawkins's Fantasyland, where atheism's greatest preachers pontificate upon this religion from its impressive peaks day and night. The good news is that one does not need to make a frontal assault on its towering crags and dangerously slippery slopes from which many have fallen to their deaths. Dawkins lets the readers of his book, *Climbing Mount Improbable*, know that the "Mount" he ingeniously conjured up can be more easily conquered from the backside. If one knows how to find it, there is supposedly a fairly easy path that will take one up this extremely important Mount more speedily.[2] That sounds like great news to the atheist, but Dawkins fails to mention the impassable swamps and impossible cliffs that must be conquered before one can reach the base of Mount Improbable.

We are told that evolution is no longer a theory but a proven fact. We would like to see the proof! Incredibly, Francis Collins, founder and former head of the Human Genome Project and now the chief of the National Institutes of Health (NIH), gains seemingly fantastic insights from DNA. Based upon a DNA comparison, he declares, "The conclusion of a common ancestor for humans and mice is virtually inescapable."[3] But where are the fossils one would expect to number in the millions (if not billions) that show the alleged evolutionary path from mouse to man? We search in vain.

Evolutionists make a great deal of the similarity between the DNA and RNA in humans and chimpanzees. Collins claims to find convincing evidence supporting man's descent from the chimpanzee.[4] He calls chimps "our closest living relative."[5] He explains that "humans and chimps are 96 percent identical at the DNA level," but what does this mean?

There is no place in DNA for enjoying an opera, a Dickens novel, or locating the genius of an Einstein. How could natural selection bridge such a vast chasm between humans and every other living thing, and why would it even try? What could be the survival value for these and so many other uniquely human qualities and enjoyments?

Collins's arguments could seem convincing until one remembers what Collins himself points out: "Investigations of many organisms, from bacteria to humans, revealed that this 'genetic code,' by which information in DNA and RNA is translated into protein, is universal in all known organisms."[6] That universality includes not only the lowest creatures such as garden slugs but also microbes and plants.

Is man also related by an evolutionary chain to celery, strawberries, peanuts, oak trees, or any particular one (or all) of the more than 800,000 known plant species? Although there is some reference in botany textbooks to evolution of plants, no proven examples are presented because there are none. Variety in plant life is simply *assumed* to be the result of evolution. The truth is, however, that we find no evidence in what is now an impressively complete and clearly defined fossil record that even one of the phyla is either the ancestor or the descendant of any other, much less that any form of plant life evolved into any form of animal life—or that animals ever evolved into plants.

LET'S SUMMARIZE SOME FACTS

In chapter 1, we took a brief glimpse at the vastness of the cosmos and now we find that inside of living things is another universe with an immensity that is equally beyond man's ability to fully explore and comprehend. Incredible as it may seem, each human body contains 1,000 times as many cells as there are galaxies in the universe.[7] Like the vastness of space making the universe impossible for man to explore, the astronomical numbers we encounter inside living creatures and within the atoms of which they are made render the theory of evolution mathematically impossible. Medical scientists have made a good start and have done much good, but it could take many centuries to fully explore the marvels of the human body or to comprehend disease. It is by no means a foregone conclusion that mankind can ever conquer microbes.

Moreover, the complexity of each cell is beyond the ability of science thus far to unravel. According to atheists, as a result of what is popularly called the Big Bang, stars were formed from condensing gasses. Later, they gave birth to planets and moons and eventually to man. Everything we see on our earth and in the universe around us—life, consciousness, conscience, morals, and ethics—must have come from the Big Bang.

Whenever anything needs to be explained and religious people refer to God as the Creator, skeptics laughingly call this a "god of the gaps," invented to explain what science hasn't yet explained. This pitiful "god" has been banished from the universe because, as Christopher Hitchens, popular journalist and bestselling author of *God Is Not Great*, loves to pronounce with great authority, "Nothing remains to be explained."[8] Hitchens would have us believe that science can supposedly fill in all of the gaps in human knowledge. How long must we wait for that to happen? And why wait, when all of the evidence points so clearly to an infinite Creator, One who is available to all who truly call upon Him? Hundreds, if not thousands, of legitimate scientists and philosophers would rise up in protest against this reckless boast.

Perhaps Hitchens, seemingly brilliant man that he may be, has hidden in a vault somewhere a secret paper he has written and will one day reveal containing the explanation of space, time, matter, energy, life, and the origin of each. Hitchens's secret paper, if it exists, will knock the props out from under the present scientific and academic world.

There are scores of other questions that most scientists agree lie beyond the reach of science and, by their very nature, can never be answered. Let's start with the few that we listed by Nobel Prize-winning quantum physicist Erwin Schrödinger in chapter 1: "Beautiful and ugly, good or bad, God and eternity. . . . Whence came I and whither go I?"

If Schrödinger and a host of other scientists and Nobel Prize winners are right, then atheism and its children, evolution and natural selection, can only be religions that one must take by faith. In spite of this obvious fact, these religions that masquerade as "science" continue to be presented in textbooks and the media as though they were thoroughly established fact. No alternative may be taught in public schools in order to "protect our children." Any dissenters are muzzled because nothing that challenges or even questions atheism, evolution, or natural selection is allowed. Is this the way atheists pursue their open-minded quest for truth?

Atheists excuse their rejection of God as Creator because (so they say) *He* would have to have a Creator, who would also require a Creator, leading to an infinite regress, *ad absurdum*. John Lennox, in his debate with Dawkins, objected to the idea that God, if He exists, would Himself have to have been created. Lennox rejected that idea as beside the point because "no one believes in created gods." By very definition, God is the uncreated Creator of all. The atheists' demand that God would have to have been created apparently doesn't apply to energy, which atheists say had no beginning and has no end. So energy becomes the uncreated creator of all—the atheists' "god."

Lennox also pointed out that not only is atheism not derived from science, it undermines science at its very foundation. The early founders of modern science were nearly all theists, and many were Christians. They believed that science was possible only because an intelligent Creator would build order into His creation. Otherwise, there would be chaos. But the whole idea of Darwinism and its natural selection is to provide a "mechanism" that eliminates the need for God. In that debate, Dawkins declared that Darwinism provides "an explanation" of life without a Creator. That belief is the foundation upon which the atheists' "faith" rests. It is certainly a major prop behind all that Dawkins believes. Lennox firmly replied that Darwinism does *not* explain life. Nor can atheism explain the origin of life or of energy, space, time, and so on.

It may seem reasonable that natural selection explains how life develops once there is a live mutating replicator. It does not, however, explain the origin of energy, out of which everything is made; nor does it explain what life is or how it attaches itself to certain lumps of matter to bring into existence the self-replicating cell needed as the vehicle of natural selection and evolution. Isn't it presumptive to speak of natural selection as the mechanism of change and development when neither this nor any other mechanism can create energy and life? When will atheists stop misrepresenting their favorite speculations as science?

MATERIALISM IS DEAD

The issue of infinite regress (a designer must be more complex than the thing designed, so who designed the designer who designed the designer, etc.) is like a dog chasing its tail. There had to be a beginning to the universe. However, it was a struggle for many scientists to admit this obvious fact. One of those for whom this admission was the most difficult was Robert Jastrow, founder of the Goddard Space Institute that sent *Pioneer and Voyager* into space.

Something or *Someone* must have existed without being created. Is energy the uncreated creator, or is God the uncreated Creator of all? Atheists declare that in the beginning there was nothing but energy, though they can't tell us why, when, or how in space and time it came into existence. Out of the Big Bang allegedly came the matter of which everything is made. There is nothing else. But what about life? Atheism is materialistic by a necessity that is proving to be ever more embarrassing.

Dawkins wrote in his 2004 book *The Ancestor's Tale*: "The fact that life evolved out of nearly nothing, some 10 billion years after the universe evolved literally out of nothing–is a fact so staggering that I would be mad to attempt words to do it justice." How can "nearly nothing" evolve, much less create "life" in the process? This is simply more speculation on the part of Dawkins, which, as usual, he expects us to accept as science just because he says it is.

Most scientists now recognize (though many of them do so with great reluctance) that materialism as a viable philosophy is dead. Why? It has become obvious that there is a non-material universe of consciousness, thoughts, ideas, and conscience. Yet in order to eliminate God, the human soul, angels, and Satan, atheists still cling to the discredited superstition that nothing exists except matter. After all, what else do they have? As we've already seen, it is impossible to describe morals, ethics, truth, justice, and so much more in material terms. This fact ought to concern materialists deeply.

It is true that our bodies are composed of some of the same elements found in the stars. Atoms are made up of numerous subatomic particles, primarily the electron, neutron, and proton. Behind these, however, are numerous smaller bits of energy—neutrinos, leptons, quarks, baryons, mesons, etc. The number of ever-smaller particles goes on and on. These form atoms that form the molecules of which matter is composed.

Without understanding their origin or being able to explain them, atheists accept the "laws" of physics and chemistry, which declare that every material thing is formed out of energy and that this makes up the stuff we call matter. They add to these scientific facts their religious belief (which must be accepted by faith) that matter is all there is, ever was, or ever will be. Of course, this raises many immediate questions. Matter is simply one form of energy, the basic component of the universe. What is energy? Scientists do not know. Where did it come from? How long has it existed? These are very basic questions, yet they remain unanswered by science.

How did the "laws" governing matter arise, and why does unthinking and unconscious matter follow them? Scientists can't say. Having rejected in our public schools even the possibility of a Creator, atheists confess that they can explain neither matter nor life.

MYSTERY PILED UPON MYSTERY

Dawkins thinks that the laws governing matter (whether solid, liquid, or gas) developed as part of an evolutionary/natural selection process. This is a classic "which came first, the chicken or the egg?" dilemma. How could the laws that govern matter have always existed in anticipation of when energy would come into existence and form into matter? What came first, the matter or the laws that energy and matter obey?

There are literally dozens of these dilemmas that science has been unable to answer. Now it's "Which came first, protein or DNA?" It takes protein to construct DNA, but it takes DNA to make protein.

Obviously, both were created at once; neither could have evolved. There are many such questions that haunt evolutionists to this day.

Dawkins thinks that matter itself is the product of a primitive "natural selection" among atoms in which the most stable molecules survived. This is pure speculation and a form of Darwinism that Darwin himself never anticipated. But what other choice does Dawkins have, as long as he excludes God from consideration by very definition?

Today's atheistic evolutionists are scrambling to deal with a host of vital questions that Darwinism stirred up but cannot answer. A growing number of scientists are convinced that matter itself has some form of consciousness. This theory is completely irrational.

Unquestionably, our physical bodies, from head to toe, inside and out, are nothing more than energy/matter, and that includes our brains. But neither the physical brain nor the electro-chemical impulses operating within it can think, in spite of theories attributing to it some form of consciousness. Then how can one's brain think? It doesn't. It certainly doesn't originate our thoughts. If it did, we wouldn't know what thoughts our brains might come up with next and impose upon us.

The brain is the most complex lump of matter in the universe, and its design and development raise further questions to which science has no answer. The list of thus far unanswerable questions lying just beneath the surface of the "impassable swamp" that bars our approach to the base of Mount Improbable is almost endless. It is as though science has stumbled into a hall of mirrors with infinitely receding images.

NON-OVERLAPPING MAGISTERIA?

It is commonly thought today that there is a battle between science and religion. Yet highly respected evolutionist, the late Stephen Jay Gould, claimed that both could be accepted and need not contradict each other. Gould believed that science and religion dealt with entirely different subjects and were like ships passing in the night.

This theory (with which Dawkins vehemently disagrees) is known among scientists as NOMA: non-overlapping magisteria.

Gould got the inspiration for this idea in early 1984, while staying in a hotel for itinerate priests at the Vatican, where he was attending "a meeting on nuclear winter sponsored by the Pontifical Academy of Sciences." Housed in the same hotel and also attending the conference was "a group of French and Italian Jesuit priests who were also professional scientists." They asked Gould why "all this talk about 'scientific creationism'?"

They wanted to know whether evolution was "in some kind of trouble" in America? One of the priests emphasized that he had "always been taught that no conflict exists between evolution and Catholic faith." Gould explained that the only conflict came from an American "homegrown phenomenon—a splinter movement . . . of Protestant fundamentalists who believe that every word of the Bible must be literally true." A lengthy discussion followed. Gould concluded, "We all left satisfied, but I certainly felt bemused by . . . my role as a Jewish agnostic trying to reassure a group of Catholic priests that evolution remained both true and entirely consistent with religious belief."[9] *Religious belief* is a vague term into which almost anything could fit. One cannot do that with *biblical Christianity,* which the Bible alone clearly defines. This is a major reason why evangelical Christians are so maligned. They simply follow the fundamentals of biblical Christianity, as we expect a CPA to follow the fundamentals of sound accounting principles in issuing certified financial statements for the corporate Board of Directors and to the stockholders. Not to do so would be a breach of trust. Why should religious leaders be held to any lesser standard? This is one of the many reasons why this volume avoids any discussions about religion and only defends *biblical Christianity.*

The truth is that both Dawkins and Gould were partially right and partially wrong. Dawkins's belief is often called "scientism," the idea that materialistic science is the only truth and therefore everything must be describable in its terms. That belief is easily refuted. If

Dawkins disputes this fact and considers belief in anything nonmaterial (i.e., spiritual) to be "nonsense," let him give the world a physical description of "nonsense." Of course he can't.

When Einstein was asked what impact his theory of relativity would have on religion (including morals and ethics) he reportedly replied, "None. Relativity is a purely scientific theory and has nothing to do with religion."[10] There are those who imagine that the ideal way to settle any dispute between religion and science would be to make a science out of religion. In fact, that ploy destroys both.

And it's right here that logic has a serious difference with Dawkins in his treatment of "religion" as a multi-headed monster instead of recognizing that each religion has its own separate body of beliefs. That is why this book is by no means a defense of religion in any size, shape, or form. *Biblical Christianity* stands firmly on one side, pitted not only against atheism but against religion as commonly understood. That includes the vast majority of what is called "Christian" because so much known as Christianity is far from what Jesus taught and modeled.

In serious disagreement with Gould's non-overlapping magisteria theory, Dawkins believes that religion and science deal with the same determination of ultimate reality. For Dawkins and the other New Atheists, the conflict is genuine, and all belief in God must be ruthlessly stamped out. That was attempted under threat of imprisonment or death in Soviet Russia and her satellite countries for 70 years. The resulting oppression, imprisonment of millions, and the murder of more than 100 million has been well documented elsewhere. Atheists attempt to deny any responsibility for these shocking statistics, but the data has been thoroughly established.

In his debate with Lennox, Dawkins attempted to whitewash the sordid history of atheism as it has been revealed in the past few decades by saying that the denial of God was only peripheral to communism and fascism and not that important. On the contrary, Victor Aksiuchitz, who knew Lenin well, wrote:

Lenin could not mention religion without damnation, for he was possessed by the need of pathological reviling of the Divine . . . every religious idea about a certain god [was] the most dangerous abomination, the foulest pest. . . . As soon as it came to religion, Lenin . . . fell into frenzy and madness. . . . In Lenin's opinion destroying religion was the most important purpose of the communist regime. Lenin launched the bloodiest and most massive religious persecution in history. . . .[11]

SEVERE LIMITATIONS OF MATERIALISTIC SCIENCE

One of today's most common misperceptions is the idea that science is all knowing and, given enough time, will eventually solve all of our problems. Yes, science has made great strides in material matters, but it is limited to material facts and figures. Most of life as we experience it lies outside the reach of physical science. We've already quoted Erwin Schrödinger, who stated succinctly that science knows nothing of all that is most important to the human soul.

Science knows nothing of justice, ethics, morals, love, and so much else that is far more important than energy or matter. Science can't even tell us why this universe about us is so beautiful, as even Dawkins admits. Tragically, in spite of much good that it has done, science has produced a race of nuclear giants who remain moral midgets. This is an extremely dangerous situation that science created but can never help to solve. There hangs over our heads the double-edged nuclear and ecological Sword of Damocles. Science cannot help us because the only solution is not scientific but moral, and the two occupy different realms.

Our brains make us very intelligent, so we imagine, separating us from all other creatures. But our brains are just matter—and as we will continue to remind readers, matter cannot think. The truth is that something other than the brain makes the difference, something that is not in our genes and that could not possibly be the product of evolution and natural selection. This intangible, nonphysical part of man that is not shared by lower creatures has also been described by religious people as the soul and spirit—but what are we talking about?

Mortimer J. Adler, co-founder of the Great Books of the Western World program, served on the Board of Editors of *Encyclopedia Britannica* from its inception in 1949 and became its chairman in 1974. He also held the position of director of editorial planning for the fifteenth edition of *Britannica* and was instrumental in completely reorganizing much that was embodied in that edition. He pointed out long ago in his groundbreaking book, *The Difference of Man and the Difference it Makes*, that there is a nonphysical barrier between man and all other living things, which evolution did not and could not cause and which it cannot cross. Working on the latter book was instrumental in bringing Adler to the acceptance of Christianity.

If thoughts do not arise from the matter of which our bodies are made, whether from the brain or the liver or a kidney, who, or what, is forming conceptual ideas and expressing them in speech? Who *is* this thinker inside each of us? If it isn't part of the physical body, does "it" survive death? Could that be the person I really am, living temporarily in a physical body? Now there's a question to ponder that carries serious consequences!

Where did the life come from that animates our bodies for a time, then leaves us at the moment of death? How did life come to fill the earth and manifest itself in such a variety of creatures? Science cannot tell us. "Never mind," says Richard Dawkins, as he sees the sandy foundation of atheism eroding around him, "we're working on that."

DAWKINS'S UNWAVERING FAITH IN DARWIN

Richard Dawkins boldly and frequently says that Darwin explained life and everything about it, including consciousness and morals. Of course, anyone who thinks clearly knows that isn't true. What is life, and how does it animate matter? No one knows. "Never mind," says the atheist, "the solution to that problem will eventually be reached."

Dawkins's life and career are devoted to destroying any belief in any god, especially the God of the Bible, for whom he reserves a special hatred. He admits that "All of us share a kind of religious reverence for the beauty of the universe, for the complexity of life, for the sheer magnitude of geological time. It's so tempting to believe that living things . . . or that stars or mountains or rivers have all been made by something. It was a supreme achievement of the human intellect to realize that there is a better explanation . . . that these things can come about by purely natural causes. . . ."[12] Dawkins recognizes that what he is saying contradicts our normal feelings when we behold the beauties of nature.

This is a damning admission for atheists. It ought to be embarrassing that the theory of evolution is what Dawkins admits is counterintuitive. How could that be? He is confessing that there is something inside us that can act contrary to our genes. Thankfully, our genes aren't as important as Dawkins made them out to be in his first book, *The Selfish Gene*. We're not, after all, just flesh and bone bags that our genes use to advance their agenda, as Francis Crick incredibly believes.

Well, then, this "intuitive" feeling that runs counter to the theory of evolution can't originate in our genes. It can't be physical. Where could this free-will, rational impulse come from, this desire for something so at odds with natural selection?

It cannot be true, as atheism's natural selection would force us to believe, that our thoughts are simply the result of the motions of atoms in our brains that all began with a "big bang" and have been proceeding without guidance ever since. Isn't this an admission that materialism does not have the answers to everything, unlike what atheists would have us believe and as Dawkins so often asserts?

So Dawkins states repeatedly with unabashed certainty that "we know essentially how life began." On the contrary, we don't even know what life is, so how could we know how it began? Until atheists can explain what life is, it is an outright deceit to pretend to explain how it "evolved." Atheists and evolutionists are playing a game of pretense, trying to build a natural-selection structure in the air without first laying the foundation. It's just a dream. As C. S. Lewis so ably argued: "If minds are wholly dependent on brains and brains on biochemistry, and biochemistry (in the long run) on the meaningless flux of atoms, I cannot understand how the thought of those minds should have any more significance than the sound of wind in the trees."[13]

A MESSAGE FROM AN EXTRATERRESTRIAL SOURCE

Most people, including many Christians, do not take the Bible seriously when it declares that God—who created everything out of nothing—formed the human body "of the dust of the ground."[14] Our bodies indeed have the same chemicals as the soil, and it is the soil from which comes the food that sustains us and all flesh.

At death, the body returns to the earth. The phrase that one often hears at funerals, "Dust you are, and unto dust you shall return," was first uttered by God to Adam and Eve.[15] That story is not fiction but history. Those who are willing to open their minds and read on will be challenged.

Atheists dare God: "Speak to us and we'll believe!" God *has* spoken in a written message outside of and longer than the Bible. Geneticists have decoded it. It's the DNA molecule. This is God's voice to mankind. There could be no other source of that amazing instruction manual for creating and maintaining the life and physical features of every living thing.

In the Bible's creation narrative, an immediate distinction is made between matter and life. Neither atoms nor molecules nor the chemicals they form have life in themselves, yet they compose bodies that are vibrantly and consciously alive. What is life? This is a mystery that science has been unable to solve. Having said that God formed the human body and "every living creature . . . out of the ground,"[16] the

Bible declares of Adam, "God breathed into his nostrils the breath of life; and man became a living soul."[17]

That statement declares that we are not just educated lumps of evolved protein wired with nerves. We are nonphysical beings temporarily living in physical bodies. The atheist does not like the concept of "nonphysical." Nevertheless, the creation of Adam stands as a challenge to any atheist who will engage it: "Explain life, and you have finally done away with any need for God."

God has thrown down the gauntlet in the opening chapters of the Bible, but today, atheists make up the rules. Though one has the freedom to mention God and creation in universities (but generally not in lower levels), to do so is likely to draw the scorn of professors and students alike because "it's not scientific." No matter how competent, theistic scientists find it extremely difficult even to get a paper before a peer group, much less to have it approved and published. Nor does the media *ever* fairly portray the God of the Bible.

Atheists, especially the new aggressive breed, are so confident that they are right and theists are wrong that they have no conscience about stonewalling and even silencing theists whenever and wherever possible. *Conscience?* What is that? How can conscience, which has no physical qualities, be explained in materialistic terms? What part of the anatomy generates the universal recognition of right and wrong? Certainly not the brain cells, any more than the cells of the cranium that holds the brain. How does the materialist explain morals and ethics in terms of matter? We're still waiting to hear.

Cambridge professor Sir Arthur Eddington described one of his lectures as an attempt to "dispel the feeling that in using the eye . . . of the soul [for] our conception of reality, we are doing something irrational and disobeying the leading of truth which as scientists we are pledged to serve."[18] Among his many brilliant and insightful statements, which, by the way, today's new aggressive materialist atheists would do well to ponder, is the following:

That consciousness is ruled by the laws of physics and chemistry is as preposterous as the suggestion that a nation could be ruled by laws like the laws of grammar.[19] In human affairs [law] means a rule . . . which may be kept or broken. In science it means a rule which is never broken. . . . Thus in the physical world what a body does and what a body ought to do are equivalent; but we are well aware of another domain where they are anything but equivalent. We cannot get away from this distinction. . . . The laws of logic do not prescribe the way our minds think; they prescribe the way our minds ought to think. . . . However closely we may associate thought with the physical machinery of the brain, the connection is dropped as irrelevant as soon as we consider the fundamental property of thought—that it may be correct or incorrect. . . . [Truth] involves recognizing a domain . . . of laws which ought to be kept but may be broken. Dismiss the idea that natural law may swallow up religion; it can't even tackle the multiplication table single-handed.[20]

ENERGY, WHAT ART THOU?

According to prevailing scientific opinion, though we don't know what energy is or why it exists and obeys certain laws, it suddenly appeared out of nothing—and then exploded in the Big Bang. This is a "once-upon-a-time" fairy tale that says that energy came into existence compacted into an infinitely small mass, which, for unknown reasons, suddenly expanded some 13-15 billion years ago. There was a huge explosion, generally described as a "colossal fireball."[21] If that was indeed the case, this universe began as completely sterilized matter. Louis Pasteur proved that life cannot arise after sterilization has taken place.

For more than a century, the law of biogenesis was accepted as established fact. If the universe had been sterilized by the Big Bang—to a degree beyond our imagination—then life could not have come from within the universe, but only by a supernatural act on the part of a Creator who exists independently of and outside the cosmos.

Though Dawkins repeatedly says that Darwinism explains life, it has nothing to say about the origin of the universe or of the energy of which everything is made. However it came into existence, we know that life and consciousness are not qualities of matter. That simple fact alone removes all hope that natural selection could bring life to inanimate objects. The attempts to explain the origin of life no more do so than did Darwin's *Origin of Species* explain the origin of even one species.

For these and many other reasons, materialism is a dead philosophy. Paul Davies and John Gribbon point out that "Quantum physics undermines materialism because it reveals that matter has far less 'substance' than we might believe."[22] They go on to assert,

> Many people have rejected scientific values because they regard materialism as a sterile and bleak philosophy, which reduces human beings to automatons and leaves no room for free will and creativity. These people can take heart: materialism is dead.[23]

Obviously, since life is not inherent in any form of matter, it must be nonphysical and have a nonphysical source. This is the only logical conclusion that the facts support. So how do atheists react? They simply deny, or ignore, a scientifically established natural law that is universally accepted, and, in contradiction of the law of biogenesis, they invent the law of *abiogenesis*—life out of death, i.e., spontaneous generation. Such a process, however, has never been observed, contradicts a known law, and would not have been invented except for the fact that this fiction is the only way to salvage atheism. This is clearly not a scientific approach.

Richard Dawkins, ignoring the established and irrefutable natural law of biogenesis in order to cling to his atheism, writes,

[B]efore the coming of life on earth, some rudimentary evolution of molecules could have occurred by ordinary processes of physics and chemistry. There is no need to think of design or purpose or directedness. If a group of atoms in the presence of energy falls into a stable pattern it will tend to stay that way. The earliest form of natural selection was simply a selection of stable forms and a rejection of unstable ones. There is no mystery about this. It had to happen by definition."[24]

By whose "definition"? By the biased "definition" that will not "allow a Divine Foot in the door"? This is nonsense. Dawkins is adding another unnecessary step to the natural selection process. He doesn't have to "breed" stable forms of chemicals by natural selection. They form automatically by the laws of chemistry. Stable molecules have existed from the very beginning, and the universe is filled with them, yet we have never observed any of them taking on life and forming living cells—not once, anywhere!

The only purpose for such fantastic speculation is to show that neither Creator nor creative act is necessary. Of course, simply to deny that there is a Creator does not prove that to be the case. Abiogenesis is not a law. Atheism has failed in its attempt to invent some means for life to come into existence out of lifeless matter. By an already established law, the law of biogenesis, every scientist knows that life comes only from life. The post-Big Bang universe is absolutely lifeless, forever incapable of spontaneously generating life. The only honest conclusion that anyone can derive from the established facts is that life arose on earth by a supernatural creative act of God. There is no way by the laws of nature to set natural selection up in the place of a Creator God. Without a Creator, neither the physical universe nor life itself could possibly exist.

There are numerous problems with natural selection, the first one being the obvious fact that natural *selection* can only *select* from what is available. No "selection" can occur until there is a living replicator;

and the probability of even the smallest living unit (i.e., the tiniest cell) forming by chance is mathematically impossible.

Dawkins states, "Natural selection is not by chance . . . it is the opposite of chance!"[25] Fair enough, but molecules come together in proper order only by obedience to the laws of chemistry, in a process that is not related at all to "natural selection." If Dawkins wants to call it that (these chemicals haven't yet "spontaneously" come to life), let him do so. The coming together of molecules, which must be according to the laws of chemistry, happens continuously and has never once produced life.

Furthermore, for there to be natural selection, there must be DNA—but now we've moved up another level. DNA constitutes the instruction manual for constructing and operating all of the nanochemical machinery in each of the 100 trillion cells in the human body. But DNA is *in writing*—and it is encoded so that only certain protein molecules can decode it!

Only an intelligence can author meaningful information and put it in writing; and the detailed instructions for constructing and operating only one cell, let alone all of them in the human body, would take a supreme intelligence, bringing us back to the Creator once again.

Natural selection can effect many changes within a species by the mingling of DNA through mating and reproduction. There can be an almost infinite variety of dogs all descended from the wolf, but natural selection cannot create a new species because that would require an infusion of new information into DNA, and information neither comes from matter nor can it be created by any evolutionary process.

From the very beginning (and ever since), information had to have been introduced into DNA by an outside intelligence. There is no other explanation for the first appearance of information (and through it, life) organizing lifeless chemicals.

NO "SPONTANEOUS" ORIGIN OF LIFE

Make up your own rules and you can win every time. Make it the rule that God cannot even be considered as a possibility, then atheism wins—but the dice are loaded, so the "winner" is disqualified. If the rule is adopted that by considering the mountains of scientific evidence for God's existence, one is engaging in *religion*, and religion is outlawed as having no scientific basis, then no matter how overwhelming the scientific evidence for God, it will not be allowed—by the very definition atheists have imposed.

Such "ostrich rules" require everyone to bury their heads in the sand and to adopt the timeworn idiots' slogan, "Don't confuse me with facts, my mind is made up." Atheism can pronounce itself the proud "winner"—again—but the victory is hollow because the victor has made up his own rules.

Scientific jargon about chemical processes that could bring about self-replicating molecules that eventually would spontaneously create life is just so much bluster on the part of Dawkins and his fellow atheists. They are desperate to escape accountability to their Creator, and the wish is father to the thought. Life couldn't and didn't originate by spontaneous generation in defiance of the law of biogenesis. In the 1920s, independently of one another, Russian chemist Alexander Oparin and British geneticist J.B.S. Haldane came up with the idea of a "primordial soup," from which everything supposedly came into existence. That theory will not, however, rescue "spontaneous generation."

In 1950, chemist Stanley Miller and physicist Harold Urey mixed gases thought to have been on the primitive earth, sparked the mixture with simulated lightning, and produced amino acids, the foundation of proteins. This created considerable excitement among evolutionists for a time, but that has now died completely. Why? Amino acids are the *building blocks* of proteins, not proteins themselves. The possible combinations of amino acids is about 10 with 130 zeroes after it, making the likelihood of accidentally hitting the right combination effectively nil. Nor could the amino acids, according to the second law of thermodynamics, *spontaneously* form proteins.

A. G. Cairns-Smith and a few other evolutionists have proposed that life didn't originate with either nucleic acids or proteins but that the "original replicators and catalyzing agents were actually crystals found everywhere in the clay that lay around the primitive Earth."[26] It was thought that crystals qualified because they "grow . . . propagate themselves . . . carry information [and] have some minimum capacity of catalyzing." Crystals may carry information, but they cannot originate it—nor can DNA.

Einstein declared that matter cannot arrange itself into information. Obviously, as Massimo Pigliucci, Professor of Ecology and Evolution at the State University of New York, points out, "crystals don't really have a metabolism."[27] For that reason, they could play no part in the formation of life. Furthermore, as biophysicist and biology/natural philosophy professor Harold J. Morowitz has explained,

> The recipe for a crystal is already present in the solution it grows from—the crystal lattice is prescribed by the structure of the molecules that compose it. The formation of crystals is the straightforward result of chemical and physical laws that do not evolve and that are, compared to genetic programs, very simple.[28]

SIR, YOU'RE BREAKING THE LAW!

In spite of Dawkins's wishful thinking, "ordinary processes of physics and chemistry," which are purely physical and not biological, will never create life. All physics and chemistry have to work with is dead matter. The law of biogenesis declares that dead matter cannot produce life. "Spontaneous generation" was proved to be a superstition without one iota of truth. This delusion was abandoned nearly 150 years ago as a result of Pasteur's discovery that when microorganisms are killed by heat no life can arise; but in the name of "science," this folklore has been promoted to the status of fact in order to defend atheism.

No matter how many or how large the new "stable forms of atoms" that are produced, they are still composed of dead matter. Dead matter does not bring forth life, regardless of how large the molecules it forms, even if "natural selection" has produced them. The only way Dawkins can continue to spin his yarn of uncreated life is to ignore the law of biogenesis. He can only bring his tale to a happy ending by a violation of that law. But universal laws of science, including the law of biogenesis, are called "laws" because they allow no exceptions. They cannot be broken.

As Dawkins admits, life requires DNA, and that contains encoded information written in words—"a digitally coded data base," as he calls it.[29] *Information, written in words and encoded, that gives directions for constructing and operating every cell in the body*—all of this incredibly detailed and complex data, beyond our capacity to understand, was devised and imprinted on DNA by natural selection? It is merely a theory, and it certainly neither thinks nor plans. That theory gave birth to Dawkin's "digitally organized data base" of information that is beyond our capability to explain? Now *that* takes faith!

Bringing life out of dead matter is more amazing than any miracle the Bible presents. Primitive self-replicating molecules cannot create information—that process takes nothing less than an intelligence. In referring to the information provided by the DNA for constructing and operating the body—all of it on the single cell from which each human begins, Dawkins declares, "When you were first conceived you were just a single cell, endowed with one master copy of the architect's plans."[30]

Architect's plans without an Architect? Dawkins has to acknowledge that DNA contains detailed, written instructions for building and operating millions of incredibly complex and ingenious nano-chemical machines in trillions of cells joined together, each in its proper place and relationship to the others and to the whole. These amazing blueprints couldn't possibly be conceived and encoded into language except by an Infinite Intelligence. But Dawkins's "definition" turns mindless matter into an engineering genius via his god, "natural selection."

EMBRACING THE IMPOSSIBLE

The fact that every living thing is composed of the same lifeless material that makes up the physical universe shows that life is not a quality of matter. That being the case, the very existence of life becomes a series of miracles. *Miracles?* That's a forbidden word, yet modern science, after decades of trying, has failed to offer the world a better explanation.

After somehow pulling themselves together, have unthinking protein molecules taken charge? At the same time, however, science denies that the miracles reported by eyewitnesses in the Bible could ever occur.

Having no other explanation, evolutionists are forced to claim that the law of biogenesis has not been proved to be universal and must have been violated at least once and probably many times. Here is what one website that purports to answer creationist arguments declares:

> Creationists represent biogenesis as a rigid law with universal scope, when, in reality, it is merely a guideline that amounts to saying that spontaneous generation (the assembly of *fully formed organisms* out of inanimate material in *short* periods of time by purely natural processes) does not occur. This kind of all-at-once process is not comparable to the slow, stepwise process of prebiotic synthesis.
>
> Perhaps in the end it may ultimately turn out that abiogenesis *is* impossible, and that the law of biogenesis *should* be taken as universal, but to take the law as having such a scope at the moment, when origin of life studies are relatively new and progressing just fine, and only all-at-once spontaneous generation has been ruled out, would be premature.[31]

Progressing just fine? Really. The author seemingly forgets five elementary and undeniable facts:

1) The molecular composition of even the smallest sub-microscopic living things is so incredibly complex that merely to assemble the right molecules in the correct order by chance (yes, chance is all there is before "natural selection" can even begin) has repeatedly been proved mathematically to be far beyond impossible;

2) Even if the laws of mathematics could be defied and the right molecular components were put together in the right order, from what source would they receive life? We don't know what life is, but we know that it involves more than the right combinations of molecules. The right components are still all together at the moment of death, but that mysterious spark of life is no longer present;

3) Any living thing, without exception, must have come from something living. Things without life cannot make themselves live;

4) As we have already pointed out, neither any part (such as the liver, kidney, blood system, eye, etc.) nor the body as a whole could be built in stages. Not only wouldn't natural selection and survival of the fittest encourage further development, it would eliminate anything only partially formed as unfit to survive before any progress could be made; and

5) The construction of every living thing follows precise DNA instructions that demand an intelligent author—instructions that make no sense except for the building and operating of a complex and complete whole, not for piecemeal constructions of nonfunctioning parts to be put together in stages over millions of years.

Atheists who try to hide behind doubletalk about "the slow, step-wise process of prebiotic synthesis" are, first of all, deluding themselves, then others. The entire DNA manual of intricate instructions would have to be conceived and written down in words *before* anything living could exist. This is *before* the atheists' god, natural selection, would have anything from which to "select." Common sense and all that science has been able to observe over the centuries make it clear that matter (as Einstein said) cannot *ever* organize itself into information. DNA is a vast storehouse of intricate information for building every living thing, from microbes to man. It could only have been placed there by an infinite intelligence.

IS "SCIENCE" BECOMING MODERN MAN'S RELIGION—EVEN HIS GOD?

How do atheistic materialists, who say that matter is all there is, defend such persistent rejection of the One to whom all the evidence points? First of all, as we have seen, the very thought of "God" is hateful and is ruled out by definition. To do so is neither scientific nor rational. Atheists are not reticent in declaring this dogma and even boasting of it as being intellectually superior. But if God does *not* exist as the Creator of all, then who or what else established the very laws of nature that scientists look to as the only explanation for how everything functions?

No, they insist, we don't need God to explain anything; energy is self-existent, without beginning or end. But this premise violates the second law of thermodynamics, which states that energy continually entropies. Were it self-existent, without beginning, it would have been here forever and would have long since reached the state of complete entropy, which it obviously has not.

Natural laws, too, they say, are self-existent. Neither lawgiver nor reason is needed. Intricate laws that govern the universe were apparently here before the universe or came into existence simultaneously with it. "This is simply the way things are," says the atheist. But is such a claim rational?

When we ask how origins can be explained without God, the reply is that they can't *yet,* but one day "science" will be able to do so.

Unlike the great scientists of the past who believed in God and built the foundation for science upon that faith, many of today's scientists worship the universe as all knowing and without beginning or end. They have nothing else to trust. Robert Jastrow has said:

> Astronomers are curiously upset by . . . the proof that the universe had a beginning. Their reactions provide an interesting demonstration of the response of the scientific mind—supposedly a very objective mind—when evidence uncovered by science itself leads to a conflict with the articles of faith in their profession . . . there is a kind of religion in science. . . .[32]

Religion in science? Of course. On July 5, 1997, "the project manager of the Jet Propulsion Laboratory renamed the *Mars Pathfinder Lander* in memory of Carl Sagan. He stated that he believed that Sagan was 'up there' watching the entire Mars landing [and] that he believed that Sagan had his hand in several of the project's miracles."[33] *Miracles?* There was no God to perform them, but somehow Sagan is managing to guide space like Obi Wan Kenobi guided Luke Skywalker? Faced with what it cannot explain without God, atheistic science has embraced pagan superstition!

For years there has been a neopaganism in the academic world called *ecotheology*. Viktor Ferkiss was a supporter of *ecotheology*, which, he said, "starts with the premise that the Universe is God."[34] As with other religions, many articles of this "faith" are held without any evidence to support them. This is especially true among evolutionists.

On November 5, 1981, British Museum of Natural History Senior Paleontologist Colin Patterson gave an informal talk to the Systematics Discussion Group at the American Museum of Natural History in New York. The most quoted part of his talk was as follows:

> For the last eighteen months or so, I've been kicking around non-evolutionary or even anti-evolutionary ideas. Now, one of the reasons I started taking this anti-evolutionary view,

well, let's call it non-evolutionary, was [that] last year I had
a sudden realization. For over twenty years I had thought
that I was working on evolution in some way. One morning
I woke up, and . . . it struck me that . . . there was not one
thing I knew about it. That was quite a shock, to learn that
one can be so misled for so long.

Now I think many people in this room would
acknowledge that during the last few years . . . you've
experienced a shift from evolution as knowledge to evolution
as faith. I know that's true of me, and I think it's true of a
good many of you in here.[35]

ISN'T THIS "SCIENTISM"?

A creationist present that day secretly and unethically taped the talk
without Patterson's permission and later released a transcript that has
caused great controversy, with evolutionists charging creationists with
misinterpreting Patterson. That led to an exchange of letters with
evolutionists in which Patterson reaffirmed his faith in evolution in
spite of its many problems.

Of course, Patterson's job depended upon his supporting evolution.
He "explained" that the famous quote had been misrepresented—that
he had not meant evolution in general but merely the "systematics"
thereof, since that was the group he was addressing. It is clear from
the transcript, however, that he was indeed talking of evolution in
general and of his disillusionment after twenty years devoted to it.
Evolutionists defend Patterson by saying that he surely knows what
he meant, but so can those who go by what he said. If words are to be
taken at face value, then what he meant in this unguarded moment is
clear—and so is his desire to deny it.

Not only cannot science explain the origin of energy, of life,
and of the many diverse species—it also has no answers to life's
ultimate questions. Nevertheless, many scientists deny this fact and
continue their determination to arrive at a "scientific" explanation

for everything—without any need for God. The following bold declaration from an atheist is only one of many examples that could be given:

> Once there was a time when nothing was explained. Since then, everything which has been explained has been found to have a natural, not a divine, explanation. Although this does not prove that all future explanations will be of like kind, it shows that it is not at all unreasonable to expect this—and it is not a very reliable bet to expect the opposite.[36]

This is not science but "scientism," the worship of science in the place of God. The truth, however, is that science never will be able to explain ultimate reality. We could quickly list dozens of common phenomenon that science has not been able to explain: light, the electron, life, love, conscience, ethics, morals, etc. In contrast to the confidence fifty years ago that physical science would soon explain everything, including mind and personality, most scientists now recognize that science can never explain the most basic elements of the universe and our existence.

Max Planck, one of the greatest physicists of the twentieth century, considered to be the father of modern Quantum Theory, frankly admitted: "Science cannot solve the ultimate mystery of nature."[37] We can't define time, or space, or matter, or energy—much less the soul and spirit. We have names by which we refer to an atom, molecule, cell, but no real understanding of their composition, and certainly not of their origin. Nor can science tell us *why* the universe exists.

Dawkins, of course, will not admit that the inability of science to explain what really matters indicates any failure to ultimately explain *everything*. The truth is that every door that science opens reveals ten unopened doors on the other side. Those who say that the universe began with a "Big Bang" cannot explain how this energy originated or why it suddenly exploded at that particular moment in the distant past.

Nor can they explain how the astonishing order we see everywhere in the universe, contrary to all logic and scientific laws, was produced by the hopeless chaos that such an explosion would unquestionably have caused.

When backed into a corner, confronted by facts that all lean in the favor of what atheists call "The God Hypothesis," Dawkins almost always hides behind what surely is his mantra, "We are working on that." He is working diligently to wipe out the memory of "the time when the world used to imagine there was a god."

SCIENCE TURNS TO MYSTICISM

Like so many other leading scientists, among them some Nobelists, George Wald thought he had rescued atheism when he opted for a mystical view of the universe, turning it into a sort of substitute "god." He wrote, "A physicist is the atom's way of knowing about atoms." This vision of a universe that is not only alive but that thinks and plans has dispensed with the law of biogenesis and common sense altogether. Wald said, "What we recognize as the material universe . . . of space and time and elementary particles and energies is . . . the materialization of primal mind . . . there is no waiting for consciousness to arise. It is [and was and will be] there always."[38]

Primal mind? What *mind* is this? Minds think! What does this mind think about? By this mystical view, there is no mystery concerning how life came out of dead elements. Matter itself is alive and active in planning its own destiny! If that is true, then who needs God for anything? No one, of course, say atheists! In order to avoid the God to whom all the evidence points, many scientists cling to the same arbitrary rejection of the facts in order not to be accountable to their Creator. Evolutionary biologist and geneticist Richard Lewontin's views are typical:

> We take the side of science *in spite* of the patent absurdity of some of its constructs . . . *in spite* of the tolerance of the scientific

community for unsubstantiated just-so stories, because we have a prior commitment . . . to materialism. . . .[39]

This is *science*? No, this is a destructive prejudice that science should not allow to get *its* foot inside the door! In spite of the fact that the majority of early scientists were theists and many of them Christians, the National Academy of Science today is heavily biased against belief in God—a far higher percentage than among scientists in general and the American population as a whole. That bias spreads its influence throughout society via the media and is enforced in the public school system, in spite of the fact that (as evolutionist Professor of Zoology and Comparative Anatomy, D. M. S. Watson, confessed), "Evolution . . . is accepted by zoologists not because it has been observed to occur or . . . can be proved by logically coherent evidence to be true, but because the only alternative, special creation, is clearly incredible."

From what these and other atheistic scientists say, there can be no question that atheism, not the facts of science, is what guides these men. There is no way that it could not also prejudice their science.

COMMITTING INTELLECTUAL SUICIDE

This passion to destroy all thought of God and all religion is widespread and growing. The theory of evolution has been adopted by scientists and nonscientists as one of the best means toward this end. Leading geneticist Francis Collins, a professing Christian who accepts evolution, says of the angry crusading atheist: "Dawkins is a master of setting up a straw man, and then dismantling it with great relish. In fact, it is hard to escape the conclusion that such repeated mischaracterizations of faith betray a vitriolic personal agenda, rather than a reliance on the rational arguments that Dawkins so cherishes in the scientific realm."[40] Mathematician J.W.N. Sullivan remains loyal to his atheism, even though he admits that his antagonism against God causes him, like Richard Lewontin, to espouse "patent absurdity":

> [By] careful experiments, notably those of Pasteur . . . it
> became an accepted doctrine [the law of biogenesis] that
> life never arises except from life. So far as actual evidence
> goes, this is still the only possible conclusion. But since it is
> a conclusion that seems to lead back to some supernatural
> creative act, it is a conclusion that scientific men find very
> difficult of acceptance. It carries with it what are felt to
> be, in the present mental climate, undesirable philosophic
> implications. . . . For that reason most scientific men prefer
> to believe that life arose, in some way not yet understood,
> from inorganic matter in accordance with the laws of
> physics and chemistry.[41]

Of course, none of the "laws of physics and chemistry" provide any basis for life to spring from lifeless molecules, no matter how much atheists *prefer* to imagine that this is the case. In fact, these laws deal only with dead matter, from which life cannot possibly arise. Nevertheless, every atheist and evolutionist, to maintain his faith in the god Chance, must defy the facts. Jacques Monod is one more typical example. A French biochemist, he shared the Nobel prize in physiology/medicine. In his book, *Le Hasard et la Nécessité* (*Chance and Necessity*, Paris, France, 1970), Monod gives at least twenty reasons why both a chance origin of life and evolution are impossible. He shows conclusively that the complex composition of living cells could exist only through intelligent design and direction, yet he ends the book with a defiant atheistic and totally irrational declaration similar to Wald's, basically saying that "our number came up in the Monte Carlo game." This is *science*?

Yes, this *is* science in the view of many scientists today—and in stark contrast to most of the founders of modern scientific theory. Pigliucci, a staunch atheist and critic of creationism, declares uncompromisingly as well as unscientifically (if science is indeed an open-minded search for the truth wherever it lies):

> No serious scientific discussion of any topic should include
> supernatural explanations, since the basic (and very
> reasonable) assumption of science is that the world can be
> explained entirely in physical terms, without recourse to
> divine entities.[42]

This is a shocking statement coming from a scientist who also has a doctorate in philosophy. The truth is that he cannot even explain in physical terms the idea he is expressing. As we point out repeatedly because of the great importance of this foregoing fact, no idea, concept, or conviction is physical. For example, "goodness" is a common idea understood by all. What does it weigh, smell like, look like, feel like, or sound like? Goodness is a concept held entirely in the mind that has no relationship to the physical world. Surely, Pigliucci would deny that he rejects God and believes in evolution because of the physical composition and configuration of his brain. Thus, his very belief that "the world can be explained entirely in physical terms" cannot itself be explained in physical terms.

At least Pigluicci is not as dogmatic as most of his colleagues. He does acknowledge that "special creation . . . although implausible . . . is still possible." However, he says it need not be considered because "though the situation is messy, it is not that desperate." Still firmly opposed to God, he momentarily tilts toward agnosticism: "It may be that the only rational position for the time being is simply a provisional and salutary, 'I don't know.'"[43] But on one point he remains unshakable: that huge area of "I don't know" is not allowed to contain a Creator.

It is amazing how the climate among scientists has swung radically to the side of atheism since acceptance of Darwin's theory gathered momentum. Of course, this became Darwin's basic motivation—and he was successful beyond his wildest hopes. This is particularly shocking when one considers that the vast majority of history's most famous scientists believed firmly in a supernatural Creator—especially those whose genius laid the foundation for today's science. They said, almost to a man, that their belief in God and thus in an orderly universe led them to discover the laws of physics, chemistry, thermodynamics, etc., for which they are still given credit today.

In fact, as has been pointed out by historians, not only were the founders of modern science Christians themselves, but it is no coincidence that they were all part of a Christian culture. Modern science would not have arisen in any other of the world's cultures. That is why these great men of science have almost no counterparts elsewhere in world history:

> Where is the Greek version of Newton? Where is the Muslim version of Kepler? Where is the Hindu version of Boyle? Where is the Buddhist version of Mendel? Such questions are all the more powerful when you pause to consider that science studies [universal] truths. . . . How is it that so many other cultures, some existing for thousands of years, failed to discover, or even anticipate, Newton's first law of motion or Kepler's laws of planetary motion? So it's not just that the Christian religion is associated with the birth of modern science [but] that modern science was not birthed in cultures which lacked the Christian religion.[44]

Yes, other cultures made valuable contributions such as the Arabic-Hindu number system and some advances in mathematics and engineering such as those used in building pyramids not only in Egypt but in South America, the South Sea Islands, and elsewhere. But these non-Christians

> . . . did not discover the laws of . . . gravity . . . thermodynamics . . . chemistry . . . heredity . . . biogenesis, etc. If you take any introductory undergraduate textbook in physics, chemistry, biology, genetics, physiology, paleontology, etc., it is not hard to point to the knowledge that is indebted to the work of these [European scientists who were staunch Christians]. But you would find very little that is indebted to Greek,

Muslim, Hindu, or Buddhist philosophers. . . . Instead of measuring energy in joules, why don't we measure it in platos or al-Asharis?"[45]

THEISM, THE FOUNDATION OF SCIENCE

Among these brilliant theist thinkers were the following: Louis Aggasiz, founder of glacial science; Sir Francis Bacon, who established the scientific method of inquiry based on experimentation and inductive reasoning; Sir Charles Bell, first to extensively map the brain and nervous system; Robert Boyle, founder of "Boyle's Law" for gasses; Nicolas Copernicus, who set forth the first mathematically based system of planets orbiting the sun; Georges Cuvier, founder of comparative anatomy; John Dalton, father of modern atomic theory; René Descartes, mathematician, scientist, and philosopher, called the father of modern philosophy; Jean Henri Fabre, chief founder of modern entomology; Michael Faraday, one of the greatest scientists of the nineteenth century, who revolutionized physics with his work on electricity and magnetism; James Joule, discoverer of the first law of thermodynamics; William Thomson Kelvin, among the first to clearly state the second law of thermodynamics; Johannes Kepler, mathematician, astronomer, discoverer of the laws of planetary motion; James Clerk Maxwell, formulator of the electromagnetic theory of light; Gregor Mendel, father of genetics; Sir Isaac Newton, inventor of the reflecting telescope, discoverer of the Law of Gravity,) and generally regarded as the most original and influential thinker in the history of science; Blaise Pascal, major contributor to probability studies and hydrostatics; Louis Pasteur, formulator of the germ theory—and too many others to name.

There were influential atheists as well, showing that these men did not merely pretend to believe in God because such a belief was popular in their day. Aggasiz, Cuvier, Fleming, Kelvin, and Linnaeus were what we now call "creationists." Kelvin openly opposed Darwinism. Newton ended his most important book with these words: "This most beautiful system of sun, planets, and comets could only proceed from the counsel and dominion of an intelligent and powerful Being. . . . This Being governs all things, not as the soul of the world, but as Lord over all; and on account of his dominion he is wont to be called Lord God."[46]

Albert Einstein, too, though he did not believe in a personal God (yet he said, "I want to know His thoughts . . . "), admitted that the universe demanded an intelligent Creator who, as Spinoza showed, "reveals himself in the harmony of what exists." That fact, Einstein believed, was the basis for science. He is famous for saying, "God does not play dice [with His universe]."

Even Stephen Hawking, certainly anything but a Christian, has said, "It is difficult to discuss the beginning of the universe without mentioning the concept of God." Commenting on Einstein's "God doesn't play dice. . . ," Hawking declared, "God not only plays with dice, He sometimes throws them where they can't be seen."

HONEST SCIENCE PRODUCES FAITH IN GOD

To say that belief in God is not "scientific" and that scientists don't believe in God is to expose both one's ignorance and bias. As we have often shown, there have always been many top scientists who had faith in God and credited science itself with arousing that faith. The same is true today. Yet, sadly and incredibly, with the advent of Darwin and evolution, atheists have increasingly taken over the scientific and academic establishment, generally control it today, and are almost exclusively consulted by the media as the official spokespersons for science.

Biology professor Dean Kenyon, author of *Biochemical Predestination*, a major university textbook for teaching evolution (which he has since repudiated), reminds us:

We tend too easily to forget that creationist views of origins predominated in scientific circles before the publication of Darwin's *On the Origin of Species* in 1859. The *leading scientists* of Europe and the United States were creationist scientists, and they defended their views with scientific evidence and argument. . . . Although students generally hear only one side on the origins question, increasing numbers of scientists are now *abandoning evolution* for a new scientific version of creationism. [His emphasis][48]

Francis Collins is another case in point. Certainly one of the foremost geneticists alive today, he was director of the National Human Genome Research Institute from 1993-2009, having "headed a multinational 2,300-scientist team that co-mapped the 3 billion biochemical letters of our genetic blueprint, a milestone that then-President Bill Clinton honored in a 2000 White House ceremony. . . . He is also a forthright Christian who converted from atheism at age 27 and now finds time to advise young evangelical scientists on how to declare their faith in science's largely agnostic upper reaches."[49]

In spite of the rampant unbelief among the general public and the efforts of atheists such as Dawkins to convince the world that faith in God is anti-science, there are still many Christians among top scientists and modern Nobel laureates:

William D. Phillips won the 1997 Nobel Prize in chemistry for using lasers to produce temperatures only a fraction of a degree above absolute zero. Phillips once quipped that so many of his colleagues were Christians that he couldn't walk across his church's fellowship hall without "tripping over a dozen physicists. . . ." Professor Richard Bube of Stanford says, "There are [proportionately] as many atheistic truck drivers as atheistic scientists." But among Nobel laureates, the number who recognize the hand of God in the universe is remarkably high.[50]

WELL-QUALIFIED SCIENTISTS ON BOTH SIDES

There are scientists who are atheists and there are scientists who are Christians. Is there a difference? As far as talents, intelligence, and qualifications go, there is no difference in favor of either side. At the beginning of the modern scientific era, scientists who were theists far outnumbered atheists and agnostics. That balance has changed in more recent times in favor of the unbelievers. But there are still many highly qualified scientists who are firm believers in God.

What then is the difference, if there is any? There is no point in counting the numbers on each side—that would prove nothing. But there is an important and obvious distinction. The central issue is, which one would be the best scientist, most likely to look at all the facts objectively? And that question is answered heavily on the side of the theists. Why?

Read Francis Crick, co-discoverer of the structure of the DNA molecule (along with James D. Watson and Maurice Wilkins), in a book he subtitles, *The Scientific Search for the Soul*. His atheism, not an honest scientific inquiry, has already predetermined what his "search" will reveal. He isn't really searching for the soul as the ordinary person would conceive it. That would be unthinkable for him as an atheist. He is searching for some mechanical, physical, or chemical "thing" that will enable him to change the minds of those foolish enough to hold the view of a nonmaterial soul. This has always been and still is the universal belief of mankind. And that pre-bias cannot but hinder his research as a scientist by preventing him from considering valuable evidence that leads in a direction he will not go.

Of course, the ordinary person would firmly oppose any attempt to describe himself and his life in such a manner. He would consider it not only astonishing but ridiculous. He knows that he is not just a lump of molecules. He is a thinking person, and jealous of his own identity, one who makes choices that he carefully weighs, who experiences joys, sorrows, hopes, ambitions, fears, remorse, and regrets that are very real.

Crick ends the book with a treatise explaining away free will as attributable to certain areas of the brain.[51] Once again, he is clearly denying what the ordinary person would consider logical, based upon his or her own experience of life. He *must* find a material explanation in the physical brain to maintain his atheism. He would not dare for a moment to consider the possibility of a nonmaterial explanation, even though many scientists who are not theists but agnostics freely admit the overwhelming evidence that thoughts are not material.

THE DIFFERENCE IT MAKES

Richard Dawkins dares to say, "I show that all the alternatives to Darwinism that have ever been suggested are in principle incapable of . . . explaining the organized complexity of life. . . . My reasoning, if it is correct, tells us something important about life everywhere in the universe."[52] *If it is correct?* He acknowledges that this is just a theory, and a shaky one at that—but that doesn't prevent him from proceeding as though it were true because he has no other hope to explain life on earth. It *must* be correct—this is the best his atheism can offer—and atheism is the one thing he will not abandon under any circumstance.

Has he shown us that Darwinism can "explain the organized complexity of life?" No, he hasn't even come within miles of doing that. Darwinism fails completely in this respect. Nor has Dawkins ever shown that creation by God could not account for the "organized complexity of life. . . ." In fact, it is the only alternative that can! But he won't even consider that possibility. So the *religion of atheism* hampers the scientist in research and judgment because it restricts him to only one point of view.

The scientist who is a Christian, on the other hand, is willing to consider every possibility. If the evidence proves that he has believed a lie, he will abandon his faith. The fact that he is confident that no evidence, when all the facts are known, could ever prove that the Bible is wrong, does not prevent him from honest investigation to see whether evolution can be supported by objective evidence or not. He is free to examine all the facts and follow them wherever they may lead.

He will not forsake His faith in God because he knows there had to be a Creator. But if the facts should prove evolution to be true, he would be willing to say, "I guess that's the way God chose to do it" —even though that would make no sense. Francis Collins is evidence of this openness.

In contrast, the atheist cannot be this open-minded. He cannot "allow a Divine Foot in the door,"[53] and that restricts his research and intellectual honesty. There is no such person as an "atheistic theist" who would be comparable to a theistic evolutionist.

Darwinian evolution is the only process we know that is ultimately capable of generating anything as complicated as creative intelligences. . . . Evolution is the creator of life.

—WALL STREET JOURNAL (WEEKEND JOURNAL),
"MAN VS. GOD," SATURDAY/SUNDAY, SEPTEMBER 12-13, 2009

We can deal with the unique origin of life by postulating a very large number of planetary opportunities. Once that initial stroke of luck has been granted—and the anthropic principle most decisively granted to us—natural selection takes over: and natural selection is most emphatically not a matter of luck.

—RICHARD DAWKINS, THE GOD DELUSION
(BOSTON: HOUGHTON MIFFLIN, 2006), 139-40

What is a big deal—the biggest deal of all—is how you get something out of nothing. . . . Don't let cosmologists try to kid you on this one. They have not got a clue either—despite the fact that they are doing a pretty good job of convincing themselves and others that this is really not a problem. "In the beginning," they say, "there was nothing—no time, space, matter or energy. Then there was a quantum fluctuation from which. . . ." Whoa! Stop right there! You see what I mean? First there is nothing, then there is something. And the cosmologists try to bridge the two with a quantum flutter, a tremor of uncertainty that sparks it all off. . . . Either there is nothing to begin with, in which case there is no quantum vacuum, no pre-geometric dust, no time in which anything can happen, no physical laws that can effect a change from nothingness into somethingness; or there is something, in which case that needs explaining.

—DAVID DARLING, "ON CREATING SOMETHING FROM NOTHING,"
NEW SCIENTIST, VOL. 151 (SEPTEMBER 14, 1996), 49

By the end of the 1960s the big bang had become almost universally accepted, and it has penetrated the popular consciousness so deeply that at times one forgets it is still just a theory.

—ANTHONY L. PERATT, "NOT WITH A BANG,"
THE SCIENCES (JANUARY/FEBRUARY 1990), 24

Only fundamentalist Christians who insist on a literal interpretation of the Bible refuse to accept the biological evidence for evolution. Most other churches, including the often dogmatic Catholic church, have by now quietly accepted the notion of evolution as a scientific fact. . . .

—VICTOR L. STENGER, "WAS THE UNIVERSE CREATED?"
FREE INQUIRY (SUMMER 1987), 26

FIVE

IN THE
BEGINNING:
THE QUESTION
OF ORIGINS

RICHARD DAWKINS ADMITS that "Darwin's answer to the question
of the origin of species was . . . that species were descended from
other species."[1] This is no answer at all! It's a far cry from *origin* of species, as the title of Darwin's first book promised, and as Dawkins claims
Darwin achieved. What was the first species, and how did it come into
existence? Darwin doesn't tell us, nor does Dawkins. Atheism, no matter how scientific it attempts to be, has nothing to contribute to the
question of origins. The answer to that question does not lie within the
province of science.

The first words in the despised and perpetually attacked book, the
Bible, just "happen" to be: "In the beginning. . . ." The Bible certainly

got that right long before science reluctantly agreed. This is either a massive coincidence, or it alone would seem to be proof that this book was indeed written by the Creator himself. For thousands of years, its wisdom has stood as a challenge to atheists and now to scientists as well. They still have no answer. Perhaps everyone, including atheists, ought to pay attention. The next two words offer the only rational solution to the problem of origins: "God created."

Scientism's pitiful substitute for this very logical declaration is, "In the beginning there was nothing. Once-upon-a-time, 'nothing' gathered itself together, squared its shoulders, and decided to explode. There was a huge noise—and here we are, after billions of years, the proud offspring of a 'Big Bang.'" Such is the preferred theory of many today, but no one yet has solved the problem of origins. The Big Bang must have required an almost infinite amount of energy. What is energy, and how did it *originate*? What about life? What is its origin? It is pointless to attempt estimates of the odds of life *somehow* coming into existence. The law of biogenesis very clearly states that life comes only from life. That brings us full circle: what is life and what is its origin?

If that is not plain enough, this law says there is *zero* possibility that life could arise out of a universe that has been totally sterilized by a huge ball of fire that evolutionists call the Big Bang. Dawkins can multiply zero possibility of life by as large a number and in as tiny steps as he can conceive, and the result will still be *zero* possibility of life. Surely, an Oxford professor knows the elementary mathematical fact that *zero* times infinity is still zero!

In these first five words of the Bible, God has issued a challenge. We are still waiting for atheists and today's scientists to provide a substantive response. In his new book, very lucidly and convincingly written, *Why Evolution Is True,* Jerry Coyne attempts to respond to the Creator's challenge. As one might have suspected, however, this highly acclaimed book doesn't even have a reference in its index to this key element: origins.

THE ATHEIST'S ACHILLES HEEL

John Lennox wrote, "[Friedrich] Engels made a very perceptive comment on the issues at stake: 'Did God create the world? Or has the world been in existence eternally? . . .'"[2] Obviously, it has not always existed because although, according to the first law of thermodynamics, energy cannot be destroyed, the second law, the law of entropy, declares that it deteriorates until it becomes utterly useless. This tells us that the universe had a beginning, or energy would have degraded to the point of total uselessness.

Lennox continued, "Stephen Hawking adopts a similar view: 'Many people do not like the idea that time has a beginning, probably because it smacks of divine intervention.'"[3] In spite of reluctance to accept the consensus that the cosmos had a beginning, the evidence cannot be denied.

Sir Arthur Eddington, when confronted with the question of a beginning to the universe, reacted as follows: "Philosophically, the notion of a beginning of the present order of nature is repugnant. . . . I should like to find a genuine loophole."[4] Clearly, however, there is no loophole through which the atheist can make any face-saving escape.

Lennox commented, "That repugnance was shared by others in the mid-twentieth century. Gold, Bondi, Hoyle, and Narlikar advanced a series of steady-state theories in which it was argued that the universe always existed, [and] that matter was continuously being created in order to keep the density of the admittedly expanding universe uniform. . . ."[5]

If energy can't be created, it must have been here forever. We know that is not possible, or all matter would have become useless by now. Every attempt that atheists make to avoid the logical consequences of the facts as we know them comes up against the stone wall of established scientific law.

Richard Dawkins has not explained anything, let alone how life began. This seems odd in view of the fact that he declares a number of times that Darwin explained everything about life. Isn't this how Dawkins says he was converted to the religion of atheism? Let me quote him again: "My final vestige of religious faith disappeared when I finally understood the Darwinian explanation for life."[6] But he has also told us, as have the other leaders of the New Atheists, that Darwinism *doesn't* explain the origin of life after all, so there was really no sound reason for his conversion to atheism! That should be more than a little disconcerting.

Nor can we be impressed with the reasons he has since accumulated in the name of science and offers to us now. Concerning the all-important question of the origin of life, he says,

> The major ingredient was heredity, either DNA or (more *probably*) something that copies like DNA but *less* accurately, *perhaps* the related molecule RNA. Once the vital ingredient—*some kind of genetic molecule*—is in place, true Darwinian natural selection can follow, and complex life emerges as the eventual consequence. But the spontaneous arising by chance of the first heredity molecule strikes many as improbable. *Maybe it is*—very, very *improbable*. . . . The origin of life is a flourishing, if *speculative*, subject for *research*. The expertise required for it is chemistry and it is not mine. [Emphasis added][7]

In fact, the "spontaneous arising by chance of the first heredity molecule" is not just improbable but impossible. This is one of those ingredients lying in wait in the impassable swamps and impossible cliffs that must be conquered before even reaching the base of Mount Improbable. Evolutionists/atheists are now telling us that the law of biogenesis isn't really a law. It has been violated not just once but millions of times all over the universe! To accept Darwinism is tantamount to rejecting the very foundations of science itself. Everything is up for grabs.

And when we come to the question of origins, the lips of science are tightly sealed. Science can't explain the origin of either matter or life. We have merely substituted new words to cover our ignorance and pretend we've made an advance. As far as ultimate reality is concerned, however, we are still where primitive man was before "science" deluded us with false hope.

One of the greatest astrophysicists of the twentieth century, Sir Arthur Eddington, frankly confessed, "We have learned that the exploration of the external world by the methods of the physical sciences leads not to a concrete reality but to a shadow world of symbols."[8] In agreement, great mathematician and astronomer Sir James Jeans declared, "The most outstanding achievement of twentieth-century physics is not the theory of relativity . . . or the theory of quanta . . . or the dissection of the atom . . . it is the general recognition that we are not yet in contact with ultimate reality."[9] Sir Karl Popper, one of the most influential philosophers of science in the twentieth century, stated that the theory of evolution is not science but "a metaphysical research programme."[10]

In his book, *God's Undertaker*, John Lennox says, "[Astrophysicist] Arno Penzias used the space platform of earth to make the brilliant discovery of the 'echo of the beginning,' the cosmic background of microwave radiation," for which he was awarded a Nobel Prize. In contrast to the increasingly belligerent New Atheists, Penzias has said, 'Astronomy leads us to a unique event—a universe that was created out of nothing, one with the very delicate balance needed to provide the exact conditions to permit life and one which has an underlying (one might say) supernatural plan.'"[11]

The more we investigate, the clearer it becomes that the New Atheists are trying to force upon the entire world a rejection of God that is contrary to what the majority are willing to believe, at least at this point.

Dawkins concedes, "There are still gaps in our understanding. We don't understand how the cosmos came into existence in the first place. . . . " This is Dawkins's standard escape hatch whenever he is confronted with the many questions for which atheism and evolution have no answer. Instead of admitting that science has nothing to say about what is good, what is evil, what is beautiful, what is ugly, where did we come from, where are we going, etc. (as many of the greatest scientists have frankly confessed), Dawkins sings the same worn-out song, "We're working on that."[12]

There are numerous books that defend evolution and natural selection. Their authors admit to many problems with these theories and propose many supposedly *possible* solutions but never give definitive answers with any degree of certainty. For example, in Stephen Jay Gould's discussion of the alleged Cambrian explosion, theory after theory is proposed, all of them based upon little evidence and much imagination. If that were not enough to expose the bankruptcy of the whole issue, one even larger and more obvious question stands out above all others: the problem of origins. That should be dealt with first, yet in a book of more than 300 pages, Gould has *nothing* to say about this most important problem for any scientist or philosopher.

As we continue to point out, it is one thing to speculate about the alleged evolution and natural selection of species once they exist. Literally thousands of volumes and scientific papers have been written on such conjecture. It is something else entirely to explain the origin of the energy out of which all living things are made (even to explain what energy is). The fact that life, as we've seen, "comes only from life" requires an explanation of how the first life began. The same is true of the fact that a cell comes only from another living cell. The atheist cannot escape these and dozens of similar "chicken or egg" puzzles. Shouldn't solving them be the top priority?

What is the point of developing theories about the evolution of something when we don't even know what is allegedly evolving, how it came into existence, and how life was imparted to it? Wouldn't it make more sense to find out what life is than to theorize about how it supposedly evolves once it mysteriously appears? Yet the origin of life is almost universally avoided in treatises about evolution, as is the origin of time, space, and matter. For example, the index to Gould's book *Wonderful Life,* about the Burgess shale, has no reference at all to origins. Nor does Crick's *The Astonishing Hypothesis,* or Hitchens's *God Is Not Great: How Religion Poisons Everything.* In their book,

Biology Revisioned, Willis W. Harman and Elisabet Sahtouris make several brave but unsuccessful attempts both to define and to explain the origin of life. The best they can do is to describe what living things *do* but not what they *are,*[13] much less how life came out of the total death left by the heat of the Big Bang.

As it is with the writings of evolutionists, so it is with those of atheists. Obviously, it is impossible to be only one or the other; these two come as a package, as Dawkins admits in declaring that Darwinism led him to atheism. In the index to Hitchens's book, he offers one reference to origins.[14] The entry is, *Origin of Species, The* (Darwin, 269-70). Those pages have nothing to do with the origin of species—nor does Darwin's entire book, though that is its title.

Hitchens refers to "the unarguable facts of evolution" but gives us none of them. Like other atheists and evolutionists, he is referring to modifications within a species—even within a bacterium. We're still waiting for an example of genuine evolution from one species to another. The abundant variety of dogs is not evidence of evolution from one *kind,* as defined in Genesis 1, to another *kind.* Clearly *"kind"* is still a division that cannot be crossed. Let us have *just one example* of evolution changing a dog into something other than a dog. No such examples are offered. As we showed in chapter 2, Colin Patterson confessed that he couldn't think of *even one!*

Atheists get excited about using "evolution" to reorganize the DNA in various bacterium.[15] But that is not evolution, although Dawkins and others continually call it that. Kenneth R. Miller's enthusiasm is almost unbounded when it comes to origins. He bluntly declares that

> . . . evolution is, by definition, a story of origins. This means . . . it really does supersede another creation story—in particular, the creation story at the very core of the Judeo-Christian narrative. The conflict between these two versions of our history is real, and . . . needs to be addressed. [But] I do not believe that the conflict is unresolvable.[16]

A story of origins? Evolution has *nothing* to say about *origins,* neither the origin of energy, nor of the cosmos, nor of the first cell, nor of the first species, nor of life.

Not unresolvable?! That is like saying that there is no real conflict between atheism and theism, between evolution and creation. Words have lost their meaning. There can be no meaningful discussion if the total contradiction of the two views is denied as though it did not exist.

When chased with a volley of facts, evolutionists attempt to hide behind "billions of years," which, if taken in tiny enough steps, they imagine to be long enough for anything to have happened, no matter how impossible. Having accepted these long periods of time for the origin of the universe, the world, and life, some scientists who otherwise accept the Genesis creation account have been forced to postulate what they call "progressive creation." Other Christians have tried to reconcile the Bible and the pseudo-science of evolution by adopting what has euphemistically become known as "theistic evolution." We will deal with both of these aberrant theologies in later chapters. The truth is that billions of years are not long enough.

It is a fact that the sun could not have been in the sky forever. It can only burn for a finite length of time. No matter how huge or of what kind, a fire will eventually die. It is true of every star and everything else that makes up the universe that all physical things deteriorate with age and ultimately become useless. Stars die, but they are not yet all dead, so they could not have existed forever.

It is self-evident that at one time the stars, planets, galaxies, and *the energy from which they are made* did not exist. All must have come into existence in the distant but finite past. Of that we can be certain. Otherwise, all stars would have burned out by now and the entire universe would be approaching absolute zero in temperature. We are driven by the second law of thermodynamics, the law of entropy, to conclude that there was a time when *no material thing existed, not even the energy from which all is made.*

Consequently, what about the first law, the law of the conservation of energy, which says that energy cannot be created and must therefore have been here forever? That law precludes a creator, ruling out God by very definition. This is arbitrary, unscientific—and unreasonable, but most of the world, led by the new atheistic science, is far down that irrational path. Although it is true that *man* can neither create nor destroy energy, common sense says that it could not have existed forever or, according to the second law, it all would have entropied long ago. Therefore, energy and all matter must have had a beginning.

Since energy could not have existed forever, where did it come from in the beginning? It couldn't have arisen spontaneously and in a vacuum. Nor could it be eternal and have been waiting billions or trillions of years to explode in a "big bang," or it would have entropied before it "banged." There is only one rational alternative: there must be an all-powerful Being who exists independently of, outside of, and is the Creator of this space-time-matter continuum in which we exist.

Atheists cannot deny this logic but reject it as "unacceptable" to them. This is hardly a good reason, and it is certainly not a scientific one. What does atheism offer as an alternative? It has nothing to offer but insists that it is "working" on the problem and "one day" will have it solved. This is not science but religion, a religion of no God—not theism but *a*-theism.

WHY THE QUESTION OF ORIGINS MATTERS

Inasmuch as life comes only from life, the origin of the first life poses an unanswerable problem for those who choose to reject God as the Creator of all things and the only source of all life. That foundational question is shoved aside and various theories of how life "evolved" are printed in textbooks for trusting young students and presented in the media as though they were fact. Having rejected God, atheists find it easy to reject facts and logic. As we have seen, even Nobel laureates such as George Wald are driven to accept utter nonsense in their desperate flight from God.

The theory of evolution tries to leapfrog over the uncomfortable question of origins. It starts off with energy/matter already in existence, out of which the universe miraculously emerged, then primitive life, which eventually progressed to what we have today. The question of origins is surely basic. No sound conclusion can be derived until we have an answer to how, from whence, and why life arrived on planet Earth. Science cannot provide this essential foundation for atheism's only possible response: that life developed by fortuitous chance from dead matter after a "big bang" had sterilized everything.

Someone will argue that a doctor doesn't have to know the origin of life in order to practice medicine; he only needs to know how life functions or malfunctions in the present. That is true, but the analogy doesn't fit. We are not discussing health issues of life already in existence but the question of how totally sterilized matter gave birth to life, and why.

Moreover, life is not only physical, as we have already shown. There is a nonphysical side to life as well. If someone says, "Nonphysical reality? That's ridiculous!" let the complainant give us a physical description of ridiculous. What about a physical description of purpose? meaning? justice? truth, etc.?

Remember what turned Mortimer J. Adler from agnosticism to belief in God: he discovered the difference between humans and all animals, a chasm that no evolutionary leap can span. What makes a human being? Not his skeletal structure or the capacity of his brain. It is the ability, said Adler, to form conceptual ideas and express them in words. Neither conceptual ideas nor the words that express them occupy physical space or have physical substance—but they are real nonetheless. Right here, in this simple truth, the atheist materialist is dealt a death blow.

Back to the question of life. What is it? Is it found in the chemical composition of the body? Obviously not. Chemicals, no matter what form they take, do not have any life in themselves nor can they give life to anything. How do we know this? Even if medical science reached the point where it could gather together, and in the right order, the exact chemicals of which the body is composed, it would take more than such incredible engineering to give life to these chemicals. Left on their own, no matter how lifelike when first sculpted, they would obviously deteriorate into a lifeless pile of what this "body" was made of—mere chemicals.

That being the case, it is quite clear that to understand what a man or woman really is, we must look beyond the physical body. The body is temporary. But what about the life, which is clearly not part of that body but gives it consciousness and meaning? Consciousness exists in a nonphysical dimension. The body did not create its own consciousness. A dead body cannot give life to itself. Life must come from another dimension, and when it leaves the body, there is no medical or scientific way to call it back.

The all-important question is whether the soul and spirit of man, which resided in the body, continue to exist even after the body is dead. If we don't know how life arose, can we be sure what happens to it when it abandons the body in death? That is the most important question we face. The answer to it all hangs on the question of origins.

Men will behave one way if they truly believe they were created by a God of infinite love who, nevertheless, holds them accountable for their attitudes, secret thoughts, and deeds on Earth and will either punish or reward them eternally after death. They will behave another way altogether if they think they were formed by blind forces that are impersonal and cannot judge, and that when they are dead, that is the end.

PANTHEISM WON'T WORK

Logic alone is sufficient to rule out pantheism, the belief that God created the universe out of Himself and it is therefore equal to God. It could not be an extension of or part of Him, or it would not be subject to the law of entropy. By itself, this fact refutes the idea of the "Star Wars Force" or of any other theory that turns God into unthinking, purposeless energy. By claiming that everything is God, pantheism reduces God to matter that is incapable of thought and is helpless in and of itself. If everything and everyone is God, then nothing is God, because the concept of God has lost its meaning.

The only sensible conclusion is that God created everything out of nothing and that the cosmos was, is, and always will be separate and distinct from its Creator.

This is exactly what the Bible declares: "Through faith we understand that the worlds were framed by the word of God, so that things which are seen were not made of things which do appear."[17] The book of Genesis gives some of the details surrounding the creation of the universe and of man and all living things on Earth, including sin and death and the worldwide flood. That judgment from God through water is verified by worldwide geological evidence today—much of it in the form of marine fossils on the tops of very high mountains.

The first eleven chapters of Genesis are ignored, mythologized, or given a non-literal meaning by many who nevertheless call themselves Christians. Yet the Genesis account of the origin of the universe and all that is within it, including man, is foundational to everything else the Bible says, including the teachings of Jesus Christ and the Christian faith. That is, of course, precisely why the Bible begins this way. John M. Cimbala, a mechanical engineer who earned his Ph.D. in Aeronautics at California Institute of Technology, explains the importance of the opening chapters of Genesis:

> I was raised in a Christian home [but] eventually rejected the entire Bible and believed that we descended from lower creatures; there was no afterlife and no purpose in life but to enjoy the short time we have on this earth. My college years at Penn State were spent as an atheist. . . . Fortunately, and by the grace of God, I began to read articles and listen to tapes about scientific evidence for creation [and] realized that the Bible might actually be true! It wasn't until I could believe the first page of the Bible that I could believe the rest of it.[18]

The abandonment of a literal interpretation of the Bible, and especially of the first eleven chapters of Genesis, has turned many professing Christians into atheists. Charles Templeton, pastor for seven years of a successful and growing church in Toronto, Canada, and at one time close friend and co-evangelist with Billy Graham,[19] abandoned the faith entirely when he decided he could no longer believe the biblical account of creation. In fact, he confesses that the foundational reason for his years of agnosticism, as it has been for many others, was: "I had always doubted the Genesis account of creation."[20]

This rejection of the Genesis record is a recurring theme throughout Templeton's autobiography, *Farewell to God.* Charles Templeton was one of the original organizers of Youth For Christ. In 1946, he was listed by the National Association of Evangelicals as among those "best used by God." Yet his doubts grew until at last Templeton told Billy:

> But, Billy, it's simply not possible any longer to believe, for instance, the biblical account of creation. The world wasn't created over a period of days a few thousand years ago; it has evolved over millions of years. It's not a matter of speculation; it's demonstrable fact.[21]

He was mistaken. What he readily accepted due to his lack of faith in the Bible is not "demonstrable fact" at all. It is tragic that through faulty evidence and reasoning he was convinced that the Bible was untrustworthy and became an agnostic and, finally, an atheist. Rejection of the Genesis account of creation was a key factor in his losing confidence in the veracity of the Bible. Such was the spiritual climate at Princeton Theological Seminary already in 1946, where many of the professors, such as B. B. Warfield and Charles Hodge accepted the "billions of years old" theory of the age of the Earth—and some, like Hodge, even embraced Darwinism. Templeton reasoned that if the Bible was in such error concerning the origin of mankind, how could it be trusted when it referred to human destiny?

Most amazing is the fact that Templeton continued to represent the National Council of Churches on "preaching missions" across the United States and Canada. In spite of the loss of his own "faith," Templeton saw an average of about 150 "converts" each night who mostly "stayed converted." Six months after his meetings in Evansville,

Indiana, for example, where 91,000 out of a population of 128,000 attended, a survey "showed that church attendance was 17 percent higher than it had been before he came. . . ."[22] Incredibly, with no faith of his own, he was for three years Director of Evangelism of the Presbyterian Church U.S.A.

Here again we see the importance of origins: as Templeton reasoned, if we cannot trust the Bible's account of the origin of man, why should we believe what it says about the destiny of man? But we could turn that statement around. If we can't believe what science says about the origin of man, why should we believe what it says about human destiny? As a matter of fact, science has nothing factual and verifiable to say about either man's origin or destiny.

WE ARE COMPELLED BY ALL THE EVIDENCE TO BELIEVE IN GOD

The fact that the cosmos exists, with life and intelligence resident on planet Earth, demands an explanation. *Nothing* cannot produce *anything*. Either some*thing* of infinite potential or *Someone* of infinite power always was, must still exist, and always will. There is no escaping this conclusion. Atheists choose to believe that some*thing* of infinite potential always existed and must still be hiding somewhere. They generally choose energy as that some*thing*. This is their god. Theists choose to believe that *Someone* always was, is, and forever will be. There are compelling reasons for believing the second alternative rather than the first.

Either the universe brought itself into existence from non-existence—or God is self-existent, always has been, and is the Creator of the universe. These are the only two alternatives: take your pick. It is beyond our finite capacity to comprehend an infinite Being without beginning or end, but it is not irrational. We are driven by logic and everything we have learned about the universe in which we find ourselves to admit the inescapable second conclusion. No matter how distasteful it is for atheists, who imagine they speak for today's scientific and academic establishments, we are driven by all of the facts to believe in God as the Creator.

There couldn't be some*thing* out of which everything came, because *things* are neither self-existent nor eternal. There had to be *Someone*, an eternal Being, without beginning or end and infinite in power, who created everything out of nothing. This One is *not* any of the pitiful, physical gods of idol-worshipers that men have made with their own hands. This is the God of the Bible. He revealed Himself to Moses with these words: "I AM THAT I AM [Yahweh-the self-existent One]"[23] and through His prophets declared, "The LORD God made the earth and the heavens."[24] The Apostle Paul challenged the Greek philosophers on Mars Hill:

> God that made the world and all things therein, seeing that he is Lord of heaven and earth, dwelleth not in temples made with hands; neither is worshipped with men's hands, as though he needed any thing, seeing he giveth to all life, and breath, and all things . . . for in him we live, and move, and have our being. . . . [He even gives breath and life to those who hate Him and reject Him, such as Richard Dawkins and the other New Atheists.]
> Forasmuch then as we are the offspring [creation] of God, we ought not to think that the Godhead is like unto gold or silver, or stone, graven by art and man's device. And the times of this ignorance God winked at; but now commandeth all men everywhere to repent. . . . [25]

Biblical declarations about God agree precisely with all of the evidence science has been able to gather. It is not religious sentiment but all the known facts that drive us to acknowledge one true God, without beginning or end, who created all from nothing. Without Him, there is no answer to the most basic question facing us: the origin of the physical universe and of life.

WHICH IS THE MOST RATIONAL?

Atheistic scientism doesn't like this conclusion, but it is inescapable. This is what all of the evidence demands. Science cannot tell us what happened "in the beginning," but it admits there surely was a "beginning" to the universe. Matter cannot spontaneously arise from nothing, nor could "nothing" birth the universe. Everything that exists could have been created only by an eternal, self-existent, nonmaterial, and infinitely personal, intelligent Being. We call that Being, God.

Atheists say that belief in God is irrational. The New Atheists declare that "Religion is not only wrong, it's evil."[26] What do they offer instead? Something even more incredible and outrageous. Their "god" is energy that operates by "natural selection." If this is true, energy logically must have all of the qualities of the God of the Bible: it must be self-existent, without beginning or end, and it must be free from all laws—from the lawmaker that put in place the law of gravity and all of the other laws of chemistry and physics. Energy must have been able to plan the atomic weights and structure of the elements, put together the chemical periodic table, impose the rules for chemical bonding upon matter, and organize every elementary particle in such a way that atoms produce molecules that can form themselves into living cells.

Though lifeless itself, energy, the evolutionists' god, must be the source of all life. It must conceive and put down in writing on DNA the "architect's plans," as Dawkins calls them, for constructing and operating every incredible nano-chemical machine within every functioning cell— "information and complexity which surpass human understanding . . . programmed into a space smaller than an invisible speck of dust."[27] Though impersonal and incapable of thought, the god "energy" must have created personal beings who can reason about it, though it cannot reason about them. These are only some of the personal, thinking qualities that energy must have in order to qualify as the originator of the universe and life.

Obviously, energy can do none of this. It does not qualify to be the creator of the universe, much less of human beings. Yet this is the *"great* god" that atheists such as Christopher Hitchens worship. They say that our thinking, willing, loving, personal, all-knowing, all-powerful God, without beginning or end, is incredible—and theirs is scientific. And Hitchens dares to title a book *God Is Not Great*! That certainly is true of his "god," but here we are, alive on planet Earth, and we need to know who we are, how we got here, and why. Atheistic, materialistic "science" cannot tell us.

THE NEW ATHEISTS

We have already pointed out the fact that many of history's foremost scientists—indeed, most of the founders of modern science—believed in God. Yet since Darwin and Freud, atheists have aggressively and dishonestly claimed to speak for the entire scientific establishment.

The New Atheists are angrily rallying all nonbelievers to close ranks in a battle to the death against "this debilitating curse: the curse of faith." The New Atheists' antagonism and determination know no bounds. They condemn not just belief in God but *respect* for belief in God.

The "curse of faith"? These critics are under the false impression that "faith" is a leap into the dark. On the contrary, biblical faith is based upon evidence. Many of the greatest historians and legal experts, not for sentimental reasons but on the basis of established scientific evidence, have turned from atheism to believe in everything the Bible declares, including the resurrection of Christ. They have come to this faith not by some mystical or emotional experience but based solidly upon overwhelming evidence that they say will stand up in any court of law.

Simon Greenleaf, co-founder of Harvard's graduate school of law, in his day the foremost expert on legal evidence, was an agnostic for years. After examining the evidence for the life, death, and resurrection of Jesus Christ, Greenleaf became a fervent Christian. In a book that is still in print,[28] he challenged fellow members of the legal profession that if they would face the facts he presented (which most of them had never considered), they would be forced by the evidence to become Christians as well. Lord Caldecote, Lord Chief Justice of England, became a believer on the basis of "strict evidence." So did Lord Lyndhurst, one of England's greatest legal minds, and Thomas Arnold, Regius Professor of Modern History at Oxford. Many more men and women of similar qualifications could be named.

Of course, their confident faith in the Bible, in Jesus Christ, His death for man's sins, and resurrection does not prove that the biblical record is true. It does disprove, however, the claim that only ignorant, uneducated people believe in God, the Bible, and Christ, and that faith is based only upon emotion and not on evidence.

THE NEW MEANING OF THE WORD "SCIENTIST"

There has been a change in the meaning of the word "scientist." Today, does it include all bona fide, thoroughly competent scientists? Certainly not included, when speaking to atheists, are any of the more than 700 who have signed their names to a statement declaring that evolution is not a scientific theory and that they oppose it on those grounds.[29] At the top of the list is the statement, *"We are skeptical of claims for the ability of random mutation and natural selection to account for the complexity of life. Careful examination of the evidence for Darwinian theory should be encouraged."*

To be accepted by the media as a "scientist" these days, one must be an atheist. By what authority is this unscientific distinction made? Whenever it is mentioned that hundreds of scientists oppose evolution, atheists smile condescendingly and say, "But there are thousands who believe in it and who do not believe in God." The truth in science is not determined by vote. In fact, one often hears it said, "No competent scientists believe in Creation or Intelligent Design." We are simply showing that the New Atheists often exaggerate in order to make their case.

Richard Dawkins made the following statement during a BBC interview in February 2009 when asked if Darwin was considered controversial in the United States:

> [Darwin] is controversial amongst people who don't know anything, but if you talk to people who are actually educated, he's not really controversial. There's no controversy about the fact we are cousins of monkeys, cousins of cows, cousins of aardvarks. That's completely non-controversial among anyone who knows anything about science.[30]

The "new" science is based on speculation, uncertainty, and wild guesses, which reveal the fact that the atheists' theories of the origin of life are not scientific. What do atheists have to show for two centuries of theorizing? *Nothing* of any substance. Still, like a fisherman who keeps going back to throw his hook into the same hole out of which no one has ever yet caught a fish, the ever-hopeful atheist scours the earth and searches the skies with one goal in mind: to prove there is no God.

We have compared the old science with the new. In the days when theists were predominant in scientific endeavors, evidence was uncovered that pointed to what became new laws of physics, chemistry, etc. Today the "new science," controlled by atheists, is not driven by evidence that has been discovered and points somewhere; it is driven by blind determination to do away with God, and never mind the overwhelming evidence to the contrary!

THE NEW CULT OF "RELIGIOUS SCIENCE"

The Church of Religious Science, founded in 1927 by Ernest Holmes, was part of the New Thought movement. The universe itself was considered to be governed by a universal consciousness, or mind, of which we are all a part and which can be manipulated by our thoughts, enabling us to tap into its infinite power. The similarity between this religious idea and what the New Atheists espouse is not merely coincidental. This thread of belief has wound its way through paganism and every primitive religion and still remains, in one form or another, in every religion except biblical Christianity. This universal mind is the god of religious science and, like the god of atheistic science, is a totally impersonal force that works through evolution.

Though they would deny it, atheists have their own religion. Atheism is a faith. It has no foundation in fact and certainly cannot be proved but must be taken by "faith." The article from *Wired* referring to the New Atheists and their crusade against belief in God is titled "The Church of the Non-Believers." It is a church to which they insist that everyone must belong because atheists alone can reason logically. In their religious fervor to destroy what they imagine is "religious faith" and to convert the entire world to their atheistic religion, they reveal an ignorance of the true faith that motivates biblical Christians.

Surely the New Atheists' writers cannot be ignorant of the fact, which Sam Harris documents very well in his writings, that the fundamentals of Islam teach that it must be forced upon the entire world by eliminating all who refuse to submit to Allah. Clearly, Christ taught and lived entirely otherwise. Yet the New Atheists persist in equating Islam and Christianity simply because each is considered to be a "faith." Such perverse reasoning is sprinkled throughout the atheists' best arguments.

Fundamentalism has gotten a bad rap. The "fundamentalism" that requires a Muslim terrorist to blow himself up in order to kill others and thereby reach Islam's paradise is not the "fundamentalism" that causes a Christian to obey the teachings of Jesus Christ and stand upon biblical principles. The issue is truth. Anyone is free to disagree with biblical Christianity, but it is unreasonable to dismiss it as "fundamentalism." One would have to prove that the fundamentals taught by Jesus Christ and throughout the Bible are erroneous before they could be dismissed.

WHAT'S WRONG WITH FUNDAMENTALISM?

Hatred of fundamentalism is either ill informed or part of a deliberate smear campaign against biblical Christianity. There is nothing wrong with fundamentalism in itself. It all depends on the fundamentals one believes. Every mathematician is a fundamentalist. Two plus two is four, always was, and always will be. It would be absurd to say, "You fundamentalist mathematicians are unreasonable. Why can't we let two plus two be five every Thursday?" Of course, if that were the case, thereafter, bridges, buildings, etc., built on Thursdays would collapse, all of the airplanes in flight would crash, etc., etc. It is not "dogmatic fundamentalism" to be unwilling to compromise the laws of physics and chemistry or the rules of mathematics. Then why is Christian fundamentalism maligned? Only if the Bible on which it is founded is proved to be wrong. What is certainly wrong is to lump all "faiths" together, ignoring the vast differences between. To do so betrays a deep bias that is disappointing when found in those who claim to speak for science and for rationality.

Unquestionably, some who have called themselves Christians (Roman Catholic popes, Eastern Orthodox leaders, the Crusaders, and not a few modern televangelists, for example) have been guilty of all manner of evil. In the process, they have violated the teachings and example of Christ. The fundamentals of true Christianity, however, promote love, freedom of choice, and forgiveness.

Sadly, self-confessed New Atheists equate Christianity with Roman Catholicism. Imagining that everyone who calls himself a Christian gives blind obedience to the pope and the Roman Catholic Church, they equate Christian fundamentalism with the Crusades and Inquisitions and thus with fanaticism and violence. The truth is that the Crusaders who waved the Cross and conquered in the name of Christ could hardly have been biblical Christians because they violated everything Christ taught, slaughtering His brethren, the Jews, everywhere they went and especially in Jerusalem. The Inquisitors were equally in disobedience of Christ.

These New Atheists seem also to be ignorant of the fact that from the days of Christ there were always multitudes of Christians who never gave allegiance to Rome but to the Bible and to Christ alone and paid for their faith with their lives. The Church of Rome martyred them by the millions over a period of centuries *before* the Reformation. The New Atheists seem to know nothing of the Protestant Reformation, with its cry of *sola scriptura*. Millions of Roman Catholics in the fifteenth and sixteenth centuries and thereafter rejected the dogmas of their Church and embraced a biblical faith in Christ alone. These defectors from the false faith that had once held them in bondage were also killed by the hundreds of thousands by the popes and their armies. To equate them and biblical Christians today, who are their successors, with Roman Catholicism (let alone with Islam) is to be guilty either of inexcusable ignorance or deliberate dishonesty. Passing along such misinformation in the name of science not only does a gross injustice to Christ and to His true followers but casts serious doubt on the honesty and motivation of those doing so.

THE NEW CRUSADERS

Richard Dawkins is the *de facto* leader of this aggressive new movement. At least he does not pretend, as do so many theistic evolutionists, that teaching Darwin's theory does not undermine the possibility of religious devotion. He forthrightly declares that "evolution *must* lead to atheism" and that "the atheist movement has no choice but to aggressively spread the good news. Evangelism [to convert the world to atheism] is a moral imperative."[31] Imagine atheist fundamentalists evangelizing to convert the world to their faith—while condemning all evangelizing by Christian fundamentalists!

Nevertheless, we applaud their honesty about where faith in evolution must inevitably lead—a refreshing honesty that rebukes those who claim to believe the Bible yet adhere to "theistic evolution" or "progressive creationism." This "science falsely so-called"[32] is condemned and disproved by the Bible in the clearest terms.

The New Atheists demand that religion should not be tolerated (except, of course, their own godless religion), especially its "colonization of the brains of innocent tykes." According to Dawkins, "It's one thing to say people should be free to believe whatever they like, but should they be free to impose their beliefs on their children? Is there something to be said for society stepping in? What about bringing up children to believe manifest falsehoods?"[33] By *their* definition of truth and falsehood, of course. This is dangerous totalitarian talk that makes one fear for parents and children alike.

Who are promoted on secular radio and TV? Who are consulted by the media as the spokespersons for science? Not consulted are the many top scientists who are Christians and every bit as competent in every field of science as their atheist colleagues. Instead, it is the atheists, who have seized the exclusive right to represent science today. Who are allowed to evangelize in public schools? Christians have been forced to establish their own schools or turn to home schooling in order to rescue their children from atheism's evangelists. Atheists are free to preach their "gospel" to children in public schools, while no one is allowed the freedom to refute their lies in that venue. Yet Dawkins complains about the "colonization of the brains of innocent tykes [and] bringing up children to believe manifest falsehoods"! Whose "falsehoods"?

The infamous and much misrepresented Scopes trial in 1925 came about because the Bible was being taught in public schools to the exclusion of atheism and evolution. A major underlying purpose of Clarence Darrow, the atheist chief defense attorney, was to force schools to allow the teaching of evolution as an alternate belief alongside the biblical account of creation. Darrow's main strategy was to discredit the Bible itself. The outcome was far beyond what the evolutionists claimed to be arguing for—an equal forum for both evolution and creation. Evolutionists have taken over the public domain and public opinion so that now the since-discredited theory stands as *proven science,* and creation may not be taught in public schools, even as an alternative.

So much for the freedom of expression in education and supposed search for truth that these "liberals" claim to espouse. Any attempt to present scientific evidence on the other side is now denied as "religion," which is not allowed in public schools, while atheists' brainwashing of our children to believe the lie that fantasy is fact when pronounced in the name of science is acceptable.

AN UNAVOIDABLE ADMISSION

Science cannot avoid the question of origins, but when it pretends to give us answers, it really has nothing to say. In spite of overwhelming scientific evidence for the only possible explanation of origins, many of today's scientists refuse to admit to a supernatural act of creation because they do not wish to be accountable to God.

Though astronomers have no explanation, they generally agree to the inescapable but difficult-for-atheists-to-swallow conclusion that there was a beginning to the universe. Of course, they say, it was a purely natural event that science will eventually explain. It ought to be embarrassing that the clear written declaration that there was a beginning and the explanation of how it happened and why has been staring mankind in the face for thousands of years in an ancient book. Although the Bible is the all-time bestseller worldwide, scientism scorns it, atheists ridicule it, and most of those who own it largely ignore it in their own personal lives.

In his debate with John Lennox, Richard Dawkins claimed not to be impressed. After all, he said, there were only two possibilities: a beginning or no beginning. And to get one of them right was no better than correctly calling a coin toss. Lennox countered, "Well, at least it [the Bible] got it right." The big difference is revealed when it comes to the nature of this beginning.

In response to the Bible's explanation that the universe began as a creative act of God, atheists counter that this is no explanation at all because it only raises a further question: Who created God? Common sense tells us that this question is absurd. For centuries, philosophers have agreed that there must be an uncaused first cause that has always existed.

The late Robert Jastrow, who hosted more than 100 CBS-TV network programs on space science, struggled for years to deny the distasteful evidence. An agnostic, he shocked many of his fellow scientists when he implied at the 144th National Conference of the Association for the Advancement of Science that the evidence seemed to demand an intelligent Creator.

Though remaining an agnostic (he denied he was an atheist), Jastrow finally arrived, along with most of his colleagues, at the inescapable conclusion that the universe came into existence at some point in the finite past. He described the embarrassing realization like this: "The scientist has scaled the mountains of ignorance; he is about to conquer the highest peak; as he pulls himself over the final rock, he is greeted by a band of theologians who have been sitting there for centuries."[34]

AGREED: THERE WAS A BEGINNING TO TIME, SPACE, AND MATTER, BUT....

Unfortunately, that gathering would not include all theologians, because many of them no longer believe the Bible—at least not all of it. And many who claim to believe it, nevertheless pick and choose what parts they accept as "inspired." Even some self-professed "evangelicals" describe the first eleven chapters of Genesis, which form the essential foundation for the rest of the Bible, as "prescientific . . . prehistory . . . myth . . . rich oral tradition . . . gathered and edited" so that "Near Eastern religious narrative and mythology were reshaped with monotheistic intent."[35] They deny the ultimate authority of Scripture and look rather to "science" and its changing and contradictory opinions. They are leaning on a "broken reed."[36]

Though the majority of today's scientists today admit there was a beginning to the universe, their views about that beginning have little in common with the biblical account. Jastrow did not believe that the universe was created by God out of nothing, as the Bible declares. Instead, he believed that the universe already existed in some unimaginable and unexplainable "pre-Big Bang" form.

Of course, Jastrow's imaginary scenario was pure conjecture— and solved nothing concerning the actual *origin* of energy or of the universe. Jastrow was trapped in the vortex of an endless speculative regression of "before that . . . and before that . . . and before that. . . ." There had to have been an actual beginning of all physical existence. Jastrow was only deferring the moment of truth. He declared:

> Recent developments in astronomy have implications that may go beyond their contribution to science itself. In a nutshell, astronomers . . . have been forced to the conclusion that the world began suddenly, in a moment of creation, as the product of unknown forces.
>
> [I]f we go back far enough in time, we find that at a certain critical moment in the past all the galaxies in the Universe were packed together into one dense mass at an enormous density, pressure and temperature. Reacting to this pressure, the dense, hot matter must have exploded with incredible violence [that] marked the birth of the Universe.
>
> The seed of everything that has happened in the Universe was planted in that first instant; every star, every planet and every living creature in the Universe came into being as a result of events that were set in motion in the moment of the cosmic explosion. It was literally the moment of Creation . . . the origin of the world—for which there is no known cause or explanation within the realm of science . . . we cannot find out what caused that to happen.
>
> This is a distressing result for scientists because, in the scientist's view . . . he must be able to find an explanation for the beginning of the Universe . . . that fits into the framework of natural rather than supernatural forces.

So, the scientist asks himself, what cause led to the effect we call the Universe . . . [and] he sees that he is deprived—today, tomorrow, and very likely forever—of finding out the answer to this critical question.

Why is that. . . ? At that time it must have been compressed to an enormous—perhaps infinite-density, temperature and pressure. . . .

The shock of that moment must have destroyed every . . . clue to the cause of the great explosion . . . to the nature of the forces—natural or supernatural—that conspired to bring about the event we call the Big Bang.

This is a very surprising conclusion. . . . The scientist . . . goes . . . back . . . feeling he is close to . . . the answer to the ultimate question of beginning—when suddenly the chain of cause and effect snaps. The birth of the Universe is an effect for which he cannot find the cause. . . .

This is why it seems to me and to others that the curtain drawn over the mystery of creation will never be raised by human efforts. . . . Although I am an agnostic, and not a believer, I still find much to ponder in the view expressed by the British astronomer E. A. Milne, who wrote, "We can make no propositions about the state of affairs [in the beginning]; in the Divine act of creation God is unobserved and unwitnessed."[37]

By Jastrow's own analysis, God is the only answer that fits all the facts—but he wouldn't subscribe to it unequivocally. Was he afraid of losing his reputation, of suffering the scorn of his atheistic/agnostic colleagues? His speculations did not answer anything but only added further questions. Where did this energy come from? How long had it been sitting there (wherever "there" was) waiting to explode? How did this bundle of energy become "packed together into one dense mass of enormous density, pressure and temperature"?

How could Jastrow or any other astronomer know this, when by his own admission "the curtain drawn over the mystery of creation will never be raised by human efforts"? And how could "every living

creature" have been "planted in that first instant" that totally sterilized everything? No life could possibly come out of the ball of fire he
describes, or the law of biogenesis is a lie! Nor could Jastrow offer any
sensible reasons why we should accept his scenario.

This is not science, but *scientism*. It is pure speculation, forced
upon scientists by their refusal even to consider the possibility that
God may exist as Creator of all—not an unreasonable idea. Nor could
Jastrow, as he honestly confessed, tell us anything concrete about the
origin either of matter or of life. He could no more have seen behind
the "curtain" he described that hides creation from human eyes than
could anyone else. Therefore, we have no reason for accepting his (or
anyone else's) speculation about what he called "the moment of creation," even though pronounced in the name of science. By his own
admission, science has nothing to offer when it comes to the origin of
the universe, but speculation often speaks with "scientific authority"
that is mistaken for proof.

Why must there be an explanation—an explanation that, admittedly, science can never produce? Are we to bury our heads in the
sand? Why not admit the obvious, that God created it all? It cannot
be argued that this conclusion is irrational unless it can be proved
that God does not exist, and almost every atheist admits that no such
proof can be found.

WHAT ABOUT THE ORIGIN OF LIFE?

Massimo Pigliucci acknowledges, "The origin of life is one question
that science will be pondering for some time to come . . . be wary of
oversimplified answers found in introductory biology textbooks."[38]
God is eliminated not by evidence and proof but by definition. What
does that leave? Scrambling desperately to get along without a Creator,
scientists offer all manner of speculation (which is all they have), as
does Pigliucci himself. Consider the following (uncertainties/guesses
are italicized):

The general path leading to the organization of life seems to have been something like this: 1. Primordial soup. . . ; 2. Nucleoproteins (similar to modern tRNAs); 3. Hypercycles [which] could have coexisted before the origin of life. . . ; 4. Cellular hypercycles . . . eventually enclosed in a primitive cell made of lipids. . . ; 5. Progenote (first self-replicating, metabolizing cell, possibly made of RNA and proteins, with DNA entering the picture later on.[39]

This is all science fiction. No one has ever seen a hypercycle, progenote, etc. "How plausible is all this?" Pigluicci asks. Bravely upholding the honor of modern science as best he can, he replies, "It certainly is *conceivable* from the standpoint of modern biology. The problem is that each step is difficult to describe in detail from a theoretical standpoint, and so far (with the exception of the formation of organic molecules in the soup) has proven *remarkably elusive* from an empirical perspective. It looks like we have several *clues*, but the overall puzzle is proving to be one of the most difficult for scientific analysis to solve . . . the events in question are so far remote in time that *there is very little we can be certain about*, making any attempt at empirical investigation hopelessly vague."[40]

His candor, however, is missing from most biology textbooks, whether in high school or university. Unfortunately, the lie that evolution is established fact continues to be popularly promoted. Rare is the person who has even heard, much less who heeds at all, Pigliucci's advice quoted above: "Be wary of oversimplified answers found in introductory biology textbooks."

ATHEISTS WON'T ADMIT THE OBVIOUS

The many scientific papers written on the subject of origins are filled with unproved and unprovable theories. They overflow with serious differences of opinion and outright contradictions among the experts, and many "ifs" without any basis for fulfillment. Material science has no ultimate answers. Stephen Hawking came very close to admitting this:

> What happened at the beginning of the expansion of the universe? Did spacetime have an edge [i.e., boundary] at the Big Bang. . .? The quantity that we measure as time had a beginning but that does not mean that spacetime has an edge. . . .
>
> If spacetime is indeed finite but without boundary or edge, this would have important philosophical implications. It would mean that we could describe the universe by . . . the laws of science alone. . . . But we do not know the precise form of the laws. . . . We are making progress [but] our powers of prediction would be severely limited . . . by the complexity of the equations which makes them impossible to solve in any but very simple situations. Thus we would still be a long way from omniscience."[41]

Expressions such as "if . . . do not know . . . severely limited . . . a long way from omniscience" certainly do not encourage confidence in what those who use such terms have to offer. But such admissions by Hawking of science's inability and ignorance fall far short of the confession he ought to make.

A MORE BEFITTING HUMILITY

When confronted by the genius and power that created the universe, we pitiful bits of protein molecules wired together with nerves find ourselves overwhelmed by a wisdom that defies our computers to unravel and the brightest among us fully to understand. We ought to fall on our faces before omniscience—the only posture we should dare to take! This is true enough when we merely contemplate the structure of the physical universe, from the innermost depths of the atom to the outermost reaches of the cosmos, but it is infinitely beyond that when we contemplate living creatures, from microbes to man.

This earth is teeming with life—a fact that is not true of any other part of the cosmos, as far as we have been able to discover. Regarding the origin of life, science can do little more than engage in hopeless speculation—though few in the scientific establishment are prepared to admit that humiliating fact. Nor can science explain why life fades and eventually dies. Nothing should age and die. Self-repairing and self-renewing living things should not be subject to the second law of thermodynamics—a now discredited argument that evolutionists once used to explain why evolution seemingly defies the second law and gathers upward momentum. In fact, death occurs because of a higher law, the "law of sin and death."[42] The Bible says death entered the universe because of man's sinful, self-willed rebellion. That act cut him off from God, the source of life, and brought the entire universe as well, including plants and animals, under the penalty of death. "Science" has no better explanation.

Theistic evolutionists have nothing better to offer. Francis Collins, for example, after telling us that the moon was torn from Earth (which we know is not true because its rocks are so diverse from Earth's), then declares that single-celled organisms appeared 3.85 million years ago, "*presumably* . . . capable of information storage, *probably* using DNA . . . were self-replicating and capable of evolving into multiple different types." He then mentions a "*plausible hypothesis*" that "at this particular time on earth, exchange of DNA between organisms was readily accomplished."[43]

After another *perhaps* and *may have*, he finally admits that what he has said is mere speculation. Collins confesses that "at the present time we simply do not know . . . how self-replicating organisms [could] arise in the first place" and that DNA "seems an utterly improbable molecule to have 'just happened.'" Instead of admitting that the God he claims to believe in could create everything out of nothing (as the Bible declares), Collins continues to speculate, suggesting "RNA as the *potential* first life form. . . ." Rejecting what the Bible clearly says ("God created man in his own image . . . male and female . . . of the dust of the ground, and breathed into his nostrils the breath of life;

and man became a living soul."[44]), Collins clings to speculations of all living things, including man, originating with "self-replicating information-carrying molecules assemble[d] spontaneously from [amino acids]"[45]—a theory as far from the biblical description of God's *creation* of man as an atheist's speculation could devise.

REASON ITSELF IS LOST

Furthermore, if everything began with a "big bang" and has been proceeding by random processes ever since, there is no basis for rational thought: "For if my mental processes are determined wholly by the motions of atoms in my brain, I have no reason to suppose that my thoughts are true."[46] Darwin himself was troubled by this problem that his theory created: "Can the mind of man, which has, as I fully believe, been developed from a mind as low as that possessed by the lowest animals, be trusted. . . ? I cannot pretend to throw the least light on such abstruse problems."[47]

In fact, this is not an abstruse problem but a very important one. C. S. Lewis argued:

> If . . . the appearance of organic life on this planet was also an accident, and the whole evolution of Man was an accident . . . then all our present thoughts are . . . the accidental byproduct of the movement of atoms. And this holds true for the thoughts of the materialists and astronomers as well as for anyone else. But if their thoughts . . . are merely accidental by-products, why should we believe them to be true? I see no reason for believing that one accident should be able to give me a correct account of all the other accidents.[48]

To the "Big Bang" materialist, our thoughts can only be the result of the present motions of atoms in our brains, which resulted from prior motions of atoms in our ancestors' brains, from chimpanzee and reptile brains, and from prior motions of atoms before there were any brains, and prior, and prior . . . all the way back to a huge explosion/expansion of matter. In other words, our thoughts themselves could have no meaning, nothing to do with truth, and would thus be untrustworthy. One cannot bring truth and meaning out of a mindless expansion of energy. How and from what source would truth and meaning have been introduced into expanding and cooling matter? The theory of evolution itself would be the result of motions of atoms in Darwin's (and other's) brains that began with that original explosion. Consequently, the atheistic theory of evolution pronounces its own lack of meaning.

If life sprang by spontaneous generation from dead matter created by a "Big Bang" and we are the result of chance plus millions of years of evolution, then our existence has no purpose. There is nothing to discuss about life, education, science, politics, hopes for a better world, or anything else because the best arguments on either side would merely be the result of chance motions of atoms in opposing brains.

On the other hand, if we are, in fact, descended from the first man and woman, who were created by God for a specific purpose, then life has meaning and involves inescapable moral responsibility to our Creator. So, knowing the origin of life is absolutely essential for any person who wants to live with some understanding and purpose. This is especially important when one arrives at the moment of death. No, that should have been decided much earlier. Death can come suddenly and doesn't always provide opportunity for last-minute decisions—which, in fact, may be considered counterfeit by our Creator if one's entire life has reflected the opposite.

One must reasonably reject the idea that our existence and our very thoughts, ambitions, frustrations, joys, and sorrows are the meaningless result of a giant explosion/expansion of energy. James Perloff put it very well when he wrote: "But remember; 'The princess kissed the frog, and he turned into a handsome prince.' We call that a fairy tale. Evolution says frogs turn into princes, and we call it science [because it takes a very long time]. . . . Is that science? Or is it, like the fraud of Piltdown Man, the forgeries of Haeckel's embryos, the misrepresentations of *Inherit the Wind*, and the coercions of the Supreme Court, merely part of a long effort to deny God?"[49]

That is the question—the most important one for every one of Earth's inhabitants to find a trustworthy answer to as soon as possible. We hope the following pages will be of help in arriving at such an answer.

The mutation rate affects not only the evolution of the human species but also the life of the individual. Almost every mutation is harmful, and it is the individual who pays the price. . . . There can be little doubt that man would be better off if he had a lower mutation rate. I would argue, in our present ignorance, that the ideal rate for the foreseeable future would be zero.

—JAMES F. CROW, "IONIZING RADIATION AND EVOLUTION,"
SCIENTIFIC AMERICAN, VOL. 201 (SEPTEMBER 1959), 138-60

An honest man, armed with all the knowledge available to us now, could only state that in some sense, the origin of life appears at the moment to be almost a miracle, so many are the conditions which would have had to have been satisfied to get it going.

—FRANCIS CRICK, *LIFE ITSELF: ITS ORIGIN AND NATURE*
(NEW YORK: SIMON & SCHUSTER, 1981), 88

In short there is not a shred of objective evidence to support the hypothesis that life began in an organic soup here on the Earth.

—SIR FRED HOYLE, *THE INTELLIGENT UNIVERSE*
(NEW YORK: HOLT, RINEHART & WINSTON, 1983), 23

Now we know that the cell itself is far more complex than we had imagined. It includes thousands of functioning enzymes, each one of them a complex machine in itself. Furthermore, each enzyme comes into being in response to a gene, a strand of DNA. The information content of the gene (its complexity) must be as great as that of the enzyme it controls.

—FRANK B. SALISBURY, "DOUBTS ABOUT THE MODERN SYNTHETIC THEORY OF
EVOLUTION," *AMERICAN BIOLOGY TEACHER,* VOL. 33 (SEPTEMBER 1971), 336

It must not be forgotten that mutation is the ultimate source of all genetic variation found in natural populations and the only new material available for natural selection to work on.

—ERNST MAYR, *POPULATIONS, SPECIES AND EVOLUTION*
(CAMBRIDGE: HARVARD UNIVERSITY PRESS, 1970), 8-9

A major problem in proving the theory has been the fossil record; the imprints of vanished species preserved in the Earth's geological formations. This record has never revealed traces of Darwin's hypothetical intermediate variants—instead species appear and disappear abruptly, and this anomaly has fueled the creationist argument that each species was created by God as described in the Bible.

—MARK CZARNECKI, "THE REVIVAL OF THE CREATIONIST CRUSADE,"
MACLEAN'S (JANUARY 19, 1981), 56

SIX

THE ETERNAL DILEMMA

THERE MUST BE A UNIVERSE in which self-replicating life already exists before evolution through natural selection can function. How the cosmos came into existence is a haunting question that atheists and evolutionists attempt to avoid. They respond to this mystery with "once upon a time" it suddenly appeared, though no one knows how. As for life, they cling to spontaneous generation as their messiah. This mythical savior miraculously arose out of the total sterilization caused by a giant fireball familiarly known as the Big Bang.

Atheists reject biblical miracles that fulfill hundreds of specific prophecies attested to by scores of eyewitnesses over a period of centuries. They do, however, accept two non-biblical miracles, though witnessed by no one: the astonishing appearance of the energy that fueled the Big Bang, and spontaneous generation of life. Evolutionists bow reverently to this two-headed Phoenix that arose mysteriously out of the giant fireball, though Pasteur long ago exposed it as mere superstition. The law of biogenesis, upon which all scientists agree, declares it to be impossible: life can come only from life.

Moreover, to form the universe by chance through a cataclysmic explosion creates numerous contradictions and raises many serious problems for which evolution offers no solutions. The universe is composed of stars and galaxies, but there is no way they could come from such an event. Jonathan Sarfati, with a Ph.D. in physical chemistry, points out, "It's vital for any cosmological theory to explain the origin of stars. But there are two major problems in this area. The first is the lack of observational evidence of the stars that should have formed first after the big bang, and the second is the mechanics of clouds [of gases] collapsing to form these first stars."[1]

Astronomers have long searched for signs of the first stars that would have formed after the initial expansion. They have been unable to find any evidence of their existence. These missing stars create a serious problem for atheists. Indeed, the fact that any stars at all exist is itself an enigma, because there really shouldn't be any. The theory is that the stars formed from condensing clouds of the gas created by the initial explosion. The way gas naturally behaves, however, is to expand, not to collapse upon itself. There are various theories to explain this odd occurrence, but they become so complex that it is the theories, not the gas clouds, which implode.

In the final analysis, the only way for gas clouds to collapse into stars hot enough at the center to ignite would be with the help of another star. Supposedly, the blast of a nearby exploding star would cause this compression. Thus, we can't even form the universe by natural means without being confronted again by the classic and perpetual dilemma, "Which came first, the chicken or the egg?" If it takes a star to provide the boost that creates a star, which came first— the clouds of gas out of which all stars are supposedly made or the stars that caused clouds of gas to turn into stars?

As we have already seen, without a Creator, the very existence of the universe itself is a solution-defying mystery. After all the centuries of observing, investigating, and theorizing, the very components of the universe defy explanation. We can deal with them by mathematical formulas, but beyond the mathematics we do not know what energy, space, time, gravity, or electrons really are. Furthermore, when it comes to life, the problems and contradictions multiply almost exponentially for those who persist in denying the existence of the Designer to whom all creation so clearly points.

C. S Lewis commented:

> You remember the old puzzle as to whether the owl came from the egg or the egg from the owl. The modern acquiescence in universal evolutionism is a kind of optical illusion, produced by attending exclusively to the owl's emergence from the egg. We are taught from childhood to notice how the perfect oak grows from the acorn and to forget that the acorn itself was dropped by a perfect oak. We are reminded constantly that the adult human being was an embryo, never that the life of the embryo came from two adult human beings. We love to notice that the express engine of today is the descendant of the "rocket"; we do not equally remember that the "rocket" springs not from some even more rudimentary engine, but from something much more perfect and complicated than itself—namely, a man of genius. The obviousness, or naturalness, which most people seem to find in the idea of emergent evolution thus seems to be a pure hallucination.[2]

THE OLD CHICKEN-AND-EGG CONUNDRUM

There are many interdependent systems in living things that present dozens of times over the old conundrum: "Which came first, the chicken or the egg?" This obvious question confronts evolutionists in many forms, and they have no answer for it, though they have given it much thought and discussion, as well they might.

Massimo Pigliucci explains protein as organizer, builder, and end product—which is really impossible, as he admits:

> It should be clear from . . . what goes on in a cell that we are indeed facing a classic chicken-egg problem. If the proteins appeared first and . . . could eventually catalyze the formation of nucleic acids, how was the information [that was] necessary to produce the proteins themselves coded? On the other hand, if nucleic acids came first, thereby embodying the information necessary to obtain proteins, by what means were the acids replicated and translated into proteins?[3]

There is no life without enzymes, although they themselves are not living things. And there are no enzymes without life, because it takes life to produce them. Which came first—the enzymes without which there can be no life, or the life without which there can be no enzymes?

Neither evolution nor the atheists who support the theory have any answer to such logical and essential questions. In fact, they *refuse* to deal with the question of origins. Darwinism can't even get out of the starting gate without life. It refuses to deal with this missing link, blithely starts off with life already in existence, while Darwinists, following a quest that began on a small ship called the *H.M.S. Beagle*, continue to chase all over the world for the wrong "missing link." Evolution should be rejected on this ground alone. It hasn't yet qualified for serious consideration.

BUILDING IN THE AIR WITH NO FOUNDATION

Any building that is erected must carefully follow the architect's plans for its construction. Those plans begin in the mind of the architect, an intelligence that even Richard Dawkins admits must exist for genes to be programmed to perform their essential role.[4] Could this "architect" to whom Dawkins refers be God?

Many different enzymes are required to translate the genetic information encoded on the DNA (deoxyribonucleic acid). Yet the enzymes are themselves encoded by DNA. The genetic code can only be translated by that which has itself been translated. This is a vicious circle that leads to only one conclusion: the molecules that encode the information and those that decode it had to exist simultaneously and from the very beginning. The only way that could happen would be through a supernatural act of creation bringing into instantaneous existence all of the essential ingredients for every living thing. Yet Darwinists vehemently proclaim that natural selection proves that God is not needed to explain life and the universe.

The incredible nano-chemical machinery in the cell is responsible for synthesizing DNA, but DNA carries the code that constructs and operates the cellular machinery. Without the DNA, there could be no cell, but without the cell, there could be no DNA. Which came first?

The genetic code has vital editing machinery that is itself encoded in the DNA. Which came first, the machinery that edits DNA or the DNA that produces the editing machinery? Clearly, all of the components had to come into existence at the same time. As a further example, the enzymes that make the amino acid histidine themselves contain histidine. Which came first—the histidine or the enzymes that manufacture it (which themselves contain histidine)?

There are more than 200,000 types of proteins in the human body. Even the simplest cells, such as the mycoplasmas of the class Mollicutes, some of which cause diseases and are resistant to antibiotics, may have as many as 750 proteins. Proteins are the basic building block of life. The DNA molecule is made of protein; but it is the DNA by which alone protein is produced (via RNA). DNA cannot function without at least 75 pre-existing proteins—but only DNA can produce these 75 proteins. Obviously, once again, all had to exist simultaneously from the very beginning. There is only one sensible answer to the classic question, "Which came first, the chicken or the egg?"

The instructions for building and operating every cell in the body are pre-encoded on the DNA. Only special proteins can decode these instructions for the cell. Only DNA can make these proteins, but it can't function without them.

Which came first? For those who are willing to admit it, the only possible answer is, "God came first, and all life comes from Him," as the Bible says. Nor can God be rejected as a purely religious hypothesis that has no part in science. It is science itself, based upon overwhelming evidence, that compels us to believe in God.

CONTRADICTIONS WITHIN
THE "PRIMARY AXIOM"

Scientist and prolific inventor, J. C. Sanford, reminds us, "Modern Darwinism is built . . . upon what I will be calling 'The Primary Axiom' . . . that man is merely the product of *random mutations* plus *natural selection*."[5] Part of the Primary Axiom is that "all genetic variation *must* come from *random* mutations, since no genetic variation by design is allowed."[6] Evolutionists, in claiming that some mutations are beneficial, use examples from genetic engineering. These are not random mutations but, in fact, are part of an intelligent design imposed upon the genome—something that evolutionists will not allow God to do in the act of creation but claim it is legitimate for genetic engineers to do.

Evolutionists often offer the development of immunity to antibiotics by bacterium as an example of evolution. But evolution is not involved at all. The bacterium is still the same bacterium. It has not evolved into anything else. Sanford explains that instead of new information being added to the DNA,

> . . . information decreases . . . in chromosomal mutations for antibiotic resistances in bacteria, where cell functions are routinely lost. The resistant bacterium has not evolved—in fact it has digressed genetically and is *defective*. Although adaptation is occurring, information is actually being lost—not added. Yet the Primary Axiom still insists that mutations are good, and are the building blocks with which evolution creates the galaxy of information that currently exists within the genome.[7]

An axiom is supposed to be established fact, but that is not the case with this one. Of course, chance mutations do occur, but they could hardly become the basis of any upward evolutionary progress inasmuch as mutations are far more likely to be harmful than helpful. This fact (sometimes disputed by evolutionists) pulls the rug from under a foundational evolutionary doctrine, but there is no denying it.

What would the mutations affect? The only way to change the organism is to change the information in the DNA, which determines the organism's composition and function. We have already quoted Richard Dawkins declaring that DNA is a digitally organized database at the heart of the cell. Imagine Dawkins's "blind watchmaker" cutting out words and letters here and there from these instructions and randomly inserting new ones in their place! Dawkins will have it no other way. There must be no intelligent direction involved. That would totally spoil his scenario.

PROMISING MORE THAN THEY DELIVER

In arguing that mutations are often beneficial, what do evolutionists give us for examples? They offer genetic engineering feats, but these are produced by geneticists playing God with nature. How can these qualify as examples of what occurs in random mutations or natural selection?

In his latest book, *The Greatest Show on Earth*, Richard Dawkins expresses his belief that genetic engineering, which he calls "artificial selection," should convince us that "natural selection" can accomplish the same thing, but using billions of years. Genetic engineers can only rearrange what is already there; they cannot originate new information nor can natural selection.

Of course, there are some examples from nature. One that first caught Darwin's attention during his voyage on the *Beagle* was the finch in the Galapagos Islands. Their "beaks change shape over time,"[8] but this has been explained as an adaptation to different food sources. Like every other example that evolutionists offer, it is a far cry from a change of one species into another.

Francis Collins suggests, "In some instances, scientists are even catching evolution in the act. . . ."[9] Incredibly, a major example he gives is the oft-mentioned finch. Another favorite is the stickleback, a fish that is found both in saltwater and in fresh. Says Collins, "It is not hard to see how the difference between freshwater and saltwater sticklebacks could be extended to generate all kinds of fish. The distinction between macroevolution and microevolution is seen to be rather arbitrary, larger changes that result in a new species are a result of a succession of small incremental steps."[10] That's theory, but where are the examples? Did any stickleback ever continue on and evolve into a swordfish or any other truly new species?

Not hard to see? There is *nothing* to see, no examples to show. But Collins persists, just look at the stickleback! Freshwater sticklebacks have virtually no armor, and those that live in saltwater are nearly covered with bony spines. This isn't even close to a change in species.

Finches remain finches and sticklebacks remain sticklebacks. If this is the best Collins can offer, isn't he engaging in wishful thinking? How could he have become a biblical Christian and at the same time reject the Creator that the Bible presents so clearly from Genesis to Revelation? It would be demeaning to accuse the God who could say "let there be light, and there was light. . . ,"[11] of taking billions of years of inefficiency and waste, leaving a worldwide graveyard filled with rotting corpses of deformed and half-developed freaks along a tortuous trail of natural selection. Was it really through this process that "God created man in his own image, in the image of God created he him"?[12]

How ironic that Richard Dawkins titled his latest book *The Greatest Show on Earth*. A large part of the original "Greatest Show," originated by P. T. Barnum, had a display of "freaks." Isn't this exactly what natural selection creates? Doesn't it leave in its trail the fossils of the wreckage it creates of malformed, pitiful creatures that were eliminated from this natural process?

The only way to create a new species is by an infusion of *new information*. And that does not happen. Man's attempt to do so is through careful breeding. Everything that was necessary for a wolf to become a tiny Pekingese is already in the wolf's DNA. Insects become immune to insecticides by adaptation through loss of vital information, but there is no transformation into a new species.

Remember Colin Patterson's response to the reader who was disappointed that in his book *Evolution* he had not included any examples of intermediary forms going from one species to another. "I will lay it on the line," he wrote in explaining this deficiency, "there is not one such fossil for which one could make a watertight argument."[13] Stephen Jay Gould said, "New species almost always appeared suddenly in the fossil record with no intermediate links to ancestors in older rocks of the same region."[14] He also stated, "The absence of fossil evidence for intermediary stages between major transitions in organic design, indeed our inability, even in our imagination, to construct functional intermediates in many cases, has been a persistent and nagging problem for gradualistic accounts of evolution."[15]

Why do we see no intermediary forms today? There ought to be millions. Why is there no sign of evolution in progress today? Evolutionists can provide no examples, but there ought to at least be some. There should be *billions* of examples in the fossil record. Moreover, among the millions of species on Earth today, surely at least a few thousand ought to show signs of being at varying stages in Dawkins's "tiny steps" process of climbing ever upwards toward the fabled summit of Mount Improbable. Yet we see no sign of these ardent mountaineers. There ought to be swarms of them climbing everywhere. Where are they? Not one is in sight!

NEW SPECIES REQUIRE NEW INFORMATION

As we have seen, information is essential to life. DNA is the detailed instruction manual for every species. These instructions are written in words in the DNA of every member of every species. Without written instructions, no living thing can exist. DNA embodies one of the most amazing communication systems conceivable.

Perry Marshall, communications/information authority, explains the obstacles to evolution by natural selection inherent within the DNA:

> In all communication systems the encoding-decoding process starts at the top with intent, goes down to the alphabet. . . . Random mutations violate the whole nature of how information is created. Language can only be improved from the top working down to the bottom. You can't randomly mutate a sentence into saying something more meaningful.[16]

Information of significance as it applies to the evolutionary steps that are necessary to turn one species into another could never be produced by random rearrangement. New information must be introduced from an outside intelligence. It would take more than a mutation of present information to create a new species. As Marshall points out, mutations can only

> . . . put fractures into your intent, your syntax, your meaning and your grammar. . . . [For example] nowhere in any communication engineering book [including those of] all the geniuses that built the Internet [is found] any formula where you could add noise to the signal and it would [improve] it. Noise is always bad. In 1948, Claude Shannon wrote [what is] probably the most important paper ever written in the field of Electrical Engineering . . . "The Mathematical Theory of Communication. . . ."[17]

Shannon explained that the mathematics behind noise in digital communication is identical to the mathematics of entropy of thermodynamics, which meant that noise equals entropy, or the degradation of what is being communicated: "When you have noise on your cassette tape, it dulls some of the music and it takes some of the information away. You can't get the information back. It's an irreversible process of degradation."

This random mutation (noise) does not *increase* information, and in the same way, random mutation in natural selection cannot increase information, so evolution of any kind still requires an intelligence to direct it. Marshall continues:

> Now I must be fair here: I have *not* disproven evolution. What I have disproven is naturalistic explanations for evolution. . . . I don't personally care [but if] the antelope did evolve into a giraffe, *I want to know how.* And random mutation is not how; absolutely not.
>
> So what are the possibilities? We haven't disproven that antelopes evolved into giraffes. It's just that random mutation does not do it [nor do] current naturalistic explanations.[18]

DAWKINS'S ATTEMPT TO DEFEND HIMSELF

Richard Dawkins is a brilliant storyteller, but that is almost all we get from him. He has an amazing imagination, but science is not developed by adult fairy tales like "Mount Improbable." The problem the atheist faces (and which Mount Improbable scrupulously avoids) is the matter of information, and this is what DNA is all about. Where does the information come from to start with a single cell bacterium and end up with the human brain? Dawkins never tells us.

He devotes an entire chapter in one of his more recent books to defending his theory that evolution does in fact increase information. He tells us:

> In September of 1997, I allowed an Australian film crew into our house in Oxford without realizing that their purpose was *creationist propaganda.* . . . They issued a truculent challenge to me to 'give an example of a genetic mutation or an evolutionary process that can be seen to increase the information in the genome.' It was the kind of question only a creationist would ask. . . . [Emphasis added]

When I eventually saw the film a year later, I found that it had been edited to give the false impression that I was *incapable* of answering the question about information content. . . . These people really *believe* that their question *cannot* be answered! Pathetic as it sounds, their entire journey from Australia seems to have been a quest to film evolutionists failing to answer it. . . . [His emphasis]

Dawkins spends the next three and a half pages in an explanation of information theory. Then he claims that all living things are descended from bacteria and expounds his belief that their genome is smaller than ours, which he attributes to their having appeared millions of years before humans. One simple question dispenses with that explanation: what if they were designed that way? Aren't they still the same as they have always been?

"So during the billions of years of evolution since that ancestor lived," continues Dawkins, "the information capacity of *our* genome has gone up . . . about a thousandfold. . . ." But wait! *Our* genome? This is a classic "shell game switch." Now he has us believing in his unproved theory that humans descended from bacteria. Dawkins is so clever that most of his readers don't realize that they are being deceived.

Dawkins covers his tracks with an impressive display of verbiage:

Should human dignity feel wounded . . . by the fact that the crested newt, *Triturus cristatus*, has a genome capacity . . . larger than the human genome? . . . The crested newt has a bigger 'hard disk' than we have, but since the great bulk of both our hard disks are unused, we needn't feel insulted. . . . Why the Creator should have played fast and loose with the genome sizes of newts . . . is a problem that creationists might like to ponder. From an evolutionary point of view, the explanation is simple. . . .

Almost all of evolution happened way back in the past, which makes it hard to study details. But we can use the "length of book" thought-experiment to agree upon what it would *mean* to ask the question whether information

content increases over evolution, if only we had ancestral
animals to look at. . . .

Supporters of "intelligent design" guiding evolution,
by the way, should be deeply committed to the view that
information content increases during evolution. Even if the
information comes from God, perhaps *especially* if it does, it
should surely increase, and the increase should presumably
show itself in the genome. . . .

The "information challenge" turns out to be none other
than our old friend: "How could something as complex as
an eye evolve?" It is just dressed up in fancy mathematical
language—perhaps in an attempt to bamboozle. Or perhaps
those who ask it have already bamboozled themselves. . . .[19]

In Dawkins's own words, "Some species of the unjustly called
'primitive' amoebas have as much information in their DNA as 1,000
Encyclopedia Britannicas."[20] A separate instruction manual of at least
similar volume would be required for every new species that came
into existence through the alleged process of evolution and natural
selection. Not one forward step could be taken in this process without
the completion of a new and massive instruction manual for the supposed new species. What would be the source of this huge amount of
intricate new information?

Everyone acknowledges that this infusion of information for
a new instruction manual is absolutely essential for any change in
species. It is not a question of merely editing or even rewriting the
existing instruction manual for the species that is supposedly in the
process of evolving. There must be a completely new set of instructions. Dawkins dares to say that natural selection itself produces this
information, apparently out of thin air.

Someone has said, "Dawkins . . . has the ability to tell very entertaining stories to illustrate ideas in a manner which indeed reflect the
underlying thinking of many evolutionists, but that's all they are—
stories. . . . The atheist must propose a solution in which inanimate
matter alone develops information."[21]

WHAT HAPPENED TO GOD?

Culture guru Theodore Roszak suggested that "so many scientists rallied to Darwin's banner" because he drove "every last trace of an incredible God from biology." Theistic evolution tries to make God the author of this inefficient, cruel, time-consuming, and death-dealing process of natural selection. Roszak went on to honestly admit that Darwinism "replaces the old God with an even more incredible deity—omnipotent chance."[22] Darwin himself appeared ambivalent concerning the existence and nature of God.

Although Darwin did on at least one occasion call himself a "theist,"[23] the vast majority of scientists interpret him exactly as did Roszak. This opinion seems clear from most of Darwin's writings. This view of Darwin and Darwinism is popularly embraced because so many are willing to espouse a "god" that can be described as a "higher power" or a creative "force." Being impersonal, it will not judge us or require submission to its nonexistent will, but we can use it to our own ends. It certainly behooves everyone to think this entire subject over very carefully before trusting one's future to the great god "chance."

What could possibly be the source of new DNA required to change to a "higher" species? Without such a change, there is no evolution. But the change cannot occur without the introduction of new information, because it is the information in the DNA that defines and distinguishes between species. The information essential to define new species could come only from an infinite intelligence. Who could that be but God?

Nobelist Ernst Boris Chain points out that "The assumption of directive forces in the origin and development of vital processes becomes a necessity in any kind of interpretation."[24] Darwin critic Phillip Johnson asks another question that stumps evolutionists:

> Are our thoughts "nothing but" the products of chemical reactions in the brain, and did our thinking abilities originate for no reason other than their utility in allowing

our DNA to reproduce itself. . . ? [M]aterialism applied
to the mind undermines the validity of all reasoning. . . .
If our theories are the products of chemical reactions,
how can we know whether our theories are true? Perhaps
Richard Dawkins believes in Darwinism only because he
has a certain chemical in his brain, and his belief could be
changed by somehow inserting a different chemical.[25]

The information written on this page in ink was not created by
the paper and ink. The means of communication does not originate the message. Professor George C. Williams of the Department
of Ecology and Evolution at State University of New York, member
of the National Academy of Sciences, and himself an evolutionist,
refers to "the separability of information and matter." He acknowledges that information (and thus the intelligence that communicates
it) is not physical but entirely nonmaterial: "The DNA molecule is
the medium, it's not the message. . . . In biology, when you're talking
about things like genes and genotypes and gene pools, you're talking
about information, not physical objective reality."[26]

There is absolutely no way that either chance or natural laws, or
both working together, could create information. This comes only
from an intelligence—and intelligence, like the information it creates,
exists outside the physical world altogether. Clearly, no evolutionary
process could add new information to the DNA molecule.

In view of Einstein's declaration that he "could identify no
means by which matter could bestow meaning to symbols,"[27] John
R. Baumgardner, with a Ph.D. in geophysics and space science from
UCLA, argues for a distinction between the brain and the mind, the first
being clearly material, and the second, just as surely, nonmaterial:

> If something as real as linguistic information has existence
> independent of matter and energy, from causal considerations
> it is not unreasonable to suspect that an entity capable of
> originating linguistic information is also ultimately non-
> material in its essential nature.

An immediate conclusion of these observations concerning linguistic information is that materialism, which has long been the dominant philosophical perspective in scientific circles, with its foundational presupposition that there is no non-material reality, is simply and plainly false. It is amazing that its falsification is so trivial.

The implications are immediate for the issue of evolution. The evolutionary assumption that the exceedingly complex linguistic structures which comprise the construction blueprints and operating manuals for all the complicated chemical nanomachinery and sophisticated feedback control mechanisms in even the simplest living organism—that these structures must have a materialistic explanation—*is fundamentally wrong.*[28]

EVOLUTION COULDN'T EVEN GET STARTED

As we have already pointed out, it is absurd to theorize and speculate about natural selection and survival of the fittest when, at the molecular level, it is mathematically impossible for evolution even to get the tiniest start. Evolutionists proceed with their scholarly treatises and bold bluffs about "evidence" that doesn't exist. All the while, they are suppressing the fact that evolution is mathematically impossible.

The probability of a single basic protein *molecule* arising at random is one chance in 1 followed by 43 zeros. One cell contains thousands of complex protein molecules, which must join together in a precise order in relationship to one another. To form the first cell, this combination would have had to come about by pure chance because nothing would yet exist upon which natural selection could act. It would be utter nonsense to imagine that a "first cell," with its thousands of complex protein molecules, could form by chance.

Consider the bacterium *Mycoplasma Genitalium*. It has the smallest genome of any known self-replicating organism: 482 genes of 1,040 nucleotide base pairs, for a total of 580,000 base pairs. The average sized protein molecule coded for by these genes contains 347 amino acids. The probability of random formation of one such protein molecule is one chance in 1 with 451 zeros after it. Carbon is an essential ingredient of amino acids and protein. If the entire earth were solid carbon, it would contain 1 followed by 50 zeros of carbon atoms. Thus, it would take 1 with 401 zeros *times* the carbon atoms in a solid carbon earth to provide sufficient carbon molecules to give this a try!

We could continue with further examples, piling impossibility upon impossibility, proving without question that the chance of producing even the smallest units of life by random construction is absolutely zero. In the examples given, we have already passed the point of the ridiculous. Nevertheless, we will persist with a variety of mathematical and logical proofs to show that evolution could never create even a single cell, let alone a human body with its 100 trillion cells. One must be very determined to escape accountability to God to cling to "chance" as the author of even the smallest living things.

MORE "CHICKEN AND EGG" DILEMMAS

The cell cannot be alive and functioning without all of its parts. But the parts cannot exist separately. They can only exist together within a functioning cell. Therefore, it would be impossible for each part to "evolve" separately while waiting for the other parts to come into existence and finally all be joined together by some unknown evolutionary process. Moreover, if that occurred, it would violate evolution's foundational principle of natural selection.

The complexity of the cell, with its thousands of interdependent parts, none of which can function until all other parts are in place and working together, poses an unanswerable problem for atheists. It is equally clear that no evolutionary process of trial and error by "natural selection" could produce even one cell. Without God as Creator, neither a cell nor its parts could exist. Biologist Jerry R. Bergman, who holds two Ph.D.s, presents the undeniable facts succinctly:

> Oversimplified, life depends on a complex arrangement of three classes of molecules: DNA, which stores the cell's master plans; RNA, which transports a copy of the needed information contained in the DNA to the protein assembly station; and proteins, which make up everything from the ribosomes to the enzymes. . . .
>
> The parts could not evolve separately. . . . Even if they existed, the many parts needed for life could not sit idle waiting for other parts to evolve, because the existing ones would usually deteriorate very quickly. . . . For this reason, only an instantaneous creation of all the necessary parts as a functioning unit can produce life. . . . A cell can come only from a functioning cell and cannot be built up piecemeal. . . .[29]

Once again, we are confronted with the same "chicken and egg" dilemma, which deals a deathblow to evolution. Just as the law of biogenesis declares that life can come only from life, necessitating a creative act by God, so the fact that it takes a cell to produce a cell also demands a creative act by God. Thus, the premise that God exists cannot be rejected as an unscientific religious idea. We are forced by science itself to believe in God.

A PROBLEM FOR EVERY PART OF THE BODY

Just as a cell cannot come into existence in stages, so it is for most of the members of the body. For example, a muscle is useless without a connecting nerve to direct its contracting activity. Both the muscle and the nerve are useless, however, without a complicated control mechanism in the brain to direct muscle contractions and correlate them with the action of other muscles. To ask which came first is ridiculous when it is obvious that one could not function apart from the others. Darwin's natural selection would eliminate any part of this complex of muscle, nerve, and cerebral control system that "evolved" alone.

The separate components of every cell and member of the body, each of which is essential to the whole process, could not have gradually and individually evolved. They all had to come into existence as functioning units at once, and only an act of creation could do that. If evolution occurred, trillions of cast-off mistakes would have been produced by trial and error—yet we see no evidence of such in the fossil record. Speaking at the 1981 Annual Meeting of the British Association for the Advancement of Science, anthropologist Edmund R. Leach told his audience, "Missing links in the sequence of fossil evidence were a worry to Darwin. He felt sure they would eventually turn up, but they are still missing and seem likely to remain so."[30]

Johns Hopkins University Professor Steven Stanley of the Department of Earth and Planetary Sciences declared, "The known fossil record fails to document a single example of phyletic evolution accomplishing a major morphologic [structural] transition and hence offers no evidence that the gradualistic model can be valid."[31] In the same vein, professor Nils Heribert-Nilsson, director of the Botanical Institute at Lund University, Sweden, declared after forty years of study:

> The fossil material is now so complete that . . . the lack of transitional series cannot be explained as due to the scarcity of the material. The deficiencies are real, they will never be filled. . . . The true situation is that those fossils have not been found which were expected. Just where new branches are supposed to fork off from the main stem it has been impossible to find the connecting types.[32]

THE EYE, DARWIN'S NIGHTMARE

In a letter to Harvard botany professor Asa Gray, Charles Darwin admitted that the development of the eye could not be explained by his theory of gradual development: "The eye to this day gives me a cold shudder. . . ."[33] Far from finding evidence of primitive eyes, some of the most advanced eyes are found in those creatures that evolutionists tell us date back almost to the beginning. Consider certain trilobites, which evolutionists claim represent some of the earliest forms of life: "These trilobite eyes had *compound lenses*, sophisticated designs for eliminating image distortions. . . . Only the best cameras and telescopes contain compound lenses. Trilobite eyes '*represent an all-time feat of function* optimization' (emphasis in original)."[34]

As Stephen Jay Gould pointed out, "Of what possible use are the imperfect incipient stages of useful structures? What good is half a jaw, or half a wing?"[35] The idea of gradual change is not viable. He admitted that, "The eyes of early trilobites, for example, have never been exceeded for complexity or acuity by later anthropods."[36] Does that sound like "evolution" from the simple to the complex? Something is wrong with that theory!

A starfish has been discovered with more than 1,000 eyes, each with an identical lens that surpasses today's technology. This creature is supposed to have appeared millions of years prior to man in the evolutionary time scale—yet its eyes are, in some ways, superior to those possessed by humans. And more than 1,000 of them for a lowly and tiny starfish? This is such a ridiculous number of eyes that they could hardly have been produced by natural selection as essential for survival. Is the Creator laughing at evolutionists? Does the following brief description sound at all like something that would have been developed by chance mutations so early in the alleged evolution process?

> Built into the starfish's tough, calcite skeleton are arrays of microscopic crystals that focus light 10 times more precisely than any manufactured micro optics. Such was the finding of Joan Aizenberg and her colleagues at Lucent Technologies and the Los Angeles County Museum of Natural History. Molecular biologist Daniel Morse, who directs the marine biotechnology program at UC [University of California] Santa Barbara, said, it's significant because it demonstrates that living organisms control nanostructures . . . with a precision beyond the reach of present-day engineering.

"Linked by networks of nerve fibers, the thousands of micro-lenses together appear to form a kind of single compound eye that covers the creature's entire body in all-seeing armor," said Aizenberg, an expert in biomaterials. . . . "The actual optical performance of these lenses is far beyond current technology."[37]

Indeed, for microengineers trying to craft infinitesimal lenses for faster optical computers, sensors, and switches, the brittlestar's [*Ophiocoma wendti*] eye is a living blueprint. It could lead to better-crafted and more efficient telecommunication systems and optical networks. Lobster eyes, with their precise geometrical relationships of individual units, have been copied by NASA X-ray telescopes.

The human eye couldn't possibly function for assistance in survival without the cornea, iris, pupil, macula, vitreous, the rods and cones, the 100 million light-sensitive cells that send information to the brain through the one million fibers of the optic nerve, the brain itself, and the 100 billion nerve cells joined by some 240,000 miles of nerve fibers and the 100 trillion connections between nerve cells in the brain. As has been pointed out, "Since the eye is obviously of no use at all except in its final, complete form, how could natural selection have functioned in those initial stages of its evolution when the variations had no possible survival value. . . ? And there are other equally provoking examples of organs and processes which seem to defy natural selection. . . ."[38]

To imagine that vision's many essential parts could have developed over millions of years while contributing nothing to survival until it all worked is wishful thinking by those who will grasp at any idea to prop up a bankrupt theory. Even Darwin, who didn't know a fraction of the eye's complexity that we understand today, nevertheless wrote:

To suppose that the eye, with all its inimitable contrivances for adjusting the focus to different distances, for admitting different amounts of light, and for the correction of spherical and chromatic aberration, could have been formed by natural selection, seems, I freely confess, absurd in the highest possible degree.[39]

Turning to another complex organ, James Perloff, author and former atheist, has reminded us, "The human heart is an ingenious structure. Blood is pumped . . . through more than 60,000 miles of vessels. To accept evolution, we must believe that human blood circulation—a wonder of engineering—was actually *constructed* by chance mutations, when actual observation demonstrates they [mutations] do nothing but damage. . . . We must believe that mutations built the human brain and every other feature of life on Earth."[40]

The same is true of the many other organs such as the lungs, kidneys, glands, stomach, intestines, etc. Any components of any of these while "in process" of evolutionary development, far from aiding survival, would be a burden and thus eliminated by natural selection. Clearly, no evolutionary process—only God—could create the eye or any of the other organs and parts of the body. Nor has anything "in process" ever been observed in the fossil record but only fully functioning organs.

Richard Dawkins, in his book *The Blind Watchmaker*, claims that an imperfect cell would somehow be able to function *at some level*, but that's not true. Even if 95 percent of the cellular machinery were in place and ready to go (an impossibility as we have seen), the cell would not be 95 percent useful. On the contrary, it would, in fact, be 100 percent useless, because cells will self-destruct in a process called *apoptosis* if every component is not present and functioning properly.

NATURAL SELECTION IS SELF-DESTRUCTIVE

It takes only a moment's reflection to realize that the idea of evolution through natural selection is self-contradictory. Evolution proposes a gradual development that would actually destroy what is supposedly being formed. The very process of Darwinian selection and survival of the fittest would eliminate as unfit any parts of the body that were "in process" and not yet united into the whole and thus not functioning properly. All living things had to be created complete and functioning the way the Bible both declares and emphasizes repeatedly: "And God saw that it was good."[41]

All available scientific evidence supports this appraisal. That is a fact for which science itself offers overwhelming proof, but most scientists ignore it in their desire to escape accountability to the Creator. For scientists who know the facts to persist in dogmatically clinging to and promoting evolution as the explanation for life is unconscionable. It is even more dishonest for them to foist their impossible theory on school children and the general public. And most reprehensible of all is the refusal to allow creation to be taught as an alternative to evolution.

We've already seen that there is something missing from all of the purely materialistic scientific inquiries and endeavors. Why are we interested in this? Why should the scientific facts about the universe leave such questions unanswered? There is a part of man that demands such answers and they will never come from the examination of the physical universe.

Cosmology is unique in science in that it is a very large intellectual edifice based on a very few facts.

—H. C. Arp, G. Burbidge, F. Hoyle, J. V. Narlicar, and N. C. Wickramasinghe, "The Extragalactic Universe: An Alternative View," *Nature*, vol. 346 (August 30, 1990), 812

Big Bang cosmology is probably as widely believed as has been any theory of the universe in the history of Western civilization. It rests, however, on many untested, and in some cases untestable, assumptions. Indeed, Big Bang cosmology has become a bandwagon of thought that reflects faith as much as objective truth.

—Geoffrey Burbidge, "Why Only One Big Bang?" *Scientific American* (February 1992), 120

If there is a purpose to the universe, and it achieves that purpose, then the universe must end, for its continued existence would be gratuitous and pointless. Conversely, if the universe endures forever, it is hard to imagine that there is any ultimate purpose to the universe at all. So cosmic death may be the price that has to be paid for cosmic success. Perhaps the most that we can hope for is that the purpose of the universe becomes known to our descendants before the end of the last three minutes.

—Paul C. Davies, *The Last Three Minutes* (London: Orion Books, 1994), 155

Was there ever really a big bang? Even as greater and greater numbers of people have come to believe that the universe began with one great eruption, others have seen a persistent weakness in the theory—a weakness that is becoming ever harder to overlook.

—Sir Fred Hoyle, "The Big Bang Under Attack," *Science Digest*, vol. 92 (May 1984), 84

Short of postulating some sort of action from outside the universe, whatever this may mean, the energy of the universe must continually lose availability. . . . Change can occur only in the one direction. . . . With universes, as with mortals, the only possible life is progress to the grave.

—James Jeans, *The Universe Around Us* (New York: Cambridge University Press, 1969), 280

The popular conception of primitive cells as the starting point for the origin of the species is really erroneous. There was nothing functionally primitive about such cells. They contained basically the same biochemical equipment as do their modern counterparts. . . . How, then, did the precursor cell arise? The only unequivocal rejoinder to this question is that we do not know.

—David E. Green and Robert F. Goldberger, *Molecular Insights into the Living Process* (New York: Academic Press, 1967), 403

SEVEN

WHY CAN'T "SCIENCE" TELL US WHY?

O NE OF THE MANY PROBLEMS with atheism is its unthinking and even unconscious supporting cast of materialism and inherent purposelessness. Because atheism acknowledges nothing but matter, what can atheists do but boast of this fact? And indeed they do. This is the thesis of Richard Dawkins's book, *The Blind Watchmaker*.

As a consequence, Dawkins and his fellow geneticists are forced to admit that DNA has no place in its structure for, and thus plays no part in, the most important aspects of human existence: purpose, meaning, morals, ethics, esthetics, a sense of accomplishment, satisfaction with achievement, appreciation of beauty, of music, of poetry, etc.

DNA pertains to the physical body, not to the mind or to the soul.

I challenge any atheists reading this book to keep reading and refute what I say if they can—but to read far enough to be fair. No one can deny that human intellect and emotions defy any physical description. How can the genius of a musician or artist or poet be physically described? Where are these abilities located in the DNA?

Here is what Dawkins himself said regarding "purpose" in his video *The Big Question: Why Are We Here?*:

> It is we who actually provide the purpose in a universe that has none.
>
> We seem to have freed ourselves from the need to spend all our time propagating our selfish genes. . . . Speech lets us share goals. The creature able to communicate its goals begins to think purposely, act purposely, create purposely. . . . An animal who invents will look at the world in a different way from any other animal. We see the world through purpose-colored spectacles. . . . Because we created things for a purpose, in the past we assumed that there was a purposeful design in nature, too. There wasn't. . . . It took Darwin to realize this. . . . For the first time an evolved creature had seen beneath nature's veil and worked out what nature was really up to.[1]

Just in these few words, we have so many contradictions. How could there be a purpose if there's "none in the universe"? Where did this "purpose" come from? *Darwin* knew about this? Well, of course, we know that Darwin is so highly regarded by Dawkins that his admiration causes him to overstate his case continually. Darwin's first book was titled *On the Origin of Species*. Any reader knows that the one thing Darwin didn't explain in his book was the origin of even one species. Here we have Dawkins praising his hero even more highly. Not only could Darwin not give us the origin of species as he promised, but now Dawkins credits his hero with having given us what even the universe can't tell us: man's underlying purpose for existence.

The basic problem in this entire discussion between atheists and theists, evolutionists and creationists, is the insistence by one party to this discussion that nothing exists but matter. Materialism is at the very heart of this problem. Does man have a soul or doesn't he? Is there a difference between the mind and the brain? Obviously, there must be. The mind thinks. The brain cannot think. Ideas are not physical. The brain is made of protein.

What is the physical description of the brilliance of the mind and the initiative behind the invention of the computer and the seemingly endless software that expands its use? How and why did natural selection program such unnatural inventiveness into the human mind? Pardon me, I should have said brain, because the mind is nonphysical. Ask the materialist what part of the brain is responsible for the initiative and genius that brought forth the astonishing inventions that fill today's world. What will the response be?

We will deal with consciousness, conscience, and morals in chapter 13. In the meantime, the atheist/materialist can be thinking of a *physical* description for these clearly nonphysical elements that are so important in the lives of every man, woman, and child.

WHAT IS MAN?[2]

When the first chapter of the Bible declares, "God made man in his image," for anyone who believes and desires to follow the Bible, the words of Jesus entirely rule out natural selection and evolution, including the "theistic" variety. "The image of God" is obviously not speaking of "physical image" because Jesus said, "God is a spirit."[3] Any attempt to represent God physically is condemned as idolatry and is thus forbidden.

In what sense, then, can man be made in God's image? Only in the moral and spiritual sense. The atheist has committed intellectual and moral suicide by necessarily denying morals and spirituality because they have no physical description. How can the atheist be consistent and still claim to be a moral person?

Yes, atheists hate the very thought of the "God" in whom they don't believe. Well, we don't believe in the ridiculous mythical "god" to which they refer either, so there's a point of agreement.

Evolution and natural selection, even if true, could deal only with the physical body. But that does not define the man that the psalmist referred to when he asked, "What is man?"[4] or that Pilate meant when, with these dramatic words, "Behold the man!"[5] he presented Jesus to the howling mob demanding His crucifixion.

Though Christopher Hitchens hates the words as glorifying the One he derides as a "heavenly dictator," *his* "soul" and that of every other atheist must be stirred by the genius of the music in Handel's *Hallelujah Chorus*, including even its climax, "And He shall reign for ever and ever and ever. . . !" The atheist who closes his ears and heart to such brilliance out of hatred for God has, as Jesus warned, lost his soul! "What is a man profited, if he shall gain the whole world, and lose his own soul? Or what shall a man give in exchange for his soul?"[6]

There are differences of opinion on the meaning of "soul," but intellectual arguments aside, we all innately know that whatever is meant cannot be described physically.

BEYOND MATERIALISM'S EMPTINESS

One is awed by the genius of a William Shakespeare or a Charles Dickens that could produce such a quantity of intellectually and morally challenging literature without computers or even typewriters! In what part of the DNA is this brilliance located? Why did natural selection create such amazing talent? What could it possibly have to do with survival of Dawkins's selfish genes or Crick's bag of molecules? In Collins's tracing human DNA back to a common ancestor with primates and even fungi, what thought has he given to the undeniably impassable chasm that Mortimer J. Adler identified as separating man from all nonhuman creatures: the ability to form conceptual ideas and express them in speech? Where is that incredible ability located in the DNA, and what is its physical description?

The Apostle Paul said that the physical world is temporary, but the unseen world is eternal. This is the world that the materialist cannot deny exists but refuses to acknowledge and is impoverished by that refusal. Of the physical world, the Apostle John wrote, "The world passeth away, and the lusts thereof: but he that doeth the will of God abideth forever."[7]

Many leading scientists acknowledge this "unseen world." In fact, one of Sir Arthur Eddington's most famous books is titled *Science and the Unseen World*. He's referring to the world that is invisible to the physical eye but very real to the soul.

Surely, in what Christ said about losing the soul, we are getting an insight into hell. The Bible speaks of those who are there as being "lost." Even non-Christians refer in sympathy to a "lost soul" as someone who refuses to accept advice and who sinks ever deeper into the morass of his own stubbornness and folly.

This is not to say that "heaven" and "hell" are only mental states that we create for ourselves here in this life. I think we will see even before the final chapter of this book that just as the very nature of the universe requires physical laws, so the nature of man requires spiritual laws. It will become very clear that just as the physical laws cannot be even temporarily suspended for someone's momentary personal convenience because of the horrible physical consequences for the entire universe that would follow, neither can the moral laws be annulled because of the even more serious moral destruction that would involve the entire human race.

Physical destruction, when it causes the deaths of those involved, cannot be undone in this life. This fact is built into the very fabric of the universe and the physical laws governing it. So it is with the moral consequences of evil in one's life. Why is this? Because we cannot turn time back and "try again," no matter the need or desire.

THE FINALITY OF TIME PASSING

When a baby, who has no idea what is happening, accidentally falls over a cliff to its death, the atheist would not expect "nature" to momentarily suspend the law of gravity. Natural laws hold the universe together, so a suspension of gravity, no matter how brief, would bring disaster upon the entire universe. So it is with moral laws that hold our lives together. The consequences could be disastrous not only for ourselves but for many others when we violate the morality with which our consciences confront us.

Time has no "replay" button. What was done was done, and there is no undoing it. The murderer can say "Sorry!" to the relatives of his victim, but that cannot change the reality of his deed. Did Hitler, by suicide, escape the judgment he deserved? Hitchens's claim, "When you're dead, that's the end" surely leaves justice in the grave also. Is that possible? Not if the God of the Bible exists. Atheism is in fact a mockery of justice!

What we call "natural disasters" cause every victim and sympathetic observer to cry out "Why?" Almost everything that happens, whether disaster or just the fact that we exist surrounded by a pitiless nature, causes every thinking person to ask the same important question, and neither atheism nor nature can respond. One asks a hurricane, or earthquake, or cyclone, or flood, or fire in vain why it has caused so many deaths and so much destruction.

What parent has not endured the endless, "*Why*, Daddy?" Or "Mommy, *why*?" almost to the point of exhaustion? Nor can one accuse a child of being unreasonable in asking that question. In fact, to ask, "*Why*," is the very foundation of thoughtfulness and reason. It is at this point that science is mute.

THEORIES ARE NO ANSWER

Annoying though such persistent questioning may be, it comes from the normal innate desire in every child to find an answer that eliminates the need for any further questions. Tragically, after varying lengths of time (depending upon the individual and circumstances), disillusionment and cynicism eventually bring the frustrating conviction that perhaps there are no real answers to life's most important questions. The fresh, youthful search after truth is drowned in a sea of disappointments and betrayals and is finally silenced by the narcotic of amusement and pleasure.

The haunting questions are deferred until some imaginary day "when there will be time" to give them serious thought. Yet that time seldom comes. With a helpless shrug, the attitude in the teens and twenties can eventually turn into *so what*! The conscience still wants a reason, but that desire gets buried deeper and deeper under piles of so much else that seems more urgent or desirable for the moment. No wonder the Bible warns, "Remember now thy Creator in the days of thy youth. . . ."[8]

In today's atmosphere, where science is worshiped, any educated person will inevitably come face-to-face with Darwinism. For many, this widely believed theory is welcomed with open arms as an "at-last-there's-an-escape-from-God" discovery!

The honest seeker after truth, however, must sooner or later admit, to the discomfort of his conscience, the glaring contradictions that Dawkins dogmatically pronounces as scientific fact. In spite of denying all purpose and meaning to his admirers, he allows two purposes to himself that consume him day and night: to justify his worship of Darwin and his rejection and hatred of the God of the Bible, in whom nearly two billion others believe.

WHY?

No one has lived very long without being confronted with situations that cause one to cry out, "Why me?" The answer to that question involves everything we've been discussing. Ultimately, "why me?" comes back to "why life?" "why existence?" and "why the universe?" Such questions reflect a groping after some reason for what has happened. Our minds cry out, *There must be some meaning!* And that recognition demands purpose. The question "Why?" is really asking, "What is the purpose?"

One would not ask a hurricane to explain its purpose in the destruction it causes. Nature knows nothing of meaning and purpose. If there is no Intelligence behind nature, then there can be no purpose. It is the manufacturer who alone decides the purpose for the object he has made. It is axiomatic that everything in existence must have meaning and, therefore, must have been made. No physical person or object in the universe can exist without some cause. This is exactly what scientists such as Einstein or philosophers like Spinoza meant when they acknowledged "something" is behind this universe. But they were reluctant to say "some*one*," nor would they call this "God" or assign to "it" any personal qualities. Basically, then, we would have to call Einstein a pagan who, like Sagan, actually worshiped nature.

Dawkins blusters that Darwinism can tell us "why," which it obviously cannot. Incredibly, he says, "Intelligent life on a planet comes of age when it first works out the reason for its own existence. . . . Living organisms had existed on earth, without ever knowing why, for over three thousand million years before the truth finally dawned on one of them. His name was Charles Darwin . . . who first put together a coherent and tenable account of why we exist. . . . We no longer have to resort to superstition when faced with deep problems: Is there a meaning to life? What are we for? What is man?"[9]

Charles Darwin was the "first [to] put together a coherent and tenable account of why we exist"? Dawkins can't be that ignorant. The truth is that even the pagan philosophers were deeply impressed with the order and beauty of the universe. Stoics spoke of a divine cosmic reason for man's existence and of providential care over humans. Pagan philosophers expressed the same belief. In the first century BC, Cicero, brilliant orator and philosopher, yet a pagan who worshipped Rome's many gods, nevertheless declared:

If any man cannot feel the power of God when he looks upon
the stars, then I doubt whether he is capable of any feeling
at all. . . . In the heavens there is nothing accidental, nothing
arbitrary . . . [only] order, truth, reason, constancy. . . .[10]

Plato, in his work, *Timaeus*, presented an elaborate account of a
divine Craftsman bringing mathematical cohesion out of chaos to form
an orderly *kosmos*, making the universe itself a living thing. After the
pagans, nearly the entire roster of philosophers prior to the nineteenth
century were Christians who argued from reason and supporting evidence for divine creation of an orderly universe. That belief became
the basis of the science established by the founders of modern scientific theories that laid out the basic laws explaining the universe as we
know it today. Yet Dawkins, in worshiping what we can only assume
is his god, declares that *Darwin* "was the first to give us a coherent
and tenable account of why we exist." Certainly many tried to give an
explanation, but Dawkins makes this ridiculous statement because he
doesn't acknowledge them as intelligent human beings—only Darwin,
Dawkins, and the other "brights" fall into that category.

Although Darwinism, for those who believed it, drove the
Creator out of his universe, Dawkins is just dead wrong in crediting
Darwin with explaining why man and the universe exist. Would he
say that Darwin's followers are now elaborating on "the purpose for
our existence"? In fact, with one voice they firmly deny any *reason* for
existence, as we have amply shown. Bertrand Russell declared that
"All the labor of the ages, all the devotion, all the inspiration, all the
noonday brightness of human genius are destined to extinction in the
death of the solar system. . . ."

Dawkins has already told us there is no meaning, either present or
possible, anywhere in the universe. Certainly, neither Dawkins's *Selfish
Gene*, which "has no foresight," nor Crick's "bag of molecules" that
rejects categorically any purpose or meaning, can supply in its place
something better than what they have scorned. With its denunciation
of a personal, thinking, and willing Creator, atheism has turned its

back on any rational basis for purpose or meaning to life. The atheist has burned his bridges. So what is there to reason about?

It seems not only simplistic but nonsensical to offer Darwinism as the answer to the primary questions that still evoke a number of contradictory responses from the deepest thinkers of our day. Neither Dawkins nor his god Darwin ever gives us a satisfactory answer to who we are and why we are here. And how can they, since in Dawkins's book *The Selfish Gene* he says we're just vehicles for our genes? That's our *purpose*? He may think this a satisfactory answer to why we are here, but few others would be happy with that "purpose" for their lives—nor could natural selection provide a *reason* for the disappointment we feel in this alleged "purpose."

It is pointless to speculate about why the cosmos exists if one is not willing to look beyond the creation to its Creator. This is the undeniable fact that hampers atheism. Matter is all that an atheist can look to for answers because, for the atheist, nothing else exists. The material of which the universe is made can, no more than the material in "Aunt Matilda's cake," tell us what it is or how it came into existence, much less *why* it exists—or what its purpose is. That fact alone ought to give atheists great concern. *If* we are here for a purpose and miss it, we have missed the very reason for which we exist—and what could be more serious than that?

DAWKINS'S CONFUSION

Paul Davies, physicist, cosmologist, astrobiologist, and a research director at Arizona State University, says: "There's no need to invoke anything supernatural in the origins of universe or in life. . . ."[11] We challenge him to give us a "natural" explanation for the origin of energy, or of gravity, or of genius, or of the will, or of life, or even of his own thoughts.

Ironically, Dawkins says he got into science because he wanted to know why we're here, why the cosmos exists.[12] But science doesn't even pretend to answer such questions—and it can't.[13] These were young

Dawkins's naïve thoughts as a fifteen-year-old boy. Yet Dawkins the man and scientist is still apparently imagining the capabilities that he immaturely credited to science.

He persists: "I consider it an immense privilege to be alive as a scientist with the opportunity to know the reason for life. . . . We naturally explain everything as having been made by someone [and] so do the same with the universe, but that is fallacious." This is a dogmatic statement, but no evidence or reason is offered.

He forgets that unarguably *nothing* has meaning without a maker. It is the maker who gives it purpose, his purpose. I challenge the reader to find an exception to that statement. Says Dawkins, naively, "It was a supreme achievement of the human intellect to realize there is a better explanation [than God], these things can come about by purely natural causes." How absurd!

What "natural cause" was responsible for the sudden appearance of energy and matter from nothing? What caused it "naturally" to explode in a "big bang" and to bring forth from that giant fireball the marvels of today's universe? What was the "natural cause" that allegedly brought forth life by spontaneous generation out of the total sterilization of the Big Bang? There is no "natural cause" that can go against the law of biogenesis. The only way life could possibly come out of death would be by resurrection. In nature, there is no room for resurrection, which is a supernatural act.

Natural selection could never bring that about. We challenge Dawkins to explain "purely natural causes" that could bring about an event, which, logically, must be outside the physical universe of nature. Spontaneous generation of life out of a totally sterilized mass of gasses is not a natural event, yet Dawkins has nothing else to offer. We do not see this happening, even infrequently, around us. Something that happened only once, and before "nature" even existed, couldn't possibly be a "natural" event.

Darwinism purports to give us an "explanation" of everything (including the purpose and meaning of life) without a Creator. This is a major point in all Dawkins says. Instead of a Creator with a mind and will who brought the universe into existence for a purpose, Dawkins offers the mindless mechanism of natural selection through a "blind watchmaker" and a "selfish gene." In fact, it would ruin everything for him and his fellow atheists if the "architect" he credits with laying out the "plans" of life in the DNA could actually think and plan ahead.[14] His "watchmaker" *must* literally be *blind* and incapable of thinking or planning anything. Such is his hatred of God that it drives him to this insanity. In fact, in Dawkins's latest book, *The Greatest Show on Earth,* he contradicts himself again. Now he says that DNA *cannot* be compared to an architect's plan.[15]

In his 2007 debate with John Lennox, Dawkins stated with the utmost confidence: "We now understand essentially how life came into being. . . . Darwinism explains life . . . and no serious scientist doubts that." Lennox strongly disagreed, pointing out that Darwinism may explain something about life *after it comes into existence,* but it cannot tell us what it is, how it originated, or why. Darwinism leaves dozens of vital *why* questions unanswered.

DOES THE UNIVERSE HAVE A "PURPOSE"?

Everyone knows that understanding *why* the cosmos exists is essential if we are to know *why* we find ourselves on this particular planet in this particular corner of the universe—a question that science has been unable to answer thus far. Could Darwinism be the *voila!* that every rational person seeks? Has a giant explosion of unknown substance and origin left us, its supposed offspring, dangling as meaningless products of billions of years of evolution and natural selection? Could that be what this entire universe and human life are all about? Dawkins says he feels very fortunate to be alive, but does the universe even know he exists, much less care? Stephen Hawking sums up all of the *why?* questions and doesn't seem to agree with Dawkins that Darwinism holds the final answer:

> The usual approach of science of constructing a mathematical model cannot answer the questions of why there should be a universe for the model to describe. Why does the universe go to all the bother of existing?[16]

That has so far proved to be an unanswerable question for both science and philosophy and doubly so for atheism. *Go to all the bother of existing?* Matter is not "bothered" by anything. Can such a question be addressed to pitiless nature? Like Dawkins's fabled selfish genes and Aunt Matilda's famous cake, natural selection does not think, plan, or know anything. Having no purpose in and of itself, how could natural selection endow its creatures with any meaning to their lives?

One might as well ask an airplane or computer why it exists as to expect the universe to explain its origin and purpose. Can there be any meaning without a maker who alone determines the purpose for which he makes things? Robert Jastrow comments:

> This is why it seems to me and to others that the curtain drawn over the mystery of creation will never be raised by human efforts. . . . Although I am an agnostic, and not a believer, I still find much to ponder in the view expressed by the British astronomer E. A. Milne, who wrote, "We can make no propositions about the state of affairs [in the beginning]; in the Divine act of creation God is unobserved. . . ."[17]

Dawkins concedes that a universe with a God would be very different from a universe without a God.[18] In attempting to define Him, what Dawkins has to say is defiantly blasphemous. It is safe to say that most theists would not believe in the god in which Dawkins doesn't believe. Yet this is the "god" he accuses theists of embracing.

How odd, then, that Dawkins says he was attracted to science because he "wanted to know why we're here, why the universe exists."[19] Perhaps he didn't know at that early age that science cannot, does not, and will not even pretend to answer that question. Before Dawkins was born, Nobel Prize winners had already declared unequivocally that science has nothing to say about purpose or meaning. After devoting his life to finding the purpose and meaning of the universe, what has Dawkins concluded about why we're here and why the universe exists? Why, it's to "make our own purpose because there is none in the universe"! The question of meaning and purpose is of vital importance, yet Dawkins tries to avoid it.

Sorry Richard, you can't escape that easily.

QUESTIONS THAT PUZZLE THE BRIGHTEST MINDS

We have seen that astronomers have generally concluded, though many of them reluctantly, that the universe of space, time, and matter had a beginning. Of course, that logical deduction immediately raises many questions: when, how, and *why* did it all come into existence? What is its purpose?

Dawkins generously says it's entirely up to each of us to give life whatever meaning and purpose it is going to have. This is a cop-out. His atheism drives him to this senseless and equally hopeless conclusion. You're looking for meaning and purpose in life? Great! Make it up as you go along. What do you want life to be? "Row, row, row your boat gently down the stream. Merrily, merrily, merrily, merrily, life is but a dream."

And what does science have to say about this undeniable beginning to the universe? It pretends to tell us how it happened—with a sudden explosion of energy. But science cannot tell us for sure whether it even happened that way, much less how it came about, nor *why*. In fact, science can't even tell us what energy *is*. As Harvard astrophysicist Margaret Geller has said, "It is clear that there is something profoundly wrong with our theories."[20] Even Massimo Pigliucci, with three doctorates (genetics, botany, and philosophy), and who is an outspoken critic of creationism, acknowledges, "The origin of life on Earth is a fundamental scientific question, but we do not know as much as many biology textbooks would like you to believe."[21]

As we have already seen (and I think it is important to keep reminding ourselves of these basic facts), we don't even know what space, time, and matter are. Nor do we know what energy is, how it came into being, or how it organized itself into the astonishingly marvelous universe in which we find ourselves. And we certainly don't know what life is.

Dawkins admits, "We don't yet understand cosmology," and then, with another reverent bow toward his favorite deity, he adds, "Cosmology is waiting for its Darwin." Dawkins has such a high regard for his god Darwin that he calls Darwinism the "greatest accomplishment of the human mind." Isn't this absurd!

One begins to suspect that Dawkins is hoping for the day when the calendar worldwide will be changed from BC (Before Christ) to BD (Before Darwin), and AD will mean, "After Darwin." The transition from BD to AD will be set at 1860, and all calendars will be revised on that basis. This milestone will be recognized as the turning point in history, when the revolution against God gained decisive momentum.

THE THUNDEROUS SILENCE OF SCIENCE ON VITAL ISSUES

In so many respects, scientists have made great strides in telling us *what* the atom and cell and DNA, for example, are and *how* they function, but they cannot tell us *why* they exist and act the way they do. As Daniel Dennett admits, "Today's cosmologists, like many of their predecessors throughout history, tell a diverting story, but prefer to sidestep the 'why' question of teleology. Does the universe exist for any reason? Do reasons play any intelligible role in explanations of the cosmos? Could something exist for a reason without it being *somebody's* reason?"[22]

Dennett is asking the right questions, questions that ought to give him and all other atheists pause. A little reflection should deliver them from their dogmatic rejection of God. The first two questions would elicit a prompt "yes" from theists and should challenge atheists to think carefully, while the only rational answer to the third one must be a resolute "no." Only personal beings with intelligence and a will can act for a *reason*. No man was there at the beginning when the universe came into existence. *Someone must have been.* This could only have been *The Creator.*

Could unexplained blind forces be the "intelligence" behind existence? Can atheism in any way answer the all-important *why* questions? The atheist's life has no meaning unless he can support an affirmative answer to that question. This is the crux of the issue with which we are dealing—and to show that materialism cannot even provide a definition of "meaning" is a major purpose of this book.

Clearly, only the One who conceived, planned, and created the cosmos could give it any meaning at all. If there is no Creator, then the universe and everything within it (including man) is without purpose. Dennett's supremely rational question must haunt atheists. Yet Dawkins, incredibly, exults in this meaninglessness. What else can atheism do?

Dennett spends the next 500 pages of his remarkably challenging book futilely trying to explain how Darwinism has done exactly that: "Darwin has shown us how, in fact, *everything* of importance is just such a product."[23] In fact, Darwin has shown us nothing of the kind. Can an unexplained and purposeless explosion of energy with a mysterious and unidentifiable origin supply any meaning to the cosmos or to our own existence? Dennett ends his supposed masterpiece, *Darwin's Dangerous Idea: Evolution and the Meaning of Life*, without providing a coherent answer to the important question he asked— and like Darwin, his idol, fails to live up to the ambitious promise of the book's title.

AN EMBARRASSING SILENCE

Darwin would not deal with origins at all—not even in *The Origin of Species*, which, in a classic cop-out, declares that all species originated from previously existent species. What could have been the origin of the *first* species? That is the answer Darwin promises and fails to give.

It is surprising that Dennett, who is praised in the *Wall Street Journal* as "a philosopher of rare originality, rigor, and wit [who] clears up conceptual muddles in the sciences,"[24] accepts Darwin's silence as great wisdom. He leaves the question, which he will spend 500 pages supposedly clarifying, still dangling unanswered at the end of the book. In his praise of Darwin, he is offering a lame excuse for the inability of *any* evolutionist to offer *any* explanation of the origin of life:

> When speculation on these extensions of his view arose, Darwin wisely chose to retreat to the security of his base camp, the magnificently provisioned and defended thesis that began in the beginning, with life already on the scene, and "merely" showed how, once this process of design accumulation was underway, it could proceed without any [further?] intervention from any Mind. But, as many of his readers appreciated, however comforting this modest disclaimer might be, it was not really a stable resting place. . . .
>
> If *re*design could be a mindless algorithmic process of evolution, why couldn't that whole process itself be the product of evolution, and so forth, *all the way down*? And if mindless evolution could account for the breathtakingly clever artifacts of the biosphere, how could the products of our own "real" minds be exempt from an evolutionary explanation? Darwin's idea thus also threatened to spread *all the way up*, dissolving the illusion of our own authorship, our own divine spark of creativity and understanding.[25]

This "retreat to the [supposed] security of his base camp" was occasioned by a debate between Samuel Wilberforce, Bishop of Oxford, and Thomas Huxley, on June 30, 1860. Sponsored by the British Association for the Advancement of Science and held at the Oxford Natural History Museum, Dennett describes it as "one of the most celebrated confrontations between Darwinism and the religious establishment."

In the debate, Wilberforce made this powerful statement, which goes to the heart of the issue. It has bothered atheists and evolutionists ever since. In spite of thousands of books offering convoluted arguments in defense of evolution, no one in that camp has yet been able to refute this simple statement by Wilberforce in 1860:

> Man's derived supremacy over the earth; man's power of articulate speech; man's gift of reason; man's free-will and responsibility . . . all are equally and utterly irreconcilable with the degrading notion of the brute origin of him who was created in the image of God. . . .[26]

"A FINE-TUNED UNIVERSE"

A growing number of scientists are concluding, many of them reluctantly, that the universe gives too many indications of having been fine-tuned specifically for the human race to deny that fact any longer. As a recent BBC science documentary pointed out, "Even those who do not accept The Anthropic Principle[27] admit to the 'fine-tuning' and conclude that the universe is 'too contrived' to be a chance event." The documentary quoted a number of distinguished cosmologists, among them Dr. Dennis Scania, head of Cambridge University Observatories, who says, "If you change a little bit the laws of nature, or you change a little bit the constants of nature . . . it is very likely that intelligent life would not have been able to develop."[28]

This is where desperation grasps at fantasy theories. The most desperate and at the same time most popular (what else do they have?) is the multiverse hypothesis first promoted by David Deutsch in his book *The Fabric of Reality*. This theory seems to be the atheist's only way of escape. Postulating the existence of an infinite number of parallel universes would mean that in at least one of them, conditions exactly like those in our universe would be inevitable by pure chance. But this, as philosopher and long-time Oxford professor Richard Swinburne points out, is madness: "To postulate a trillion-trillion other universes, rather than one God, in order to explain the orderliness of our universe, seems the height of irrationality."[29]

Nor is there the least scientific evidence that this multitude of universes exists. It certainly is not a *necessary* condition for the existence of life on Earth or anywhere else. This is wild speculation that violates Occam's Razor[30] and multiplies questions. No one has yet explained the origin of energy that supposedly exploded in the Big Bang, as a result of which this universe now exists; nor has anyone explained what life is, much less how it can emerge from lifeless matter contrary to the law of biogenesis. If atheistic science can't even do that for this one universe, how will it handle an endless number of universes? Eminent quantum theorist John Polkinghorne rejects this multiverse nonsense:

> Let us recognize these speculations for what they are. They are not physics, but . . . metaphysics. There is no purely scientific reason to believe in an ensemble of universes. . . . To my mind greater economy and elegance would be that this one world is the way it is because it is the creation of the will of a Creator who purposes that it should be so.[31]

The BBC documentary went on to say, "The scientific establishment's most prestigious journals, and its most famous physicists and cosmologists, have all gone on record as recognizing the objective truth of the fine-tuning." Nobel Laureate high-energy physicist (a field of science dealing with the very early universe) Professor Steven Weinberg, an agnostic, reflects on "how surprising it is that the laws of nature and the initial conditions of the universe should allow for the existence of beings who could observe it. Life as we know it would be impossible if any one of several physical quantities had slightly different values."[32] How different?

Weinberg describes how "a beryllium isotope having the miniscule half-life of 0.0000000000000001 seconds must find and absorb a helium nucleus in that split of time before decaying. This occurs only because of a totally unexpected, exquisitely precise energy match between the two nuclei. If this did not occur, there would be . . . no carbon, no nitrogen, no life. One constant does seem to require an incredible fine-tuning. . . . The existence of life of any kind seems to require a cancellation between different contributions to the vacuum energy, accurate to about 120 decimal places."[33]

Michael Turner, widely quoted astrophysicist at the University of Chicago and Fermilab, describes the fine-tuning: "The precision is as if one could throw a dart across the entire universe and hit a bullseye one millimeter in diameter on the other side."[34]

Roger Penrose, the Rouse Ball Professor of Mathematics at the University of Oxford, and renowned for his work in mathematical physics, in particular his contributions to general relativity and cosmology, with honors, degrees, books and published scientific papers too numerous to list, calculates that the likelihood of the universe having stable energy at the creation is one chance in one followed by a "million billion billion billion billion billion billion billion billion billion billion billion billion billion billion zeros. Even if we were to write a zero on each separate proton and on each separate neutron in the universe . . . and on every other particle as well . . . we should fall far short of writing down the figure needed."[35]

Writing of the origin of the universe, Stephen Hawking declared: "The remarkable fact is that the values of these numbers (i.e., the constants of physics) seem to have been very finely adjusted to make possible the development of life. . . . It would be very difficult to explain why the universe should have begun in just this way, except as the act of a God who intended to create beings like us."[36]

STUMPING SCIENCE

Why? is a question that demands purpose and meaning, and science cannot provide it. What does our survival for a few years on this planet matter to an impersonal and deteriorating universe? Does *anything* really matter? If so, *why*? Once again, that persistent question intrudes to trouble atheists. No rational person can avoid its logic, though most close their consciences to the frightening, unwanted implication that Hawking recognizes: *God*!

Atheistic scientists become especially uncomfortable when one asks *why*, and for this very reason: without God there is no answer to that question. Yet the desire to know why we even exist, much less why we are on this particular planet, when supposedly there is similar life on numerous planets throughout the cosmos, pops instinctively into the average person's mind. This haunting and compelling question cannot be avoided.

Atheists, however, even the brightest and best, continually circle widely around this uncomfortable and unanswerable (for science) dilemma. We've already seen that Hoyle pretends to answer, with a bit of further speculation, the question of how life arose on planet Earth and why we are here: well, of course, we were brought here by creatures from another planet. This is no answer at all. Who put them *there*, and so on, endlessly?

Pigliucci goes a bit deeper with this question, "Why do we care?" In spite of his doctorate in philosophy, his response is both childish and biased. First of all, he suggests that if we discovered that "life originated elsewhere and was then somehow 'imported' to Earth, [then] this would automatically imply the existence of life as a widespread phenomenon in the cosmos [and] it is hard to conceive of a more compelling blow to anthropocentrism. . . ." His "answer" answers nothing and in fact reveals that the only thing he cares about is to protect his atheist bias. So what if life is widespread throughout the cosmos—that still wouldn't say *what* it is, *how* it got there, and *why* it is there.

No less disappointing from such a highly educated and intelligent man is the following: "Second, and perhaps more relevant, humankind would finally have an answer to the question 'where did we come from?' which, like it or not, has been vexing our philosophy, art, and science since the beginning of recorded history. . . ."[37] Would this tell us *where* we came from and *why*? Of course not. Those same questions would only have been transferred to other creatures and other places but would not be answered either for them or for us.

Pigliucci recognizes this obvious fact and later in the article writes: "Finally, it has to be realized that even if we do admit that life originated outside Earth and was then imported here, we really would not have an answer to how life started. We would have simply shifted the question to a remote and very likely inaccessible realm, an intellectually unsatisfactory state of affairs."[38] Still left hanging would be that persistent question, "*Why* are we here?"

Without solving this perplexing puzzle, atheists press on in their crusade against "god" and all "religion." Edward O. Wilson, often called "one of the most outstanding evolutionary biologists of our time," has optimistically declared:

> The final decisive edge enjoyed by scientific naturalism will come from its capacity to explain traditional religion, its chief competition, as a wholly material phenomenon. Theology is not likely to survive as an independent intellectual discipline.[39]

Nor is this ridiculous philosophy that he proposes likely to survive, because it takes us nowhere, as any thinking person can see.

If every phenomenon is proved to be "wholly material," then in the parade of that triumph, truth will be trampled under the boots of atheism. In the same ruins, next to truth will lie the smashed remnants of justice, morality, conscience, ethics, kindness—all exposed as delusions created by Crick's "bag of molecules" of which we are composed, and Dawkins's "selfish genes" that cleverly use us to their own selfish ends. The new liberating "truth" (can't we escape that concept!) will be that these fantasies somehow helped us to survive to enjoy a few brief moments of meaninglessness before oblivion. How unthinking bits of protein can give birth to *ideas* and *ideals* in the mind—thoughts that seem both true and real to those who can think—is a mystery that atheistic materialism has created but cannot solve.

The atheist has a death wish, deliberately plunging himself (though a firm alternate path is available) into a bog of meaninglessness and despair, without hope of ever knowing the reason for existence. In fact, any meaning must be denied. This vacuum is the only possible escape from accountability to the Creator. The atheist actually flees from meaning as though it were an enemy because he is fleeing from God. This sentiment is expressed by the main character in Jean-Paul Sartre's novel, *Nausea*:

> Here we sit . . . eating and drinking to preserve our precious existence and really there is nothing, nothing, absolutely no reason for existing. . . . I know that the world exists. That's all. It makes no difference to me . . . every existing thing is born without reason . . . and dies by chance. . . . I do not believe in God; His existence is belied by science.

MATERIALISM'S PRACTICAL AND FRIGHTENING CONSEQUENCES

This whole despairing admission that life is a delusion can be laid at the door of the materialistic view of the world that prevails in our day, primarily because of Darwin and Freud, and which reached its zenith in Nazi Germany and Soviet Russia. According to modern psychological theory (which, in its desire to be recognized as "science," has attempted to apply the laws of physics and chemistry to human personality), man is just a piece of highly evolved and educated beefsteak wired with nerves. The brain accounts for everything in human experience and thus can be manipulated to change ambitions, motives, and actions. Of course, every tyrant in modern history has believed that as well. That "scientific" belief has become the basis for brainwashing through torture and reward.

Forcing someone to say they believe something, however, does not mean that they really believe it. A society that is founded upon force or psychological pressure to conform must be maintained by the same tactics. Thus, the Iron Curtain, with its Berlin Wall, had to be constructed in order to maintain the Soviet system. It no more changed the real beliefs of those it imprisoned than does prison time change the minds and characters of criminals today.

Tragically, without even subscribing to materialism, this is the means of "conversion" utilized by Islam from its very beginning and spread by the sword from France to China: "Either confess that 'There is no God but Allah, and Muhammad is his messenger/prophet,' or suffer the consequences—death." This remains the foundation of Muslim terrorism to this day—a fact that the West, to its own destruction, refuses to face. Nor does it matter to Islam, any more than it did to Muhammad, its founder, that forcing someone, under threat of death, to "confess" this belief does not mean they really believe it. This is why Saudi Arabia is a closed society where no other religion may be practiced, even in secret. There is no freedom to question Islam, and any Muslim who converts to any other faith is beheaded. Yes, this is still happening *in the twenty-first century* in obedience to Muhammad, who commanded, "Whosoever relinquishes his faith, kill him!" After Muhammad's death at the vengeful hands of a widow whose husband the "prophet" had murdered, the "Wars of Apostasy" were fought to force defecting former Muslim Arabs back into the "faith." At least 60,000 were murdered in the enforcement of the above command by Muhammad. Opposed to the reality, however, our president and other world leaders repeat the "good news" that Islam is peace!

The refusal to face the truth about Islam is merely a reflection of the same stubbornness that will not allow atheists to relinquish their irrational attachment to evolution and natural selection. In contrast, the God of the Bible does not force anyone to *say* they believe, because He desires a love relationship with man that comes from the heart: "Thou shalt love the LORD thy God with all thine *heart*, and with all thy *soul*, and with all thy might."[40] From beginning to end, the Bible makes a clear distinction between what someone says they believe and what they really believe. As Christ declared: "Well hath Esaias [Isaiah] prophesied of you hypocrites, as it is written, This people honoreth me with their lips, but their heart is far from me."[41]

Atheistic materialism makes no such distinction, because a "big bang" and the matter produced by it have neither morals nor motives. Matter just *is*, and the brain is just matter that supposedly originates what we call "thought" and controls the body. The entire person is just a stimulus-response charade. Any idea that there is some purpose, meaning, or sincerity involved in any action is a delusion, according to Dawkins and classic atheism.

No rational and honest person could believe what Crick can only call an *Astonishing Hypothesis*: that our thoughts, ambitions, hopes, fears, loves and hates, likes and dislikes, fondest desires, admiration or contempt for others, are meaningless feelings with which the unthinking molecules of our bodies have deluded us.

SCIENCE ATTEMPTS AN ANSWER

We find ourselves on this tiny planet, barely a speck of dust in the Milky Way, which itself is just one of a trillion similar galaxies scattered across the cosmos. A *trillion*? How many is that? That's a million million, or a thousand billion!

Our galaxy is one-trillionth of the galaxies, which is one ten-billionth of one percent of the galaxies in the universe—and our solar system is one two-hundred-billionth of that. From whence comes the pride that makes space scientists imagine that they have really learned much from examining our solar system when it represents such a miniscule sample of the universe as a whole: one two-hundred-billionth of one ten-billionth of one percent? How can any individual (an infinitesimal bit of flesh in the cosmos) feel that he or she is worth more than any of the other 6 billion people elbowing their way through life on planet Earth—or animals or insects, as Dawkins says, for that matter? But man is a proud creature, unwilling to bow before His infinite Creator or even to acknowledge His existence.

The Bible says it was in the Garden of Eden that Adam and Eve, deciding to follow Satan, rebelled against God and set themselves up as "gods," with the intent to run their own lives and rule over others as well. That was when "self" had its awful birth and took the throne away from God in the human spirit. Adam blamed Eve and she blamed the serpent—and the proud "blame-someone-else" game has only grown fiercer, lurking behind every quarrel, crime, and war that has happened since. That the Garden of Eden and what happened there is not myth but history is proved by this pair's descendants' persisting in the same rebellion against God and engaging in deadly quarrels with each other *ad infinitum*.

But how did the whole thing begin—and *why*? The Bible says that God created the universe and pronounced it "very good."[42] Out of a good universe, how could such a cesspool of evil arise—and what might be the solution? A great question! We've hinted briefly at the answer and will delve into it in more depth later. But right now, we're examining further what science has to say in response to the logical question, "*Why?*"

SCIENCE CAN'T OFFER US A REASON

Science says that it all began with energy compacted into an infinitely small space and suddenly exploding in a "big bang." We have already mentioned some of the multitude of questions this theory creates. How does anyone know this? What was the *reason* for the existence of the energy in the first place, and *why and how* did it become infinitely compacted and then explode? What *caused* it to explode *at that moment*? And not just *how* but *why* did exploding energy arrange itself into atoms, molecules, and eventually the human brain?

There is a huge difference between "how" and "why"—a difference that science cannot deal with and won't even acknowledge. Science brushes questions of "reason" and "why" aside as metaphysical, philosophical, or religious considerations with which it doesn't deal. Big Bang supporters even claim that such questions are meaningless. But aren't these the really important issues? Who could deny that fact? Yet concerns about purpose, meaning, and reasons for anything couldn't possibly result from a "big bang" or evolution through natural selection, nor could they be found anywhere in the DNA.

Science can only deal with matter, but matter is no part of justice, truth, goodness, or evil, so science cannot deal with these very real but abstract concerns. Such concepts (which form the foundation for meaning in our lives) could not originate in the matter that makes up the brain because they cannot be described in terms of the five senses with which we experience the physical universe around us. Justice has no taste, truth has no texture, goodness has no weight, etc.

There's a great deal more to human existence than the physical energy-become-matter from which our bodies and everything else is made. Materialistic science has no means of dealing with nonmaterial questions, the really important ones—as Erwin Schrödinger said so well. Many other scientists have said the same.

Materialistic, atheistic science has a multitude of unanswerable questions that it pushes off as not within its province. In fact, the theory of the Big Bang alone has raised more unanswerable questions than its proponents can handle. These questions are being increasingly raised by those who once accepted this theory but who now doubt its validity from a purely scientific standpoint.

WILLINGLY BECOMING FOOLS

It does not take modern discoveries to see God's power and wisdom in the surrounding universe. Thoughtful men everywhere have always recognized this fact. Evolutionists complain that creationists falsely accuse them of postulating the origin and development of life by chance, when they actually assert that natural selection functions on a reasonable basis and not by chance. That is a false accusation. We have already shown that there is no reason in nature. When one denies that God is the Creator of the universe, other explanations must be invented, which can be nothing but myths at best and lies at worst. Take it from arch atheist, Richard Dawkins. He acknowledges, "The account of the origin of life that I shall give is necessarily speculative;

by definition, nobody was around to see what happened." So what is the point of speculating? And isn't it all meaningless, anyway?

Dawkins then offers bold assertions intermingled with a litany of uncertainty. Typical are the following words and phrases, all within one page: "probably . . . we do not know . . . must have . . . perhaps . . . at some point . . . formed by accident . . . may not necessarily. . . ."[43] He continues his speculation about how (but not *why*) life began:

> This may seem a very unlikely sort of accident. So it was. It was exceedingly improbable. In the lifetime of a man, things that are improbable can be treated for practical purposes as impossible [but] we are not used to dealing in hundreds of millions of years.[44]

Here come billions of years to the rescue again, that deep silk hat from which the atheist magician pulls his theories! Lies become truth if we just give them enough time. The Bible warns, "When they knew God [through the evidence in the universe], they glorified him not as God, neither were thankful; but became vain in their imaginations, and their foolish heart was darkened. Professing themselves to be wise, they became fools, and changed the glory of the incorruptible God into an image made like to corruptible man . . . and worshipped and served the creature more than the Creator, who is blessed forever, Amen."[45]

Those who instinctively could see the need for a Creator as they stood awestruck before the visible universe all around them turned their backs on what their hearts and minds told them must be true and became nature worshipers. Here, then, is the problem with atheistic, materialistic evolutionists: the universe is all there is, but it can neither explain itself nor justify its existence. Since by its own power and wisdom it allegedly brought into existence the marvels it manifests, then, they reason, we ought to bow before it. And so mankind does every time atheists credit evolution, with its natural selection, of producing a single cell, much less the human brain.

If the brain and all that we are were produced by evolution, which all began with a giant explosion/expansion of energy, can we excuse ourselves by blaming our wrong behavior on the alleged Big Bang that started it all? Instead of "the Devil made me do it," the criminal can tell the judge, "The Big Bang and natural selection made me do it!" Science robbed us of something vital when it took the answer to "*why*" away from us.

ATHEISM'S DEADLY EFFECT

Scientific materialism denies the existence not only of God but also of the nonphysical dimension of the mind as separate and distinct from the physical brain. This head-in-the-sand attitude is rigorously maintained in spite of much evidence, which, according to numerous neurosurgeons, affirms the nonphysical reality. Atheism's assertion that the physical matter of which the universe is made is all that exists turns man into a mere object, no matter how highly evolved it credits him with being. Speaking as a scientist who is not caught in the materialist trap, Peter Breggin warns:

> What happens when we start viewing a human being as an object? We lose our own capacity for rationality and for love. It is impossible to reduce a person's emotional suffering to biochemical aberrations without doing something psychologically and morally destructive to that person. We reduce the reality of that individual's life to a narrowly focused speculation about brain chemistry. . . . Thus, in their efforts to be "objective" and "scientific," biological psychiatrists and doctors end up doing very destructive things to people, including themselves. . . .[46]

Isn't that exactly what the entire idea of evolution does—reduce us to the chemicals that make up our bodies? If we are the products of unthinking forces that were set in motion by a huge explosion, can we have any significance at all? How can humans differ—and *why*—

from other lumps of matter that also came out of the Big Bang? Dawkins agrees that there is no difference between a fungus and a man. Atheistic materialism has made us the prisoners of our material bodies and brains, as we wonder what ideas our brains will think of next. That must be the case if our thoughts are caused by chemical processes in our brains.

No one, at least not yet, has thought of blaming their aberrant or criminal conduct on the Big Bang, or on their "selfish genes" or chemical composition, although that would be logical if this atheistic theory were true. But millions are encouraged by their doctors to blame a "chemical imbalance" in the brain—as though our thoughts and deeds are not our own but are merely the result of chemical reactions in the brain and nervous system. Dr. Breggin exposes that folly with the scientific facts:

> No biochemical imbalances have ever been documented with certainty in association with any psychiatric diagnosis . . . their existence is pure speculation, inspired by those who advocate drugs. . . .[47]
>
> There are no known biochemical imbalances and no tests for them.[48]

But this delusion continues its moral destruction of lives because it is backed by "science." Behind it all is the idea foundational to materialism that Francis Crick expressed in the opening and "comforting" words of his 1994 book, *The Astonishing Hypothesis: The Scientific Search for the Soul.*

Crick wasn't honestly searching for the soul. He had already concluded that it didn't exist and was trying, in the name of science, to destroy belief in the soul for all time. But if we are merely a bundle of chemical reactions, one wonders why the chemicals of which Crick is made spent the time and effort to explain away the soul in a book. What does it matter? Isn't human existence meaningless anyway, as well as very brief?

In spite of the fact that science turns man into a blob of purposelessness, it has actually done much good, for which we must give it credit. But there is too much that is wrong because of its atheistic foundation to let it proceed unchallenged to spread its poison and infect further generations. We will examine its premises in more detail, beginning with a closer look at the so-called Big Bang.

Following the pied piper of materialism, society has lost its soul. If *why* is not a legitimate question, we have sunk into the quicksand of insignificance and are no longer distinguishable from any animal, insect, or plant, all of which have the same "selfish genes." In fact, we have quoted Dawkins declaring with the authority of "science" that man is in no way of greater significance than any other species, because we all share the same DNA. Crick's astonishing hypothesis is a form of insanity that seems to afflict only atheists, evolutionists, and materialists—and does so to their own intellectual and spiritual destruction.

The inflationary model of the universe provides a possible mechanism by which the observed universe could have evolved from an infinitesimal region. It is then tempting to go one step further and speculate that the entire universe evolved from literally nothing.

—ALAN H. GUTH AND PAUL J. STEINHARDT, "THE INFLATIONARY UNIVERSE," *SCIENTIFIC AMERICAN*, VOL. 250 (MAY 1984), 128

We are told that matter is being continually created, but in such a way that the process is imperceptible—that is, the statement cannot be disproved. When we ask why we should believe this, the answer is that the "perfect cosmological principle" requires it. And when we ask why we should accept this "principle," the answer is that the fundamental axiom of science requires it. This we have seen to be false, and the only other answer that one can gather is that the "principle" must be true because it seems fitting to the people who assert it. With all respect, I find this inadequate.

—HERBERT DINGLE, "SCIENCE AND MODERN COSMOLOGY," *SCIENCE*, VOL. 120 (OCTOBER 1, 1954), 515

Few cosmologists today would dispute the view that our expanding universe began with a big bang—a big, hot bang—about 18 billion years ago. Paradoxically, no cosmologist could now tell you how the Big Bang—the explosion of a superhot, superdense atom—ultimately gave rise to galaxies, stars, and other cosmic lumps.

—BEN PATRUSKY, "WHY IS THE COSMOS 'LUMPY'?" *SCIENCE*–81 (JUNE 1981), 96

I am an atheist, out and out. It took me a long time to say it. I've been an atheist for years and years, but somehow I felt it was intellectually unrespectable to say one was an atheist, because it assumed knowledge that one didn't have. Somehow it was better to say one was a humanist or an agnostic. I finally decided that I'm a creature of emotion as well as of reason. Emotionally I am an atheist. I don't have the evidence to prove that God doesn't exist, but I so strongly suspect he doesn't that I don't want to waste my time.

—ISAAC ASIMOV, INTERVIEW BY PAUL KURTZ: "AN INTERVIEW WITH ISAAC ASIMOV ON SCIENCE AND THE BIBLE," *FREE INQUIRY*, VOL. 2 (SPRING 1982), 9

EIGHT

WHAT ABOUT THE BIG BANG?

T HE ATHEIST HAS DUG HIMSELF into a deep hole with his Big Bang. Dawkins admits:

> Modern physicists sometimes wax a bit mystical when they contemplate questions such as why the big bang happened when it did, why the laws of physics are these laws and not those laws, why the universe exists at all, and so on. Sometimes physicists may resort to saying that there is an inner core of mystery that we don't understand, and perhaps never can; [or] say that perhaps this inner core of mystery is another name for "know the mind of God." The trouble is that God in this sophisticated, physicist's sense bears no resemblance to the God of the Bible . . . a being capable of forgiving sins . . . who might listen to prayers . . . [or] a being capable of imposing a death penalty on His son to expiate the sins of the world. . . .[1]

The so-called Big Bang is the atheist's last hope to explain everything without God. It is also the *sine qua non* of theistic evolution. For both atheistic and theistic evolution, the Big Bang, with its lengthy cooling-down period, provides a rationale for the billions of years needed for life to have arisen out of the completely sterilized universe so that evolution and natural selection could begin and eventually produce the forms of life we have today. Hoping to hide behind billions of years, evolutionists ignore the law of biogenesis.

There is growing opposition to the alleged Big Bang from many scientists, yet its proponents continue to promote this questionable theory authoritatively and optimistically. Richard Carrier says:

> Scientists have amassed a wealth of evidence confirming that the universe *we can see* began about fourteen billion years ago as an incredibly hot, dense, kernel of energy, which inflated under pressure, expanding and cooling . . . from which scientists can explain almost everything that has happened since . . . billions of complex galaxies . . . billions of stars . . . billions of planets . . . on at least one of those, life [arose] by a natural accident, evolving into us. . . . The facts support it fairly widely and well."[2]

No, many of the most thoroughly established facts, far from supporting this theory, contradict it. To get from the white-hot chaos of a "big bang" to living things is impossible no matter how tiny the increments and no matter in how many billions of years, according to three simple facts: 1) the law of biogenesis; 2) not even a cell, the smallest living unit, could be built in stages because none of the components that chanced into existence could survive apart from the whole, and 3) nothing gradually built by natural selection (eye, wing, kidney, liver, brain, etc.) could contribute to survival until it actually worked as part of the whole. It would be eliminated by the very natural selection that atheists preach. As Professor Jerry R. Bergman points out:

The origin of life could not have occurred by a gradual process but must have been instantaneous [because] every machine must have a certain number of parts for it to function. . . . Even most bacteria require several thousand genes to carry out the functions necessary for life. . . . The simplest species of bacteria, Chlamydia and Rickettsia [which are] about as small as it is possible to be and still be living . . . require millions of atomic parts. . . . All of the many macromolecules necessary for life are constructed of atoms . . . composed of even smaller parts . . . and the only debate is *how many* millions of functionally integrated parts are necessary. . . .

Overly simplified, life depends on a complex arrangement of three classes of molecules: DNA, which stores the cell's master plans; RNA, which transports a copy of the needed information contained in the DNA to the protein assembly station; and proteins, which make up everything from the ribosomes to the enzymes. Further, chaperons and many other assembly tools are needed to ensure that the protein is properly assembled. All of these parts are necessary and must exist as a properly assembled and integrated unit. . . . The parts could not evolve separately and could not even exist independently for very long, because they would break down in the environment without protection. . . . For this reason, only an instantaneous creation of all necessary parts as a functioning unit could produce life.

No compelling evidence has ever been presented to disprove this conclusion, and much evidence exists for the instantaneous creation requirement. . . . A cell can come only from a functioning cell and cannot be built up piecemeal . . . to exist as a living organism, the human body *had* to be created fully formed.[3]

The evolutionist's confident response is *natural selection*! It doesn't all have to happen at once but in gradual stages over millions and billions of years. Dawkins mocks the creationist's rhetorical question, "What is the use of half an eye? What is the use of half a wing?"

Dawkins makes that which is not just improbable but *impossible* sound very probable—gradual and tiny steps up the gentle evolutionary slope, but he fails to mention that an *Impassable* swamp had to be crossed and *Impossible* cliffs had to be scaled just to reach the base of Mount *Improbable*. The "half a wing" has to be attached to some living thing—a creature composed of atoms, molecules, cells, and DNA, which are only lumps of useless chemicals, unless they have somehow been made alive. The mathematical odds against the molecules needed for the smallest cell coming together by chance are off the chart, and to "evolve by slow . . . gradual degrees" is impossible because natural selection can't do its job at that early stage. So we are dealing with *chance* that cannot be ruled out by natural selection. Moreover, there would be only blobs of chemicals at this stage. Where did the life come from? We don't know what life is or how it invades, or attaches to, or animates lifeless matter.

Furthermore, seemingly forgotten is the fact that if the universe began with a "big bang," life could never arise thereafter even in a trillion years. Contrary to atheist Richard Carrier's claim, absolutely no "facts support" spontaneous generation of life out of dead matter. The law of biogenesis has not been overturned. Certainly, no facts support life arising spontaneously from matter that has endured temperatures hotter than the center of our sun. Instead of evidence, atheists offer speculation—and speculation that flies not only in the face of the universally acknowledged law of biogenesis but in the face of other laws as well.

SAND CASTLES WASHED INTO A LIFELESS COSMIC OCEAN

With the extinction of the universe, there will be no record left of human history, no one to mourn man's passing, with his unfulfilled ambitions, corporate dreams, and schemes. There will be no one to be impressed with the accumulation of endless volumes of speculation and ingenious inventions, and no one to care one whit that all of it has become like sand castles washed into a cosmic ocean of nothingness. Cosmologist Edward Harris wrote, "Tens of billions of years pass in the growing darkness . . . of a universe condemned to become a galactic graveyard." Isn't this a cheerful prospect that natural selection promises to us?

That epitaph, of course, is pronounced in advance upon all that Russell wrote as well. So why did he spend the time and energy writing what his own philosophy declared to be a complete waste of time? Is there some faint spark of hope even among atheists, perhaps some intuition that something of man continues after the death of the body? Otherwise, why such great effort expended in this life to stave off death a short while longer in order to leave some meaningless record of one's having been here?

If we are nothing more than containers of molecules, whose lives, fondest ambitions, and greatest accomplishments mean nothing at all, then why cling to life in a world that has a way of making mere existence difficult? Why not rather commit collective suicide than keep up this pretense of smiles and enjoyment? In a foolish attempt to find a silver lining in the cloud of gloom and doom that atheism hangs over our heads—something worth living for—Richard Dawkins writes:

> In *Unweaving the Rainbow* I tried to convey how lucky we are to be alive, given that the vast majority of people who could potentially be thrown up by the combinatorial lottery of DNA will in fact never be born. . . . We are staggeringly lucky. . . . However brief our time in the sun, if we waste a second of it, or complain . . . couldn't this be seen as a callous insult to those unborn trillions who will never be offered life in the first place?
>
> As many atheists have said it better than me, the knowledge that we have only one life should make it all the more precious. The atheist view is correspondingly life-affirming and life-enhancing, while at the same time never being tainted with self-delusion. . . .[4]

Whatever can Dawkins be talking about? We are "lucky" to have a brief millisecond on the cosmic time scale of meaninglessness only to pass into oblivion? No, it is not we who are "lucky" but our selfish genes and molecules, who hold our meaningless destiny in their hands. Do they have any concept of luck or what it means to be alive, even for a moment?

Why, then, would natural selection endow us with the instinct of self-survival to keep ourselves working at an eight-to-five job and entertaining ourselves in our brief time off before we fall exhausted into bed, only to awaken for another meaningless day? All this to escape the ultimate truth of our fast-approaching demise and passage into oblivion? Why endure the sweat and pain of life, plodding through university, earning advanced degrees, and engaging in laborious research and endless writing and speaking in order to be famous or to help future generations? Why should we care? Whence this pride and ambition?

Surely, if there is no God, the old saying, "Let us eat, drink, and be merry, for tomorrow we die," makes more sense, but how can one engage in merriment while carrying the weight of this misbegotten philosophy? Something within even atheists must rise up in anger against this nihilistic philosophy of their own making.

The fact that death is not the end but rather just the beginning of something more has been the universal hope, or dread, of all races at every strata of society as long as man has been on this earth. Man is an incurably religious being. As a result, another huge and impassable chasm yawns between man and all lower forms of life that evolution cannot possibly bridge. Confirmation of this fact is found everywhere among primitive peoples and continues in every race and culture to this day. Modern science has rejected belief in God. What has been the result? Ironically, it has been a return to the superstition of nature worship that once prevailed before science became totally materialistic and pronounced the death of God.

LOST WITHOUT GOD

Rejection of the Creator leads to two realities: 1) the hopelessness expressed above because, as Professor Paul Davies, formerly of the Australian Centre for Astrobiology at Macquarie University in Sydney and now a research director at Arizona State University, aptly said, "No agency, intelligent or otherwise, can delay forever the end of the universe. Only a supernatural God could try to wind it up again"; and 2) a return to primitive worship of the cosmos. After all, if the cosmos is all there is, and if, after displaying its power in a fantastic explosion of energy that created all the elements, it formed itself into stars and galaxies and living things, shouldn't we worship it as the god that made us? Such is the backward thinking of many scientists today.

This is exactly what Carl Sagan believed and did as he followed atheism and evolution to where they logically led him. This was also where Pierre Teilhard de Chardin, once a Jesuit priest, ended up through his embrace of evolution: "If . . . I were to lose in succession my faith in Christ, my faith in a personal God, and my faith in spirit, I feel that I should continue to believe invincibly in the world. The world (its value, its infallibility and its goodness)—that, when all is said and done, is the first, the last and the only thing in which I believe. It is by this faith that I live."[5]

These men, who seem so brilliant in other ways, rebel against conscience and reason in order to deny God in spite of the abundant evidence He has placed all around them in the universe that He made. They excuse themselves for not believing in God because they say that such a belief would open the door to miracles, which can't possibly happen as it would violate the laws of nature. Then they attribute miracles to the universe itself. Paul Davies exposed the embarrassing irony. He said that the Big Bang

> . . . represents the instantaneous suspension of physical laws, the sudden abrupt flash of lawlessness that allowed something to come out of nothing, it represents a true miracle—transcending physical principles. . . .[6]

The Big Bang is a philosophical theory that has been "corrected" many times, is not backed by scientific consensus, is contradicted by recent observations, and has aroused increasing opposition among many scientists. It represents one more desperate effort for atheists to escape God. *Desperate?* Yes. Without that necessity, the biblical declaration, "In the beginning God created the heaven and the earth," would find universal acceptance.

One thing is certain: very little in astronomy is certain. The almost endless contradictions among the world's great astronomers are reason enough for us to have little confidence in any theory they propose concerning the origin of the universe. We will present a very simple and easily verifiable proof that the Bible is true from Genesis to Revelation, proof that gives us every confidence in the validity of its opening statement (just quoted above) and in all that follows, to the last word of the Bible. In the meantime, let's see what scientists have to say as they contradict one another.

THE "BIG BANG" RUNS INTO A WALL OF OPPOSITION

Opposition to the Big Bang theory has been underway almost since it was first proposed. More than eighteen years ago, an article in an international news magazine declared, "A spate of articles in both the popular and scientific press point to disturbing discrepancies between recent astronomical findings and the Big Bang theory."[7] That opposition has steadily increased among scientists. Numerous scientific studies and entire books have been written against it such as *Bye Bye Big Bang: Hello Reality* by cosmologist William Mitchell and *Big Bang Blasted* by physicist Lyndon Ashmore, a book written for laymen.

There are enough problems with the Big Bang to fill several volumes. For example, our galaxy, the Milky Way, has supposedly rotated only 50-60 times since the alleged Big Bang, far too few rotations and too short a time to have developed its spiral shape. Other galaxies that are calculated to be so close to the time of the Big Bang that they have rotated only two or three times are nevertheless shaped like ours. Furthermore, galaxies very close to the occasion of the supposed Big Bang are much farther apart than they should be, according to that theory. There are galaxies so close to the alleged moment of the Big Bang that they couldn't have had time to mature, yet they have.

The very idea of some galaxies being closer to the Big Bang and others much farther away is itself suspect. How could some fragments of the Big Bang be "closer" by billions of light years to the original point where the explosion supposedly took place? Everything that came out of the Big Bang ought to be at relatively the same distance from that point in time and space—certainly not separated by billions of light years. It makes more sense for the stars and galaxies to have been created in place, as the Bible declares.

The structure of the entire universe contradicts the theory of a "big bang." We can't even fit the formation of our own solar system into the Big Bang. For example, "Examining the faint light from an elderly Milky Way star, astronomers have detected a far greater abundance of beryllium atoms than the standard Big Bang model predicts."[8] Nobel laureate in physics, Hannés Alfven, argued that since it is without empirical support, the Big Bang "is only a myth that attempts to say how the universe came into being. . . ."[9] Malcolm Longair, Jacksonian Professor of Natural Philosophy in the Cavendish Laboratory, Cambridge University, England, cites several basic problems related to the Big Bang that remain unsolved:

1. The origin of the baryon asymmetry in the universe.

2. The origin of the spectrum of fluctuations from which galaxies and clusters form.

3. The origin of the isotropy of the universe. . . .[10]

Questions are legion. Is there, or isn't there, a spacetime continuum? Are space and time curved? Does "mathematical space" have a "fractional number of dimensions"? Is it a "lattice"? Are there, perhaps, no spacetime points at all? There is no agreement in response to such problems. Scientists have a multitude of questions with few definitive answers. As Chris Isham, Professor of Theoretical Physics at the Blanket Laboratory, Imperial College, London, England, confesses, "We simply do not know."[11] One critic writes:

> And the myths we are told . . . start with the Big Bang, which *somehow* begets stars and galaxies. Galaxies *somehow* contrive to form spirals. . . . Stellar nebulae *somehow* beget planets from a disk of dust and gas. The Earth *somehow* finds itself with a lot of water and a large moon. Venus *somehow* is hellishly hot, has no moon and spins slowly backwards. "*Somehow*" is the operative process in modern cosmology. Perhaps we shouldn't be surprised that *somehow* we are giving Nobel prizes to those responsible for revitalizing this nonsense. . . .
>
> We don't understand the real nature of matter or its interactions via gravity or light. . . . And as for the tests of the Big Bang hypothesis, they are viewed through the distorting lens of preconception. Afterwards theory is bent to fit. That may explain the "Alice in Wonderland" appeal of cosmology— "*Why, sometimes I've believed as many as six impossible things before breakfast.*"
>
> It is not that most of the matter and energy in the universe is dark, but that most cosmologists are totally in the dark about the real nature of the universe.[12]

In spite of the unanswered questions and the mounting opposition, this theory keeps being resurrected. More amazing is the fact that the Nobel Prize in Physics 2006 went for research that supposedly bolstered support for the Big Bang. It was awarded to George Smoot from the University of California, Berkeley, and John Mather, the Goddard Space Flight Center's head COBE scientist, "for their co-discovery of the blackbody form and anisotropy of the cosmic microwave background radiation." Meanwhile, opposition to this theory continues to mount throughout the scientific community.

Some critics point out that in 1947, George Gamow, a Manhattan Project scientist (after observing that an A-bomb explosion created new elements), was the first to suggest that the universe began with a giant explosion that created the matter we have today. These critics suggest that it was his talent for promotion and his immensely popular book, *One, Two, Three, Infinity,* that caused his theory to catch on quickly and become the predominant cosmology. It was his detractors who jokingly provided the label, "Big Bang."

Those who have devoted decades of their lives to supporting the Big Bang and whose professional careers depend upon its survival are not likely to open the door to those who oppose it. Big Bang critic Eric Lerner declares, "Entire careers in cosmology have been built on theories which have never been subjected to observational test, or have failed such tests and been retained nonetheless." Consequently, opposition is stifled by lack of peer review that closes the door to grants for further study and by the reluctance of the best journals to publish such papers. Reportedly, for example, Halton Arp "was squeezed out of his Palomar telescope assignment because the allotment committee would not permit telescope time to any non-Big Bang project."[13] Is there a scientific "mafia" protecting Big Bang promoters?

STILL, PROBLEMS PERSIST

Things are not as they ought to be in the universe had it all begun with a "big bang." An explosion of that magnitude should send its fragments uniformly flying in all directions. Yet there are billions of huge "lumps" in the universe, with no explanation as to how that came about.[14] If one applies the laws of physics to the Big Bang model, the universe ought to be "a cosmic vastness of evenly distributed atoms with no organization of any kind."[15] But, of course, it is anything but that. Lerner, not popular among mainstream cosmologists, points out,

> In 1986 astronomers discovered that galaxies compose huge
> agglomerations a billion light-years across; such mammoth

clustering of matter must have taken a hundred billion
years to form [in contrast to 15-20 billion years back to the
Big Bang]. . . . These enormous ribbons of matter, whose
reality was confirmed during 1990 . . . (The most dramatic
work was that of Margaret J. Geller and John P. Huchra of
the Harvard Smithsonian Center for Astrophysics, who . . .
in 1989 [discovered] what they called the "Great Wall,"
a huge sheet of galaxies stretching in every direction . . .
more than 200 million light-years across and seven hundred
million light-years long . . .) also refute a basic premise of
the Big Bang—that the universe was, at its origin, perfectly
smooth and homogeneous. Theorists . . . can see no way to
get from the perfect universe of the Big Bang to the clumpy
. . . universe of today. As one leading theorist, George Field
of the Harvard-Smithsonian Center for Astrophysics, put
it, "There is a real crisis."[16]

Others agree that "There shouldn't be galaxies out there at all, and
even if there are galaxies, they shouldn't be grouped together the way
they are."[17] Fred Hoyle concluded, "The main efforts of investigators
have been in papering over holes in the big-bang theory, to build up
an idea that has become ever more complex and cumbersome. I have
little hesitation in saying that a sickly pall now hangs over the big-bang
theory. When a pattern of facts becomes set against a theory, experience shows that the theory rarely recovers."[18] Ivars Peterson agrees:

> In its simplest form, the Big Bang scenario doesn't look like
> a good way to make galaxies. It allows too little time for
> the force of gravity to gather ordinary matter—neutrons,
> protons and electrons—into the patterns of galaxies seen
> today. Yet the theory survives for want of a better idea.[19]

Another problem is the rotary motions of galaxies: "Galaxy rota-
tion and how it got started is one of the great mysteries of astrophysics.
In a Big Bang universe, linear motions are easy to explain: They result
from the 'bang.' But what started the rotary motions?"[20] Adding to the

mystery is the fact that, whereas planets, moons, or satellites ought to rotate in the same direction as the bodies from which they were supposedly thrown off, Venus rotates backward to its orbit.

Not only is the "lumpiness" not explained but neither is the vastly varying chemical makeup of suns and planets that are allegedly related to one another. Earth and the other planets in the solar system were supposedly ejected from the sun into their orbits, but the sun is more than 98 percent hydrogen and helium—hardly good stuff for creating the earth or other planets. Nor do moon rocks give evidence of coming from the earth because their chemical makeup is so much different. Yet evolutionists persist in the belief that a giant asteroid or meteorite "tore the moon loose from earth."[21] How could a huge explosion sort out the chemicals into such distinct groups?

There are so many problems with the Big Bang theory that we can't cover them all. Walt Brown points out:

> One might also ask where the "cosmic egg" came from if there was a big bang. Of course, the question is un-answerable.... [Furthermore] if a tiny "cosmic egg" existed, consisting of all the mass in the universe, it should not explode, based on present understanding. Claiming some strange, new phenomenon caused an explosion (or inflation) is philosophical speculation. While such speculation may or may not be correct, it is not science.[22]

A major problem, as we have already noted and will comment upon further, is the fact that the universe does not have anything like the mass it ought to have if it resulted from the Big Bang. Years have been spent searching for it, but the missing mass has not been found. Numerous studies have, in fact, concluded that the missing mass simply does not, nor ever did, exist. "The observed universe just doesn't appear to have enough matter in it to explain the way it behaves now, nor the way theorists predict it will evolve."[23]

By so many observations and careful calculations, the present universe couldn't be the result of a "big bang," but read on.

EVEN MORE PROBLEMS WITH THE BIG BANG

According to the second law of thermodynamics, the law of entropy, the universe is going from order to disorder. But that doesn't fit with a theory that starts everything off with chaos of the ultimate kind, a huge explosion of everything. One cannot deny that if the universe steadily goes from order to less order, it must have been more highly ordered at its beginning than it is now. For the universe to have begun with a huge explosion (which itself is the ultimate disorder, and to have been sliding ever since into less order) couldn't have brought about today's highly ordered cosmos.

From the structure of the atom to the farthest reaches of the galaxies, we see an amazing picture of design that couldn't possibly have come about through an explosion of the material of which everything would be made by chance motions of atoms. Though not a creationist, molecular biologist Michael Denton stated it well:

> It is the sheer universality of perfection, the fact that everywhere we look, to whatever depth we look, we find an elegance and ingenuity of an absolutely transcending quality, which so mitigates against the idea of chance.
>
> Is it really credible that random processes could have constructed a reality, the smallest element of which—a functional protein or gene—is complex beyond our own creative capacities, a reality which is the very antithesis of chance, which excels in every sense anything produced by the intelligence of man?
>
> Alongside the level of ingenuity and complexity exhibited by the molecular machinery of life, even our most advanced artifacts appear clumsy. We feel humbled, as Neolithic man would in the presence of twentieth-century technology.[24]

Furthermore, this unimaginably huge explosion would produce at that instant a universe composed of nothing but expanding gas, but the random motions of hot gas surely have no information content, which of course comes only from an intelligence. For that reason also, to start it all with a "big bang" doesn't fit the life we see on Earth today, every part of which is dependent upon complex and exhaustive *written* information/instructions that directs every part of every living thing in its incredible functions and operation. Without doubt, the universe reflects the supreme power and organizational genius of an intelligence that transcends our finite comprehension.

The universe is filled with information, most of it far beyond man's present capabilities to duplicate or comprehend, even with the most advanced technology. How did a giant explosion of all that existed produce the astonishingly detailed, incredibly complex, and ingeniously organized information that combined atoms and molecules throughout the universe so that everything works together in such precision with everything else, and all by chance, with only energy to guide it? How did the structure of a single living cell, so amazing in its complexity, get injected into a universe that began in lifeless chaos? The cell and the life it exhibits certainly could not be the result of a giant explosion.

Such vast and brilliant information, which has organized this entire universe from the innermost depths of the atom to every living thing and on to the farthest galaxies, could come only from the One whose "Foot" scientism will not allow in the door.

MORE AND MORE PROBLEMS

The troubled theory that the universe began with a "big bang" some 15-18 billion years ago is placed in question by much additional scientific evidence to the contrary. We now know that when particles are brought into existence by a burst of energy, "pair production" occurs, creating an equal number of electrons and positrons, protons and antiprotons. Yet the universe is observed to have "an extreme dominance of matter over anti-matter, which contradicts the notion that a 'big bang' produced the matter that we see in the universe around us."[25] Jonathan Sarfati reminds us,

So if there is no matter to start with, and energy is converted to matter, the number of pluses must balance the number of minuses. But our universe is almost entirely matter.[26]

There is a further problem. The first law of thermodynamics tells us that no natural process can create energy. The foundation of the universe, however, is energy, and it could not have been here forever, according to the second law. There is only one conclusion we can come to, short of turning energy into a self-existent god to be worshiped: energy must have been brought into existence by some agency or power outside of, and independent of, the natural universe. Clearly, there can be no natural explanation for the universe. Again the evidence points us to a supernatural Creator. No wonder Stephen Hawking says it is difficult to contemplate the origin of the universe without reference to a Creator.

It is now estimated that a trillion galaxies exist, each with hundreds of billions of stars. That would mean there are *hundreds of billions of trillions of stars*. What a universe! Though the public is periodically propagandized with accounts of "the formation of stars," the truth is that astronomers have no workable explanation for how even one star formed! Harvard University astrophysicist Abraham Loeb, a leader in the search for extraterrestrial life, admits that "we don't understand star formation at a fundamental level."[27] University of Toronto Professor J. Richard Bond, Director of the Canadian Institute for Theoretical Astrophysics and Canada's most highly cited cosmologist, likewise acknowledges, "It's a huge mystery exactly how stars form."[28]

Nothing would seem to be more basic to the universe than stars and galaxies, yet leading astronomers confess that the origin of stars represents one of the most fundamental unsolved problems of contemporary astrophysics.[29] One can no more explain how stars came from a "big bang" than how life resulted from it. Once again, the only explanation that avoids these many contradictions necessitated by atheism is a simple belief in the Creator to whom all the evidence points—but that admission would pull the rug out from under the atheistic majority who claim to speak for science today.

The major hypothesis has the expanding gas from the force of the explosion clumping together to form clouds that would attract other clouds until the mass would become great enough to attract additional gas and eventually collapse upon itself. The laws of physics would preclude such lumping of matter in what should be a homogeneous expansion. The gas would have to contract in order to form clusters, and to do so would contradict the laws of physics, which declare that gas expands rather than contracts. University of South Carolina Physics and Astronomy Professor Danny Faulkner elaborated on the problem in an interview:

> Stars supposedly condensed out of vast clouds of gas, and it has long been recognized that clouds don't spontaneously collapse and form stars; they need to be pushed somehow. . . . There have been a number of suggestions to get the process started, and almost all of them require having stars to start with [to ignite the cloud of condensed gas]. . . .[30]

Not only is the formation of stars a mystery, but the rapid change that has been observed in some has been startling and certainly not what astronomers have predicted from a "big bang." Sarfati gives a particularly interesting example of a star in the constellation of Sagittarius that was discovered by the Japanese amateur astronomer Yukio Sakurai in February 1996:

> In 1994 this star was most likely a white dwarf . . . with a diameter about the same as earth's. . . . But a team of astronomers [from the USA and Sweden] have observed it change to a bright yellow giant . . . about 80 times wider than the sun. This means that the diameter has increased by a factor of 8,000 and the volume by a factor of over 500,000 million. The astronomers expressed great surprise at the rapidity at which this change occurred.
>   But [by] 1998, it had expanded . . . to a red supergiant with a diameter of 210 million km, 150 times that of the sun.

But as fast as it grew, it shrank, releasing much debris. By 2002, the star itself was invisible even to the most powerful optical telescopes. . . .

This is a good lesson. . . . Astronomers have not observed stars changing over millions of years, but now they have observed them changing over months![31]

So maybe the billions of years are, after all, part of an elaborate myth concocted to support the fantasy of evolution!

AND GALAXIES?

The same contradiction arises in the clumping of stars into galaxies. In addition, the European Space Agency recently discovered that "rather than being randomly distributed in space," galaxies themselves tend to cluster together[32]—a fact that also defies the Big Bang. Although James Trefil, professor of physics at George Mason University, Virginia, accepts the Big Bang, he highlights a major problem:

> The problem of explaining the existence of galaxies has proved to be one of the thorniest in cosmology. By all rights they just shouldn't be there, yet there they sit. It's hard to convey the depth of frustration that this simple fact induces among scientists.[33]

The same European Space Agency study indicated that galaxies had formed far earlier in the "evolution" of the universe than had been postulated previously. Of course, the only reason for furrowed brows among astronomers caused by the many contradictions this theory creates is their refusal to admit that God created the universe this way from the very beginning. With that honest admission, all of the contradictions would disappear. As Sarfati points out,

> A biblical solution is that the spiral galaxies did not evolve, but were created that way. God could easily have created

galaxies with different degrees of spiraling, bars, and ellipticals, and the variety would have declared "the glory of God." (Psalm 19:1)[34]

Genesis chapter 1 gives us the simple, straightforward, uncomplicated answer to every problem caused by this unworkable theory. The Bible does not describe a "big bang," though some Christians have imagined that it does. It presents the purposeful creation and orderly arrangement of the heavens and earth to support life on planet Earth. What Genesis describes is exactly what we see reflected in the universe all around us.

Did this amazing order in atoms and stars come about by chance, and all from a huge explosion? It simply isn't rational to believe such a fantasy, but this is the atheist's only hope if he is to escape accountability to a Creator.

PROBLEMS, PROBLEMS, PROBLEMS. . . .

It would take several books just to quote the many astronomers and astrophysicists who have written about the seemingly insurmountable problems that beset the theory of a "big bang." Why so many problems? Because the more we learn about the universe, the more certain it becomes that it could not have begun with a giant explosion of energy. The entire theory is under attack by eminent scientists:

> Astronomy, rather cosmology, is in trouble. . . . It has departed from the scientific method and its principles, and drifted into the bizarre; it has raised imaginative invention to an art form; and has shown a ready willingness to surrender or ignore fundamental laws, such as the second law of thermodynamics and the maximum speed of light. . . .
>
> Perhaps no "science" is receiving more self-criticism, chest beating, and self-doubt; none other seems so lost and misdirected; trapped in debilitating dogma.[35]

As noted above, the total mass of the universe is a very critical factor. For one thing, it would take a definite mass for galaxies to form, and it isn't there. In fact, "The estimated mass of the visible universe is less than a tenth of this critical value. [Yet] stars and galaxies exist. Therefore, the big bang probably did not occur. Faith in the big bang theory requires believing that a vast amount of invisible, unmeasurable mass is hidden somewhere."[36] After years of diligent searching, the missing mass cannot be found.

Nevertheless, to salvage this theory, scientists generally agree that most of the matter in the universe is invisible. They call it *dark matter*. It supposedly consists of some exotic particle that is yet to be discovered. So how do they know? That is quite a leap of faith to take to rescue a troubled theory. Its supporters take another leap into what they say is "an even more mysterious entity called *dark energy*."[37] This was an offshoot of Einstein's cosmological constant, a "fudge factor" that he invented in 1917 to accommodate the prevailing opinion at that time of a static universe and later abandoned as a "blunder" he regretted—but astronomers still cling to it as essential to the Big Bang theory.[38]

Theories are put forth, later facts prove them wrong, yet they survive. As stated, it is still widely accepted that the moon was torn off from the earth—but we now know that the chemical composition of its rocks is entirely different from those on Earth. More than twenty of the sixty-plus moons in our galaxy orbit backwards, compared to their planets' orbit around the sun—with no known explanation for this anomaly.

Once the solar system seemed simple, but it has become extremely complex, with increasing questions being raised. Today, its formation is more of a mystery than ever. Proponents of the Big Bang must explain the formation of our solar system on that basis, but they cannot. Stuart Ross Taylor, Emeritus Professor of Geology, Australian National University, has declared, "The ultimate origin of the solar system's angular momentum remains obscure."

The more information we accumulate about our solar system, the more questions arise. For example, while "our sun has over 99 percent of the mass of the solar system, it has only 2 percent of the angular momentum,"[39] a fact that doesn't fit the theories relative to the Big Bang and is only one more of an increasing array of facts that don't bode well for the survival of the theory. It seems increasingly difficult to reconcile our solar system with a "big bang" that occurred billions of years ago. Sarfati mentions another problem, and the solution:

> The sun's known energy source should make the sun shine ever more brightly over time. But this means that if billions of years were true, the sun would have been fainter in the past. However, there is no evidence that the sun was any fainter at any time in the earth's history. Astronomers call this the "faint young sun paradox," but it is no paradox at all if the sun is only as old as the Bible says—about 6,000 years.[40]

All of the problems related to explaining the origin of the cosmos have one thing in common: they refer to conditions that could not have come about through any known natural processes, least of all by a huge explosion of all matter. All of them demand a supernatural explanation. "In the beginning God created," if accepted by astronomers, would answer and eliminate every one of the questions that the Big Bang theory raises.

Why such reluctance to accept this obvious and certainly rational solution? It is not to protect any particular theory—but to protect *themselves* from a Creator to whom atheistic materialists would have embarrassing moral obligations.

AN OPEN LETTER

In spite of the many problems with the Big Bang that we have mentioned, most of the scientific establishment remains married to this theory. Those who oppose it are increasingly squeezed out of funded research. On May 22, 2004, *New Scientist* published "An Open Letter to the Scientific Community." Since then, hundreds of researchers around the world have added their signatures to this protest. In part, the letter said:

> The Big Bang theory can boast of no quantitative predictions that have subsequently been validated by observation. The successes claimed by the theory's supporters consist of its ability to retrospectively fit observations with a steadily increasing array of adjustable parameters, just as the old Earth-centered cosmology of Ptolemy needed layer upon layer of epicycles. . . .
>
> Big Bang proponents have won the political and funding battle so that virtually all financial experimental resources in cosmology are devoted to Big Bang studies. Funding comes from only a few sources, and supporters of the Big Bang dominate all the peer-review committees that control the funds. As a result, the dominance of the Big Bang within the field has become self-sustaining, irrespective of the scientific validity of the theory. . . .

The open letter resulted in a conference, "The First Crisis in Cosmology: Challenging Observations and the Quest for a New Picture of the Universe." It was held in Monçao, Portugal, June 23-25, 2005. One report reads:

> Three dozen physicists and astronomers reviewed the evidence for and against the Big Bang theory. . . . The conference, organized by the Alternative Cosmology Group, was a response to a flood of new observations that challenge the predictions of the Big Bang, the dominant theory of cosmology, and that have led increasing numbers of astronomers to think that the field has entered a crisis.
>
> Important new data was presented at the conference for the first time. Observation on globular clusters analyzed by Riccardo Scarpa of the European Southern Observatory cast doubt on the existence of dark matter, a key component of the Big Bang theory. . . .

The very basis of the Big Bang, the expansion of the universe, was called into serious question by data presented by Eric Lerner of Lawrenceville Plasma Physics, the conference chair . . . using new data from the Hubble Ultra Deep Field images, which show the most distant known galaxies. . . . The Big Bang predictions that distant galaxies would appear to have hundreds of times less surface brightness was completely contradicted. "The data clearly show that the universe is not expanding, and that the redshift of light must be due to some other cause. . . ." A third new result also contradicted the idea that the universe is expanding. . . .

Other scientists at the conference reviewed recently announced results that posed other serious challenges for the Big Bang [by] Francesco Sylos-Labini of the Enrico Fermi Institute . . . Glenn Starkman of Case Western Reserve University [and] Tom van Flandren of Meta Research [who] pointed out the growing gap between observations and the Big Bang predictions of light element advances, another key test to the theory. . . .

The Big Bang theory has long been characterized by an increasing array of hypothetical entities, like dark matter and dark energy that have been added to overcome contradictions with observation. Mike Disney of Cardiff University [showed why] the theory makes few or no meaningful predictions. . . . Geoffrey Burbridge of the University of California, San Diego, elaborated on the same point, showing that at critical junctures, evidence claiming to verify Big Bang predictions in fact did not. . . .

There were lively discussions and disagreements. Alain Blanchard of the Astrophysical Laboratory of Tarbes and Toulouse [made] a spirited defense of the Big Bang. . . . Participants intensely discussed how the pervasive fear especially young researchers face in criticizing the Big Bang can be overcome. . . .[41]

One critic who believes that the evidence against it is over-whelming and is eager to write its obituary has said: "So it is with a sigh of utter relief, we can dispose of all the whimsical nonsense accompanying the Big Bang hypothesis—the invisible dark matter, the dark energy, the expanding universe (whatever that meant) and creation of matter from nothing. (And cosmologists can don sack-cloth and ashes and admit their profound ignorance—while pigs perform aerobatics overhead and the Nobel committee asks for their prize money back.)"[42]

THE MOST IMPORTANT QUESTION REMAINS

The fundamental disagreement among scientists that we have been documenting is evidence that something very basic is wrong with some of the major theories. The key issue is *why* does the universe exist? So long as that vital question is shoved to one side, the confusion will continue. It should be abundantly clear by now that the explanation of how the universe works and why it exists is not to be found within the cosmos itself—but outside of it. There is no *natural* explanation that will unite all of the data. The evidence points inescapably to only one unifying answer: the cosmos came into existence by a supernatural, creative act of God.

Hawking suggests that when we discover "why it is that we and the universe exist . . . it would be the ultimate triumph of human reason—for then we should know the mind of God."[43] In a later book, Hawking hypothesized, "You still have the question: why does the universe bother to exist? If you like, you can define God to be the answer to that question."[44] But that is not an answer at all. What does he mean by *God*? That "god," not being personal, transcen-dent, and distinctly separate from the universe, could not possibly answer the question of why the universe exists. Moreover, if the true God, Creator of all, exists, He must have existed eternally before creating the universe, which surely is only one of His infinite deeds and therefore could not define God. For all of his brilliance in other directions, when it comes to God, Hawking stumbles badly.

Nature is neither self-existent nor conscious. Obviously, it could not create itself and cannot provide the reason for its own existence, nor could any "god" that is identical to nature. Only a Creator who is personal and exists separate and distinct from His creation could provide the answer that scientists seek to find within the cosmos itself. Furthermore, would it not make sense that this God has constituted the cosmos so as to frustrate every attempt to find a *natural* explanation—and has done so in order to force scientists, no matter how reluctantly, to acknowledge His existence?

Scientists invoke the magic of large numbers . . . knocking a few noughts off for reasons of ordinary prudence, a billion billion is a conservative estimate of the number of available planets in the universe. Now suppose the origin of life, the spontaneous arising of something equivalent to DNA, really was a quite staggeringly improbable event . . . so improbable as to occur on only one in a billion planets. . . . But here we are talking about odds of one in a billion. And yet . . . even with such absurdly long odds, life will still have arisen on a billion planets, of which earth, of course, is one.

—RICHARD DAWKINS, *THE GOD DELUSION*, 137-38

Take religion, for instance. If religion is all a pack of lies—a muddle of myths—why would natural selection allow religion to survive? How could natural selection allow a behavior that has nothing at all to do with the real world to develop in the first place?

—FRANK R. ZINDLER, "RELIGION, HYPNOSIS AND MUSIC: AN EVOLUTIONARY PERSPECTIVE," *AMERICAN ATHEIST*, VOL. 26 (OCTOBER 1984), 22

It is certainly true that one would be most unlikely to develop a functioning flying insect, reptile or bird by a chance collection of changes. Some sort of guidance is necessary. And in these cases, of course, natural selection is the only mechanism we know of to produce a workable combination of characteristics.

—DAVID M. RAUP, "CONFLICTS BETWEEN DARWIN AND PALEONTOLOGY," *BULLETIN*, FIELD MUSEUM OF NATURAL HISTORY, VOL. 50 (JANUARY 1979), 26

It seems to me that sociobiology [the idea that human social behavior can be explained by genetic and evolutionary background] aggravates its opponents by the ingenuity with which it produces explanations to make observations fit a theory. . . . Perhaps those who disbelieve and spurn sociobiological teachings may be responding to a genetic trait. The struggle against pre-ordained fate could in itself have a survival value. This struggle may include the rejection of theories that tell us we are in the grip of determinism imposed by our genes.

—THOMAS H. JUKES, "ON SOCIOBIOLOGY," *NATURE*, VOL. 270 (NOVEMBER 17, 1977), 203

In the meantime, the educated public continues to believe that Darwin has provided all the relevant answers by the magic formula of random mutation plus natural selection—quite unaware of the fact that random mutations turned out to be irrelevant and natural selection a tautology.

—ARTHUR KOESTLER, *JANUS: A SUMMING UP* (NEW YORK: VINTAGE BOOKS, 1978), 185

NINE

FROM BIG BANG TO LIFE?

W<small>E EACH BEGIN LIFE</small> as a single cell about the size of the period at the end of this sentence. That tiny, frail structure of billions of atoms and molecules, as Nobelist Linus Pauling pointed out, is more complex than New York City. It would have to be. In addition to its own ingenious and intricately complex chemical machinery, it contains the directions for forming and operating every part, process, and mechanism inside the 100-plus trillion cells that the mature body will comprise. These amazingly conceived and detailed *written and encoded* instructions are found at the nucleus of every cell (the smallest living unit) in what has come to be known as DNA (deoxyribonucleic acid), which also synthesizes RNA (ribonucleic acid). DNA molecules contain the formula for every living entity, whether plant, insect, animal, fish, or human.

Every kind of living thing follows its own particular DNA instruction manual. These are "chains of nucleotides [sub-microscopic molecules] . . . twisted together in an elegant spiral; the 'double helix'; the 'immortal coil,'" as Richard Dawkins calls it. He comments further:

> The nucleotide building blocks come in only four different kinds, whose names may be shortened to A,T,C, and G. These are the same in all animals and plants. What differs is the order in which they are strung together. [The] G building block from a man is identical in every particular to a G building block from a snail. But the *sequence* of building blocks is not only different from that in a snail. It is also different—though less so—from the sequence in every other man (except for the special case of identical twins).[1]

The organizational genius behind DNA is breathtaking. Consider the nearly infinite possibilities of this arrangement of molecules. Using only four letters, and the same ones for plants, animals, and man, distinction is maintained not only between all kinds of living things but between individuals of each kind. As we all know, no two members of the human race except identical twins have the same DNA—a fact invaluable in identifying remains left from disasters, in solving crimes, tracing ancestry, etc. This ingenious arrangement sets bounds that make it impossible for DNA of one kind to change into DNA of another kind. The similarity between man's DNA and that of all animals is no more evidence that man evolved from animals (as evolutionists insist) than is the similarity in human and plant and insect DNA evidence that man evolved from insects and plants.

How can one explain the incredible genius in the organization and operation of DNA of which Dawkins speaks? Atheists must attribute this to the DNA itself, but that is no answer to what we confront in this amazing organization of matter. In fact, it is absurd! As we have already mentioned, Einstein explained that there is no way for matter to arrange itself into information.[2] The explanation of that fact is rejected out of hand by atheists, without any evidential reason for doing so. Here we are, back to the foundational argument between chance and reason, between atheism and God. This argument is inescapable and of course consumes a large part of this book.

Had Darwin known about DNA, he might never have come up with his theory. He assumed an evolutionary relationship between species on the basis of similarities in physical appearance and common functions he had observed. The same mistake is still made today by evolutionists. That is like saying that all automobiles, airplanes, and everything else that has an engine must be related. In a sense they are, but only because common functions require common designs—not because one evolved into the other. It is the purpose of the machine and the environment in which it is to function that dictates its design. And that, simply, is why all land creatures large enough have hearts, lungs, brains, and limbs, etc. A far better explanation of the similarity in design, rather than being proof that all evolved from a common ancestor, would be that they have all been designed by one Creator to function on the same planet.

SLAMMING THE DOOR ON EVOLUTION

One of many mysteries surrounding DNA is the strange fact that the slightly greater number of genes in man compared with those in lower forms of life is nowhere near proportional to man's far greater complexity. Francis Collins writes, "Many of us were stunned to discover that God writes such short stories about humankind. That was especially shocking in the context of the fact that the gene counts for other simpler organisms such as worms, flies, and simple plants seem to be in about the same range [as humans] . . . around 20,000."[3]

Even so, most of the capacity of the genome is left unused, a fact that seems to deal a serious blow to evolution. How, and *why*, did natural selection develop a huge DNA capacity in man that it never needed or used? For theists, why God did this is also a question, but He is free and more than able to do what He pleases for His own reasons, which we may only later discover with further analysis.

There is so much that we are discovering about the body that we didn't previously know, particularly about what had long been thought of as useless vestigial parts. One recent discovery is the "primary cilia."

These tiny slivers (about 1/1000 the size of the cell) protrude from most cells in the body and have been ignored heretofore as of no use. Now we know that they play a key role in the development of the fetus, for example, and throughout the life of the body. They act as almost microscopic antennae that sense what is going on in the body and send signals shaping the fetus, signaling division of cells, and making certain of normal adult cell growth. They heal wounds and grow cells. If they malfunction, they could cause cancer. This is only further evidence of how little we know about the human body, from a single cell to the millions of cells that make up the body.[4]

Natural selection, on the other hand, supposedly produces only what is essential for survival. Collins writes:

> Some observers have taken this as a real insult to human complexity [but] clearly gene count must not be the whole story. By any estimation, the biological complexity of human beings considerably exceeds that of a roundworm, with its total of 959 cells, even though the gene count is similar for both.[5]

The genome contained in the tiny dot of matter that signals the beginning of each person as a living being comprises the DNA. Here we have in this microscopic bit of matter detailed directions for the construction and healthy operation of *each* of the thousands of different kinds among the 100 trillion-plus cells that together make up the human body. "To view just half of your genome, you would have to view 10 nucleotides every second for 40 hours per week for 40 years! The apparent simplicity of this language system is deceptive."[6]

Nowhere is the potential for diversity seen more clearly than in the genome. Natural selection is not evolution at work; it is simply the result of the near-infinite variety built into the DNA. With the copying errors that have accumulated over the past 6,000 years, some of the offspring will be more suitable to cope with the environment than others, but none will escape the genetic restrictions and become another kind of creature.

The possible variety of human sperm and egg cells is about 25 times the number of atoms in the known universe. Multiply that possibility (1 followed by 2,017 zeroes) by the astonishing genetic potential for variety within each sperm or egg cell, and the possible assortment of physical characteristics among humans is beyond imagination. The same is true, to varying degrees, in all living things. This is why Noah didn't need to bring more than one pair of each kind of creature into the ark.

The exhaustive instructions, written in words on DNA molecules, point unmistakably to an intelligent source beyond human comprehension. Could any natural process create the information contained in DNA? Absolutely not! It is indisputable that the intelligent Author of the information that DNA contains could only be nonphysical and of infinite wisdom and knowledge.

Thomas Jefferson was not a Christian by any stretch but a confirmed materialist who did not believe in souls, spirits, angels, or devils. He declared: "To talk of immaterial existences is to talk of *nothings*. To say that the human soul, angels, god, are immaterial, is to say they are nothings, or that there is no god, no angels, no soul. I cannot reason otherwise. . . ."[7]

The shallowness of Jefferson's thinking is very disappointing, coming from someone we admire in so many other ways. Ideas such as "kind," "ingenious," "thorough," are obviously nonphysical, as must be the mind that holds them. If ideas only exist in the physical brain, and if humans are merely stimulus-response mechanisms, what was it *physically* that caused the reaction *nothings* in Jefferson's mind?

To Einstein, the sharp distinction between matter and information indicated that language is a nonmaterial reality distinct from energy or any other physical form. Therefore, the unbridgeable chasm between matter and language/information is commonly known among linguists as the "Einstein gulf."[8] This "gulf" marks the difference between the idea itself and the medium that conveys it, whether computer, CD, DVD, paper and ink, or any other physical object upon which the idea is recorded. That distinction carries serious consequences for atheistic materialists.

It is indisputable that the written instructions that are obeyed by the cells and inscribed in DNA no more originated the information their word arrangement conveys than did the ink and paper originate the ideas expressed upon the page you are now reading. The gene neither understands the detailed and complex instructions that it follows nor makes a choice to do so. Furthermore, being nonmaterial (as all ideas are, though of necessity communicated by physical means), the written information contained in the language inscribed in the DNA could neither be caused nor modified by natural selection, which can only affect material things. DNA, in fact, slams the door in evolution's face. Mathematician and information scientist Andrew McIntosh put it like this:

> The major obstacle to evolutionary theories of origins is that information cannot be defined in terms of physics and chemistry. The ideas in a book are not the same as the paper and ink, which constitute the book. . . . Meaning cannot spontaneously arise, since meaning presupposes intelligence and understanding. To argue that this [information in the DNA] came by chance is scientifically preposterous . . . there is no mechanism in Darwinian evolution to add new information to a species at the macro level. . . . As Professor Gitt has stated: "No information can exist without an initial mental source. . . ." Thus the very existence of the DNA-coded language stalls evolution at the first hurdle.[9]

THE LANGUAGE OF THE CREATOR?

Geneticists have only recently learned to read—in a limited way—the encoded text of this fantastic manufacturer's instruction manual. Collins calls it "the language by which God spoke life into being." No scientist has any explanation for how the code was conceived and put into DNA. Acknowledging that it is "a language we understand very poorly," Collins adds, "it will take decades, if not centuries, to understand its instructions. . . ."[10] How, then, does each cell identify and follow its particular instructions? One thing is certain: unthinking natural processes could not create the intricate and exhaustive information in this ingenious blueprint of life—and there is no life without it.

There is *nothing* in Darwinism to account for this complex instruction manual. How could there be, when Darwin knew nothing of DNA? Its language wouldn't be even partially decoded until more than a century after Darwin's death.

Natural selection is a theory that attempts to show that DNA was actually the engine of evolution. This is the same underhanded reasoning that the evolutionist routinely uses: a "big bang" without any explanation of the origin of the energy involved or how this giant explosion occurred, much less why; a theory of what happens in the alleged evolutionary development of species without any explanation of how the first living cell came into existence; silence about the origin of the atoms and molecules that make up the cells, organs, and species that natural selection influences; exhaustive study of the coded message in DNA by which natural selection allegedly develops species, while denying that language itself requires an intelligent source; denial that nothing less than an infinite intelligence could be the author of the ingenious directions in that fantastic instruction manual, etc. Sadly, like Francis Collins, many other professing Christians are guilty of this same intellectual dishonesty.

One is reminded of the story of the group of atheists who challenged God: "We can do anything you can do, so we don't need you as an explanation any more."

God asked, "Can you make a man?"

The atheists replied, "Of course we can! You made a man out of dirt—we'll make a man out of dirt."

The determined group then discussed at length among themselves where they might collect the most promising soil samples from around the globe.

"Oh, no," God sternly interrupted. "You make your own dirt."

DNA: A CURE FOR ATHEISM

Announcing that the human genome code was finally cracked (though it possibly may take centuries to *understand* its instructions), in a statement that did not endear him to atheists but with which most Americans agreed, former President Clinton declared, "Today we are learning the language in which God created life."[11] On that point, at least, Clinton was right. His conclusion, as we shall see, was logically inescapable from the evidence, yet it is harshly denounced by those who have sworn not to acknowledge God's existence.

In spite of his own atheism, Richard Dawkins concedes, "The genetic code is truly digital, in exactly the same sense as computer codes. This is not some vague analogy; it is the literal truth."[12] Neither Dawkins, however, nor his fellow atheists have been able to propose a rational explanation of how the encoded information originated and became part of the first DNA. It takes a mind to design the desired structure, create the alphabet, and write out the instructions in code. No evolutionary/natural selection process could ever do that. To conceive and write blueprints and codes takes a personal intelligence, not a natural process.

Nor could it be an ordinary mind but one that is all-knowing. The plans for, let us say, a high-rise office building must be completed *before* construction begins. The body is far more complex than a high-rise building. Blueprints don't write themselves; they are conceived and written by a personal intelligence. The plans exist in the mind of the architect before they are put into a computer, to be adhered to by the construction crew. Clearly, the DNA instructions for every living thing had to exist in the mind of the ultimate Intelligence who is the supreme architect of all living things. This seemingly endless store of written instructions (which had to be written in advance) could not be devised by anyone less than the Creator himself. They could not be "written" by any other agent.

It was at New York University, in May 2004, that Antony Flew, at that time still known as the world's most notorious atheist, shocked the academic world. He had been almost a cult figure to atheist intellectuals. At this, his last public debate, says Flew, "I announced that I now accepted the existence of God." Stating that "recent work on the origin of life pointed to the activity of a creative Intelligence," he went on to explain in a book:

> What I think the DNA material has done is that it has shown, by the almost unbelievable complexity of the arrangements which are needed to produce (life), that intelligence must have been involved in getting these extraordinarily diverse elements to work together. It's the enormous complexity of the number of elements and the enormous subtlety of the ways they work together . . . which looked to me like the work of intelligence.[13]

Unwilling to lose one of their most famous stars, the atheists have tried to discredit this book by Flew. There have been suggestions that he is elderly and senile, unable to write the book himself. On at least one occasion, during a panel discussion, Dawkins himself publicly stated that Flew fell into the hands of unscrupulous Christians who actually wrote the book and put Flew's name on it. The recognized atheist authority for the claims that Flew's book wasn't written by him is one of the "New Atheists," Richard Carrier, author of *Sense and Goodness Without God*, whose biography states that he was raised going to Sunday School, became a Philosophical Taoist at age 15, and a secular humanist atheist at age 21.[14]

Has Flew become a Christian? Not as of the date he wrote the book, but as a Deist he is investigating the claims of Christ with an open mind, willing to face the truth. The testimony to that fact is in Flew's inclusion of more than 26 pages of arguments for the resurrection of Christ by his friend N. T. Wright. Is this book a fraud, as Dawkins claims? I do not believe so. HarperCollins would never issue such a book carrying its imprint. Here is a press release from the publisher, issued November 7, 2007, quoting Flew:

> My name [Antony Flew] is on the book and it represents exactly my opinions. I would not have a book issued in my name that I do not 100 percent agree with. I needed someone to do the actual writing because I'm 84 and that was Roy Varghese's role. The idea that someone manipulated me because I'm old is exactly wrong. I may be old but it is hard to manipulate me. This is my book and it represents my thinking.

Harper One deputy publisher Mark Tauber added, "We stand behind this book. Roy Varghese took Tony's thoughts and put them in publishable form. This is not an unusual practice." Tauber adds, "Unfortunately, the *NYT Magazine* writer generalized from Flew's aphasia to senility—which is far from accurate. Additionally, the *NYT* writer completely skipped the philosophical content of the book, dismissing Tony's arguments for God's existence in one word, calling it 'pseudoscience' and so insulting both Tony and anyone persuaded that these arguments might be true."

FOLLOWING "THE ARCHITECT'S PLANS"

To credit natural processes with the invention and implementation of a "digital code" is tantamount to worshiping nature as all-knowing and all-powerful. Not only are those instructions written down in a digitally encoded language, but only certain protein molecules can decode and read them. Dawkins demonstrates further his bias and refusal to face undeniable proof for the existence of God:

> As an adult, you consist of a thousand [it should be 100] million million cells, but when you were first conceived you were just a single cell, endowed with one master copy of the *architect's plans*. This cell divided into two, and each of the two cells received its own copy of *the plans*.
>
> Successive divisions took the number of cells up . . . into the billions. At every division the *DNA plans* were faithfully

copied, with scarcely any mistakes. . . . The *coded message* of the DNA . . . is *translated* . . . into another alphabet . . . the alphabet of amino acids, which *spells out* protein molecules. . . . Proteins not only constitute much of the physical fabric of the body; they also exert sensitive control over all the chemical processes inside the cell, selectively turning them on and off at precise times and in precise places. *Exactly how this eventually leads to the development of a baby is a story which it will take decades, perhaps centuries, for embryologists to work out.* [Emphasis added][15]

The italicized words are those Dawkins is forced to use in order even to talk about what DNA and the protein of which it is made accomplish in the construction and operation of any cell. Yet the very words he uses unavoidably spell out *purpose*, the one thing he steadfastly denies because that could come only from a personal God. Purpose on God's part is also denied by Francis Collins even more firmly than by other theistic evolutionists. Collins's "God" only foreknows what will happen but keeps hands off and lets natural processes take their course.

Incredibly, though claiming to be Christian, Collins rejects the first eleven chapters of Genesis. Therein the Bible clearly declares that God created man in a specific act, not over billions of years, as Collins claims. Elevating evolution above God, Collins, instead of crediting God with a specific act of creation, attributes to Him merely the foreknowledge that this would all happen through natural selection! He credits God with

> . . . knowing the precise outcome of the formation of the universe even before it started . . .
>
> . . . foreknowledge of a planet near the outer rim of an average spiral galaxy that would have just the right characteristics to allow life . . .
>
> . . . foreknowledge that that planet would lead to the development of sentient creatures through the mechanism of evolution through natural selection.[16]

This is an astonishing statement from a man who professes to be a Christian. The "God" Collins believes in knows what is going to happen, but he neither causes nor controls the actual creation of man and lower creatures. Collins's theory contradicts the Genesis account of creation of all species, including mankind. It downgrades God from Creator to passive observer watching the alleged marvel of natural selection taking its cruel, inefficient, laborious, time-consuming, deadly, and wasteful course over "millions of years" that should have left billions of carcasses of "missing links." Such inefficiency and waste of life could all have been avoided had Collins's "God" followed the Genesis creation account!

AN "UNSATISFACTORY GOD"?

Dawkins is perfectly willing to attribute, as did Einstein, God-like powers to nature. He quotes with full approval Carl Sagan's statement, "If by 'God' one means the set of physical laws that govern the universe, then clearly there is such a God."[17] Although this is what Dawkins means when he refers to *architect's plans* and *apparent purpose*, such concepts do not fit impersonal nature. The fact that what the evolutionist chooses to call "natural selection" can only be described in such terms points unavoidably to an *architect* who is capable of thinking, planning, foreseeing, making, and executing such plans—yet inexplicably doesn't. This is certainly not the "selfish gene."

Dawkins takes refuge behind "natural selection" to escape the creationists' proof that mathematically the probability of life and species developing by chance is zero. He points out that natural selection does not operate by chance. But natural selection doesn't even come into play before there is a functioning cell or organ. The components of even one cell (let alone the many complex workings of a heart, liver, or kidney) could not be held in suspense waiting for all to evolve and join together.

There is no purpose in matter (or nature), yet this is all the materialist says we are. This leads Dawkins into a dead end with no escape except to turn around—which he will not do. He has agreed that "natural selection has built us and it is natural selection we must understand if we are to comprehend our own identities." On the contrary, "natural selection" is an impersonal and unthinking process. Nature knows nothing of *personal* "identities" and can provide no understanding of our identity for us. This is why Sagan had to admit that this nature-is-God idea "is emotionally unsatisfying . . . it does not make much sense to pray to the law of gravity."[18]

Just the word *unsatisfying* reveals an impassable gulf between humans and nature. If natural selection has made us, why would we find that belief to be an unsatisfying idea? The fact that to "pray to the law of gravity" is so obviously ridiculous shows that the very concept of prayer could not be the product of natural selection. If, in fact, natural selection is the god that created us, wouldn't we all be content with this belief? Why should atheists have to write books and engage in debate in order to convince the rest of us that they are right? Shouldn't natural selection have already programmed that belief into our genes? And if natural selection did so, why should it be true? Why should natural selection also deliberately delude us with producing what *appears* to be design but couldn't possibly be?

Of course, medical researchers legitimately want to understand how the fetus develops in order to combat disease and any problems that could arise in the womb. Atheistic geneticists such as Dawkins, however, pursue their research, hoping to discover a purely materialistic, naturalistic explanation for life that would once and for all relieve them of any accountability to the personal God of the Bible. Why should they find the idea of such an unsatisfactory "god" *satisfying*? Are they really searching for Ponce de León's fountain of youth? Is the atheist's ultimate hope that science will at last conquer the atom, space, and disease so that man can rule as the immortal sovereign over all the forces of nature? Is that what makes Nature more acceptable than God—that it is susceptible to conquest so that we can use it to accomplish our will?

What Dawkins does not tell us is that the interrelationship of nucleotides and interaction between two or more genes (called *epistasis*) is "*infinitely complex* and virtually impossible to analyze, which is why geneticists have always conveniently ignored it."[19] The word *epistasis* is not found even once in the index of *The Selfish Gene*, nor does Crick discuss it in *The Astonishing Hypothesis*. Dawkins has one passing "could be" reference in *The Extended Phenotype*, without any explanation of how it "could" work. There is nothing in *The Blind Watchmaker, Climbing Mount Improbable,* or *The Greatest Show on Earth.* Such key omissions betray the fact that evolution cannot honestly pose as science because no one could possibly either explain or test it at this essential level.

A CHALLENGE ATHEISTS FAIL TO MEET

If geneticists are to understand what life is, how it functions, or where it came from, it must ultimately be at this molecular-cellular level. For evolutionists to defend their theory, they must find at the very foundation of all living things a non-supernatural origin for the information digitally encoded in a written language in the DNA. They must find a natural explanation of how the completely sterilized chaos of the alleged "big bang" could produce life.

They must explain how a natural process could conceive and print in an encoded language via DNA the massive yet microscopic instruction manual that tells each cell how it is to construct and operate the incredibly complex and delicate chemical nano-machinery it contains, and how to function thereafter in relation to every other cell and to the whole body. It is right here that those who reject a personal God have failed most miserably, because a natural explanation for DNA is impossible—an undeniable fact that even some atheist evolutionists reluctantly admit.

Though they boast of "cracking" the genetic code, geneticists cannot explain how this language could arise through any natural process to write and maintain this amazing instruction manual. Dawkins calls it "the architect's plans." Crick, in speaking of the structure of the brain and nervous system, says they "are built according to the same general plan."[20] But neither genes and DNA nor matter of any kind can make "plans." If atheism is to be defended, its champions *must* explain the Architect's instructions in written language and the compilation and communication of organized information without an intelligent, purposeful architect or planner.

It is self-evident that the written instructions on DNA, which Collins describes as "the most significant of all biological texts" and which create in him "an overwhelming sense of awe," could only originate with a conscious, intelligent author. Atheism has no plausible explanation for the origin of the coded language in DNA.

Furthermore, it is virtually impossible for an atheist to describe the astonishing function of DNA without using language that is incompatible with evolution/natural selection but which, instead, implies creation by a personal God (*architect's plans . . . general plan . . . apparent design*). This seems extremely odd. If, in fact, there is not a *personal* Creator of all things, why is there so much about the universe that points to one?

WHY SUCH PREJUDICE AGAINST A PERSONAL GOD?

Dawkins's writings present many examples of "God language," which he seems to find necessary in describing DNA, evolution, and natural selection in particular. Given his obvious hatred of the very thought of a personal God, one would think he would carefully avoid such language—but apparently, he finds that desirable course impossible to take, given the facts. He calls biology "the study of complicated things that *give the appearance of having been designed* for a purpose."[21] He writes, "Natural selection . . . has lifted life . . . to the dizzying heights of complexity, beauty and apparent design that dazzle us today."[22] While making it very clear that he doesn't believe in design because he doesn't believe in a supernatural designer, he cannot escape this language because it describes the cosmos, and particularly his field of genetics, as they seem to be.

One can only wonder why the way the entire universe so obviously *seems* to be isn't really the way it is at all; why, if the cosmos really *wasn't* designed, it (and particularly intelligent life) have an unmistakable *appearance* of having been designed; and why nature creates in man such an overwhelming sense of awe, to which even atheists attest? This is odd, indeed. No less perplexing is why anyone would profess awe at what *seems to represent* design and yet reject out of hand the strong implication of a designer. Is there, perchance, some prejudice involved and fear of the truth?

Atheists are generally willing to concede that there is some mysterious "force" behind the order we see all around us—but not a personal God. Is that because a force is impersonal, amoral, and nonjudgmental? Is a force appealing because it will not trouble us with moral standards or hold us accountable for failing to do what we know is right?

Whether a force is appealing for this reason or for some other, it is irrational to attribute to a "force" what unmistakably could only be the result of an infinite intelligence. To what "force" could atheists be referring—gravity, electricity, atomic energy? It is foolishness to attribute to *any force* whatsoever the composition of the brilliantly conceived and encoded information and instructions contained in DNA. Why would anyone attribute this to a force except out of prejudice against a personal, supernatural God, who alone could be the cause of the "apparent design"? After all, nature cannot have designed itself, but why should it give what atheists claim is the false "appearance" that *seems* to demand a supernatural designer?

Dawkins denies any "design or purpose or directedness,"[23] which, of course, he must in order to maintain his atheism. He wants to believe that appearance lies; that the brain, nervous system, and eye (to mention a few examples that surely have a purpose) came about by chance plus billions of years of natural selection. Yet he cannot

describe the genome except with words that imply design and purpose. Those words are italicized in the following from Dawkins:

> A notable *advance* was the evolutionary *"invention"* of
> memory. . . . The memory, or store, is an essential part
> of a *digital computer*, too. Computer memories are more
> reliable than human ones, but they are less capacious,
> and enormously less *sophisticated* in their *techniques of
> information-retrieval.* One of the most striking properties of
> survival-machine *behaviour* is its apparent *purposiveness.*"[24]

STUBBORN IRRATIONALITY

No matter how clear it is that each of the thousands of complex
processes inside each cell, as well as among trillions of cells working
cooperatively together, aims at a very clear and specific purpose,
Dawkins cannot admit it because of his prior commitment to atheism.
He can only acknowledge *apparent* purposiveness. Yet he honestly
confesses what every geneticist knows very well: the nucleus of *every
cell* contains "a digitally coded data base larger in information content
than all 30 volumes of the *Encyclopedia Britannica* put together."[25]

Dawkins would have us believe that encyclopedias only *appear*
to have a purpose. He would also have us believe that given enough
millions or billions of years, an encyclopedia or any textbook on any
subject could write itself—and that evolution has accomplished this
feat billions, if not trillions, of times in bringing life to dead matter
and from an unconscious beginning, evolving lower creatures and
on up to man. Such is the utter irrationality in which every atheist is
trapped. Though he hates the very thought of God and claims that
theism is the greatest of evils, Dawkins nevertheless falls helplessly
into "God language" at times, because the phenomena he is describing can be expressed in no other way.

Even beyond the mystery of DNA's *somehow* imprinting itself
with intelligent information, an even greater cause for wonder is how

the written instructions direct themselves to individual and vastly different cells and *why* these instructions should be followed by any cell. How are the construction and operating instructions (an encyclopedic amount of exceedingly complex information) for trillions of cells not mixed up but transmitted unerringly to just the right cells as they come into existence and in precisely the right order? Remember the biblical declaration: "As thou knowest not . . . how the bones do grow in the womb of her that is with child: even so thou knowest not the works of God who maketh all."[26] Surely DNA, which among many other tasks directs the growth of the fetus in the womb, cannot be explained except as one of "the works of God who maketh all." And that God cannot be Nature!

WHAT HAPPENED TO HEALTHY SKEPTICISM?

Of course, the atheist credits this entire amazing process (which no one can adequately understand) with conceiving, organizing, and operating itself. Common sense, however, says that the DNA instructions could not possibly result from survival of the fittest because the instructions on how to build a cell must have been in place before the cell existed and thus before any "natural selection" could occur. The undeniably incredible idea that natural selection could change the DNA before it even existed is passed along as something that everyone ought to immediately realize was the only way it could have happened. Daniel Dennett, one of the Four Horsemen of the New Atheists, declares,

> The fundamental core of contemporary Darwinism, the theory of DNA-based reproduction and evolution, is now beyond dispute among scientists. It demonstrates its power every day, contributing crucially to the explanation of planet-sized facts of geology and meteorology . . . ecology . . . agronomy, down to the latest microscopic facts of genetic engineering. . . . It is securely tied by hundreds of

thousands of threads of evidence anchoring it to virtually every other area of human knowledge.[27]

Beyond dispute among scientists? If not outright dishonesty, that statement is at least an irresponsible exaggeration birthed by wishful thinking. From the very beginning, there have always been numerous scientists who opposed Darwinism. Their numbers have grown (and are still growing) to include hundreds of credible scientists who vigorously challenge Darwinism today as an unworkable theory that should have been discarded by the scientific community long ago. On the internet, one can find a periodically updated and growing list of, at this time, nearly 800 highly qualified scientists from numerous countries and disciplines who have signed "A Scientific Dissent From Darwinism."

One of the signatories, celebrated brain surgeon Dr. Michael Egnor, professor of neurosurgery and pediatrics at State University of New York, Stony Brook, in his dissent declares, "Darwinism is a trivial idea that has been elevated to the status of the scientific theory that governs biology." Others who have signed include scientists from the U.S. National Academy of Sciences, Russian, Hungarian, and Czech national academies, as well as from universities such as Yale, Princeton, Stanford, MIT, UC Berkeley, UCLA, and others. They declare:

> We are skeptical of claims for the ability of random mutation
> and natural selection to account for the complexity of life.
> Careful examination of the evidence for Darwinian theory
> should be encouraged.[28]

The fact that Dennett dares to make the bold statement that Darwinism's "fundamental core [of] the theory of DNA-based reproduction and evolution is beyond dispute" is beyond belief! Darwin never heard of DNA! *It is securely tied by hundreds of thousands of threads of evidence anchoring it to virtually every other area of human knowledge*? Dennett's obsequious praise of Darwinism leaves fact and reason far behind.

The truth is that *none* of those (Christian, non-Christian, or atheist) who praise natural selection as the marvelous way that new species have been repeatedly created can give *one* example—even a hypothetical one—of natural selection creating a new *kind*. No one has been able to disprove the repeated declaration in Genesis, chapter 1, that each living thing will "bring forth after its kind." They only cite those micro-evolutionary changes that by natural selection create variety within a species. They can cite nothing that goes beyond the bounds set by the DNA that defines "kind," as God declared. Varieties of dogs, for example, are now carelessly called species, but they are still dogs—a fact that does not contradict Genesis by differing in "kind" from any other dogs.

Over time, many species have developed a great variety among individual members, but they always remain what they have always been within the bounds set by the DNA of that *kind*. DNA is programmed to replicate itself perfectly, thus maintaining the species. The only known changes (and the only ones possible) arise either from a loss of genetic information through copying errors, or from recombinations through sexual reproduction of the genetic material already existing within the genome of each kind.

Botanist Nancy M. Darrall points out that "the addition of further coded information [is required] to make another organism with new and different structures. . . ."[29] It is axiomatic that the information in the DNA of every species defines that species, and to change one species into another is impossible without the introduction of new information to replace the information for the previous species.

Asked to give examples of changes in organisms that have occurred by the addition of new information, Dawkins has been unable to do so. Nor has any other evolutionist been able to provide such examples. As Lee Spetner, biophysicist and opponent of evolution, points out, "The failure to observe even one mutation that adds information is . . . evidence against the theory. . . . My main arguments against evolution are well illustrated by the human eye: Where would the new information come from to provide the genetic blueprint for this new structure?"[30]

DON'T JUMP TO CONCLUSIONS BASED UPON INSUFFICIENT EVIDENCE

A tremendous amount of information must originate from some infinitely intelligent being to be programmed into DNA in order to get from an alleged Big Bang to the human brain. Information is information in whatever form (DNA, DVD, CD, radio or TV broadcast, movie script, etc.) Even the simplest information can originate only from an intelligent source; it cannot be created by natural selection. As Jonathan Sarfati explains: "None of the alleged proofs of 'evolution in action' to date provides a *single* example of functional new information being added to genes. Rather, they all involve sorting and/or loss of information. . . . The origin of information is an insurmountable problem for the GTE [general theory of evolution]."[31]

There is *no known case* of information being added to the genome by a copying error or other mutation—yet this is the only way "higher" and more complex forms of life could evolve from lower forms. Spetner has quipped, "Whoever thinks macroevolution can be made by mutations that lose information is like the merchant who lost a little money on every sale but thought he could make it up on volume."

To get a new species of a different kind would require the input of new DNA information, and that can come only from an intelligent source, not from natural selection through the life experiences of the individual members of the species—and certainly not from copying errors, much less from the chaos of a "big bang!" Nevertheless, the atheist's "faith" in Darwin and natural selection approaches worship. Gerald A. Kerkut, Dean of Science, Chairman of the School of Biochemical and Physiological Sciences, and Head of the Department of Neurophysiology (though himself an evolutionist), pointed out seven evolutionary assumptions that in his opinion lacked sufficient evidence to support them. He defined evolution as

> . . . the theory that all the living forms in the world have arisen from a single source which itself came from an

inorganic form. . . . The evidence which supports this is not sufficiently strong to allow us to consider it as anything more than a working hypothesis.[32]

He's putting on a brave front, hoping that evidence to support evolution will come some day. Geneticist James S. Allan writes, "I had believed in the theory of evolution for nearly 40 years . . . [before] I became a Christian. . . . One day . . . my wife . . . asked me whether . . . there was any reason why God should not have created all forms of life as 'variations on themes' and so have provided the observed orderly degrees of genetic and phenotypic resemblance as evidenced in taxonomic classification. . . ? The theory of evolution . . . infers that species, genera, families, orders, etc., are genetically related. They all do carry some genes with similar structure and function, yes, but does this imply genetic relationship in the normal, within-species sense. . . ? Was there any reason why God should have created different species, genera, etc., in completely different ways and with completely different genes?"

Such questions as these led Allan into a series of studies to determine whether the Bible, which had proved to be true in every other area he could investigate, could also be true in its clear contradiction of a theory about the origin of life and species that was accepted so widely in the scientific community. He focused on the protein cytochrome-c because "There are no differences in the cytochrome-c taken from humans and from chimpanzees, and only one difference . . . from the Rhesus monkey. . . ." Evolutionists take this one cytochrome-c relationship as evidence of a common ancestor in spite of at least 5,000 other genetic differences.

Allan calculated that for the claimed genetic relationship, the 5,000 differences would require at least "150,000,000,000 forerunners of 'modern man' . . . often represented as belonging to small groups of cave-dwelling hunters called australopithicenes who roamed the African savannah. . . . [This is] both physically and Scripturally unrealistic."[33]

THE ORIGIN OF SPECIES?

Dennett, a Humanist Laureate of the International Academy of Humanism and a Fellow of the Committee for Skeptical Inquiry, nevertheless throws caution to the wind when it comes to Darwinism. He elevates his admiration for Darwin's theory to the level of absurdity as though it were the key to everything and the infallible word of a god who knows all. His praise knows no bounds. He goes on page after page in almost worshipful adoration of what he admits are Darwin's "groping" and "speculation" to explain species—which he acknowledges Darwin never could achieve.

Although Darwin's first book (1859) was titled *On the Origin of Species*, Dennett admits that "Darwin doesn't even purport to offer an explanation of the origin of the *first* species, or of life itself."[34] Of course not. Natural selection can't create life, nor can it function until species already exist. As inorganic chemist Stephen Grocott points out,

> If one believes in evolution, then one has to also account for the origin of life—the very first step. Without this, the whole subject of evolution hangs on nothing. . . . The weight of evidence against the spontaneous origin of life on earth is, in my opinion, overwhelming. . . .
>
> Suppose you could go back in a time machine to a time when, according to evolutionists, a lifeless world existed. Assume that you have taken with you an ocean full of organic precursors of life. What would happen to them? They would all decompose to simpler and simpler molecules and mostly would end up as lifeless common inorganic substances. . . .
>
> The complexity of the simplest imaginable living organism is mind-boggling. You need to have a cell wall, the energy system, a system of self-repair, a reproduction system, and means for taking in "food" and expelling "waste," a means for interpreting the complex genetic code and replicating it, etc., etc. The combined telecommunications

systems of the world are far less complex, and yet no one believes they arose by chance.[35]

Unquestionably, natural selection can only work on something that exists as a living unit, not on the proposed parts before they are functioning together. As geneticist Timothy G. Standish points out, "A living organism must have many functional proteins, all of which work together in a coordinated way. . . . For natural selection to occur, all proteins on which it is to act must be part of a living organism composed of a host of other functional protein machines. In other words, the entire system must exist prior to selection occurring, not just a single protein."[36] Obviously, then, to speak of natural selection causing the components of a cell (upon which it cannot operate) to come together is not talking science.

The chance that such facts, however, will find a chink in a confirmed atheist's defiant armor is about as likely as a .22 caliber bullet stopping an M-1 battle tank. Allan confesses that during the nearly 40 years that he accepted evolution as fact, the numerous problems that would raise red flags didn't concern him at all—didn't even get his attention. This is characteristic of almost any cult member because to doubt is simply out of the question for insiders. One dreads being shunned by those who remain within the cult. So it is with atheistic evolutionists. To admit the many obvious flaws in Darwinism would make one essentially an outcast from the scientific community.

One begins to despair of reasoning with fanatics like Dennett. It seems clear that no amount of evidence will ever deliver him (and multitudes of others) from the grip of Darwin's religious cult. Yes, cult. The fact that Dennett attributes to Darwin virtually the same infallibility for which cult members worship their gurus is undeniable. Consider the following:

> Let me lay my cards on the table. If I were to give an award for the single best idea anyone has ever had, I'd give it to Darwin, ahead of Newton and Einstein and everyone else.

In a single stroke, the idea of evolution by natural selection unifies the realm of life, meaning, and purpose with the realm of space and time, cause and effect, mechanism and physical law. . . . My admiration for Darwin's magnificent idea is unbounded. . . .

Not only does Darwin's dangerous idea apply to us directly and at many levels, but the proper application of Darwinian thinking to human issues—of mind, language, knowledge, and ethics, for instance—illumines them in ways that have always eluded the traditional approaches, recasting ancient problems and pointing to their solution. Finally . . . what really matters to us—and ought to matter to us—shines through, transformed but enhanced by its passage through the Darwinian Revolution.[37]

Meaning and purpose? Natural selection has nothing to say about *meaning and purpose*—a subject that scientists themselves agree science cannot even address. Nor can Darwinism apply at all to *mind, language, knowledge, and ethics.* Language and knowledge, like the mind that conceives and uses them, are nonphysical. In contrast, Darwinism deals only with the physical and has nothing to do with, or say about, thoughts such as "justice," "good," "evil," "right," or "wrong." Natural selection neither created these nonphysical concepts held in the mind, nor could it possibly change them, as thousands of years of human history attest. *Ethics*? Nature has no ethics. Dennett has glorified natural selection and Darwinism beyond all reason. Nor could reason itself, which he claims to use with unusual expertise, be a product of natural selection. If it were, it would be meaningless.

What really matters to us—and ought to matter to us—[is] transformed [and] enhanced by its passage through the Darwinian Revolution? The desire to know the meaning of life and what happens at death ranks at least near the top of what really matters to us. Darwinism has nothing to say about these vital issues—except to tell us that they are meaningless. How does natural selection solve all problems about the meaning and purpose of life? Where does Darwinism explain why we exist, where the universe came from, and whether God exists? The blunt truth is that it doesn't and couldn't. One is left speechless that Dennett could credit Darwinism with accomplishing that which it so obviously has not and cannot!

UNANSWERABLE QUESTIONS
FOR THE ATHEIST

In summary, as we have seen, the only way for life to come out of a "big bang" (had this giant explosion actually occurred) would be by a supernatural act of a Creator. This the atheist will not accept, so he must ignore or deny the law of biogenesis because a "big bang" (as already noted) would have sterilized everything a billion times over, making it impossible (according to that well-established and universally accepted law) for life to appear ever thereafter anywhere in the cosmos. The Big Bang theory is the prevailing opinion today, leaving the atheist in an untenable position.

The haters of God can only plead, "But there must be some exception to the law of biogenesis . . . please? If there isn't, then we're forced to believe in God, and we absolutely refuse to do that!" I can hear the atheist who jumped out of an airplane but forgot to strap on a parachute, "There has to be at least *one exception* to the law of gravity . . . please, God, just one exception? If you'll do that for me, then I'll believe in you! You can't do this to me! Richard Dawkins promised me there were millions of exceptions to the law of biogenesis all over the universe. Why couldn't there be at least *one e*xception to gravity? Please . . . just one?" From the God who allegedly is not there comes only silence.

The problems facing the atheist are insurmountable. Where did the energy come from of which everything is composed? What about life? It is certainly more than energy or protein molecules. What is it, and how does it animate matter?

The evolutionist tries to explain the forms life takes as resulting from natural selection. But that begs the question both of the *origin* of life and the formation of the first living cell before there was any living thing upon which natural selection could work. The silence on the part of the evolutionist surrounding the origin of energy, protein, and life, and of the first living cell is deafening—and ought to be embarrassing. Nor can the vital questions that Darwinism can never answer be quietly swept under the rug.

Who (it couldn't be *what*) conceived the instructions to build cells and bodies and imprinted them into the DNA of every living thing? Instructions have to be written in words, and that is exactly what DNA is: words strung together in a precise order. Furthermore, they must be written in advance of each species being formed.

Words express ideas, and ideas are nonphysical, yet the words inscribed in the DNA affect the physical body. They are the only source of information the 100-plus trillion cells in the human body have of how they are to construct themselves and how they are to function as part of the whole body. How was this information conceived, and how did it become the very structure of DNA? Why and how do each of the trillions of cells in the body follow this incredibly complex instruction manual written in a coded language?

None of these vital questions can be escaped in explaining the journey from Big Bang to DNA, and none of them is answered by natural selection or evolution. Is there an answer?

I had motives for not wanting the world to have meaning, consequently assumed it had none, and was able without any difficulty to find satisfying reasons for this assumption. . . . The philosopher who finds no meaning in the world is not concerned exclusively with a problem in pure metaphysics; he is also concerned to prove there is no valid reason why he personally should not do as he wants to do. . . . For myself, as no doubt for most of my contemporaries, the philosophy of meaninglessness was essentially an instrument of liberation. The liberation we desired was simultaneously liberation from a certain political and economic system and liberation from a certain system of morality. We objected to the morality because it interfered with our sexual freedom.

—Aldous Huxley, "Confessions of a Professed Atheist," Report: Perspective on the News, Vol. 3 (June 1966), 19

So I began to lose my faith. And the more I lost it, the better I felt. I mean, it starts out with this notion that we're all horrible. We're all born with sin and we're so bad that this wonderful person . . . and I'm sure Christ was a wonderful person . . . had to come down here and suffer and die on the cross so that with his blood our sins would be washed away. Weird man, I'm telling you.

—Ted Turner, "Humanism's Fighting Chance," The Humanist, vol. 51 (January/February 1991), 13

Pekka-Eric Auvinen, a Finnish schoolboy who murdered eight people at his high school in November 2007, wrote on his blog that "stupid, weak-minded people are reproducing . . . faster than the intelligent, strong-minded" ones. Auvinen thought through the philosophical implications of Darwin's work and came to the conclusion that human life is like every other type of animal life: it has no extraordinary value. The Columbine killers made similar arguments. One of the shooters, Eric Harris, wore a "Natural Selection" shirt on the day of the massacre. These are examples of how easily Darwin's writings can lead to very disturbed ways of thinking.

—Dennis Sewell, author of The Political Gene: How Darwin's Ideas Changed Politics, in an interview with Eben Harrell, "The Dark Side of Darwin's Legacy," Time.com (November 24, 2009)

Under ordinary conditions, no complex organic molecule can ever form spontaneously but will rather disintegrate, in agreement with the second law [of thermodynamics]. Indeed, the more complex it is, the more unstable it is, and the more assured, sooner or later, is its disintegration. Photosynthesis and all life processes, and life itself . . . cannot yet be understood in terms of thermodynamics or any other exact science.

—George P. Stravropoulos, Letter-to-the Editor, re Weisskopf, "The Frontiers and Limits of Science," as published in July 1977 issue of American Scientist, vol. 65 (November-December 1977), 674

TEN

DESCENT INTO COLLECTIVE MADNESS?

A THEISTS HAVE BECOME the toast of the West. Many are brilliant scientists or university professors, and, most important of all, have best-selling books to their credit—books that are influencing millions.

There is also an aggressive and growing vocal and written opposition to atheism by many Christians whose scientific credentials and educational qualifications are equal, and in some cases superior, to those of the leading atheists. In public debates and published works they have challenged atheists (though so far, their books have not come close to the popularity enjoyed by those of their opponents). Most of these debates are available as CDs or DVDs. Far from being dull and academic, they are fascinating and informative. We have quoted from some of these debates, two between Richard Dawkins and John Lennox, also an Oxford professor (see footnote for list of others)[1] and, in my opinion, Lennox not only holds his own against Dawkins but gives him more than he can handle.

Trying desperately to explain away the many evidences of design and the seemingly inexplicable opposition to Darwinism by the majority of Americans, including hundreds of scientists, Dawkins has offered some truly bizarre and one would think embarrassing excuses for the steadfastness of his faith in evolution. He has written (as we've already noted): "It is almost as if the human brain were specifically designed to misunderstand Darwinism, and to find it hard to believe."[2]

This is an astonishing yet oft-repeated admission. We are supposed to be, from head to toe, inside and out, the products of evolution by natural selection. Yet, incomprehensibly, the very processes that have supposedly made us have also produced a brain and mind in man that rejects them!

Dawkins does, after all, believe in design. Not by God, however, but by natural selection. He calls it an *illusion* of design, yet with an apparent *purpose* of deluding man into imagining that we were designed after all, when in fact that is not the case. Mystifying, isn't it? One wonders why the all-powerful god of natural selection decided that an illusion of design would enhance man's chances of survival. I've tried without success to find where Dawkins explains this theory. Nor can I understand why natural selection would give me the curiosity to wonder about it. Furthermore, what could that curiosity have to do with my survival and that of mankind?

HERE WE GO AGAIN . . .

How could the brain of man, by following the "architect's plans," which Dawkins credits with guiding evolution and natural selection, so firmly reject the very theory that supposedly created that brain? That theory doesn't make any sense, but these are the *facts*. This is an honest admission by Dawkins, and every other evolutionist must agree.

"Scientists invoke the magic of large numbers . . . knocking a few noughts off for reasons of ordinary prudence, a billion billion is a conservative estimate of the number of available planets in the universe."[3] Really? How could anyone arrive at this figure? How does one define "available planets"? The scientific consensus is that this earth is uniquely suited for life, which is not true of any other planet yet discovered in the cosmos. Dawkins continues to mix wild speculation with the large numbers he loves, imagining this will provide an escape from the creation "myth":

> Now *suppose* the origin of life, the spontaneous arising of something equivalent to DNA, really was a quite *staggeringly improbable* event . . . so *improbable* as to occur on only one in a billion planets. . . . But here we are talking about odds of one in a billion. And yet . . . even with such absurdly long odds, life will still have arisen on a billion planets, of which earth, of course, is one. . . .
>
> Even accepting the most pessimistic *estimate* of the *probability* that life *might* spontaneously originate, this statistical argument completely demolishes any suggestion that we should *postulate* design to fill the gap. [Emphasis added][4]

Are atheists playing mind games? *Suppose* spontaneous generation "really was a quite staggeringly improbable event"? But wait. By the law of biogenesis, spontaneous generation is not merely "staggeringly improbable" but *absolutely impossible!* This fact has been accepted by generations of scientists!

How could life, in defiance of this law, arise like a Phoenix out of the thoroughly sterilized and totally dead residue of a fireball hotter than the inside of the hottest sun? To deny the resurrection of Jesus Christ, testified to by numerous eyewitnesses, and to accept an even greater miracle—not the resurrection of a dead body but life where scientifically there could *never* have been any—would not be worthy of the scientist Dawkins claims to be.

What established science declares to be *impossible* is audaciously redefined as *inevitable* and could happen on a billion planets. The law of biogenesis is universally accepted, but atheists deny this scientific fact and pretend that it could be violated billions of times.

At the beginning, there was nothing at all for natural selection to work on. The first cell hadn't yet been formed and this is where it all must start. Natural selection, however, was supposedly behind the chemical processes that formed the first molecules. Is this transition possible? It is foundational to atheism, but is it a basic law of chemistry, established by experiment and cited in chemistry books?

Dawkins often refers to evolution by "slow . . . gradual degrees" over billions of years, but isn't this wishful thinking without first explaining what life is and how it began in a sterile universe? Neither Darwin nor Dawkins nor any other atheist has explained how the first life arose. Always the evolutionist must begin with life, unexplained and already present. Isn't that cheating?

Let's look at Dawkins's explanation of how life got started:

> Darwinian evolution proceeds merrily once life has originated. But how does life get started? The origin of life was the chemical event, or series of events, by which the vital conditions for natural selection first came about.[5] [What chemical event?]

It is axiomatic that natural selection is impossible without the prior existence of some living thing that can replicate itself. The first cell, therefore, had to come about by pure chance. That is mathematically impossible for many reasons. John R. Baumgardner declares:

> It is sheer irrationality for anyone to believe that random chemical interactions could ever identify a viable set of functional proteins out of the truly staggering number of candidate possibilities. In the face of such stunningly unfavourable odds, how could any scientist with any sense of honesty appeal to chance interactions as the explanation for the complexity we see in living systems? To do so with conscious awareness of these numbers, in my opinion represents a serious breach of scientific integrity.*

THE NEW EVANGELISTS

Why is it necessary to check the odds? It is not necessary to do so for a theist who believes in the Creator God, One who made all according to His will and pronounced it "very good."[7] We only show these facts for the benefit of atheists. Dawkins actually states that the "Watchmaker" is not only blind but *has* to be blind. He exchanges the Bible's intelligent, loving, purposeful Creator for the blind forces of nature and considers that to be a "major emanicipation."[8]

Today's atheists have become blatantly militant. They are determined to stamp out the very memory of God. What could be their motive? Why such a diligent campaign against a God who they argue doesn't even exist? Why the tireless effort that includes books, debates, television appearances, internet articles, etc., to accomplish that goal on the part of those who say there is no purpose, no meaning, no goal? Where are they leading us? And why do they care, if there is no meaning

---

* "[If we take] 10 to the 80th [1 followed by 80 zeros] as a generous estimate of the total number of atoms in the cosmos, 10 to the 12th [1 followed by 12 zeros] for a [very] generous upper bound for the average number of interatomic interactions per second per atom, and 10 to the 18th seconds (roughly 30 billion years) as a very generous upper bound for the age of the universe, we get 10 to the 110th as a very generous upper limit on the total number of interatomic interactions which could have ever occurred during the long cosmic history the evolutionist imagines.

"Now if we make the extremely generous assumption that each interatomic interaction always produces a unique molecule, then we conclude that no more than 10 to the 110th unique molecules could have existed in the universe during its entire history. Now let us contemplate what is involved in demanding that a purely random process find a set of about 1000 protein molecules needed for the most primitive form of life. [And] suppose that somehow we already have found 999 of the 1000 different proteins required and we need only to search for that final magic sequence of amino acids which gives us that last special protein.

"Let us restrict our consideration to the specific set of 20 amino acids found in living systems and ignore the hundred or so that are not. Let us also ignore the fact that only those with left-handed symmetry appear in life proteins.... [Considerable] theoretical and experimental evidence indicates that in some average sense about half of the amino acid sites must be specified exactly. For a relatively short protein consisting of a chain of 200 amino acids the number of random trials needed for a reasonable likelihood of hitting a useful sequence is then in the order of 20 to the 100th power with 20 possible candidates (100 amino acid sites with 20 possible candidates at each site), or about 10 to the 130th trials. This is a hundred billion billion times the upper limit we computed for the total number of molecules ever to exist in the history of the cosmos! No random process could ever hope to find even one such protein structure, much less the full set of roughly 1000 needed in the simplest form of life."[6]

or purpose in life and our sun and planet are heading for destruction that will leave not even a memory and no one to remember? They are taking the unsuspecting on a descent into collective madness!

Dawkins, Harris, and other atheists put belief in God in the same category as belief in Santa Claus and the tooth fairy. It is clear that they do not actually believe such accusations. Their actions betray the fact that they consider belief in Santa Claus and the tooth fairy far less dangerous than belief in "the monster of the Bible."[9] They don't write books, give lectures, and appear on radio and TV to denounce Santa Claus, but no effort is too great to take advantage of an opportunity to malign the God of the Bible. For a man who admits to lacking 100 percent proof that God does not exist, Dawkins expends an inordinate amount of energy and time fighting to convince others of what he can't fully prove to himself.[10] Why? He doesn't just want nothing to do with God, but like the other New Atheists, Dawkins *hates* Him.

Like some prominent American evangelists, the new atheist evangelists have their publicity agents, a growing following of millions, and an expensive campaign to advertise to the general public their gospel of hatred against God. In the fall of 2008, the British Humanist Association launched a massive advertising crusade. Richard Dawkins agreed to match all donations up to 5,500 [British pounds] (nearly $8,000). Within six weeks, British citizens had donated more than 120,000 pounds. Interestingly, one of the enthusiastic donors trumpeted, "I hope to God this helps!"

The atheist ads were in response to Christian ads promoting faith in God. The ads began to appear in Britain on the sides of buses, with enthusiastic organizers declaring, "We are going to expand all across the UK [plastering] buses, trains, billboards—the sky's the limit!" Early ads read "THERE'S PROBABLY NO GOD. NOW STOP WORRYING AND ENJOY YOUR LIFE." Logically, it seems that atheists would want a little more assurance than "probably," considering the risk involved in case God does exist and doesn't take too kindly to these slogans mocking Him. Meanwhile, as of June 2009, signs have been appearing in Washington, D.C., New York City, New

Orleans, Texas, Philadelphia, etc., with the good news, "Why believe in a god? Just be good for goodness' sake," and "Don't believe in God? You're not alone," and the number of these "testimonies" is growing.

PRIDE VS. HUMILITY

In contrast, consider the humility expressed by Einstein in an interview in 1929. It would seem to rebuke the cockiness of Dennett, the angst of Crick, and the brash contempt and open animosity of Dawkins, Harris, and Hitchens:

> We are in the position of a little child entering a huge library filled with books in many different languages. The child knows someone must have written those books. It does not know how. It does not understand the languages in which they are written. The child dimly suspects a mysterious order in the arrangement of the books, but doesn't know what it is.
>
> That, it seems to me, is the attitude of even the most intelligent being toward God. We see a universe marvelously arranged and obeying certain laws, but only dimly understand those laws. Our limited minds cannot grasp the mysterious force that moves the constellations.[11]

The theist thinks Einstein is on his side. In a way he is—somewhat. On the other hand, like so many other scientists who have used similar language, Einstein did not believe in a personal God, much less the God of the Bible. He repeatedly made that very clear:

> If something is in me which can be called religious, then it is the unbounded admiration for the structure of the world so far as our science can reveal it. . . . I am a deeply religious nonbeliever. This is a somewhat new kind of religion. . . . What I see in Nature is a magnificent structure that we can comprehend only very imperfectly, and that must fill a thinking person with a feeling of humility. . . . The idea of a personal God is quite alien to me and seems even naïve.[12]

By the time of Einstein's death, it is not likely that he knew much of anything about DNA. Had he known what we know today, he would have had a very good reason for believing in a personal God. Einstein did acknowledge that matter could never arrange itself into information. Information demands an intelligent, and thus a personal, author. Certainly this fact would have been sufficient to convince Einstein, had he known it, that the God who created all had to be a personal being.

Modern geneticists, in a sense, are repeating the mistakes of earlier evolutionists who followed Darwin's faulty reasoning. Then it was visible physical similarities that were taken as proof of one species evolving into another; now it's invisible similarities in the DNA. I can't challenge Francis Collins's knowledge of genetics, but it is clear that he is contradicting the Bible, which he surely must believe is God's Word, when he says that a chimpanzee is man's closest relative and that even a mouse shares a common ancestor with humans.

EVIDENCE FOR GOD, NOT FOR EVOLUTION

To believe that living things have many common features (arms, legs, stomachs, eyes, etc.) because they were designed by God to function on the same planet makes more sense than that they evolved, species after species, from common ancestors—except to those who have ruled God out by very definition. But natural selection and evolution cannot work on the chaotic super-heated matter coming out of a "big bang" and turn it into a single cell, much less into the human brain. Nor could any form of life ever come out of matter of any kind.

The information required for the simplest living cell cannot be produced by nature or by any evolutionary process. When one sees information, no matter how it is communicated, one knows that an intelligent being with a mind and will is behind it. In the case of DNA, only an *infinite* intelligence could have conceived, organized, and produced it.

It is here that the atheist confronts an insurmountable problem that Dawkins forgot to include in his model of Mount Improbable. Certainly it would be a violation of the law of biogenesis for any life ever to come out of the Big Bang—if that really was how the universe began. A related and also insurmountable problem is the fact that there can be no life without DNA, yet there can be no DNA without life. There is no escaping the fact that DNA and the life it defines had to come into existence simultaneously—and only an act of creation could accomplish that. This is an obvious dilemma that no atheist can solve unless he converts to faith in God.

Just as it takes life to produce life, only a cell can produce a cell. No one has ever presented a theoretical exception to this fact, let alone a physical example of its happening. Long-time Cornell University professor, researcher, and plant geneticist J. C. Sanford explains some of the mind-boggling complexity of the genome:

> The genome is not just a simple string of letters spelling out a linear series of instructions. It actually embodies multiple linear codes, which overlap and constitute an exceedingly sophisticated information system, embodying what is called 'data compression' . . . plus multiple, overlapping, linear, language-like forms of genetic information [with] countless loops and branches—like a computer program. It has genes that regulate genes that regulate genes . . . genes that sense changes in the environment, and then instruct other genes to react by setting in motion complex cascades of events that can then modify the environment.
>
> Some genes actively rearrange themselves . . . *changing portions of the instruction manual. . . !*
>
> The bottom line is this: the genome's set of instructions is not a simple, static, linear array of letters; [it] is dynamic, self-regulating, and multi-dimensional. There is no human information system that can even begin to compare to it.
>
> The genome's highest levels of complexity and interaction are probably beyond the reach of our understanding. . . . All this mind-boggling information is [located] within a genomic package that is contained within a cell's nucleus—a space much smaller than the smallest speck of dust.[13]

In contrast to Sanford, who firmly opposes evolution, geneticist Francis Collins still embraces it. Collins surely knows that DNA, with all of its ingenious complexity (only a small part of which is described above), could not be formed without intelligent direction that is beyond our capacity even to imagine. He also knows beyond question that information is not a quality of molecules nor can it come into existence through natural selection. The information must already be programmed into the DNA for natural selection to occur—and it cannot escape those bounds.

Collins claims to believe in the infinite Creator of all, a Creator who certainly doesn't need billions of years to do anything but who could create the entire universe and all its life in a moment. Yet Collins writes, "No serious biologist today doubts the theory of evolution to explain the marvelous complexity and diversity of life. In fact, the relatedness of all species through the mechanism of evolution is such a profound foundation for the understanding of all biology that it is difficult to imagine how one would study life without it."[14] On the contrary, everything that he has pointed to (certain gaps in the genes appearing in the same odd positions in human and mice genomes, for example[15]) could be explained as similar copying errors or could be normal for reasons we don't yet understand.

His statement that "no serious biologist today doubts the theory of evolution" simply isn't true. We just quoted such a biologist extensively a few paragraphs above. There are many hundreds, if not thousands, of top scientists, and among them many "serious biologists," who reject evolution entirely and do so on the basis of overwhelming scientific evidence. Among just the 50 scientists whose papers refuting evolution are included in the book, *In Six Days: Why 50 Scientists Choose to Believe in Creation*, six are biologists and eleven more are in fields closely related, such as biochemistry, medical research, genetics, botany, and medical physics.

Furthermore, we have been pointing out why Darwinism offers *no* explanation of living things. How could evolution be a better explanation than creation by God? It couldn't, except to those who will not allow God even as a hypothesis. Then why does Collins, who believes in God, call evolution, with its billions of years of inefficiency and wasted time and lives just to make tiny "advances," better than instantaneous creation by God? Is it because to deny evolution would lower his esteem in the eyes of so many colleagues and make it more difficult, if not impossible, to gain the approval of peer review committees? That this sad fate has been the nemesis of many qualified scientists in various fields who dare to use the term "Intelligent Design" is vividly shown in the live interviews in the documentary *Expelled*, to which we've already referred.

WAS DARWIN JUST A HAIR BELOW GOD?

Collins admits that Darwin really had no physical evidence for his theory of evolution. To a staunch believer in the Darwinian religion, however, that fact elevates Darwin all the higher as someone who must have had a secret "revelation." Collins says that "Darwin's insight was all the more remarkable at the time. . . . It took a century of work to discover just *how* there could be modifications in life's instruction book" in order to support Darwinism.[16] He goes on to say,

> One can therefore think of DNA as an instructional script, a software program, sitting in the nucleus of the cell. Its coding language has only four letters in its alphabet. . . . A particular instruction, known as a gene, is made up of hundreds of thousands of letters of code. All of the elaborate functions of the cell, even in as complex an organism as ourselves, have to be directed by the order of letters in this script.[17]

An instructional script, a software program . . . coding language . . . made up of . . . thousands of letters of code . . . the elaborate functions of the cell . . . directed by the order of letters . . . ! These words cry out, "Intelligent authorship and direction!" Collins uses terms that require God to be guiding the process, but as a believer now, no longer an atheist. So God *must* be involved at least behind the scenes. Again, we ask why God would employ natural selection and survival of the fittest in order to inefficiently accomplish, over billions of years, what He could do with one creative act. Consider the following:

> The DNA information that makes up a specific gene is copied into a single-stranded messenger RNA molecule [that] moves from the nucleus of the cell (the information storehouse) to the cytoplasm (a highly complex gel mixture of proteins, lipids, and carbohydrates), where it enters an elegant protein factory called the ribosome.
>
> A team of sophisticated translators in the factory then read the bases protruding from the . . . RNA to convert the information in this molecule into a specific protein, made up of amino acids. Three "rungs" of RNA information make one amino acid. It is proteins that do the work of the cell and provide its structural integrity. . . .
>
> This brief description only scratches the surface of the elegance of DNA, RNA, and protein, which continues to be a source of awe and wonder.
>
> Investigations of many organisms, from bacteria to humans, revealed that this "genetic code," by which information in DNA and RNA is translated into protein, is universal in all known organisms. . . .[18]

A CALL TO REASON

Collins appeals to Christians to use reason in facing the issue of whether or not God used evolution to create man. His "plea for reason" asks believers not to attach their "position to a flawed foundation." We appeal to Collins in the same spirit. Many scientists would consider his position to be highly unreasonable, and some of them use rather harsh language. Geophysicist Ker C. Thomson, former Director of the U.S. Air Force Terrestrial Sciences Laboratory, declares:

Is there available a scientifically observable process in nature which on a long-term basis is tending to carry its products upward to higher and higher levels of complexity? Evolution absolutely requires this. . . . The Second Law of Thermodynamics states that there is a long-range decay process, which ultimately and surely grips everything in the universe that we know about. That process produces a break-down of complexity, not an increase. This is the exact opposite of what evolution requires. . . .

If the evolution or creationism discussion were decided by sensible appeals to reason, evolution would long ago have joined the great philosophical foolishnesses of the past, with issues such as how many angels can dance on the head of a pin, or the flat-earth concept.[19]

The evolutionists' answer to the entropy imposed upon the universe by the second law is to say that natural selection is able to defy that law, at least temporarily. The obvious problem of entropy is given a wide berth by most evolutionists. Dawkins rarely ever mentions it, nor does Dennett. It is an inescapable fact, however, that even as supposed upward development is advancing a species, all the while the second law is inexorably at work. The DNA of every creature is deteriorating through accumulating copying errors. Furthermore, these come at such a rapid rate that life could not have been on Earth a fraction of the time evolutionists say it has. We will come back to that subject later, but for the moment, consider the following from one of the foremost experts on entropy's effect on living organisms:

The nature of information and the correctly formulated analogy of the genome as an instruction manual, help us see that the genome must degenerate. This common-sense insight is supported by information theory. . . . The very consistent nature of mutations to erode information helps us see that the genome must deteriorate. . . .

For decades biologists have argued on a philosophical level that the very special qualities of natural selection can essentially reverse the biological effects of the second law of thermodynamics [so that] the degenerative effects of entropy in living systems can be negated. However . . . mutational entropy appears to be so strong within large genomes that selection cannot reverse it. This makes eventual extinction of such genomes inevitable. . . . Genetic entropy . . . is a logical conclusion derived from careful analysis of how selection really operates. . . . Mutation/selection cannot even stop the loss of genomic information—let alone *create* the genome. . . .

Selection occurs on the level of the whole organism and cannot stop the loss of information due to mutation . . . happening on the molecular level.[20]

By all of the facts, reason tells us that life couldn't even begin, let alone evolve. The supposed Big Bang's explosion would have created total chaos. How could such ultimate disorder, left to itself, and in defiance of the second law, ever turn into the highly ordered universe of the present? Atheistic evolution cannot account for this transition by the laws of physics and chemistry, much less by the laws of thermodynamics. There is no scientific answer to the question we have repeatedly asked: How did the matter of which the universe is made—matter that had been sterilized a trillion times over by the Big Bang—give birth to life? Impossible, says science. Yet the evolutionist says, "From the chaos of the Big Bang to the human brain? No problem, it just took a lot of time." We can label such reasoning as totally without scientific merit. To call impossible events possible, given enough time, is surely a descent into madness!

Researchers at Cambridge University isolated the short part of the control region of a gene that made the difference between a fruit fly with "two rows of bristles on the thorax and one with four rows. . . . By [some gene] swapping they could turn a two rows fly into a four rows fly. Scientists were elated to declare that such experiments *may* 'tell us how different organisms evolved.'"[21] Is this a triumph of scientific engineering—to build another row of bristles on fruit flies?

The amount of time and effort that has been expended in persistent pursuit of proof for the bankrupt theory of evolution is staggering.

Why do brilliant men and women continue to beat this dead horse? Why such diligence? They *must* prove that God does not exist, or their world of fantasy castles will dissolve like mist under the first rays of sunlight. How ironic it is that its founders built modern science upon belief in an intelligent Creator because of the orderliness of the universe they had observed—and now their successors are building a "new order" with the single-minded goal of sweeping that foundation away!

Only those who are seeking for an excuse to explain life without God could grasp at such straws as engineering another row of bristles in fruit flies. Every item like this is hailed as further proof of evolution, when, in fact, this has nothing to do with changing a fruit fly even into a dragonfly, let alone showing that evolution from one kind to another ever occurred or ever could occur. Yet devout Darwin worshippers happily claim that every living thing is the result of billions of years of laborious and inefficient evolution from a common parent through natural selection. Is this the *sound reason* for which Collins appeals?

Collins declares, "Truly it can be said that not only biology but medicine would be impossible to understand without the theory of evolution."[22] On the contrary, the theory of evolution was formulated by Darwin without any knowledge of the genetics behind biology and medicine. Nor did Darwinism lead to any genetic discoveries that could not have been made without such a theory. In fact, the more we learn about DNA and genetics, the more compelling the evidence becomes that evolution from one kind of creature to another (such as dog-like creatures to horse, as irresponsibly shown by artists' illustrations in many textbooks) could *not* occur. The organization of DNA, with its safeguards to protect the integrity of the species, far from facilitating evolution from one kind to another, prohibits it.

NATURAL SELECTION: YES! EVOLUTION: NO!

Skeptics often ask, "What about the amazing variety we see all around us in nature? Isn't that evidence of evolution?" Every snowflake is different, as is each crystal, but they don't evolve. These are patterns that occur in nature. Natural selection can occur within a species in living creatures to create variety, but no comparison can be made between adaptations in *living* things by the natural selection process and naturally occurring patterns in *nonliving* things. The possible variety of patterns in nature is virtually infinite, but that doesn't mean that snowflakes, crystals, stalactites, stalagmites, etc., were personally designed by God. These come about by the elements of God's creation: temperature changes, moisture content, gravity, wind, time, minerals, etc. Such patterns in nature cannot be compared to *designs*, which come only by intelligent direction. This is why creationists often speak of "Intelligent Design," exhibited in nature, as evidence that God does exist, because only He could be its author.

Though Collins is the leading expert on DNA, his claim that DNA supports evolution is irrational. That belief could only have been birthed by his predisposition to evolution. As proof of "macroevolution," he refers to the "stickleback" fish, which, in saltwater, has "a continuous row of three dozen armor plates extending from head to tail." He cites the fact that sticklebacks in fresh water "have lost most of these plates. . . . It is not hard to see how the difference between freshwater and saltwater sticklebacks could be extended to generate all kinds of fish."[23] But fish are still fish, and the stickleback is still a stickleback.

No creationist doubts that genetic copying errors can cause all kinds of varieties of dogs or cats or fish—or that they can produce strains of bacteria and parasites that have developed immunity to medications designed to combat them. But this is not evolution from one kind to another. Nor does Collins in his entire book (in spite of touting mistakes in copying DNA as proof of Darwinism) offer *one* example of a genuine change in *kind* through copying errors. DNA of one kind of creature has never been known to evolve into the DNA of a different kind. No evolutionist has ever found such an example. Then how can anyone claim that this is the way evolution, through natural selection, has created the limitless variety of species of creatures of all kinds? Impossible!

We plead with evolutionists, please don't tell us about the stickle-back fish and the finch's beak again! We've heard enough about them! Is this the best you can produce? Don't you have some *real* evidence? Aren't you embarrassed to keep showcasing these two creatures?

DEFYING LAWS AND LOGIC

About 4,000 species of fruit flies exist, but with all their variations they are all still fruit flies. The examples that Collins and others cite as evidence of evolution are of this nature. Nearly every variation is due to a *loss* of genetic information through mistakes in copying a gene sequence. No case has ever been found of information being *added* that would cause a fish to evolve into a lizard or a chimpanzee into a man. Dawkins tried in two full chapters in two different books (*Unweaving the Rainbow*, and *A Devil's Chaplain*) to explain how information is added to the genome in the process of natural selection. He failed. Yet Collins dares to say that "the distinction between macroevolution [change from one kind to another] and microevolution [variety within one kind] is . . . rather arbitrary; larger changes that result in a new species are a result of a succession of smaller incremental steps."[24]

Such statements echo Dawkins's illustration of climbing Mount Improbable and begin to erode our confidence in Collins. He has given us no example of a gradual change in DNA leading to a new species and knows that he can't. In saying that a "succession of smaller incremental steps" is the way one species allegedly evolves into another, he is only echoing the worn-out mantra of Darwinism. But this is theory, not fact—and it is theory that goes against information science and for which the evolutionist has never produced one example of its actual occurrence.

In summation, is it possible to go from a "big bang" to the human brain, the most complex mechanism in the universe, whose construction and operation is spelled out in written language in the DNA and requires an intelligent author? Natural selection could play no part until self-replicating molecules with primitive DNA in place had somehow come into existence *by chance*—and that has been proven to be mathematically out of the question. No theory has ever been proposed nor any model shown how the information in DNA could be written except by an author of infinite intelligence. The very structure of DNA itself, which is based upon *information*, declares the addition of information to be *impossible*.

Moreover, how this transformation from the total chaos of the Big Bang to the human brain (over no matter how many billions or trillions of years) could eventually develop through mistakes in the DNA copying process—that is the question that must be answered. Evolutionists have yet to give us a coherent response.

BEYOND CREDULITY

In fact, we are *morally responsible* for our actions. There is far more to what makes a human being than the composition of the physical brain. Human personality and ambition are not physical, nor are they produced by electrical current or chemical reactions in the brain, glands, or nervous system. Nor can any explanation for them be found in the DNA. Evolution from lower species to man must cross that impassable gulf that Mortimer J. Adler so eloquently explained in *The Difference of Man and The Difference It Makes*.

The human brain ought to be treated with the utmost respect and care because it is the most complex structure in the known universe. It "contains more than 100 billion neurons, each linked to as many as 10,000 others." A single human brain has more electrical connections than all of the electrical appliances in the world put together. To throw drugs at the incredibly finely tuned and intricately fashioned brain is worse than dangerous, especially when it is impossible to predict exactly what the outcome years down the line may be. Yet this is the "remedy" of choice in today's overmedicated society.

As the brain of the human fetus grows, billions of neurons migrate along glial cells (which will eventually number as many as 5 trillion) to their final destinations. The brain develops its astonishing connection to the eye through the optic nerve, with its 1,200,000 fibers. More than 500 million cells in the visual cortex, 5-6 million cones and 120-140 million rods all play their part in bringing the eye's visual image to the brain. The aqueous humor in the eye must be turned over 15 times a day and the essential blood supply to the retina constantly maintained through the central retinal artery and the choroidal blood vessels, the arterial intraretinal branches that supply three layers of capillary networks that reach into the inner part of the nerve fiber layer. These few facts, including the development of the complete fetus in the womb, is beyond present comprehension. It has taken decades of research to discover this amazing network, and there is much more to know.

We have two options: to say with Samuel Morse, as he did on May 24, 1844, in that first telegraph message ever sent, "What hath God wrought!";[25] or to say with atheist evolutionists (and sadly with Christians, among them Francis Collins), "What hath Darwin wrought!"

It strains credulity to imagine that this astonishingly complex and intricately organized computer network, finely tuned and operated with software beyond our capability presently to understand, is the product of a giant explosion plus billions of years of evolution through natural selection. Are we to believe that it was put together somehow by chance until finally, when it began to function enough to aid in "survival of the fittest," it could then contribute at last to "natural selection" and be developed to what it is today? Is this truly more reasonable than to believe that Dawkins's "architect," instead of being "blind," is an infinite Intelligence who planned and created it all?

Following the pied piper of materialism, society has lost its soul. If *why* is not a legitimate question, we have sunk into the quicksand of meaninglessness and are no longer distinguishable in any meaningful way, as Dawkins would have us believe, from any animal, insect, or plant—which all have the same "selfish genes."

SPECULATIVE DECEPTION?

Dawkins believes that even the impossible can be made possible if it is taken in one infinitely small step at a time and spread out over billions of years. The likelihood of that ever happening is zero.

To show how the impossible can become possible, Dawkins suggests, "Could the human eye have arisen directly from something slightly different from itself, something that we may call X. . . ? Clearly *yes*, provided that the difference between the modern eye and its immediate predecessor X is sufficiently small."[26]

What is this "X" Dawkins suddenly introduces? Where did it come from? What is *its* evolutionary history? This is like saying, "Anybody can climb Mount Everest. Even I can! Just take me up by helicopter to about 10 feet below the peak on a beautiful, clear, windless day, and I can do it!" This is nonsense. He is not explaining how evolution could occur through natural selection. He even defines "X" exactly as I have described my conquering of Mount Everest. Here is Dawkins's explanation:

> X is *defined* as something very like a human eye, sufficiently similar that the human eye could plausibly have arisen by a single alteration in X. . . . By the same reasoning [reasoning?] we must conclude that X could plausibly have arisen, directly by a single change, from something slightly different again, which we may call X'. . . .
>
> Obviously we can then trace X' back to something else slightly different from it, X", and so on. By interposing a large enough series of Xs, we could derive the human eye from something not slightly different from itself but *very* different . . . provided we take small-enough steps.
>
> We are now in a position to answer [another] question. Is there a continuous series of Xs connecting the modern human eye to a state with no eye at all? It seems to me clear that the answer has to be yes, provided only that we allow ourselves a *sufficiently large* series of Xs. . . . Given,

say, a hundred million Xs, we should be able to construct a plausible series of tiny gradations linking a human eye to just about anything! [His emphasis]

So far, by a process of more-or-less abstract reasoning, we have concluded that there is a series of *imaginable* Xs, each sufficiently similar to its neighbors that it could *plausibly* turn into one of its neighbors, the whole series linking the human eye back to no eye at all. . . .

Considering each member of the series of hypothetical Xs connecting the human eye to no eye at all, is it *plausible* that every one of them was made available by a random mutation of its predecessor?

This is really a question about embryology, not genetics. . . . The smaller the difference between X" and X', the more embryologically *plausible* is the mutation concerned. . . . Whatever problems may be raised. . . we can at least see that the smaller we make the difference between any given X' and X", the smaller will be the problems. My *feeling* is that, provided the difference between neighboring intermediates in our series leading to the eye is *sufficiently small* [his emphasis], the necessary mutations are *almost* bound to be forthcoming. [Emphasis added][27]

Yes, a cow *could* jump over the moon! Surely a good animal trainer could teach a cow to jump over a bar placed half an inch above the ground. Starting at that low height, it must be *plausible* that if we raise the bar a centimeter, the cow could still jump over it. Now, following Dawkins's impeccable logic, it is certainly *plausible* that we could train any ordinary cow to fulfill the nursery rhyme of jumping over the moon, provided the increments between jumps were sufficiently tiny and there were enough of them, and billions of years to accomplish this—unless the moon had moved in the meantime!

Now let's ask ourselves: did Dawkins tell us what is involved in these tiny natural selection steps from no eye to the incredible mechanism of a fully operating eye and the brain to which it is connected?

Well, come to think of it, he didn't! Did he offer any physical proof that such a thing had ever happened—or could ever happen? No, he did not. This is all imaginary, the stuff of fairy tales that has given Dawkins his world-famous reputation as a brilliant geneticist. It seems almost as amazing as a cow jumping over the moon that so much of the scientific world (that is, the atheistic, materialistic segment) goes right along with this madness!

Going back to Mount Everest, what Dawkins is saying is that anybody can climb this highest peak in the world—and easily. If I can make it from two feet below the peak, surely I can make it from three feet—especially with the assistance of a helicopter— and so forth. Remember, anything is possible in small enough steps. Wouldn't it be a legitimate climb of Mount Everest if the motor kept running on the helicopter and every three feet I just stepped out and stepped back in—and *voilà*! I conquered Mount Everest in record time without suffering frostbite or overexerting myself. Well, let's see what other difficult tasks I can accomplish in this manner! I'm out to break world records!

THE HEART OF THE MATTER

There is far more to what Eccles has called *The Wonder of Being Human: Our Brain & Our Mind* than neural activity in the brain. During most of the last century, materialism was the dominant belief among physical scientists and even neurologists, a prejudice clearly expressed by Lord Adrian: "The final aim of brain research must be to bring behavior within the framework of the physical sciences."[28] It is not honest science to insist that one's experiments reach a predetermined result. Adrian was echoing the *Manifesto* already issued by Carl Ludwig, Emil du-Bois-Reymand, and Hermann von Halmholtz: "All the activities of living material, including consciousness, are ultimately to be explained in terms of physics and chemistry."[29]

Why this prejudiced and unscientific demand? Materialism is the atheist's last fortress. If that must finally be surrendered, the materialist's final hope is gone. That surrender to truth and reality could precipitate a burst of discovery and advancement. True science has far too long been hog-tied by the determination not to allow that "Divine Foot in the door."[30]

Atheism and materialism go hand-in-hand, supporting one another in their denial of God. Increasingly, however, toward the end of the last century, even leading physical scientists such as physicists, chemists, physiologists—and especially neurologists—began to see that materialism did not explain the data that was coming in. Inescapably, it all pointed to a nonphysical source of thought. *Mind had to be distinct from brain.* Chemical and electrical reactions in the brain could not explain the whole person. Eccles pointedly observed, "It is not at all clear how 'natural selection' has somehow selected for Bach's 'Partitas' . . . or for a system of justice that will let a thousand guilty men go free lest one innocent man be constrained of his liberties."

After extensive interviews in Europe and America, philosophy-of-science professor John Gliedman wrote:

> Several leading theorists have arrived at the same startling conclusions: their work suggests a hidden spiritual world, within all of us. . . . From Berkeley to Paris and from London to Princeton, prominent scientists from fields as diverse as neurophysiology and quantum physics are coming out of the closet and admitting they believe in the possibility, at least, of such unscientific entities as the immortal human spirit and divine creation.[31]

Materialistic science has nothing to say about the *mind* (except to deny its existence), which famed neurosurgeon Wilder Penfield described as "outside [and] independent of the brain."[32] Penfield, during his lifetime known as "the greatest living Canadian," taught for years at Montreal's McGill University and the Royal Victoria hospital. Obviously, anything governing human behavior that is outside and independent of the brain must be nonphysical—a scientific conclusion confirmed by many experiments that rankles materialists.

Sir John Eccles confirms, with his own research, Penfield's conclusions. He describes the brain as a machine that a ghost can operate, by which he ordinarily means the human spirit.

To believe that an infinite Creator, without beginning or end, brought the entire universe and all life into existence and wrote the DNA code is, admittedly, too much to comprehend. It is not unreasonable, however, and no other explanation fits all the evidence. To believe the only alternative, that energy is the self-existent, eternal, all-knowing, and all-powerful god behind everything is surely unreasonable. Indeed, it is unbelievable—except to atheists—and it violates the laws of thermodynamics as well as mountains of evidence to the contrary.

We are back to our only two options: either *Someone* of infinite wisdom and power always existed and created the universe and all in it or some*thing*, such as energy, meets these requirements. We will continue to face the evidence on both sides, from which we must each form an opinion in attempting to answer this question.

Furthermore, beyond atheistic evolution, the burden of proof rests squarely upon the theistic evolutionists to provide one sound reason why God would choose to use the inefficient, cruel, and wasteful-of-life process of evolution over a period of billions of years to accomplish what He could do in a moment.

Generalizations employing terms denoting probability or possibility, however, far out-number generalizations of universal form in the geologic literature. A striking feature of geologic discourse is the frequency with which such word and phrases as "probably," "frequently," and "tends to" occur in generalizations.

—DAVID B. KITTS, "THE THEORY OF GEOLOGY,"
IN FABRIC OF GEOLOGY, ED. C. C. ALBRITTON, JR.

We really need Darwin's powerful [theory] to account for the diversity of life on earth and especially, the persuasive illusion of design. . . . We can deal with the unique origin of life by postulating a very large number of planetary opportunities. Once that initial stroke of luck has been granted . . . to us natural selection takes over. . . .

—RICHARD DAWKINS, THE GOD DELUSION, 139-40

Darwin expected that his book would arouse violent criticism from the scientific world, and it certainly came from that quarter. According to his own account, most of the leading scientists of the day believed in the immutability of species.

—FRANCIS GLASSON, "DARWIN AND THE CHURCH,"
NEW SCIENTIST, VOL. 99 (SEPTEMBER 1, 1983), 638

The very fact that the universe is creative, and that the laws have permitted complex structures to emerge and develop to the point of consciousness—in other words, that the universe has organized its own self-awareness—is for me powerful evidence that there is "something going on" behind it all. The impression of design is overwhelming. Science may explain all the processes whereby the universe evolves its own destiny, but that still leaves room for there to be a meaning behind existence.

—PAUL C. DAVIES, THE COSMIC BLUEPRINT
(NEW YORK: SIMON AND SCHUSTER, 1988), 203

Faith is the great cop-out, the great excuse to evade the need to think and evaluate evidence. Faith is belief in spite of, even perhaps because of, the lack of evidence.

—RICHARD DAWKINS

One reason education undoes belief is its teaching of evolution; Darwin's own drift from orthodoxy to agnosticism was symptomatic. Martin Lings is probably right in saying that "more cases of loss of religious faith are to be traced to the theory of evolution . . . than to anything else."

—HUSTON SMITH, "EVOLUTION AND EVOLUTIONISM,"
THE CHRISTIAN CENTURY, VOL. 99 (JULY 7-14, 1982), 755

ELEVEN

SELFISH GENES, SELFISH PEOPLE

IF ATHEISTS COULD PROVE spontaneous generation leading to evolution, it would be the grand climactic corroboration of their theory that God did not create anything. They could then support their claim that God does not exist and certainly is not needed to explain the existence of any form of life today. This would also bolster the idea that in spite of the law of biogenesis, all life began by spontaneous generation. Dawkins, in fact, claims that this has already been proved:

> Most people, I believe, think that you need a God to explain the existence of the world, and especially the existence of life. They are wrong, but our education system is such that many people don't know it.[1]

Atheists pretty much have control of the education system, which explains why so many Christians have gone to home schooling or have created their own schools. So if the "education system" under their control fails to do what they want it to do, atheists have no one to blame but themselves. Is it possible that even young school children already have more common sense than to believe the myths atheists promote?

Richard Dawkins has set out to "evangelize" the schools in the UK more diligently, as the following press release reveals:

"FREE DAWKINS DVD FOR ALL SECONDARY SCHOOLS TO CELEBRATE DARWIN 200"

Every school in England and Wales is to receive a free DVD of 'Growing Up in the Universe', Professor Richard Dawkins' 1991 Royal Institution Christmas Lectures for children. The DVD is being distributed by the British Humanist Association with funding from the Richard Dawkins Foundation for Reason and Science to celebrate the 200th anniversary of the birth of Charles Darwin and the 150th anniversary of the publication of 'On the Origin of Species', which both fall in 2009.[2]*

Evolutionists are desperate to show that this myth is really fact. They *must* do so. They are digging all over the earth in their extreme anxiety to demonstrate that evolution is more than just theory. They talk about examples of evolution, but the average person who has believed their propaganda would be nonplussed by the "examples" they offer. There are plenty of fossils representing millions of distinct species but *none* to show any transition from species to species along this incredible "billion-year journey" from bacterium to man.

This same lack of fossil evidence persists across the entire spectrum of evolutionary theory. Here is a puzzling fact that haunts evolutionists honest enough to face it. Darwin tried to explain away the embarrassing absence of intermediary forms as "the extreme imperfection" of the fossil record. If evolution is true, however, there literally ought to be in the fossil record billions of these "missing links" that, far from aiding survival, were a detriment to the species and therefore were eliminated by natural selection.

We have uncovered millions of fossils since Darwin's day, but there are no "missing links" of any consequence among them. Nor has even one of the billions of imperfectly formed creatures that were supposedly cast off in the upward evolutionary struggle (if "natural selection" is fact) ever been discovered. Colin Patterson tells of his search to find evolutionists who could provide some fossil evidence or explain the lack thereof:

> I've tried putting a simple question to various people and groups of people. Question is: Can you tell me anything you know about evolution, any one thing, that is true? I tried that question on the geology staff at the Field Museum of Natural History and the only answer I got was silence. I tried it on the members of the Evolutionary Morphology Seminar in the University of Chicago, a very prestigious body of evolutionists, and all I got there was silence for a long time and eventually one person said, "I do know one thing—it ought not to be taught in high school."[3]

These facts should be admitted in high school and college text-books. Instead, the embarrassing truth is suppressed. The very "artistic license" shunned by Patterson in his book has been for more than 100 years the major textbook means of promoting the bankrupt theory of evolution by natural selection as an established fact of science. It is reprehensible to lie to young students whose opinions are being built on a false foundation.

It is undeniable that the DNA alphabet (not the order in which it appears) is identical for every living thing. There should be just as much emphasis upon the evolution of the 800,000 species of plants and the transition from at least a few of them to fish or mammals of some kind. Generally, however, the alleged evolution of plants to animals, then on to man, is scarcely mentioned in high school or even college textbooks. Could that be because at that age not enough "higher learning" has been acquired to override common sense?

LET'S LOOK AT THE "PROOF" THEY OFFER

The average person would not consider significant the few examples evolutionists habitually offer as identifying a transition from one species to another. For example, the stickleback fish that we have already discussed has some different physical features depending on whether it is in freshwater or saltwater, but it is still a stickleback fish. This is not evolution from one species to a new one.

Another example given is the beak of a finch, until we get tired of hearing about it. Atheists say, "Look! A new species of finch!" This is still a finch but with a slightly different beak—a far cry from evolution from one species to another, which is absolutely essential if they are to support evolution through natural selection. As Dr. Gary Parker, biologist/geologist, explains:

> All we have ever observed is what evolutionists themselves call "subspeciation" (variation within a species), never "transspeciation" (change from one kind to another). Evolutionists are often asked what they mean by "species," and creationists are often asked what they mean by "kind." Creationists would like to define "kind" in terms of interbreeding, since the Bible describes different living things as "multiplying after their kind," and evolutionists also use the interbreeding criterion. However, scientists recognize certain bowerbirds as distinct species *even though* they interbreed, and they can't use the interbreeding criterion *at all* with asexual forms. So, both creationists and evolutionists are divided into "lumpers" and "splitters." "Splitters," for example, classify cats into 28 species; "lumpers" (creationist *or* evolutionist) classify them into only one![4]

We've already given the example of the tiger and the lion. At one time, all we had were lions. Because of a geographical separation that developed, we now have tigers and lions. Atheists call this an example of evolution. No, this is *speciation*, a change in some characteristics while remaining within the same species. These are simply divisions among the cat family. Tigers are cats. Lions are cats. Great Danes and Chihuahuas are called different species by evolutionists (they are desperate to find examples of new "species" being formed) but like German Shepherds and Yorkshire Terriers, they are still dogs. There has been no evolution in the real sense, though Dawkins and his fellow atheists want us to believe otherwise.

Dawkins admits that "Darwin's answer to the question of the origin of species was . . . that species were descended from other species."[5] This was a pitiful statement to be found in a book titled *The Origin of Species*. Darwin gives the example, to which we earlier referred, of tigers and lions, but this is not evolution in the sense that would ordinarily be expected.

How about from mouse to tiger? That would be *real* evolution, but such examples are not offered. Better yet, what about from mouse to *man*? Francis Collins, today's leading authority on DNA, tells us that the DNA sequence proves that the mouse is one of man's closest ancestors:

> There are AREs [Ancient Repetitive Elements] throughout the human and mouse genomes that were truncated when they landed, removing any possibility of their functioning. In many instances, one can identify a decapitated and utterly defunct ARE in parallel positions in the human and the mouse genome. . . . The conclusion of a common ancestor for humans and mice is virtually inescapable. . . .
>
> The placement of humans in the evolutionary tree of life is only further strengthened by a comparison with our closest living relative, the chimpanzee. The chimpanzee genome sequence has now been unveiled and it reveals that humans and chimps are 96 percent identical at the DNA level.[6]

But what does that mean? The conclusions Collins derives from DNA are simply preposterous. Similarities in DNA sequences are not proof at all of what he claims! There are vast differences that do not appear in the DNA sequences. Even Dawkins admits that DNA cannot define the person. At least we know that a chimp is not capable of writing Collins's book. Surely this is an extremely important distinction, and there is no way to identify it in the DNA. One needn't be a great geneticist but simply possessed of a little common sense to realize that theorizing in the new "science" of speculation has spun out of control.

DEBUNKING A FOUNDATIONAL DOCTRINE

What *is* the difference that Mortimer J. Adler identified as the impassable "chasm separating man from all other species"? It is "the ability to form conceptual ideas and to express them in words." Such a defining difference, though it is so crucial, *does not show up in the DNA*. Consequently, the conclusions that Collins imagines he derives from similarities in the positioning of certain glitches in a mouse's DNA and a man's DNA are meaningless. The capability of a mouse and its animal instincts and behavior are so far from human abilities and behavior that Collins's conclusions are ludicrous.

There is a huge difference between the physical *brain* and the nonphysical *mind*. DNA defines man's physical brain, but there is no place in the DNA for the human mind. This battle that materialists waged for centuries, i.e., to prove that nothing but matter exists, spread to many fronts: Freud was a materialist, and though he talked about "mind," his theories had a strong Darwinian/materialist flavor. Freud was a medical doctor, and his theories were based on the medical model of man, which treated even the mental side of man as merely his body. Of course, Freud talked about the id, ego, and super-ego. Like the evolutionists' theories, these are simply inventions of Freud's mind. Jung's major emphasis was on the unconscious, yet it can no more be defined than consciousness.

It cannot be disputed that ideas are not physical. Ideas are not found in the DNA, so what is their origin? Most evolutionists, knowing there is no answer, avoid such questions, but it is dishonest to continue to present evolution as proven fact by skirting such vital issues as these.

None of the important moral and spiritual differences between man and all other living creatures appear in the DNA. DNA is physical and cannot reflect the most important essence of man, a part of which is nonphysical and indeed presents an impassable chasm between homo-sapiens and every other life-form.

We have already quoted a defining piece of wisdom from A. S. Eddington. He points out that there is a vast difference between physical laws, which *must* be obeyed, and moral and spiritual laws, which *ought* to be obeyed. As Eddington declared, "*Ought* takes us outside of physics and chemistry."

GRANDPA CARROT, GRANDMA ZUCCHINI

Collins calls chimps "our closest living relative"[7] because "humans and chimps are 96 percent identical at the DNA level." His arguments could seem convincing until one remembers what he himself points out: "Investigations of many organisms, from bacteria to humans, revealed that this 'genetic code,' by which information in DNA and RNA is translated into protein, is universal in all known organisms."[8] That universality includes not only the lowest creatures, such as garden slugs, but also microbes and even plants. It was a German chemist, Robert Feulgen, who discovered that DNA and RNA are in every human, animal, and plant cell—with the DNA always in the cell's nucleus and the RNA outside of it.

Sixty percent of our DNA is shared with bananas. So what? Does this mean that man is also related by an evolutionary chain to celery, strawberries, peanuts, oak trees, or any particular one (or all) of the more than 800,000 known plant species? Although there is some ref-erence in botany textbooks to evolution of plants, no proven examples are presented. Variety in plant life is simply assumed to be the result of evolution. The truth is, however, that we find no evidence, in what is now an impressively complete and clearly defined fossil record, that even one of the phyla is either the ancestor or the descendant of any other, much less that any form of plant life evolved into any form of animal life—or that animals ever evolved into plants. How can evolutionists be sure which came first?

Based upon the reasoning applied to the alleged evolution from lower creatures to man, shouldn't the fact that plants have the same DNA alphabet as humans yield some examples of evolution from plants to animals and then on to man? Googling "evolution of plants" brings more than 4 million hits. Typical is the following: "about 550 million years ago, the Cambrian Period began. During this period, life "exploded," developing almost all of the major groups of plants."[9] Another author writes, "About 425 million years ago, algae began to change into plants."[10] There is even a chart showing the development followed by the alleged gradual evolution of plants from the simple to the complex beginning 510 million years ago, "Plants begin to appear on land"; 440 million years ago, "land plants . . . cuticle . . . vascular tissues" appeared; 408 million years ago, "vascular plants diversify," all the way to 130 million years ago, when "flowering plants appeared," etc.

Definitive numbers attached to millions of years are thrown around with such confidence as to give the impression that these are verifiable facts and dates. The truth is, these figures are no more than guesses. One can only wonder, if man evolved from animals, and plants have the same DNA as both, why isn't a similar evolution traced between vegetables and blackberries and pine trees and on to animals before ultimately connecting to animals and on to man at the end of this long "evolutionary process"?

One is reminded of Ernst Heinrich von Haeckel's genealogical tree that came mostly from his imagination because there was nothing else available to support his thesis of evolution from the small to the large or from the simple to the complex. Haeckel's artistry presented the alleged relationship of all forms of life before the discovery of fossils verifying any part of this "Tree." Such has been the *modus operandi* of evolutionists ever since: bold assertions, with artists' renderings of forms of life never seen, attached to dates going back millions and billions of years, for which the evidence exists only in the evolutionist's imagination.

Talk about missing links! Where are the intermediate plant-animal fossils of which not one example has ever been discovered? Who could imagine such grotesque creatures? Yet they are essential if natural selection is to demonstrate itself. Remember, sponges, corals, jellyfish, some worms, and even sea anemones are classified as animals. So where are the intermediary forms between these plant-like creatures and plants?

Books and articles wax eloquent concerning dates going back hundreds of millions of years and boldly telling us what forms of life emerged in this age and that. Under the heading "Evolution of Plant and Animal Life," one encyclopedia declares:

> The Lower Cretaceous is characterized by a revolution in the plant life, with the sudden appearance of flowering plants (angiosperms) such as the ancestors of the beech, fig, magnolia, and sassafras. By the end of the Cretaceous such plants became dominant. Willow, elm, grape, laurel, birch, oak, and maple also made their appearance, along with grass and the sequoias of California.
>
> Closely associated with the angiosperms were insects, including a form of the dragonfly, and most were similar to today's insects. This prepared the way for the increase in mammals in the late Cenozoic.
>
> The marine invertebrates of the Cretaceous included nautiluses, barnacles, lobsters, crabs, sea urchins, ammonites, and foraminifers. Reptiles reached their zenith, including the dinosaurs Triceratops, Tyrannosaurus, Stegosaurus, Apatosaurus (Brontosaurus), and Iguanodon, and ranged from herbivores to carnivores. Flying reptiles such as the pterosaurs were highly developed, while in the sea there were ichthyosaurs, plesiosaurs, and mosasaurs.

Other reptiles living in this period include crocodiles and giant turtles; snakes and lizards made their first appearance at this time. True mammals, which had already appeared in the Triassic period, were rare, as the Cretaceous reptiles dominated.[11]

Typically, evolution is suggested, and vague outlines of the appearance and disappearance of plants in certain periods are given but with no proof to support the assertions. Crude animal-like characteristics are cited for certain species of plants, and photos are shown. One is left wondering, however, when some concrete links between plants and animals will be presented. Notably, no evidence is offered that animal-like plants and plant-like animals have any closer relationship than superficial similarities that characterize all things living on Earth, all of which have certain basic needs to sustain life.

Other than no missing links found or even imagined, there are other huge problems. What kind of "adaptability" could gradually turn a tree or bush or vine into a spider or mouse? This is the stuff of fantasy films. Why would a plant *need* to evolve into a creature? What survival or adaptability necessity would drive such natural selection? It will take another Darwin-Dawkins partnership to evolve that fantastic tale!

WHAT ABOUT THE EYE?

One of the major challenges evolutionists face is to show the development by natural selection of almost any organ in the human body. Dawkins relies upon billions of years and tiny incremental changes to move along the alleged evolution of complex organs such as heart, lungs, circulatory system, nervous system, digestive system, etc. How could these possibly develop by small steps when the "organ in process" could not contribute to survival until it was fully developed and therefore would be eliminated by natural selection before it ever began functioning? A perfect example and one of the most difficult for evolutionists to deal with is the eye. Richard Dawkins, in the DVD series that he is distributing to the UK schools, says:

Here's how some scientists think *some eyes may have* evolved: A simple light-sensitive spot on the skin of *some* ancestral creature gave it *some* tiny survival advantage, *perhaps* allowing it to evade a predator. No one can explain what this sensitivity to light might have been, how it could have provided this slight survival advantage in evading predators, or what that advantage may have been. [This is not science supported by evidence. This is desperate speculation.]

Random changes then *somehow* created a depression in the light-sensitive patch, a deepening pit that made "vision" a little sharper. [Wait a minute! *Vision* without any lens or eye? This is the basic problem with evolution. We see it also in Darwin's *The Origin of Species*.]

At the same time, the pit's opening *inexplicably* gradually narrowed, so light entered through a small aperture, like a pinhole camera. Every change had to confer a survival advantage, no matter how slight. Eventually, the light-sensitive spot evolved into a retina, the layer of cells and pigment at the back of the human eye. Over time, a lens formed at the front of the eye. It *could have arisen* as a double-layered transparent tissue containing increasing amounts of liquid that gave it the convex curvature of the human eye. In fact, eyes corresponding to every stage in this sequence have been found in existing living species. The existence of this range of less complex light-sensitive structures supports scientists' *hypotheses* about how complex eyes like ours *could* evolve. [Emphasis added][12]

PROBLEMS AND CONFUSION

There are a number of reasons why we do not need to go into a detailed analysis of DNA to conclude that, in spite of Francis Collins's expertise, hard work, and the apparently impressive evidence that he offers, we can dismiss the possibility of evolution on the basis of DNA similarities for a number of reasons.

1. If one believes in God at all (which Collins claims to and for whose existence there is conclusive evidence presented elsewhere in this volume), He must, by very definition, be all-knowing and all-powerful. Therefore, He would not need to use evolution to create man and it would cheapen his majesty if He did so.

2. God would not only have to be capable of creating everything out of nothing but must have done so in the creation of the universe, not needing a "big bang" and billions of years to turn energy into gasses, gasses into stars, flung-off planets, etc. The language in Genesis and throughout the Bible, when taken at face value, precludes that idea ("God said, "Let there be light: and there was light. . . . God said . . . " over and over).

3. It is not rational that God, who could create living creatures with a word, would, instead, employ the inefficient, cruel, and costly method of evolution through natural selection over millions of years that would leave in its wake billions of partially formed "missing links," cast off because they could not contribute to survival.

4. The theme of Genesis 1 is, "God said, and it was so." That does not sound at all like theistic evolution. Genesis 1 sounds rather like a repudiation of it. In fact, it is the very antithesis of evolution of any kind.

Collins makes no mention of the evolution of plants. There isn't even a reference to plants or botany in the index of *The Language of God*. Surely if any evolution occurred at all, it must have begun with life forms such as plants, which have no consciousness. Most Hindus have no conscience about pulling up a carrot, yet the DNA of plants, like that of animals, is exactly the same as human DNA. It is only the sequence of letters that differs. There are so many important differences between man and *all* other creatures, regardless of their DNA, that one marvels that this fraud has deceived so many millions and can continue to do so.

During a debate to determine who would be the Republican presidential candidate in the 2008 elections, U.S. Senator Sam Brownback, former Arkansas Governor Mike Huckabee, and U.S. Representative Tom Tancredo were the only ones among the ten candidates who raised their hands to signify their firm rejection of the theory of evolution.

Tom Teepen, a columnist for *Cox Newspapers*, said the three were "volunteering their ignorance. So far has the Republican Party fallen into a sink of anti-intellectualism. Indeed, into fantasy. You might as well ask the candidates whether they believe in ghosts, fairies, and calorie-free doughnuts."

Such sarcasm revealed the columnist's ignorance and prejudice. There are hundreds of the best scientists who reject evolution, as do the overwhelming majority of Americans. Yet not one of them, as a consequence, believes in "ghosts, fairies, or calorie-free doughnuts." Such insults may have entertained the audience, but they were nothing but foolish bravado.

Teepen continued, "Charles Darwin published his seminal *Origin of Species* in 1859. It was quickly understood by a major part of the scientific community. . . . But here we are, about 150 years later, and American politics still cringes before Biblical literalists who insist upon a finger-snapping God who popped creation into being in six days about 6,000 years ago."

Nowhere does the Bible even suggest that God created the universe by "snapping his fingers." On the contrary, God *spoke* the entire universe and everything in it into existence. It is demeaning to God and to those who believe in Him to use such language and will hardly forward the cause of honest scientific inquiry.

Polls show that the three Republicans were well within the mainstream of American opinion. A recent Gallup Poll found that 48 percent of U.S. adults believe that God made humans "pretty much in the present form at one time within the last 10,000 years or so."

A Harris poll in June 2005 found that 64 percent of adults believe that "human beings were created directly by God," while 22 percent say humans "evolved from earlier species." Of course, although an honest poll gives us the opinions of groups of people, truth is not determined on the basis of how many people believe this or that.

Huckabee, for one, didn't back down: "If you want to believe that your family came from apes, that's fine . . . " he told the *Des Moines Register*. "I just don't happen to think that I did."[13]

Christopher Hitchens states, as though he has definitive scientific backing, that

> Religion comes from the terrified infancy of our species. . . . [It] is innately coercive as well as innately incoherent. Because it's man-made, there's an infinite variety of it for them all, and these sects proceed to quarrel among themselves, religious warfare having been one of the great retardances of civilization of the time we've been alive and very much to this day.
>
> I think there're a very great number of people . . . who are fed up with religious bullying and coercion and clerical lecturing and with the damage being done to civilization by faith. They want to find a way of pushing back at it.[14]

This is rhetoric designed to impress unthinking people. There's no question that great damage has been done in the name of "religion." The Bible, however, is not a "religious" book, nor is it about religion. We are not defending religion of any kind. Atheists have an inherent problem of lumping all religions together. Whether it is Christian or any so-called "faith," atheism condemns them all. A Christian is maligned as a fundamentalist because he believes in the physical, bodily resurrection of Jesus Christ and, upon overwhelming evidence for this event, follows His teaching.

Hitchens has issued in public debates, in writing, and to the media a challenge that we have cited earlier. It is elementary and easily answered, as we have already shown. Let me issue a challenge as well. There are literally hundreds of biblical prophecies concerning Israel. These are not in the cryptic language of a Nostradamus or of his modern pseudo-Christian imitators, who are acclaimed and avidly followed by their gullible Christian admirers today. We've exposed them in other books. In a later chapter we will cite numerous biblical prophecies and their fulfillment concerning Israel and we challenge anyone—whether atheist or believer in any kind of god or follower of any religion or denomination—to disprove their fulfillment and to offer comparable prophecies that could stand in their place.

The distinguishing feature of science—the thing that makes it different from fields like literary criticism—is its unrelenting demand that all ideas and claims about the universe be checked by experiment on or observation of the universe itself. No matter how clever, an idea can't survive unless it meets this test. I don't think it's going too far to say that if a statement can't be subjected to experimental or observational test, it simply isn't a part of science.

—JAMES TREFIL, "WAS THE UNIVERSE DESIGNED FOR LIFE?"
ASTRONOMY, VOL. 25 (JUNE 1997), 56

Is evolution a theory, a system or a hypothesis? It is much more: it is a general condition to which all theories, all systems, all hypotheses must bow and which they must satisfy henceforward if they are to be thinkable and true. Evolution is a light, illuminating all facts, a curve that all lines of thought must follow.

—PIERRE TEILHARD DE CHARDIN, THE PHENOMENON OF MAN
(NEW YORK: HARPER AND ROW, 1965), 219

The scientific humanist holds that humans are natural creatures living in a natural universe. Evolved from stardust by cosmic processes, humans emerged from creatures that adapt themselves to nature into the self-directive agents who re-create that nature to serve the needs of their own progressive enlightenment. There are in this universe not god and humans, masters and slaves, but human beings in various stages of development, all born of the Earth-womb.

—LLOYD MORAIN AND OLIVER REISER,
"SCIENTIFIC HUMANISM: A FORMULATION," THE HUMANIST, VOL. 48
(SEPTEMBER/OCTOBER 1988), REPRINTED FROM SPRING 1943 ISSUE

[Sir John] Eccles drives home his controversial conclusion: "If I say that the uniqueness of the human self is not derived from the genetic code, not derived from experience, then what is it derived from? My answer is this: from a divine creation. Each self is a divine creation."

—ECCLES, CITED IN JOHN GLIEDMAN, "SCIENTISTS IN SEARCH OF THE SOUL,"
SCIENCE DIGEST, VOL. 90 (JULY 1982), 77

My guess is that the popular theory of evolution appeals precisely as an alternative to the Christian view of man, which not only demands faith but imposes moral obligations. People who adopt Evolutionism are not driven to it by consideration of the evidence; they like it without respect to the evidence, because they are passionate creatures, and it offers no moral impediment to their passions.

—JOSEPH SOBRAN, "THE AVERTED GAZE, LIBERALISM AND FETAL PAIN,"
HUMAN LIFE REVIEW (SPRING, 1984), 10

TWELVE

THE RIDDLE
OF "LIFE"

FORCED BY THEIR ATHEISM to reject the very idea of biblical miracles and in a complete disconnect from rational thinking, many scientists opt for an even greater miracle: a breach of the law of biogenesis billions of times all over the universe! In the name of "science," many Nobelists do the same.

Consider the following BBC article that is supposedly the latest word in science. In fact, it is the latest fraud that atheists are trying to persuade their followers to believe in the name of science.

> There *could be* one hundred billion Earth-like planets in our galaxy, a U.S. conference has heard. [On the basis of what evidence? This is the speculative, unfounded stuff of science fiction.] Dr. Alan Boss of the Carnegie Institution of Science said many of these worlds *could be* inhabited by simple lifeforms. [This statement is pronounced in the name of science as though there were some evidence and authority behind it.] He was speaking at the annual meeting of the American Association for the Advancement of Science in Chicago.

So far, telescopes have been able to detect just over 300 planets outside our solar system. Very few of these would be capable of supporting life, however. Most are gas giants like our Jupiter, and many orbit so close to their parent stars that any microbes would have to survive roasting temperatures.

But, *based on the limited numbers of planets* found so far, Dr. Boss has *estimated* that each Sun-like star has *on average* one "Earth-like" planet. [This is pure fantasy. How does the fact that there are "limited numbers of planets" become justification for calling them "Earth-like"?] This simple calculation means there *would be* [not *might be*?] huge numbers capable of supporting life. [This "simple calculation" is not supported by any evidence, mathematics, or logic.]

"Not only are they *probably* habitable but they *probably* are also going to be inhabited," Dr. Boss told BBC News. [What is his basis for making such a rash statement? This is wishful thinking, not science.] "But *I think* that *most likely* the nearby 'Earths' are going to be inhabited with things which are *perhaps* more common to what Earth was like three or four billion years ago." That means bacterial lifeforms.

Recent work at Edinburgh University tried to quantify how many intelligent civilizations *might* be out there. The research *suggested* there *could be* thousands of them. [Emphasis added][1] [The *research*? What research has been done to support this wild statement?]

WHERE IS THE PROOF?

What happened to the law of biogenesis? How can scientists, who supposedly accept this law, even speculate about the existence of life forms on planets all over our galaxy?

Ordinary common sense demands proof. When, where, and how was this wholesale breach of accepted scientific law proved to have occurred? Demanding and never receiving satisfactory answers to the most basic questions, we rise up in protest, refusing to join this open insurrection against natural law. It is undeniable that no life can exist without *information*, and information cannot come except through an intelligent source. The real question then becomes not *what* is the source of this information but *who* is the Intelligence that wrote this astonishing amount and variety of *information* into the genome—information that is essential to life?

In similar defiance, despite overwhelming evidence and logic to the contrary, Christopher Hitchens writes, "The real 'miracle' is that we, who share genes with the original bacteria that began life on the planet, have evolved as much as we have."[2] Behold the unabashed dishonesty that prevails among those who reject the existence of God! Atheists offer such tidbits as these, hoping that the crumbling sand of "maybe, perhaps, possibly, tiny baby steps over billions and billions of years," etc., can somehow be passed off as science.

So Hitchens, and presumably other atheists, believe in miracles after all, and they put evolution in that category. They don't concede that the origin of life is a miracle, because that would involve God. They dance around the question of origins of time, space, energy, life, etc., and excuse their unwillingness to admit the truth.

Dawkins carries the dishonesty a step further by claiming that his god Darwin, in 1859, told us how life began and its purpose, though he knows very well that Darwin did nothing of the kind. Let's call Dawkins's subterfuge what it is: one of his many blatant misrepresentations. He knows better!

Evolutionists make a great deal of the similarity between human DNA and that of all other life forms. But this is no proof of an evolutionary relationship. A better explanation would be that the same mind designed this amazing instruction manual that forms the basis of all life. As we have already noted, DNA contains detailed information in the form of instructions that could neither originate nor be modified by any evolutionary or natural selection process. Information can originate only with a mind, not with nature.

ALWAYS A THEORY, NEVER A LAW

After 100 years, evolution is still far from gaining unanimous acceptance among scientists. In fact, the number of scientists, including geneticists, who refuse to accept it is growing. From the very beginning, many leading scientists opposed Darwin and his theory. Adam Sedgwick, Darwin's geology professor, criticized Darwin for the materialistic and amoral nature of his theory, as well as for his failures in inductive logic. In 1859, Louis Agassiz, Harvard Geology professor, wrote that Darwin's theory was "a scientific mistake, untrue in its facts, unscientific in its method and mischievous in its tendency." Pierre Flourens, permanent secretary of the French Academy of Science, complained, "What metaphysical jargon clumsily hurled into natural history! What pretentious and empty language! What childish and out-of-date personifications."[3]

Among Darwin's many other opponents at that time were Karl Friedrich Schimper, German botanist; John Herschel, astronomer; Roderick Murchison, geologist; William Whewell, an ardent creationist and founder of the British Association for the Advancement of Science; James Dwight Dana, Yale geologist; Richard Owen, anatomist/paleontologist, who frequently debated Darwin and T. H. Huxley. Since Darwin's day, instead of gaining full acceptance, the opposition to Darwinism among leading scientists has grown as knowledge of the scientific facts has increased.

Evolution is not a physical science such as physics or chemistry, fields of inquiry in which theories are proposed, verified, and become law. That fact seems odd, because evolution is all about physical creatures and physical modifications. Medicine has become a science with its own verities that no one disputes. Yet *not one law* has been established through evolution. After more than a century, it is still all theory.

WHAT A DIFFERENCE!

The theories first propounded by the founders of modern science, such as Boyle, Mendel, Newton, Pasteur, Pascal, et al., were not established in order to prove that God existed but were demanded by the overwhelming scientific evidence pointing to the existence of the God in whom these men believed. Not one established law of any branch of science was discovered due to *rejection* of belief in God. Atheism cannot be credited with even *one* advance in science except evolution—and we are in the process of showing that evolution cannot be dignified as a "science."

Common descent of all living things from one ancestor is sometimes called an evolutionary law. In fact, it is not a law but a hypothesis that could not possibly be proved or falsified and with which hundreds of leading scientists have always disagreed. There is no opposition to the law of gravity, but there is much rejection of the attempts to establish phylogenetic trees. There are rules of thumb, such as "maximum parsimony" (the belief that truth is not established by endless complications but in simplicity of argument, for which there can be no substitute) in trying to establish relationships, but there is not one true scientific law that has been established through evolution, a fact that ought to give the scientific and academic communities cause for concern. The truth is that atheism forces evolutionists into maximum *violation* of the principle of maximum parsimony. Denial of the simplicity of "God created" opens up an endless series of phylogenetic problems that can't be solved.

Consider once again the huge difference between the old theistic science and the new atheistic "science." Of course, there must be some basic assumptions. For science as it was, tried and proven for centuries, the assumption was the existence of an all-powerful and all-knowing Creator. As a consequence, it seemed logical that the order and apparent design so clearly manifest in the universe would be defined and governed by laws that could be discovered and understood. Dawkins himself admits, "A universe with a God would look quite different from a universe without one. A physics, a biology, where there is a God is bound to look different."

And what is the difference? The purpose of Dawkins's book *The Blind Watchmaker: Why the Evidence of Evolution Reveals a Universe Without Design* is to show not only that there is no design and no designer but that this is the way it *must* be. It is heresy for Dawkins's "religion" to admit design. Yet Dawkins is forced to confess repeatedly that scientists are confronted everywhere by creatures that *appear* to have been designed! Of course, Dawkins's atheism will not allow him to accept the evidence but forces him into complicated rabbit trails in attempting to explain design away. This is not science but mythology.

IT'S DAWKINS, NOT THE WATCHMAKER, WHO IS BLIND

The numerous declarations by atheists concerning the *appearance of design* should embarrass not only Dawkins himself but all of his atheist colleagues. How often have we heard him say in a debate or read in one of his books, "One of the greatest challenges to the human intellect over the centuries has been to explain how the complex, improbable appearance of design in the universe arises."[4]

Of course, any unbiased person observing the "appearance of design in the universe" would come to the most obvious conclusion: that the universe had been designed! Let us go back in time and place ourselves 100 years before Darwin. Would anyone living at that time, from observing the overwhelming evidence of orderliness and exquisite design, have rejected this evidence and insisted that the universe must have originated at the hands of an unconscious and unthinking "blind watchmaker"? For such an idea to invade anyone's consciousness at that time would have been unthinkable.

It is equally incomprehensible how anyone today could reject the overwhelming evidence and refuse to admit that the universe had to have a designer/creator. Of course, we see this in the beauty and order-liness of nature visible all around us, which, even Dawkins admits, brings an almost irresistible urge to worship whoever or "whatever" made it. Those parts of creation that are invisible to the human eye are even more astonishing. We will give many examples in other chapters, but having just mentioned "design," let's look at another aspect of it.

The design of the human body, including, of course, the brain, clearly implies a designer. There could not be a designer who doesn't have a purpose for his design. The purpose for a house is hardly com-plete until the house has been built, following the architect's plans.

The same must be true of the cosmos. If it has the *appearance* of design, which most atheists concede, implicit in that "appearance" must also be a *purpose* that will be accomplished through the archi-tect's or designer's plans. One could liken the DNA molecule to the plans because it contains the entire instruction manual for construct-ing and operating the bodies of every physical creature on Earth.

In other words, there are two reasons why evolution and nat-ural selection could not be responsible for DNA. First of all, and most obvious, this is *information* contained in written words, which Francis Collins described in his book of this name as *The Language of God*. John R. Baumgardner explains the significance of *information*: "Einstein pointed to the nature and origin of symbolic information as one of the profound questions about the world as we know it.[5] He could identify no means by which matter could bestow mean-ing to symbols. The clear implication is that symbolic information, or language, represents a category of reality *distinct* from matter and energy. Linguists today, therefore, speak of this gap between matter and meaning-bearing symbols as the 'Einstein gulf.'"[6] Secondly, the whole idea of evolution and natural selection is that they produce the desired result not by planning ahead but by random change.

As opposition to Darwinism gathers momentum among scien-tists, the propaganda from its supporters, who have the media and academia on their side, gathers credibility among the unscientific. Even lawmakers are affected, producing bizarre legislation. On June

25, 2008, the Spanish parliament expressed support "for the rights of great apes to life and freedom. . . . Parliament's environmental committee approved resolutions urging Spain to comply with the Great Apes Project, devised by scientists and philosophers who say our closest genetic relatives deserve rights hitherto limited to humans."[7] Do we open the zoos, give the animals social security, a little money for shopping, and voting rights?

Francis Collins believes that the similarities in the DNA of humans and animals indicate a common ancestry, and Dawkins says that a common heritage of 3 billion years of evolution removes any distinction between man and the lowliest creatures, including the insentient ones. Man's intellectual prowess however, is so far beyond the capabilities of all such "relatives" that similarities in the DNA are meaningless.

Here we have, once again, confusion between matter and spirit. Collins himself pointed out that DNA does not define what it means to be human. One need hardly argue that similarities in DNA sequence cannot establish any moral or spiritual relationship between man and chimps or mice—or great apes. Were the significance of this fact clearly understood, the rash of weird legislation taking animal rights to an extreme would never have been enacted.

Just as the theory of evolution leads to untenable ideas and legislation, so that belief has become the basis for a number of other bizarre ideas. The fact that professing Christian Francis Collins, the former head of the Human Genome Project, remains an evolutionist cannot help but color his interpretation of DNA sequences. That underlying belief had to weigh heavily upon the conclusions he arrived at during his 20-plus years of making detailed comparisons and contrasts between the DNA sequences in humans and in many other creatures.

His unwillingness to abandon evolution as the foundation of his genetics is expressed in his statement, "Nothing in biology makes sense except in light of evolution."[8] In fact, many other competent geneticists disagree. Collins cannot deny that evolution contradicts the Bible and Christianity at its most basic level.[9] Clearly, Jesus considered Adam and Eve to have been historic persons and vouched for the validity of the Genesis account of their creation. If evolution is a fact, then Jesus could not contradict it and yet be the Son of God, able to pay the penalty for the sins of the world.

The Apostle Paul wrote, "By one man sin entered into the world and death by sin."[10] That statement, which does away in one stroke with "billions of years of fossils," cannot be inspired of God if the theory of evolution is true. But if it is true, then the Bible is wrong on the very foundation of the gospel. These facts (and many others revealing equally serious contradictions between evolution and the biblical foundations of the Christian faith) raise the solemn question as to what "kind" of Christian Francis Collins could be. Certainly he cannot believe both in evolution and in *biblical Christianity*, but that is the only kind of Christianity we will defend in these pages.

WHAT ABOUT THE FOSSIL RECORD?

We mentioned in the previous chapter that there are serious problems for evolutionists in the fossil record. Species are seen becoming extinct, never just beginning as mutations from another species:

> This regular absence of transitional forms is not confined to mammals, but is an almost universal phenomenon, as has long been noted by paleontologists. It is true of almost all orders of all classes of animals, both vertebrate and invertebrate. *A fortiori*, it is also true of the classes, themselves, and of the major animal phyla, and it is apparently also true of analogous categories of plants.[11]
>
> The geologic record did not then and still does not yield a finely graduated chain of slow and progressive evolution. In other words, there are not enough intermediates. There are very few cases where one can find a gradual transition from one species to another and very few cases where one can look at a part of the fossil record and actually see that organisms were improving in the sense of becoming better adapted.[12]

Dr. Niles Eldredge, an invertebrate paleontologist at the American Museum of Natural History, states: "The smooth transition from one form of life to another, which is implied in the theory is . . . not borne out by the facts. The search for 'missing links' between various living creatures, like humans and apes, is probably fruitless . . . because they probably never existed as distinct transitional types . . . no one has yet found any evidence of such transitional creatures.

"This oddity has been attributed to gaps in the fossil record, which gradualists expected to fill when rock strata of the proper age had been found. In the last decade, however, geologists have found rock layers of all divisions of the last 500 million years and no transitional forms were contained in them. If it is not the fossil record which is incomplete then it must be the theory."[13]

CONFUSION AMONG THE LOYALISTS

The entire cosmos and everything in it is made of atoms, which, in turn, are composed of numerous subatomic particles. Ultimately, everything is made of energy. Yet atheistic science, as we have already seen, in spite of its proud and grandiose claims, cannot tell us what energy is, where it came from, or how long it has existed—much less *why*. This elementary knowledge would seem to be essential for any true understanding of the universe, yet it eludes every effort to discover it. Could it be that no analysis of the universe will reveal its ultimate secret because its Creator has designed it that way?

Why is the universe the way it is, and how could a "big bang" have created it? Francis Collins acknowledges, "What we cannot discover, through science alone, are the answers to the questions 'Why is there life anyway?' and 'Why am I here?'"[14] Science has no answer to any of these vital questions. However, not afraid to offend the atheists, Stephen Hawking suggests that if we could "find the answer . . . then we would know the mind of God."[15]

If we can't even discover what energy is, although the entire universe consists of it, and if science has no idea *why* energy and the universe exist, isn't it foolish to stagger ahead with alleged explanations of the supposed role of evolution in turning energy into millions of species of living creatures? What horrible blunders we could be making, and how many mistakes some of our "discoveries" could involve without our even knowing it!

Life itself is the greatest mystery. We simply do not know what it is or why some combinations of nonliving matter manifest life. We know that life is not a quality of matter, because most matter is inanimate. How inanimate matter becomes alive remains a mystery. No atom or elementary particle has life. Yet many different combinations of atoms can be alive. Christ is declared to be the Creator of everything: "All things were made by him. . . ."[16] In agreement with the established law of biogenesis, which says that "life comes only from life," the Bible explains, in grand yet simple logic, that life comes only from Christ, for: "In *him* was life."[17]

Unable to fault the Christian's claims, the atheist reacts with his usual time-worn clichés or scornful silence.

WHAT IN THE WORLD IS LIFE?

As we have seen, Darwinism is locked in a frustrating silence, having nothing to say about the origin either of life or of the universe in which life is found. That would seem to be a crucial shortcoming. Yet evolutionists avoid questions about origins as though they were of little importance. Not true! They boldly propose theories of natural selection and organic evolution *after* energy somehow appeared. Evolution and its close partner, natural selection, hang suspended in a never-never land of conflicting theories and make-believe assumptions.

What about the atom, itself lifeless, yet the basic building block of everything that has life? It is neither fair nor sensible to claim to understand the purpose of life when we cannot explain the atom. Yet Richard Dawkins (like so many other atheists) dares to teach school children and to boast on radio, television, and in print that we no longer need God because Darwinism explains the meaning of life and how we got here. That is a blatant misrepresentation of the facts as we know them. Reading and hearing the praise from evolutionists for Darwin, one gets the distinct impression that they worship this god as the one who rescued them from the God of the Bible. Darwinism is a religious cult that entraps its followers in a great delusion.

Walt Brown explains:

> The first law of thermodynamics tells us that the total energy in the universe, or in any isolated part of it, remains constant. In other words, energy (or its mass equivalent) is not now being created or destroyed; it simply changes form. . . .
>
> A corollary of the first law is that natural processes cannot create energy. Therefore, energy must have been created in the past by some agency or power outside and independent of the natural universe. Furthermore, if natural processes cannot produce mass and energy—the relatively simple inorganic portion of the universe—then it is even less likely that natural processes can produce the much more complex organic (or living) portion of the universe.[18]

The composition and origin of energy, the basic material of the cosmos, is a mystery whose solution remains beyond the reach of science. For scientists who claim to know so much and who are certain that the universe was not created by God, it should be upsetting not to know what energy is—or space, time, gravity, electricity, an electron, or any other basic element in the structure of the universe. And this is nothing compared to the questions of consciousness and conscience, which we will confront later.

DELIBERATE BLINDNESS

Atheists and evolutionists might, at first blush, seem to have some hope of substantiating the development of bodily organs, nerves, and tissues by means of "natural selection." However, as we have seen, when we look more deeply into the human body at the more than 100 trillion cells of which it consists (each one's complexity beyond imagination), we discover a detailed and complete written instruction manual for constructing and operating every nano-chemical machine in every cell and putting it all together to form a complete body and to keep it healthy.

Dawkins emphasizes that the *information* contained in DNA is digital, in a very real sense. Neither Darwin nor anyone else in his day had ever heard of such a thing and wouldn't have understood what it meant if they had. Yet Darwin explained the meaning of life? Such a claim is blatantly wishful thinking.

It is right here—in DNA—that atheists are confronted with a challenge that Darwin could not have imagined, would certainly not have known how to handle, and for which today's evolutionists still have no answer. Furthermore, it is unarguable that the information in DNA is so limitless and ingenious that it could have come only from an infinite intelligence. As everyone knows, this information is presented in *written words—words* that lie at the foundation of, and are absolutely essential for, all life! Clearly, no natural process could ever produce the information contained in DNA.

Darwin knew nothing of that incredible foundation of all plant, animal, and human life. He likely would never have proposed his theory of evolution had he known of DNA and the role it plays. Yet his worshipers, who now know the truth, close their eyes and blindly push ahead with research that they are determined will yet explain life without God.

Through radio telescopes strategically located around the world, mankind has been seeking a coherent message from space that would assure us we are "not alone" in the universe. For decades, we have listened hopefully, yet in vain, for rational patterns that stand out from the chaotic noise of space and would therefore signal a meaningful communication from an intelligent source. Yet all the while, trillions of *written* messages meeting that criteria—written in a language we have decoded and can now read, though we understand it imperfectly—confront us in our own bodies and in every living thing.

If such an ingenious message as is contained in the DNA of the smallest microbe were picked up on a radio telescope probing space, it would make headlines in every newspaper and be trumpeted in every scientific journal as the most exciting discovery in the history of science! The entire world would be repeating the momentous find: "We are not alone! Some other intelligence exists somewhere in the universe! We must establish communication!" Such indeed would be the reaction to any intelligent message, no matter how brief, received from space.

GOD'S INSTRUCTION MANUAL

We have now decoded, as Dawkins himself declares, not just a brief message but a mass of incredibly brilliant intelligent information. Yet scientists are not attempting to establish a relationship with the astonishing Mind that authored these directions for life! Why not? Because this cleverly encoded, ingenious instruction manual (surely a message to mankind!) didn't come from space but is in our genes. Atheists, therefore, insist that it must not have been authored by a personal being but by the unthinking and unconscious process of natural selection.

Is this a rational reaction? Atheists are unwilling to admit that the source of this vast store of undeniably intelligent information could come only from a personal being, not from nature or from any natural process.

To admit that irrefutable fact, the atheistic evolutionists who have appointed themselves the high priests of science, before whose authority all mankind must bow, would then have to admit that God exists, which they are determined not to do. The atheist reads these brilliant instructions in the DNA for building and operating every cell in the body and exclaims in wonder, "Look how marvelous natural selection is!" Collins exclaims over the genius of the DNA molecule instead of bowing before the God who made it and in whom he now claims to believe. This is idolatry, the worship of nature in its most sophisticated form—the DNA molecule.

The Apostle Paul indicted the Greeks and Romans with having rejected the evidence of God that they saw in the universe about them:

> For the invisible things of him from the creation of the world are clearly seen, being understood by the things that are made, even his eternal power and Godhead; so that they are without excuse: Because that, when they knew God, they glorified him not as God, neither were thankful; but became vain in their imaginations, and their foolish heart was darkened. Professing themselves to be wise, they became fools, And changed the glory of the uncorruptible God into an image made like to corruptible man, and to birds, and fourfooted beasts, and creeping things.[19]

God's indictment includes all those today who reject the evidence for His existence so clearly seen in the universe around them. He calls it willful and inexcusable blindness. The evidence that we see in nature all around us is very clear, but the discovery of DNA has made this proof even more powerful.

Natural selection cannot originate information but can only mishandle it, which it does, continually, in obedience to the second law of thermodynamics. This fact is a major hurdle that evolutionists can't jump and therefore attempt to ignore. Their defense used to be that the second law did not apply to life because living things can counter the law through growth. The truth is, however, that the second law does indeed apply and manifests its effect in the errors that appear during copying DNA from one generation to the next. A certain percentage of errors slip through the editing safeguards.

The human race and all living things are deteriorating slowly but at a pace too fast for life to have been on Earth any longer than the Bible indicates—about 6,000 years. At the rate in which copying errors occur from one generation to the next by the effect of natural selection, the human race is headed for a genetic Armageddon.

Mutations cannot create new species but only downward spiraling variations of the same species. They do not introduce new information; they only *lose* function and information.[20] As we've already seen, these accumulating "glitches in the genome," far from guiding an upward evolutionary process through natural selection, cause genetic defects such as "sickle cell anemia, galactosemia (an often-fatal inability to tolerate milk products), and Down's syndrome,"[21] and similar defects, which could shorten the individual's life and ultimately threaten the survival of the race. Such are the consequences of loss of DNA information, a loss that is occurring at a steady, unstoppable rate. The human race (along with every other species) is doomed by the second law.

Incredibly, Francis Collins agrees with atheists. Instead of glorifying the Creator, Collins praises the "marvelous DNA molecule"[22] and pays tribute to evolution for our existence. This is an irrational reaction to the evidence presented by DNA and all of nature. Worst of all (for a professing Christian), it flies in the face of biblical truth, from Genesis to Revelation.

Attempting to remain loyal to the Big Bang and evolution, Collins clearly contradicts the Bible. He accurately reasons that "if God exists . . . He is supernatural [and] not limited by natural laws." His further reasoning, however, raises serious questions concerning who this God is in whom he claims to believe: He "could exist before the Big Bang and know the precise outcome of the formation of the universe even before it started." *Could exist*? Even *before it started*? Instead of "God created [and] . . . all things were made by Him," the universe *somehow* got "started." And although the universe got started without Collins's "God," He is credited with knowing in advance its "precise outcome." That is indeed a generous concession for a mere man to make!

MANUFACTURING THE DEIST'S "GOD"

It gets worse. Says Collins, "He [God] could have foreknowledge of a planet . . . that would lead to the development of sentient creatures through the mechanism of evolution through natural selection."[23] Collins's God has nothing to do with what happens. "Natural selection" is in charge—but "God" knows how it will all turn out. How does He know that? If He's all-knowing, why isn't He all-powerful? Why doesn't He *cause to happen instantly* what He knows will happen? Instead, He lets "nature take its course." Is He keeping His hands off because He is powerless to intervene in the tortuous, inefficient, hit-or-miss, and incredibly slow process of natural selection? Any "God" who would do that is either too weak to be God or too cruel to merit our trust! Could *this* be the way that God "created man in his image"?

DNA, THE ATHEIST'S NEMESIS

This *digitally organized database* transcribed onto the DNA in the form of written and encoded instructions could not have arisen naturally before nature existed or in advance of their utilization. Nor could it have been added to by natural selection during any stage of development. Here we have further evidence of the perversity of atheism. As we have noted, scientists would readily recognize and, in fact, would hail most enthusiastically, the smallest intentionally ordered sounds from space as having originated with intelligent life. Yet atheists reject out of hand the same explanation (the only one possible) for the Architect's written plans found in every cell.

Chemicals neither think nor plan; they simply obey the laws of physics and chemistry. Dawkins admits this same limitation for the chemically composed gene. That fact sounds the death knell for natural selection's having anything to do with the origin of any DNA molecule into which the plans of Dawkins's *architect* have been woven *in advance* of everything it will create and supervise. Would that even be possible?

As it is with the chemical components of every living cell, so it is with the laws that govern them. Laws can neither create the information that defines life and species nor the DNA molecules in which it is written in code. The fact that some chemical bonding leads to larger molecules is not evidence that chemicals can form themselves into living cells. No one has ever seen this happen in nature; nor has anyone been able to create life out of chemicals in the laboratory.

Furthermore, life is not merely dependent upon the right combination of chemicals but upon the *information* in the DNA, which must be planned and written out in advance—and that points inescapably to what Dawkins can give no lesser title than an all-knowing and all-powerful *architect*. Christians call this thinking, choosing, planning, all-knowing, and all-powerful Being, God. Dawkins calls it a "blind watchmaker." A Christian commentator reminds us of what we all innately know:

> Common sense tells us that information does not occur without an intelligence to organize it, any more than the hardware of a computer can create its own software. All scientists know this. Otherwise, how could SETI (Search for Extraterrestrial Intelligence) researchers ever hope to distinguish between radio signals generated by some natural process and those sent from the hoped-for aliens? Again, we see that the most plausible explanation for the information in DNA is that an Intelligent Designer put it there.[24]

THE GENIUS OF LIFE

Consider, for example, Professor Paul Davies. His research includes the origin of the universe and life, properties of black holes, the nature of time, and quantum field theory. None of this advanced scientific knowledge, however, can create life. As we have reminded readers several times, life is not a quality of matter. All of the right material ingredients are still together at the moment of death, but the body lies cold because that vital mysterious "something" we call "life," but can't explain, has fled. Professor Davies admits:

> Trying to make life by mixing chemicals in a test tube is like soldering switches and wires in an attempt to produce Windows 98. It won't work because it addresses the problem at the wrong conceptual level.[25]

Although Davies is not a Christian, he mentions God often—a term he cannot avoid in trying to describe life's origin and ingenious processes. Other atheistic evolutionists also refer to God, though less frequently. They generally do not mean, however, the transcendent God of the Bible and of Christianity but some vague "higher power" within nature to which Einstein also referred, as does Dawkins.

Why is the God of the Bible relevant to our discussion? If the universe was not created by a direct act of God, there is no *reason* for its existence, no explanation as to how and why it came into existence, and no purpose for mankind. Moreover, if God is not the giver of life, there is no explanation for inanimate matter becoming animate, no ultimate judgment after death, and thus the wicked have gotten away with their crimes.

The God of the Bible claims to be the giver of life. Unquestionably, life is not the product of spontaneous generation, nor has it sprung from some power innate in nature. There is no physical explanation for life arising out of the totally lifeless product of a huge ball of fire. We remind ourselves again, the Bible, in perfect agreement, says of Christ, "All things were made by him . . . in him was life."[26]

There is a further insurmountable problem for the atheist-evolutionist: conscious life. Consciousness is not physical, and physical science thus cannot have anything to say about it. Yet materialists keep trying to find a purely physical basis for life. Molecules can come to life only when they have the essential information programmed into them on DNA by an infinite intelligence. The language of DNA stops evolution before it can begin, and it sets a requirement for the origin of life that only the God of the Bible can fulfill.

Life is a mystery. Dawkins says that all it takes is tiny steps over billions of years to achieve it. Evolutionists feel confident that this would be sufficient time to produce a human from a single cell, but they cannot begin their science fiction without life already in existence. We are still waiting for them to tell us how, when, and where these tiny steps began.

THE ASTONISHING DNA CODE

Collins details the incredibly ingenious and complex workings of DNA and the fact that this "'genetic code,' by which information in DNA and RNA is translated into proteins, is universal in all known organisms, from bacteria all through the insect and animal species to man."[27] Why not admit that the facts point to creation by God, not to species evolving into other species while the all-important question of the origin of the first species is left hanging?

One of the objectives of DNA research has been to discover the genetic cause of various diseases. This process gathered momentum for cystic fibrosis (CF) when,

> . . . to the astonishment and delight of scientists and families alike, in 1985 [it was] demonstrated that the CF gene must reside somewhere within a 2 million base-pair segment of DNA on chromosomes 7. But the hard part had really just begun. . . . The search [would be] like looking for a single burned-out light bulb in the basement of a house somewhere in the United States.

It took years, but

> . . . one rainy day in May 1989 . . . data from that day's work in the lab [showed] unequivocally that a deletion of just three letters of the DNA code (CTT, to be exact) in the protein-coding part of a previously unknown gene was the cause of cystic fibrosis in the majority of patients. . . .

[T]his mutation and other less common misspellings in this same gene, now called CFTR, account for virtually all cases of the disease. . . . The next steps proved harder than expected, and the story of CF is regrettably still not history. But the gene finding . . . started CF research on a course toward what we all expect will be ultimate victory. . . . It had taken ten years and more than $50 million to identify this one gene for this one disease. And CF was supposed to be one of the easiest—since it was a relatively common disease that followed Mendel's rules of inheritance precisely.[28]

Setting aside the undeniable fact that DNA does not define what it is to be human, and thus no help can be found there for evolution, there is no question that it can be the source of many discoveries in the medical field.

Scientists have now told us that love comes from chemical reactions in the brain.[29] Isn't that comforting? Of course, we can't be sure whether we have those chemical reactions, although if you want to subject your brain to a particular scan, it supposedly can be identified. If the scan revealed that you had this right combination, would that strengthen your resolve to stick it out if you were contemplating divorce? Or would it be better to realize that the Bible tells us simply that love is a command, with no excuses allowed?

Jesus was asked by a lawyer who was trying to trap Him, "Master, which is the great commandment in the law?" He replied, "Thou shalt love the Lord thy God with all thy heart, and with all thy soul, and with all thy mind. This is the first and great commandment. And the second is like unto it, Thou shalt love thy neighbor as thyself. On these two commandments hang all the law and the prophets."[30]

Such love, far from contributing to the survival of the fittest, would work against the theory of natural selection. This is the love that God has for us as His creatures, it is the love He expects from us toward Him and toward our fellows, and it is the love that even the atheist must admit is the ultimate human experience. Atheism knows nothing of such morality.

The Big Bang offers atheists no explanation for these human qualities that cannot be described in terms of energy or matter. Moreover, that which we value most highly (love, joy, integrity, justice, truth, ethics, morals, unswerving loyalty, and a host of like qualities honored and admired by all mankind) could not possibly be the offspring of a huge explosion that supposedly brought the cosmos into existence.

Not only could not the human qualities that we value most highly have come out of a "big bang," but if that event actually occurred, it would deny their significance. All human experience, had it resulted from a giant explosion, would be meaningless. Anyone who imagined there was purpose and meaning to life would be the victim of a cruel hoax.

George Wald added his special touch: "Three billion years ago, life arose upon the earth. It is the only life in the solar system. About two million years ago, man appeared. He has become the dominant species on the earth. All other living things, animal and plant, live by his sufferance. He is the custodian of life on earth, and in the solar system. It's a huge responsibility."[31] One would think that Wald's simplistic conclusions could hardly resonate with intelligent seekers after scientific truth.

No matter how much knowledge and wisdom you acquire during your life, not one jot will be passed on to your children by genetic means. Each new generation starts from scratch.

—RICHARD DAWKINS, *THE SELFISH GENE*, 23

Man has evolved from ancestors that were not human. . . . The creation of God's image in man is not an event but a process, and therefore the moral law is a product of an evolutionary development.

—THEODOSIUS DOBZHANSKY, "ETHICS AND VALUES IN BIOLOGICAL AND CULTURAL EVOLUTION," ZYGON, THE *JOURNAL OF RELIGION AND SCIENCE*, AS REPORTED IN *LOS ANGELES TIMES*, PART IV (JUNE 16, 1974), 6

Where then shall we find the source of truth and the moral inspiration for a really scientific socialist humanism, if not in the sources of science itself, in the ethic upon which knowledge is founded, and which by free choice makes knowledge the supreme value—the measure and warrant for all other values? . . . The ancient covenant is in pieces; man knows at last that he is alone in the universe's unfeeling immensity, out of which he emerged only by chance. His destiny is nowhere spelled out, nor is his duty. The kingdom above or the darkness below: it is for him to choose.

—JACQUES MONOD, *CHANCE AND NECESSITY* (NEW YORK: ALFRED A. KNOPF, 1971), 180

The hellish vapors rise and fill the brain,
Till I go mad and my heart is utterly changed.
See this sword?
The prince of darkness
Sold it to me. For me he beats the time and gives the signs.
Ever more boldly I play the dance of death.

—KARL MARX, CITED IN RICHARD WURMBRAND, *MARX AND SATAN* (WESTCHESTER, IL: CROSSWAY BOOKS, 1987), 15

At one time man had scarcely more brains than his anthropoid cousins, the apes. But, by kicking, biting, fighting . . . and outwitting his enemies and by the fact that the ones who had not sense and strength . . . to do this were killed off, man's brain became enormous and he waxed both in wisdom and agility if not in size. . . .

—ALBERT EDWARD WIGGAM, *THE NEW DIALOGUE OF SCIENCE* (GARDEN CITY, NY: GARDEN PUBLISHING CO., 1922, CITED IN *PERSPECTIVES ON SCIENCE AND FAITH*, BY JERRY BERGMAN (44, 1992, 116)

THIRTEEN

CONSCIOUSNESS, CONSCIENCE, AND MORALS

HAVING DEFIED AND PUBLICALLY DENIED God via bestselling books, the New Atheists feel a sense of self-importance unknown to the relatively few atheists there were in the days of Newton, Boyle, Pasteur, Mendel, et al. Their current status emboldens them to defy not only God but to disregard long-established natural law. Feeling invincible, the Four Horsemen are riding the crest of a wave of newly found popularity. As mentioned before, Christopher Hitchens boasted, "I've just made a lot of money with a God-bashing book."[1]

A tsunami of truth is about to wipe out their seemingly invincible kingdom. Richard Dawkins is the master storyteller, with George Wald not far behind. Recognizing the fact that the law of biogenesis makes evolution and natural selection impossible, the latter proclaimed, "One exception [to this law] is all that was needed, and it happened right here on earth." How does he know this?

How many millions or billions of years ago did this alleged exception occur? How did Wald learn about it? Has he any scientific proof? What verification has there been from witnesses? Such simple logic bounces off the atheists' armor like rounds of tiny BB shot.

This alleged exception to established scientific law is worse than wishful thinking. One might as well wish for just one momentary suspension of the law of gravity. Of course, in that nanosecond, the universe would fly apart. Nor would a momentary suspension of the law of biogenesis have less disastrous consequences. Who knows what monsters might be conceived during that brief time? Wald says that only one exception was needed and that it occurred here on Earth. Dawkins must get his genetics from a different source. He says that this law has been violated billions of times all over the universe.

Law? A strange "law" that can be violated with impunity! Dawkins writes (italics added to highlight his uncertain gropings):

> The origin of life *may have been a highly improbable event*. Darwinian evolution proceeds merrily once life has originated. But how does life get started? The origin of life was the *chemical event*, or series of events, whereby the *vital conditions for natural selection first came about*. The major ingredient was *heredity*, either DNA or (*more probably*) something that copies like DNA but less accurately, *perhaps* the related molecule RNA. Once the vital ingredient—*some kind of genetic molecule*—is in place, true Darwinian natural selection can follow, and *complex life emerges as the eventual consequence*. The spontaneous arising by chance of the first hereditary molecule strikes many as *improbable*. Maybe it is—*very, very improbable*. . . .
>
> The origin of life is a flourishing, *if speculative*, subject for research. The expertise required for it is chemistry, and it is not mine. I watch from the sidelines with engaged curiosity, and I shall not be surprised if, within the next few years, chemists report that they have successfully midwifed

a new origin of life in the laboratory. Nevertheless, it hasn't happened yet. And it is still *possible* to maintain that *the probability of its happening is, and always was, exceedingly low*—although *it did happen once*![2]

Let me comment briefly on the italicized words and phrases:

1) *Highly improbable*? Excuse me, Richard, it's *impossible*! This is not even clever; this is a blatant denial of the long-established law of biogenesis that life comes *only* from life! Just like that, Richard, with a stroke of your pen, you've swept a proven scientific law aside and without so much as a hint to your admiring followers of your grave deception!

2) *Chemical event*? There is no life inherent in chemicals. Far from telling us the origin of life, you are avoiding the subject.

3) *Vital conditions for natural selection first came about.* Really? Tell us about them: what were they, how did they come about, and when? I await a response.

4) *Heredity*? Pardon me. Heredity before we even have life? Who are the ancestors of these nonexistent beings? I remind you, life was not yet established.

5) *More probably*? *More* doesn't turn impossible into *probably*! We need scientific facts.

6) *Perhaps . . . some kind of genetic molecule*? Perhaps you could describe and explain it for us. Where did it come from? Who was the discoverer of this amazing molecule that was apparently overlooked by Pasteur? Surely you, Richard Dawkins, the former Simonyi Professor for the Public Understanding of Science must know and have been keeping it a secret.

7) *Complex life emerges as the eventual consequence?* Sleight of hand is out of place when we're trying to deal with facts. *Complex life?* Shouldn't we have somewhat of an explanation of *what complex life* is and how it emerged? *Eventual consequence* explains nothing.

8) *If speculative?* Let's admit it. Have you or any of the other brights ever offered anything on the origin of life *except* speculation?

9) *It did happen once?* Yes, life exists on Earth, but it didn't just "happen." You say God doesn't exist, though you admit you cannot prove that assertion. We agree that it happened once but not that it "happened by chance" or was somehow infused into the totally sterilized remnants of the alleged "big bang." But to put it bluntly, Richard, you are engaging in gross deception and with complete disregard for the moral and spiritual welfare of your millions of readers.

Furthermore, the pretense of calculating odds measuring the possibility of life appearing spontaneously without cause out of lifeless matter is so much dust thrown in our eyes. What is life? Science does not know, after centuries of trying to define it. How, then, can you possibly measure the odds for its spontaneous appearance!

THE MORAL BANKRUPTCY OF ATHEISM

Atheism, as we have seen, denies the existence of anything but matter. From atheism, it follows logically that consciousness and conscience (with the latter's sense of right and wrong) must reside in the molecules of the brain (unless they've lately been discovered hiding in some other part of the body). But to suggest any bodily location whatsoever is clearly untenable. Consciousness and conscience have no relationship to the physical universe; they belong to a nonphysical dimension of existence. That fact is proven by one's inability to supply a physical description of "nonsense"—or of literally thousands of other words found in dictionaries and encyclopedias for which there is absolutely no physical description.

The rejection of this nonphysical dimension necessarily denies the existence of the God of the Bible, who Jesus said is "a Spirit."[3] It also denies the soul and spirit of man, thereby turning man into Skinner's stimulus-response mechanism. This denial puts the atheist in the desperate position of abandoning reality for foolish statements. Consider this from Professor Steven Weinberg:

> With or without [religion] you would have good people doing good things and evil people doing evil things. But for good people to do evil things, that takes religion.[4]

What is the definition of "good people"? How does Weinberg define "*good*," or "*evil*," or "*religion*"? Does atheism promote goodness, compassion, love of truth? Does atheism offer a better basis for the equality and freedom that the Declaration of Independence promised the citizens of the United States? It was founded upon the belief that such rights are endowed by their Creator! Does atheism provide a better endowment?

Is the appreciation of music, poetry, or the beauty of a sunset located somewhere in the genes? Is it physical? If not, how could it be the product of evolution and natural selection? Many musicians refer to music as having "soul." We all know what that means, but no one can give a physical description of what we can only describe as "appreciation."

In a generous mood, Dawkins says, "We must respect the other fellow's religion, but only in the sense and to the extent that we respect his theory that his wife is beautiful and his children smart."[5] Very clever. What is he trying to say?

As for "respect," can the materialist provide a physical description of it? What part of the anatomy, or what gene, determines what or whom we "respect"? How did this capability develop through evolution and natural selection? What is the physical description of the previous sentence? We're just asking sincere questions. What could Dawkins, the dogmatic materialist, be talking about?

Respect another's religion? Isn't this a contradiction, considering how often Dawkins has told us that religion must be stamped out and Hitchens has said that religion is evil and should not be taught to children? The Four Horsemen even hint about the government taking complete control of the education of children to eliminate any religious influence.

In contrast to today's acceptance of natural selection, Sir John Eccles declared: "The facts of human morality and ethics are clearly at variance with a theory that explains all behavior in terms of self-preservation and preservation of the species."[6] Yet there are numerous examples of military men and women saving their fellows' lives by sacrificing their own. These moral acts could not have been "impulses" created by natural selection, because they directly contradict it.

YOU DON'T NEED A BOOK

Second only to the atheists' favorite mantra, "We're working on that," Hitchens, Dennett, and most other atheists love to repeat, "You don't need a book to tell you what is right and what is wrong." We agree.

In March 2007, thirty-six freshman cadets were caught cheating at the Air Force Academy. They obtained answers to a test and forwarded them by email. The cadet honor code forbids lying, stealing, cheating, and covering up for anyone who does.[7] Did natural selection develop this honor because individuals survive longer to have more children if they follow it? On the contrary, it is not about individual survival in the world but survival at the academy. Surely, it was a sense of shame that caused one guilty cadet to voluntarily withdraw. Isn't it amazing that natural selection apparently knows all about survival at the academy and how that will ultimately affect the physical survival of many of the cadets who will go on to become parents!

The Christian does not deny the fact that no matter what one's religion may be, there exists something in all of mankind, something that we all know is there. It manifests itself first in very young children. We call it the conscience. In what part of the DNA is it located? Certainly, the conscience is not located in any physical organ, nor is it anywhere in the DNA.

Of course people can and do perform moral deeds. They also perform immoral deeds and know it. We frequently hear in the news of public figures, whether politicians, church leaders, lawmen, etc., who fall into some moral failure. It ends their careers. Everyone knows that such immoral behavior is wrong. Why?

The atheist has no explanation. The conscience could not possibly have been produced by natural selection. It certainly would not assist in our survival but, in fact, has caused many to expend much time and effort and even the sacrifice of one's life to save others. As Jesus said, "Greater love hath no man than this, that a man lay down his life for his friends."[8]

Consider the following:

> President Bush awarded the military's highest honor to a 19-year-old soldier who was killed in Iraq after falling on a grenade to save his fellow soldiers. Private Ross McGinnis, of Knox, Pa., was killed in a Baghdad neighborhood on Dec. 4, 2006, when a grenade was thrown into the gunner's hatch of the Humvee in which he was riding. . . . Private McGinnis had enough time to jump out and save himself but instead dropped into the hatch and covered the grenade with his own body, absorbing the fragments. He was killed instantly. All four crewmembers were saved.[9]

There are innumerable such acts of self-sacrifice down through history, including quite a number of them in recent years. Dawkins has "explained" none of them. Certainly this heroic impulse didn't come from a "selfish gene." Nor could it have been developed by millions of years of natural selection. Could Jesus' explanation about "no greater love" be the right one? Dawkins says that this is the only life you have, so live it to the fullest.[10] If that is true, it is not rational to sacrifice that one and only life to save the lives of others. Nor could such self-sacrificial love lurk somewhere in the DNA.

Such amazing love can only be a rational act for those who truly believe that man is more than his body and that his soul and spirit survive his death. We have already established that man is more than the molecules of his body and not merely a physical being. The real person who has inhabited the body continues to live endlessly, either in God's presence or in the horror of eternal separation from Him, accompanied by the torment of a guilty conscience that will forever haunt the damned.

THE HARSH STAMP OF ABSURDITY

The conscience is clearly part of that impassable barrier between man and all animals, a barrier that cannot be crossed by any evolutionary process. This chasm, which we all know is there, puts the harsh stamp of absurdity upon the efforts of all the fossil seekers who are trying to find some physical proof that man's body is similar to the bodies of numerous animals. As already mentioned, *of course it is, having been designed to function in the same physical environment.*

The same stamp of absurdity marks the efforts of geneticists, such as Francis Collins, who tirelessly pursue some evidence in the DNA for man's alleged ascent from lettuce and carrots and garden slugs and even a fungus clinging to a tree.

Neither bodily structure and functions nor the DNA that governs man's physical components has anything to do with who human beings really are. Evidence of man's incredible brilliance in music, poetry, mathematics, science, engineering, architecture, etc., will never be found in the physical parts of man, including the DNA, upon which the scientists focus. So all attempts to find a missing link between the animal world and human beings, by digging and searching, are wasted effort.

WHAT COULD BE THE SOURCE OF THIS COMMON CONSCIENCE?

Natural selection could not develop, over no matter how many millions of years, our common sense of right and wrong. Here we come back to a major problem for the evolutionist/atheist: there is no place in the philosophy of materialism for morals or even for ideas.

On the *Mike Dickin Show* [in England], in his introduction of Dawkins, Dickin said, "The religious among us claim that without religion there is no morality. What utter nonsense." What utter nonsense for Dickin to make such a statement! No religion has a monopoly on morality, nor can any religion take credit for writing God's law in every conscience. This is something *God* has done.

Furthermore, as we have already stated, we are not defending *religion*. We have shown that the Bible is not a book about religion. We are only defending *biblical Christianity*, and there is much "Christianity" that is far from biblical. The conscience, which is common to all mankind, is an undeniable reminder that God made man in His image and that this one true God, who wrote His laws in stone on Mount Sinai, has also written them in every human conscience.

Dawkins said, "It's a bit weird to base your belief on a text, and when you're asked why you believe it you respond 'because it says so here.' It's a complete circle of an argument and the authentication is contained within the book. So if you ask why you believe, the answer comes back, 'Because it says so in the Bible.'"

This is an unfair reduction of all Christians to the level of unthinking robots. Biblical Christians accept what the Bible says as true because, on the basis of careful verification, they believe it is the Word of God. They find in the Bible, in history, and in science more than sufficient proof for accepting what the Bible says. This is what biblical apologetics is about. Later, we will give irrefutable proof that the Bible foretells the future without error. We challenge atheists specifically to refute that chapter.

THE ATHEISTS' WEIRD WORLD
OF MATERIALISM!

Atheists are materialists. Matter is all they know. Nothing immaterial exists—no mind, no soul, no hope, because these are not material. Thus, there can be neither *thinker* nor *experiencer*. How can they even accept the reality of love? They might respond, "Of course everyone accepts that!" But why? Many atheists, such as Nobelist George Wald, also claim that all matter is conscious. In India, there is a holy day when everyone worships the implements of his trade. Secretaries worship their typewriters, taxi drivers worship their taxis. Banners and various ornaments are attached to the instrument of one's trade to show that this is one of the "gods" Hindus worship.

No one experiences love, joy, peace, patience, goodness, kindness, or any of the other human qualities that are expressed in the most moving literature, drama, or music as purely physical. If sex is merely physical, that is no more than what animals experience. In other words, it's mere lust.

In his book, *The Selfish Gene*, in trying to explain how his imaginative invention, the supposed "god meme," perpetuates itself, Dawkins writes, "Psychological appeal is appeal to brains, and brains are shaped by natural selection of genes in gene pools. They [genes] want to find some way in which having a brain like that improves gene survival."[11] Dawkins is claiming that the genes are in charge of everything we say and do, and apparently they supervise our "evolution." He offers no proof.

This is not only a horrible thought, but it is irrational. Rejecting the God of love, the One who knows all and can even foresee the future, Dawkins (without giving us sufficient reason for doing so), turns to an imaginary "meme" that may represent nothing more than the latest style—or the latest popular lie. If that is not irrational, then what is? This rebellion is of such proportion that it can only arise from a deep and prejudiced hatred of God.

You are not in charge of your brain, your genes are? And they are trying to reshape your brain for their own purposes? Has anyone ever experienced *anything* in daily life that would even suggest that something like this was going on, so that instead of doing one's own thinking, he or she is left to wonder what the brain and selfish genes would think of next? Rationally and consciously, we know that we are each in charge of our brains and that we ourselves, not our genes or brains, do make genuine choices!

This is incredible stuff from Dawkins. There is a "psychological appeal to *brains*," not to the *thinking persons* to whom the brains belong? And genes are engineering this appeal? Again, we are forced to say that Dawkins, one of the brightest of the brights, is talking such nonsense that even we lesser lights recognize that fact. Brains are composed of protein molecules—molecules that are as incapable of responding to a "psychological appeal" as the protein molecules in any other part of the body.

Sir John Eccles, Nobel Prize recipient for his research on the brain, explains that the brain does not originate our thoughts: "We are a combination of two things or entities: our brains on the one hand; and our conscious selves on the other."[12] He added that the brain is a precious "instrument," a "lifelong servant and companion," providing "lines of communication from and to the material world."[13]

Materialistic (i.e., atheistic) science has nothing to say about the *mind*, which renowned neurosurgeon Wilder Penfield described as "outside [and] independent of the brain."[14] As we've already noted, anything "outside and independent" of the brain can only be *nonphysical*. Numerous scientific experiments confirm this, effectively pulling the rug from beneath materialism as a viable belief system.

Surely, Dawkins ought to be bright enough to recognize these simple facts. They have been rephrased by many other neuroscientists and widely quoted. We lesser intellects certainly understand the distinction that must be made between the physical brain and the nonphysical mind, but for Dawkins to admit the dual nature of existence would be tantamount to renouncing his materialism. That would be like committing intellectual suicide after all the harsh words he has spoken against God and how far out on the atheist limb he has crawled.

PERSONIFYING THE IMPERSONAL

Who are "*they*" to whom Dawkins refers as using us as their caretakers to fulfill their own ambitions? "They" are the "selfish genes," of course, and these selfish genes "want to find some way" to use the brain for their own survival. Dawkins talks as though "selfish genes" are independent, conscious entities that think and plan ahead and consciously seek ways to manipulate *us* in order to accomplish *their* own selfish goals. How else could he use this terminology?

Dawkins has no other way to express his theory than to personify the impersonal and unconscious. This one fact alone disproves his impersonal, materialistic theory. He has, however, already disproved it himself by having gone on record in his first book, *The Selfish Gene*: "Genes have no foresight. They do not plan ahead. Genes just *are*."[15] Which of these contradictory statements are we to believe: if genes don't plan ahead, how can they "guide" our evolution or direct our thoughts and desires?

Dawkins teeters uncertainly on the very brink of admitting the necessity of a creator, whom he calls the *architect*, but that would ruin the whole "natural selection" scam. He would have to confess that all of this scientific-sounding verbiage about natural selection, genes, and memes doesn't merit being called a theory but is just so much fantasy from the neverland that Dawkins periodically visits in order to pull out another theory.

What is the physical description of "psychological" or of "foresight" that would fit somewhere in the physical matter of the brain or in the DNA? Is there an apparatus in the gene that is responsible—a gene, or part of a gene, that originates not only the idea of "desire" but a different gene for every desire and even for each shade and nuance of meaning? Since the brain is a physical organ, how can it understand, much less originate and organize, nonphysical concepts such as these?

Here we have just a small glimpse of the folly of rejecting non-physical reality. Dawkins would have us believe that the idea that man has a "soul" and "spirit" is nothing but foolishness because only matter exists.

CREDITING NATURAL SELECTION WITH WHAT IT CANNOT DO

Can such complex mental and emotional processes as goal setting, which involve motivation, ambition, determination, morals, and ethics be identified in the genes and developed by natural selection? This is ludicrous. The fact that there *must be a physical basis* for natural selection to act upon forces the atheist to make ridiculous statements.

Furthermore, having no foresight, how can Dawkins's selfish genes or Darwin's natural selection play any role in *goal seeking*? Doesn't goal seeking demand a mind, which neither genes nor natural selection have? This is a personal quality of mankind, a fact that even atheists admit. Staunch defender of atheism Douglas J. Futuyma, professor of ecology and evolution at the State University of New York at Stony Brook, declares:

> Since natural selection is totally an impersonal process that is nothing more than a difference, generation by generation, in the reproductive success of one genome over another, there's no way that it can look forward to the future or guard against the possibility of extinction. What individuals have right now that gives them superior adaptation may lead to disaster tomorrow.[16]

In spite of its adamant rejection of any "higher power," atheism is not completely without its own gods. It is not difficult to see that natural selection is really the god that Dawkins worships:

> We, all of us, share a kind of religious reverence for the beauties of the universe, for the complexity of life, for the sheer magnitude of the cosmos, the sheer magnitude of geological time. And it's tempting to translate that feeling of awe and worship into a desire to worship . . . a person, an agent. You want to attribute it to a maker, a creator.
>
> What science [through Darwinism] has now achieved is *an emancipation* from that impulse to attribute these things to a creator—and it's a *major* emancipation because humans have an almost overwhelming desire to think that they've explained something by attributing it to a maker. We're so used to explaining things in our own world—these television cameras . . . the lights . . . the clothes we wear, the chairs we sit on—everything we see around us is a manufactured object. And so it's so tempting to believe that living things, or the stars or mountains or rivers, have all been made by something.
>
> It was a supreme achievement of the human intellect to realize that there is a better explanation for these things— that these things can come about by purely natural causes.[17]

Well, that's what this debate is all about, and we theists have enough intelligence to reject this statement by Dawkins. He makes such pronouncements as though they represent "science" and are beyond contradiction. Nothing could be further from the truth. There are hundreds, if not thousands, of scientists who take strong exception to Dawkins's dogma.

One thing that both sides can agree upon is that it is the maker alone who gives meaning to the object made. Indisputably, if there is no maker, there can be no purpose for the object, and without a purpose for its existence, the object can have no meaning. Dawkins objects to carrying this fact over to the world of nature, but he cannot produce a valid reason for his objection.

Of Jesus Christ, who is God in the biblical meaning of that word, we are told, "All things were made by him; and without him was not anything made that was made."[18] Consistent with their adamant rejection of a personal Creator, atheists declare that the energy out of which the universe unquestionably is made is self-existent, without beginning or end. Astronomers, however, are now in almost unanimous agreement that the universe had a beginning. It couldn't possibly have been in existence forever nor could it be self-existent.

The unanimity among astronomers that the universe had a beginning creates serious problems for those who deny a personal Creator-God. As we have already pointed out, there appears to be a conflict between the first and second laws of thermodynamics. The first law—the law of conservation of energy—declares that energy can neither be created nor destroyed. The second law—the law of entropy—declares that energy, though it has not been destroyed, has deteriorated in usability.

For example, to tap into the energy in a log of wood, we use some for building furniture, some for cooking our food, and some to warm ourselves. Of course, this has changed the nature of the wood. Some of it remains as ashes, but the heat into which the log was mainly transformed has dissipated, some of it absorbed by our bodies or by matter within range of the heat, but much of it has gone into the atmosphere. Has it been destroyed? No, it has not been destroyed. It would be impossible to gather it up again, but it has not been destroyed.

Both laws are apparently true, but there is also no question that they contradict one another. If energy cannot be created, it must have been here forever. If it cannot be destroyed, it must be eternal. There is no question, however, that the law of entropy is equally valid. Both are true. Entropy is all around us: the rusting of metal, the death and ultimate decay of bodies, whether plant, animal, or human. Thus, energy must have had a beginning, or it would all be unusable by now.

LIFE IS MORE THAN PHYSICAL

Living things, from a materialist standpoint, are simply conglomerations of the right chemicals in the right combinations in the right places. There must be more than mere chemicals involved in the formation of a body. Chemicals don't just gather together to form bodies or anything else. Some *mind* must be in charge of the process. Of course, the essential elements could not possibly be assembled by chance in the right order and relationship with one another— not even for a single cell, the smallest unit of life. The mathematical impossibility of chance arrangement is off the charts, as we have seen. Let's assume that all of the physical elements essential for a single cell could somehow be assembled in the right order by a geneticist's expertise. Even this would still not *create* life.

Obviously, at the moment of death, all of the chemistry that was once alive is still there, but life has gone. We know what that means, but we don't know what the spark of life is that vanished. It is certainly *not* an innate quality of matter or the right arrangement thereof.

The Bible says that man's life comes from God. That statement cannot be contradicted on any scientific basis—and how could it be by those who don't even know what life is? Moreover, the Bible declares that life is not only physical but also spiritual—a fact that every thinking person knows from personal experience. Jesus said, "A man's life consisteth not in the abundance of the things which he possesseth,"[19] Wealth does not bring happiness. The wealthiest people are often the most miserable because they have reached the pinnacle of success and realized all their dreams, only to discover that they are still unfulfilled.

Why would this be? It could only be because man is more than the material body in which he lives temporarily while on Earth. That emptiness inside cannot be satisfied with material things because God created us in His moral and spiritual image, having given a soul and spirit to each person. As a consequence, we can no more satisfy that inner longing with material things than we can duplicate the beauty of a symphony by filling our stomachs with the tastiest food. The only way the universe as it is and human life within it can be explained that fits all of the facts is by a supernatural act of creation that formed man in the moral and spiritual image of his Creator. Anything else falls far short of explaining man as he is and as he experiences life.

Moral and spiritual values do not come out of an explosion of energy nor are they related at all to material things. By very definition, the most important qualities of human life are denied by atheistic materialism. Crick says we are just containers for molecules and our highest thoughts are a delusion. Dawkins says basically the same: we are just vessels for our selfish genes to use for their own survival. This is, as Crick says, "astonishing," against all common sense, but he offers it as the meaning of life. We have every right to reject such a hypothesis as the height of absurdity.

The desire for truth and justice and the longing for meaning and fulfillment cannot be explained by alleged "big bangs," evolutionary forces, or natural selection. Such desires are not a function of atoms and molecules and cells. Can we prove this scientifically? No, but it needs no such proof, any more than we should be obligated to prove scientifically that joy and sorrow are not the same thing, nor are they mere illusions. Everyone knows this is true. In vain the materialist mocks "faith" and searches for an explanation of all human experience in materialistic science. It can't be found there.

"A KIND OF SOMETHING IN THE AIR"

Dawkins tries to answer the questions we have just asked above. He says,

> There does seem to be a kind of universal acceptance that certain things are right and other things are not. . . . It almost amounts to common sense. You certainly don't need a holy book to tell you. . . . I think that it comes partly from our evolutionary past . . . there was a time in our evolutionary past . . . when we lived in small kin groups . . . where good deeds

could expect to be reciprocated. And under those conditions, we developed a kind of lust to be good, which was parallel to the lust for sex, which has a Darwinian advantage.[20]

How does Dawkins know this? He is pulling definitive statements out of the air, which are of great importance, if true. Unfortunately, he has nothing to support this astonishing bit of information. Even so, he sounds so authoritative, as though he has no doubts about the validity of what he is saying.

So Dawkins acknowledges common sense, something that everyone possesses, and the very thing we've been emphasizing, but he doesn't tell us what it is or how it got into everyone's consciousness. Is common sense something that comes through the genes? He claims that it was put there by some evolutionary process. Common sense says, "Wait a minute, Richard! How do you know all of this? What evidence do you offer? How do you know what happened millions of years ago? No trace of ideas, moral standards, or other beliefs could possibly be found in the fossil record, nor can it be found in the lettering sequences of the DNA. We demand to know the basis for this statement!"

Dawkins continues with this note of absolute certainty:

> We no longer live in small clans; Darwinism's pressure to be good is no longer so strong. . . . The point is that our evolutionary past built into us a lust for sex . . . and a lust to be good . . . to be friendly . . . to cooperate, to be sympathetic toward suffering. But it also comes from something less easy to define. I call it the shifting moral zeitgeist . . . a kind of *something in the air*, some other force, something which we can't understand with sufficient sociological, psychological sophistication. Whatever else it is, it isn't religion.[21]

This is remarkable! Dawkins doesn't know what is behind what most people would consider to be admirable qualities, but he's sure *it isn't religion*. Might there be a little bit of prejudice involved? *We* are equally sure that friendliness and sympathy are not "something in the air." What would that mean—*something in the air?* This sounds rather sophomoric. Isn't there something more definite that atheistic science can offer?

We've already explained that we are not defending religion but are opposed to it. We agree with the Four Horsemen that religion is an invention of man. On the other hand, we would deny that friendliness, cooperativeness, sympathy toward those who suffer, etc., are not genuine but are no more than bogus feelings that we have somehow inhaled from the atmosphere.

A kind of something in the air. Now isn't that profound! It seems a pity that the scientist who had promised to provide the public with an "understanding of science" apparently lacked "sufficient sociological and psychological sophistication" to give us the explanation.

An understanding of *science?* For Dawkins and his cohorts, *science* is the savior that will rescue mankind from all of its ills. Most scientists, however, would not agree with this almost worshipful attitude toward science and especially to Darwinism as its standard bearer. The reverent awe with which Darwin is treated turns Darwinism into a religious cult. Einstein, however, was very definite that science and religion had nothing to do with one another. Likewise, repeating the wisdom of Erwin Schrödinger:

> [Science] knows nothing of . . . good or bad, God and eternity.
> . . . Whence came I and whither go I? That is the great unfathomable question. . . . Science has no answer to it.[22]

Dawkins says this sense of right and wrong is "*some other force . . . we can't understand with sufficient sociological, psychological sophistication. . . .*" Wasn't this common understanding supposedly dropped into our consciousness by natural selection? How is it that this evolutionary force didn't finish the job by *giving* us an understanding? And how, or from what source, did natural selection gain this profound "sociological and psychological sophistication" in order to pass it on to us? Moreover, how did Dawkins know about this "something in the air"?

It would also be helpful if Dawkins would tell us *where* "in the air" this "something" hides so that we might know how to get it into our lungs and bloodstream to enlighten us! It's really amazing that Dawkins has discovered something so profound and important, yet all one needs to do is to take some deep gulps of air to get it. What else of this intangible and moral nature might be "in the air"? How does one catch these things floating about? Is it like catching a cold? This is awesome stuff!

Dawkins is doing his ingenious best to keep up a brave front while passing on the inadequacy of the "wisdom" that atheism provides. The really insulting irrationality it offers leaves Dawkins little choice. I suppose we ought to compliment him on his ability to make something out of nothing and thank him for the profundities he caught in a deep breath as they floated past him on the wind.

NATURAL SELECTION'S DENIAL OF GENUINE CHOICE

One of the key issues in the debate between creationists and evolutionists is whether human personality and the ability to make free choices can all be explained by neurological activity in the physical brain. If so, then it could be claimed that the mind is not distinct from the brain and thus that we humans have no genuine freedom of choice, nor is there any objective purpose or meaning to life that we voluntarily pursue. In that case, our thoughts are simply the result of motions of atoms in our brains that all began with a giant explosion and fireball and that have proceeded randomly ever since and thus have no meaning. Of course, evolution and natural selection entered, and our genes are now causing our thoughts, motives, and passions. So we're still robots.

How could criminals be held accountable for crimes that have been programmed into their genes by millions of years of natural selection? Dismiss the judges and juries and shut down the courts and law schools—and prisons! Yes, shut everything down. What is the point of any discussion? It's all a deception and delusion foisted upon us by our molecules. So said Crick to his dying day, but no one with any capacity for reason actually believes this stuff, and those who do deserve our pity.

We dimwits are going to push atheists on this point. We demand consistency. They must demonstrate in their lives that they really believe the farfetched statements they make. If this is what they insist the rest of us believe, then we insist that they live by their theories. Is it possible that everything we experience in our lives is a delusion imposed upon us by natural selection?

Can it really be true that our ambitions and love for our spouses and children and our willingness to suffer for the good of others are delusions that the molecules of our physical bodies trick us into experiencing? Well, if the genes are clever enough to disguise within the process of natural selection an "appearance of design" that deceives even the most dedicated atheist, it would seem that there is literally nothing our ingenious genes cannot do.

Common sense compels us to reject this nonsense. We refuse to let our genes, no matter how clever they are, deceive us. After all, we have the brains, and the genes don't. It really is puzzling how our genes can tell us what to think and do.

A CHOICE TO BE MADE

The Christian believes the statement in Genesis 1:27 that God "created man in his own image." Christopher Hitchens and his fellow atheists prefer to believe that we are the offspring of unthinking, unknowing forces of nature and our supposed predecessors, which these forces have created. Atheists refuse any voluntary relationship with the One whom Hitchens loves to call a "heavenly dictator" who imposes his will on his creatures. Instead, atheists prefer to be led about with a ring through their noses, with the end of the chain held by Crick's "vast assembly of nerve cells and their associated molecules" and Dawkins's "selfish genes."

Both Dawkins and Crick admit that their similar theories run contrary to common sense and the universal intuition of the race. We repeat here the obvious question that this insanity has forced us to ask: If this is what evolution has made us, why should we think it astonishing? How could the highly evolved protein molecules that make up our bodies hold thoughts that not only challenge but directly contradict what evolution has made us, even giving *"the appearance of design"*?

Wouldn't this fact alone seem to indicate that our thoughts are independent of our brains—that brain activity does not *produce* thought but is the *result* of thought? Among the few Jews in Germany who had the foresight to leave shortly after Hitler came to power in 1933, Michael Polanyi went on to become one of the world's leading physical scientists and philosophers of science. He was Chair of the Physical Chemistry department at the University of Manchester. He left that post in 1948 to pursue the philosophy of science. Polanyi vigorously opposed the positivism so popularly accepted in his day. He affirmed that consciousness cannot be explained by physical science because it exists in another dimension:

> The most striking feature of our own existence is our sentience [consciousness]. The laws of physics and chemistry include no conception of sentience, and any system wholly determined by these [physical] laws must be insentient.
>
> It may be to the interests of science to turn a blind eye on this central fact of the universe, but it certainly is not in the interest of truth.[23]

On the one hand, it seems that Polanyi is clearly criticizing the materialists among his colleagues. On the other hand, his use of the word "science" seems to credit the atheists with being true scientists. Read almost any article in newspapers and popular magazines that are not scientific journals, and see how "science" is always given an atheistic flavor. In other words, one rarely encounters the word "science" in *Time* magazine, or in *Newsweek,* or *U.S. News and World Report,* without being given the impression that it refers to anything other than atheistic materialism.

THE IRRATIONALITY OF MATERIALISM

There are many reasons for rejecting the materialists' insistence upon identifying mind and all thought and ideas with the physical brain. This facet of materialism was stripped of any possible claim to rationality by physicist A. S. Eddington (1882-1944), born to Quaker parents, who authored *Mathematical Theory of Relativity*, which Einstein called "the finest presentation of the subject in any language." Much of his writings challenged the materialism so popular in his day and even more so now. He could explain issues in such a brilliant and understandable way that there is no excuse for anyone's devotion to materialism. Eddington pointed out that

> . . . the word law . . . in science means a rule which is never broken. . . . Thus in the physical world what a body does and what a body ought to do are equivalent; but we are well aware of another domain where they are anything but equivalent. We cannot get away from this distinction. Even if religion and morality are dismissed as illusion, the word 'Ought' still has sway. The laws of logic do not prescribe the way our minds think; they prescribe the way our minds ought to think. . . . However closely we may associate thought with the physical brain, the connection is dropped as irrelevant as soon as we consider the fundamental property of thought—that it may be correct or incorrect.[24]

This is an important statement by Eddington. As we have already noted, he states that the word "ought" takes us outside the realm of "chemistry and physics." There is a battle between materialism and dualism (the belief that there is a nonphysical part to man). We have mentioned this several times and will continue to do so because the issue is extremely important. If matter is all that exists, then God is a myth and Dawkins and Crick are absolutely right in what they say. I think every reader understands the horrendous consequences if nothing exists except matter. Instead of having a mind—a mind that is capable of thinking—we have DNA molecules, glands, nerves, and "selfish genes."

If this materialistic view is true, then there is no meaning to anything. We might just as well follow the logic of those in Scripture who didn't believe in an afterlife: "eat . . . drink, and be merry, for tomorrow we die."[25] One wonders what it would mean to be "merry" while espousing this hopeless philosophy. In the final analysis, it means that our lives have no meaning. Life and death would ultimately be of equal value.

Hardcore materialists such as Crick, Dawkins, Harris, Hitchens, and many others we have not named, have adopted a theory they cannot rationally maintain. The ultimate proof would be if they could manufacture and demonstrate artificial intelligence, but they never will be able to do so. Intelligence does not reside in any part of the brain, much less in an artificial one.

MIND OVER MATTER

Here we encounter one of the vast differences between man and machine. Every artificial "intelligence" must first of all be programmed to act "intelligently." Freedom of choice is impossible for a machine because anything that it does, any reactions it makes, must have been programmed into it. Skinner attempted to turn man into a machine. Intelligence involves much more than the ability to add, subtract, and divide numbers. Intelligence must include something known as *wisdom*. There is no way to program wisdom into a computer. We're back to B. F. Skinner and his hardcore behaviorism.

> Skinner put forth the notion that Man had no indwelling personality, nor will, intention, self-determinism or personal responsibility, and that modern concepts of freedom and dignity have to fall away so Man could be intelligently controlled to behave as he should.[26]

Who would decide what "should" means? To control the answer to that question has been the goal of every totalitarian system. Obviously, Skinner was not a dualist. Like every consistent atheist, he was a materialist. It seems odd that anyone would take such theories seriously—seriously enough even to argue about them. It is difficult to understand how Skinner himself or anyone else capable of rational thinking could possibly believe that man has no individual choice in what he does. Who or what else other than Skinner himself decided to write the books he has written? Where did his ideas come from, if not from his own personal initiative? Everyone demonstrates the ability to make choices at least dozens, if not hundreds, of times each day. It seems folly to deny free will and especially so to make us the prisoners of our genes.

In Congress, July 4, 1776
The unanimous Declaration of the thirteen
United States of America

WHEN IN THE COURSE of human events, it becomes necessary for one people to dissolve the political bands which have connected them with another, and to assume among the powers of the earth, the separate and equal station to which the Laws of Nature and of Nature's God entitle them, a decent respect to the opinions of mankind requires that they should declare the causes which impel them to the separation.

We hold these truths to be self-evident, that all men are created equal, that they are endowed by their Creator with certain unalienable Rights, that among these are Life, Liberty, and the pursuit of Happiness.

FOURTEEN

MORALS AND MEANING WITHOUT GOD

THE UNITED STATES OF AMERICA began with a revolution, as all Americans know. Its successful conclusion could have been part of the inspiration for the French Revolution (1789-1799), which began with excitement and high hopes for a new beginning for a financially and morally bankrupt France. It was to have ushered in a golden age of economic, political, and social reform, with liberty for all. That noble ideal disintegrated into a Reign of Terror scarcely equaled in human history.

Many, if not most, of the political dreamers, who, in their idealism, had helped to foment the Revolution and had sought to purify it as they saw it veering off course and out of control, perished as its tragic victims at the hands of fellow revolutionaries. Not the least of these victims was Madame Roland, a member with her husband of the more moderate Girondist faction of the revolutionary movement. The two had presided in their Paris home over a salon of socially prominent intellectuals.

As the Revolution gained momentum and became more radical, the Girondists fell out of favor. In the frenzy of fanaticism, Madame Roland was arrested (her husband succeeded in escaping). While confined in prison for several months, she refused to accept any of the secret plans for her escape. Her fate was sealed when the Girondists leaders, after a seven-day trial, were found guilty of counterrevolutionary activities and were executed on October 31, 1793.

Madame Roland's trial before the Revolutionary Tribunal followed on November 8. Pronounced guilty of "conspiracy against the unity and indivisibility of the Republic, and the liberty and safety of the French people," and allowed no word of defense on her own behalf, she was ordered to be executed that very afternoon.

After being carried on a tumbrel to join the nearly 1,400 victims who were guillotined just in Paris during the last six weeks of what became known as the "Red Terror," Madame Roland mounted the stairs to the platform. Before placing her head on the block, she bowed to the sculptor David's famous statue of Liberty nearby (a copy of the original stands at the entrance to New York harbor). "Oh, Liberty," she exclaimed, "What crimes are committed in thy name!" This was her farewell to a France that was sinking ever deeper into madness.

Hearing of her death, her fugitive husband, 20 years her senior, set out for Paris on foot to make one last appeal for the Revolutionary Tribunal to live up to its popular slogan, "Liberty, Equality, Fraternity." At last, too weak to continue the journey, Jean Roland took his own life in a lonely field in the French countryside. Tragically, the atheistic leaders of the revolution seemed unaware that they had become the betrayers of the very ideals they claimed to represent.

The Enlightenment of the Eighteenth Century had prepared the way for the French Revolution and largely shaped its policies and ideals. Maximilien Robespierre came to power shortly after the Revolution began. He led in curbing the power of the Roman Catholic

Church, reducing its property holdings and wealth, imposing limitations on the clergy, and turning France into a largely atheistic country. The Revolution brought atheism out of the salons of the wealthy intellectuals into the streets of Paris, and, as it would be with the Communist Revolution later, the denial of God became a major driving force. French society remains almost completely atheistic to this day.

THE RELIGION OF ATHEISM

The heady "freedom" from God that atheism promised spawned the new anti-god religion inherited by today's average Frenchman. No longer is atheism the passion of most French citizens as it once was. Today, it is just an inbred belief for most, a way of life to which, with a shrug of the shoulders, they confess to following. With little understanding or real conviction of their own, these lost souls are ripe for conversion to Islam, which is slowly but surely taking over French society and politics. Today, it would be impossible to become president of the Republic of France without the Muslim vote.

It is a surprisingly easy step for those without any real convictions to convert from atheism to Islam. Muslims active in the conversion process, following Muhammad's example, do not insist that new converts actually believe the uncomplicated required confession: "There is no god but Allah and Muhammad is his messenger (or prophet)." Millions have made this conversion under threat of death. In Westernized countries it has not yet come to that state of control that the Muslims ultimately intend—but it will, unless the West awakens from its present stupor.

What will become of the New Atheists, including their leaders, when the Muslims find that, although partnering with the West's nominal "Christians" was relatively easy, the same cannot be said of partnering with militant atheists? The latter may face a test of their "faith" for which they are not prepared. Will they have the moral courage to die for *their* faith, as have true Christians, who died in many horrible ways for theirs down through the centuries? This life-or-death choice could well be the challenge that will test the strength of the atheists' boast that no "god" or "holy book" is needed to decide what is right or wrong. Are atheists willing to die for the belief that morals are simply a product of evolution? Nor can we blame Hitler or his underlings who ran the extermination camps for simply doing what was programmed into their genes. If ethics and morals and our sense of what is right and wrong are a product of natural selection, how can evil be blamed on anyone?

The speculative guess that we've "all evolved over 3 billion years," even if true, is not an acceptable *reason* for putting man on the same level as lower creatures, as evolutionists attempt to do. What this philosophy leads to was expressed earnestly by Jonas Salk, who believed in it with a passion: "We do not have to survive as a species. What is important is that we keep evolving."[1]

How can our evolution be important if it doesn't matter whether or not we survive as a species? The Declaration of Independence attributes every individual's right to "life, liberty, and the pursuit of happiness" not to nature but to nature's *God*. Equality is nowhere found in nature. It could never be the outcome of natural selection or survival of the fittest, the underlying principle of which is inequality.

Stephen Jay Gould acknowledged: "Souls represent a subject outside the magisterium of science. My world cannot prove or disprove such a notion, and the concept of souls cannot threaten or impact my domain." He goes on to say, "I surely honor the metaphorical value of such a concept both for grounding moral discussion and for expressing what we most value about human potentiality: our decency, care, and all the ethical and intellectual struggles that the evolution of consciousness imposed upon us."[2]

Those who accept such doubletalk have lost the very "soul" to which Gould refers. In fact, Gould himself could not have explained what he meant by "soul." When he enters the realm of morality, the evolutionist has nothing meaningful to say. He is a materialist, acknowledging the existence of nothing except matter. For the evolutionist, nothing has any meaning. If everything began with a "big bang" and has simply proceeded from that point, from whence would it derive its meaning? Evolution cannot supply meaning to anything that it supposedly produces.

Consciousness is nonphysical, so how could it evolve? The same is true of ethics and intellect, which likewise have neither physical description, substance, nor spatial location. How could evolution have imposed ethical and intellectual struggles upon us? Common sense immediately recognizes that the insistence that nothing but matter exists is irrational, but the atheist dares not admit that fact for fear of being ostracized by the scientific community and losing his job, if he is in the academic world.

C. S. Lewis, addressing the Oxford Socratic Club in 1943, declared:

> Was . . . the whole vast structure of modern naturalism . . . devised not to face facts and truth but to avoid facing God? . . . I mean the belief . . . that morality springs from savage taboos, adult sentiment from infantile sexual maladjustments, thought from instinct, mind from matter, organic from inorganic, cosmos from chaos. . . . It seems to me immensely implausible. . . .
>
> One is driven to think that whatever else may be true, the popular scientific cosmology at any rate is certainly not. I left that ship not at the call of poetry but because I thought it could not keep afloat. Something like philosophical idealism or Theism must, at the very worst, be less untrue than that. And idealism turned out, when you took it seriously, to be disguised Theism. And once you accepted Theism you could not ignore the claims of Christ. And when you examined them it appeared to me that you could adopt no middle position. Either he was a lunatic, or God. And He was not a lunatic. . . .
>
> Granted that Reason is prior to matter and that the light of that primal Reason illuminates finite minds, I can understand how men should come, by observation and

inference, to know a lot about the universe they live in. If, on the other hand, I swallow the scientific cosmology as a whole, then not only can I not fit in Christianity, but I cannot even fit in science. If minds are wholly dependent on brains, and brains on biochemistry, and biochemistry (in the long run) on the meaningless flux of the atoms, I cannot understand how the thought of those minds should have any more significance than the sound of the wind in the trees.

And this is to me the final test. The scientific point of view cannot fit . . . even science itself. I believe in Christianity as I believe that the Sun has risen not only because I see it but because by it I see everything else.[3]

Sir John Eccles explains the impossibility of reconciling mankind's unique spiritual values and experiences with Darwinism:

Since materialist solutions fail to account for our experienced uniqueness, we are constrained to attribute the uniqueness of the psyche, or soul, to a supernatural spiritual creation. . . .

We submit that no other explanation is tenable; neither the genetic uniqueness with its fantastically impossible lottery nor the environmental differentiations, which do not *determine* one's uniqueness but merely modify it.[4]

Evolutionists would dearly love to find a genetic basis for homosexuality, because that would prove that the sense of right and wrong and the entire moral and ethical side of man are not in the conscience (and thus spiritual in nature) but in the genes, and purely physical. As we have already shown, *all ideas* are nonphysical. *No idea* about *anything* has any weight, color, smell, texture, sound, or taste. To state it another way, tissues know nothing of issues, and there is no way to compare them to each other.

According to a 2009 American Psychological Association publication, there is no homosexual "gene"—meaning it's not likely that homosexuals are born that way. The new statement appears in "Answers to Your Questions for a Better Understanding of Sexual

Orientation & Homosexuality," and states the following:

> There is no consensus among scientists about the exact reasons that an individual develops a heterosexual, bisexual, gay or lesbian orientation. Although much research has examined the possible genetic, hormonal, developmental, social, and cultural influences on sexual orientation, no findings have emerged that permit scientists to conclude that sexual orientation is determined by any particular factor or factors. Many think that nature and nurture both play complex roles. . . .

That contrasts with the APA's statement in 1998: "There is considerable recent evidence to suggest that biology, including genetic or inborn hormonal factors, plays a significant role in a person's sexuality."[5]

As we've been attempting to show throughout this book, men are confused. They make pronouncements but have to retract them. It is difficult to retain confidence in what the evolutionists and atheists say when they are only voicing opinions yet love to speak as though they know what they are talking about. There is always a flurry of excitement about the latest fossil find that seems to be a further link in the evolutionary chain from microbe to man. But the experts always forget that, as we have repeatedly pointed out, what a human being really is is not to be found in the skeletal structure nor even in the physical brain, cells, or DNA. There is a *spirit* in man that the atheist and evolutionist try desperately to deny, but it cannot be avoided in any intelligent considerations of the subject we've been pursuing.

Sam Harris says that his book, *Letter to a Christian Nation*, was written "to arm secularists . . . who believe that religion should be kept out of public policy. . . ."[6] *Should?* We will charitably avoid accusing Harris of being part of an aggressive group of atheists who want to dictate the way others must think and act. Instead, we'll credit him with being sincere in his desire to improve society. Why does he care, anyway, considering that, according to his atheistic belief, it's all meaningless?

On what moral basis do we have *should* as part of the thinking in the chemical brains between the ears? What proud delusion gives such grandiose thoughts to mere specks of dust on a doomed planet in a meaningless universe that resulted from a chance explosion of energy we can't define or determine its origin, why it exploded, or why at that precise moment?

Should is a moral imperative. Dawkins and his fellow atheists think that not believing in God is far better for society than believing in God. They tell us why they don't believe in God—but what is their moral criteria for judging atheism to be better than theism? They cannot offer a pragmatic reason.

Are Christians less cheerful or happy than atheists? Are they less likely to survive than atheists, who are free of what Dawkins seriously and authoritatively calls the *"God Delusion"*? That is doubtful. Nor have Dawkins, Harris, or any of the other New Atheists shown that to be true. Theism doesn't seem to bring poverty or disease, so what is their concern?

ARE MORALS BASED UPON A DESIRE FOR HAPPINESS?

Dawkins and his "new atheist" friends say that religion is evil—but by what moral criteria? Yes, Islam is definitely evil in promising paradise and special rewards for murdering innocent people. But there is not another religion on Earth today that doesn't oppose murder in any form, so Islamic evil cannot be blamed on *religion* itself. And that is a basic and reprehensible flaw in Harris's reasoning: he is so fanatically opposed to God and religion that he damns all religions together, without distinguishing their widely differing beliefs even on fundamentals and behavior.

Furthermore, why should atheists care what anyone else thinks? What does it matter? Let these theists wallow in their delusion if that makes them happy. Harris says the fact that "love is more conducive to happiness than hate" is the key to "the moral order of our world."[7] So morality depends upon what makes one happy? Any child whose parents have disciplined him at all knows that isn't true. This is only the tip of the iceberg. The saddest thing is that not only Harris but the multitudes who have read and at one time turned his book into a bestseller, high on *The New York Times* list, really imagine they have escaped from God.

Apparent happiness is the best "moral" reason Harris can offer. It turns out, however, that for whatever purpose he might admit there could be for our existence, *should* is not the result of any objective standard to which we must all bow but is merely the opinion of atheists, for which they have no moral rationale but a great deal of prejudice.

Harris has a very shallow rationale for his "morals," namely his desire for "happiness in this world"—a world that, according to atheism, has no meaning, is a mere accident, is only temporary, and one day will be as though it had never been. Exuding his particular wisdom, he says: "But we can easily think of objective sources of moral order that do not require the existence of a lawgiving God. For there to be objective moral truths worth knowing, there need only be better and worse ways to seek happiness in this world. If there are psychological laws that govern human well-being, knowledge of these laws would provide an enduring basis for an objective morality."[8]

"*If* there are psychological laws. . . ." What is a "*psychological* law"? Who says they exist and who decreed these "laws"? How will everyone know about them and agree with them, and why should anyone obey them? Most important, what if there *aren't* any such laws? Well, Harris, our new "Moses," who is going to lead us to the promised land of "freedom from the God who doesn't exist," will surely be able to tell us. That must be why he wrote the book. Here is the guidance he offers, for which all good atheists have been eagerly waiting:

> While we do not have anything like a final, scientific understanding of human morality, it seems safe to say that raping and killing our neighbors is not one of its primary constituents. Everything about human experience suggests that love is more conducive to happiness than hate is. This is an *objective* claim about the human mind, about the dynamics of social relations, and about the moral order of

our world. It is clearly possible to say that someone like Hitler was wrong in moral terms without reference to scripture.[9]

We're relieved to know that Harris and apparently the New Atheists as well, like everyone else, agree that raping and killing are wrong and that Hitler was not a good role model. That can never be argued, however, from natural selection. In fact, the year before the Scopes trial, Clarence Darrow "had saved two rich child murderers" from the death sentence with these words:

> This terrible crime was inherent in his organism, and it came from some ancestor. . . . Is any blame attached because somebody took Nietzsche's [evolutionary] philosophy seriously and fashioned his life upon it? It is hardly fair to hang a 19-year-old boy for the philosophy that was taught him at the university.[10]

Such is the "morality" inherent in atheism and evolution. Is it possible that the near-unanimous agreement on basic morals exists precisely because the Bible is right when it says that God has written His moral laws in every conscience? Now *there's* a possibility for the 95 percent of Americans who believe in "God" to ponder—but of course not for the 5 percent who claim to be smarter than all the rest of us put together and want to persuade us to think as they do.

In another burst of profundity, Harris adds, "While feeling love for others is surely one of the greatest sources of our own happiness, it entails a very deep concern for the happiness and suffering of those we love."[11] "*Feeling* love"? What does that mean? With deep feelings of love, a young man says to an attractive young woman, "I love you with all my heart!" What he may really mean, although neither of them realizes it, is "I love me, and I want you!"

If this is what his selfish genes and the molecules in his brain are causing him to think, who could blame him? Clearly, the logic of atheism, evolution, and natural selection will inevitably bring us to the day when no one can be blamed for anything. In fact, blame will have lost all meaning. The physical construction of our brains will have to bear the responsibility. But surely we all believe that genes are selfish, don't we? Richard Dawkins said so! How could natural selection, which caused such ideas, be *wrong*? Common sense demands that we reject this amorality that now governs the ethics and morals of so many.

Harris says, "It seems rather unlikely, therefore, that the average American will receive necessary moral instruction . . . " from the Ten Commandments. Then how will anyone receive moral instruction from "psychological laws" that Harris can neither recite nor of whose existence he can be certain?

Harris criticizes the Bible for condoning slavery.[12] He deliberately ignores the fact that in biblical days the only other alternative for those taken captive in war was death. Those hopelessly in debt didn't have the modern escape of bankruptcy; they had to sell themselves into slavery. Nor was the solution as simple as setting a slave free. Where would the freed slave go? For many, this was the only means of "employment." As society changed and other possibilities developed, Christians led the way in freeing slaves. Christ did not come to reform earthly society but to die for the sins of the world so that we could be forgiven and live in heaven eternally. The teachings of the Bible, had they been followed, would have caused both slave and master to act with respect and even love toward each other.

Francis Collins confesses that in his case, at least, his atheism was an escape from moral accountability to someone other than himself: "This realization [that God might exist] was a thoroughly terrifying experience. After all, if I could no longer rely on the robustness of my atheistic position, would I have to take responsibility for actions that I would prefer to keep unscrutinized? Was I answerable to someone other than myself? The question was now too pressing to avoid."[13]

Collins only became more confused by attempting to examine the various beliefs of world religions, but a Methodist minister loaned him *Mere Christianity* by C. S. Lewis. He hadn't read far until he realized that his arguments against faith in God "were those of a schoolboy."[14] Collins was particularly impressed with Lewis's argument presented in the title of Book One, that the universal sense of "Right and Wrong Is a Clue to the Meaning of the Universe."

President Dwight Eisenhower said, "Our government makes no sense unless it is founded in a deeply felt religious faith—and I don't care what it is."[15] Ike had the right to express his own opinions, but his position of leadership obligated him to make rational pronouncements—and that statement makes no sense. There are differences in religion so great that they contradict one another. Islam's belief that Allah is the only god and the Qur'an's teaching that Christ neither died on the cross nor resurrected surely contradicts the very foundation of Christianity.[16] Ike was accepted as a Christian by many evangelicals, and he attended church regularly (a politically correct stance for presidents). Clearly, however, what he really believed and publicly expressed contradicted Christ's declaration, "I am the way, the truth, and the life: no man cometh unto the Father, but by me."[17]

Many who call themselves Christians implicitly accept the superiority of science over the Bible. Thus, whenever "science" disagrees with the Bible, as its generally accepted dogmas so clearly do with regard to the creation of the universe and source of life, they surrender their faith in Scripture (which is really a surrender of their faith in God, its Author) or attempt to twist what it says in order to make it seem that the Bible agrees with atheism's Big Bang and the evolutionary account of man's descent from fish and reptiles and chimpanzees. In a sense, they become partners with atheists, incredibly allowing them to dictate the terms of the discussion. For example, Fuller theological Seminary philosopher, Nancey Murphy has said:

> Christians and atheists alike must pursue scientific questions in our era without invoking a Creator. . . . For better or for worse, we have inherited a view of science as *methodologically* atheistic.[18]

In his book, *Reason in the Balance*, Phillip Johnson argues that only creation by God can account for man's moral conscience. Nature has no morals. Man's sense of ethics and morals cannot contribute to, but would work against, survival. If evolution is true, we ought to shut down all hospitals, cease all medications, and let the weak die to strengthen the race. Kindness and compassion cannot be reconciled with survival of the fittest. Man is compelled by conscience and compassion to sacrifice for others—proof that he is made in the image of a God of mercy and love. Natural selection doesn't fit that scenario.

PERSONALITY, MORALS, ETHICS . . .
FROM A GIANT EXPLOSION?

According to Dawkins, "the atheist movement . . . has no choice but to aggressively spread the good news. Evangelism is a moral imperative."[19] Really? What is Dawkins's source for the idea of "evangelism"? The Greek and Latin roots mean basically "gospel of good news." The Christian gospel is the good news about Jesus Christ, who died for our sins, resurrected, and is coming again. The atheists' "good news gospel" is that nothing exists but matter and we're just lumps of protein molecules, without meaning or destiny except a brief and often miserable life—then oblivion. How could this "gospel" be good news that ought be preached to the world? Who would be willing to die for this philosophy, as millions of Christians have for Christ?

If the Big Bang theory is correct, then the sentence I'm typing into my computer now came out of, and is a product of, this giant explosion. Every thought and theory (including the greatest scientific discoveries, the worst political blunders), plus every ambition and emotion—all resulted from the Big Bang. From what other source could anything, including our highest and lowest thoughts, have come? This is the absurdity that we must embrace with this theory that removes all meaning from life. Whatever anyone believes, decides, says, or does, good or bad, is simply the result of the chance antecedent motions of the atoms in their brains, all of which began with a senseless giant explosion that has been pushing matter away from its epicenter ever since.

On the other side, human existence involves morals, ethics, ambitions, purpose, meaning, hopes, love and hate, jealousy, self-sacrifice, pride and humility, frustration and patience, anger, a sense of right and wrong, justice and injustice, compassion, forgiveness, and so forth, endlessly. How could such qualities of human existence have attached themselves to exploding matter? Not only does the Big Bang offer no explanation for these human qualities, which have no relationship to energy and matter, but it denies their significance. All human experience, having resulted from a giant explosion, would be totally meaningless if it were the product of billions of years of natural selection, caused by mostly harmful mutations. Anyone who imagined otherwise would be scorned as the victim of a cruel hoax. And finally—so what?

Ah, but evolution took this exploding matter and turned it into what we are today. Really? *Time* magazine's cover story the first week in October 2006 claimed that there really isn't a chasm between man and animals but only "tiny differences, sprinkled throughout the genome." So we don't really experience love and joy, fulfillment, a deep concern about injustices in the world, but our "selfish" genes cause us to have these delusive feelings? Is it our genes, too, that cause us to reject this statement because it reduces humans to programmed robots? The summary of the article, posted on CNN.com, explained:

> As scientists keep reminding us, evolution is a random process in which haphazard genetic changes interact with random environmental conditions to produce an organism somehow fitter than its fellows. After 3.5 billion years of such randomness, a creature emerged that could ponder its own origins—and revel in a Mozart adagio.[20]

So there you have it: we are what we are as a result of "3.5 billion years" of purposeless "randomness." Then why have an education? What are governments and elections about? Why do we care about anything? Why is it that this "randomness" exuding from a giant explosion eons ago produced such different results in different people, including firm convictions that cause arguments, anger, and even wars against one another—and finally the despair of the gospel of oblivion to climax lives that have been an illusion? Such are the prospects offered to youth by our current atheistic/evolutionist education.

There wouldn't be one in a million people who experience the reality of life who would not be insulted to be told that their deepest convictions and greatest joys and fears are merely phantoms of their genes—or perhaps something from our simian ancestry or surfacing from a reptilian corner of the brain. Yet they will embrace such theories when pronounced in the name of science without realizing that this is where atheism leads.

Those who promote this theory have no explanation for the unanswerable questions it raises. What about logic and convictions? Could they, as well, be the result of a giant explosion and in the end be but delusions created by our "selfish genes"?

BIBLICAL MORALITY AND CHRISTIAN BEHAVIOR

Why not believe the Bible, since its statements are supported not only by prophecy but by vast amounts of evidence? As we have already seen, many of the greatest scientists of all time, who discovered the principles foundational to today's science, were firm believers not in a "big bang" but in a God who created the universe. Faith in God and His Word, the Bible, was the foundation of their lives. The same is true of many of today's space scientists and astronauts. Wernher von Braun, founding director and for many years head of NASA's space flight center, was always eager to testify:

> Manned space flight . . . has opened . . . a tiny door for viewing the awesome reaches of space. An outlook through this peephole at the vast mysteries of the universe should only confirm our belief in the certainty of its Creator. I [cannot] understand a scientist who does not acknowledge the presence of a superior rationality behind the existence of the universe. . . .[21]

Atheistic evolution has many close allies in the environmental (sometimes known as "Green") movement. In 1993, Mikhail Gorbachev, former Soviet leader, founded the Green Cross International, headquartered in the Hague, to build upon the work started by the 1992 Earth Summit in Rio de Janeiro, Brazil.

Green Cross? The biblical Cross was stained with the blood of Christ when He died for the sins of the world, including those who mocked and crucified Him. The "Greening of the Cross" is a growing movement worldwide. Gorbachev says that the main purpose of the Green Cross is "to bring nations together . . . to stimulate the new environmental consciousness . . . returning Man to a sense of being a part of Nature."

The idea that man must be persuaded to act like he's "part of Nature" is, in itself, an admission that he is not. Nature's creatures need no such urging. This return to nature, however, is a powerful factor in encouraging the immorality of today's world.

There is no "right" or "wrong" in nature. Clearly, it is not "wrong" for a volcano to spew forth poisonous gases. Whatever nature and her offspring do is simply "natural." If man is a product of nature through evolution, then whatever he does must likewise be natural. No one complains about the destruction wrought upon the environment by parasites, or creatures that destroy entire forests, or hurricanes and tornadoes and floods that wreak terrible destruction. These phenomena are all "natural," and no objection can be made against anything Nature does. But if man is the product of evolution, then he, too, is a child of Nature, and whatever he does should be as "natural" as the actions of any creatures in his evolutionary ancestry or of his present evolutionary "relatives" all around him today, most of whom would poison or devour him.

And what about the great concern among environmentalists over the possible extinction of so-called "endangered species"? Once again, man reveals that he is not a product of natural forces. *Endangered species?* Isn't that how evolution works? Hasn't evolution been doing away with species through natural selection and survival of the fittest for millions of years? Why should man, if he is simply a product of evolution (and one that has only lately arrived on the scene), be working against evolution while claiming to believe in it and to be its offspring?

One cannot logically believe both in evolution and the environmental movement. Evolutionists should neither be concerned for "endangered species" nor for the ecological well-being of this planet. If man, as a result of the evolution of his brain and nervous system, succeeds in destroying the earth in a nuclear holocaust or ecological disaster, that must be accepted as a natural act in the evolving universe.

The mere fact that man can reason about ecology and the survival of species is proof enough that he is not the product of such forces but, having the power to interfere with them, must have a higher origin. Man was created in the image of God. Only an intelligent Creator could have brought mankind's reasoning powers and moral and ethical concerns into existence. Consequently, the solution to the problem of evil on this earth is not in hugging trees or getting in touch with nature or listening to the earth. The true message of the bloody Cross, as explained in the Bible, which gives an accurate account of that watershed event in human history, is man's only hope.

The "Green Cross" and environmental movement invading the church is one more attempt to redefine Christianity in humanistic terms and to turn the gospel into just another human effort to once again transform the earth into a paradise.

It is important to be aware that there is no one theory for the origin and subsequent evolution of the Solar System that is generally accepted. All theories represent models which fit some of the facts observed today, but not all.

—NASA, Mars and Earth (US GPO, NF-61, August 1975), 1

DNA cannot do its work, including forming more DNA, without the help of catalytic proteins, or enzymes. In short, proteins cannot form without DNA, but neither can DNA form without proteins.

—John Horgan, "In the Beginning," Scientific American, vol. 264 (February 1991), 119

It has been estimated that . . . chance errors occur at a rate of about one per several hundred million in each generation. This frequency does not seem to be sufficient to explain the evolution of the great diversity of life forms, given the well-known fact that most mutations are harmful and only very few result in useful variations.

—Fritjof Capra, The Web of Life (New York: Anchor Books, 1996), 228

At all events, anyone with even a nodding acquaintance with the Rubik cube will concede the near-impossibility of a solution being obtained by a blind person moving the cubic faces at random. [There are 4×10^{19} possible scramblings of the Rubik cube (that is, ten billion billion).] Now imagine 10^{50} blind persons, each with a scrambled Rubik cube, and try to conceive of the chance of arriving by random shuffling of just one of the many biopolymers on which life depends. The notion that not only the biolpolymers but the operating programme of a living cell could be arrived at by chance in a primordial organic soup here on the Earth is evidently nonsense of a higher order. Life must plainly be a cosmic phenomenon.

—Sir Fred Hoyle, "The Big Bang in Astronomy," New Scientist, vol. 92 (November 19, 1981), 527

From my earliest training as a scientist, I was very strongly brainwashed to believe that science cannot be consistent with any kind of deliberate creation. That notion has had to be painfully shed. Each found that the odds against the spark of life igniting accidentally on Earth were . . . "10 to the power of 40,000." They did calculations based on the size and age of the universe (15 billion years) and found that the odds against life beginning spontaneously anywhere in space were "10 to the power of 30." At the moment, I can't find any rational argument to knock down the view which argues for conversion to God. . . . We used to have an open mind; now we realize that the only logical answer to life is creation—and not accidental random shuffling.

—C. Wickramasinghe, Professor of Applied Math & Astronomy, University College, Cardiff, Interviewed in the London Daily Express (August 14, 1981)

FIFTEEN

AGAINST ALL ODDS

Richard Dawkins writes, "Entities that are complex enough to be intelligent are products of an evolutionary process. [How does he know that? What evidence or experimental data does he offer?] No matter how god-like they may seem when we encounter them, they didn't start that way. . . . The laws of probability forbid all notions of their spontaneously appearing without simpler antecedents."[1]

Though this world-renowned geneticist is not a professor of mathematics, he surely knows better than to make that declaration about "odds." Dawkins is (again) practicing the old shell-game switch and ought to be held accountable by every scientist, especially by mathematicians! The simple truth is that the mathematics of probability has *absolutely nothing* to say either for or against life spontaneously appearing. It greatly disturbs me to see what Dawkins has done, and it disturbs me even more that thousands of readers allow him to get away with this deceit without rising up in mass protest!

Is Dawkins pretending to make a concession to rationality and logic—a "baby step" in the direction of a denial of spontaneous generation? No, he's just trying to deceive his readers into thinking that's what he's doing. Instead of a denial of spontaneous generation, it's a reaffirmation of this bogus theory, which he has slipped in through a back door in order to push his evangelistic-style crusade for promoting atheism. He's actually saying, "Of course spontaneous generation is a fact! Never mind that the law of biogenesis declares in the plainest language that life comes *only* from life."

Stephen Jay Gould, before his death, May 20, 2002, was one of the chief spokespersons for evolution in the twentieth century. He took Dawkins to task for attempting to use evolution as a proof for atheism. Gould wrote:

> The great American botanist, Asa Gray, who favored natural selection . . . was a devout Christian. Move forward 50 years: Charles D. Walcott, discoverer of the Burgess Shale fossils, was a convinced Darwinian and an equally firm Christian, who believed that God had ordained natural selection to construct the history of life according to His plans and purposes. Move on another 50 years to the two greatest evolutionists of our generation: G. G. Simpson was a humanistic agnostic, Theodosius Dobzhansky, a believing Russian Orthodox. Either half my colleagues are enormously stupid, or else the science of Darwinism is fully compatible with conventional religious beliefs—and equally with atheism.[2]

Of course, among those colleagues we find Francis Collins, who criticized what he called "Christianity's history of opposition to scientific advancement." There is nothing of the kind in history, if we are talking about biblical Christianity. This failure to distinguish biblical Christians from those who claim to be Christians but do not accept the inerrancy of the Bible from Genesis to Revelation is a common error among critics of "Christianity."

Generally, the example that is given is Galileo's forced agreement that the sun revolved around the earth. Collins lays the Crusades and Inquisitions at the door of "the church," apparently unaware that there were millions of Christians who were never part of the Roman Catholic Church, who never gave allegiance to the pope or his bishops and priests, and who were slaughtered by that Church literally by the millions long before the Reformation added another million victims to Rome's account. Of course, some "Protestants" fought back and did their share of the killing—all of it in *disobedience* to Christ's teaching and example. True Christianity and the Bible do not oppose true science.

WHAT ABOUT THE AGE OF EARTH?

Daring to contradict the Bible, some "old earth" creationists agree that it all began with a giant explosion of energy some 15-18 billion years ago. Of course, they attribute the Big Bang and its alleged results to God. On the other hand, "young earth" creationists accept the biblical age of the earth, which rules out any Big Bang because it allows far too little time for cooling and order to take place. There are compelling scientific reasons why the earth could not be more than 10,000 years old. With clear insight that he couldn't possibly have had in his day, except from God, Solomon wrote: "All the rivers run into the sea; yet the sea is not full; unto the place from whence the rivers come, thither they return again."[3]

From the genealogies it gives of Adam and his descendants, the Bible indicates that man was created approximately 6,000 years ago. In fact, the latest discoveries in physical science and also in genetics confirm this timetable. One example is found in the influence of the second law of thermodynamics on DNA.

Errors do occur (though rarely) in transmission of DNA to offspring. "It has been estimated that those chance errors occur at a rate of about one per several hundred million cells in each generation."[4]

Of course, changes that are not caused by errors inevitably occur from generation to generation by the mixing of both parents' DNA, and it is impossible to tell from which parent a given change comes. There is one kind of change, however, that can be traced. On the outside of each cell are thousands of tiny energy-producing components called mitochondria, each having a circular strand of DNA. This mitochondrial DNA (mtDNA) is passed on to the next generation *only from the mother*. The rare and random changes in mtDNA allow geneticists to identify families. Scientist and author Walt Brown explains:

> For example, if your grandmother experienced an early mutation in her mtDNA, her children and any daughters' children would carry the same changed mtDNA. It would differ, in general, from that in the rest of the world's population. In 1987, a team at the University of California at Berkeley published a study comparing the mtDNA of 147 people from five of the world's geographic locations. They concluded that all 147 had the same female ancestor. She is now called "the *mitochondrial Eve*."
>
> In 1997 it was announced that mutations in mtDNA occur 20 times more rapidly than previously thought. . . . Using the new, more accurate rate, *mitochondrial Eve lived only about 6,000 years ago.* [His emphasis][5]

Yes, but isn't it true that the light from distant galaxies has taken billions of years to get to Earth? That certainly contradicts the idea of a universe only 10,000 years old, doesn't it? There are a number of reasons why that is not the case. If light originally traveled at a much faster rate than it does today, the light from distant stars could have reached the earth in thousands instead of billions of years.

According to Walt Brown, this appears to be the case:

> M.E.J. Gheury de Bray, in 1927, was probably the first to propose a decreasing speed of light. He based his conclusion on measurements spanning 75 years. Later, he became more convinced and twice published his results in *Nature*,

possibly the most prestigious scientific journal in the world. He emphasized, "If the velocity of light is constant, how is it that, *invariably*, new determinations give values which are lower than the last one obtained . . . There are twenty-two coincidences in favour of a decrease of the velocity of light, while there is not a single one against it." [Emphasis in original]

Although the measured speed of light has decreased only about 1% during the past three centuries, the decrease is statistically significant, because measurement techniques can detect changes thousands of times smaller. While the older measurements have greater errors, the trend of the data is startling. The farther back one looks in time, the more rapidly the speed of light seems to have been decreasing. Various mathematical curves fit these three centuries of data. When some of those curves are projected back in time, the speed of light becomes so fast that light from distant galaxies conceivably could have reached Earth in several thousand years.

No scientific law requires the speed of light to be constant. Many simply assume that it is constant, and of course, changing old ways of thinking is sometimes difficult. Russian cosmologist, V. S. Troitskii, at the Radiophysical Research Institute in Gorky, is also questioning some old beliefs. He concluded, independently of Setterfield, that *the speed of light was 10 billion times faster at time zero*! Furthermore, he attributed the cosmic microwave background radiation and most redshifts to this rapidly decreasing speed of light. Setterfield reached the same conclusion concerning redshifts by a different method. If either Setterfield or Troitskii is correct, the big bang theory will fall (with a big bang).[6]

There are other possibilities. Adam was not created a baby but a mature man who would have taken many years to reach that stage had he not been God's special creation. It is not likely that all trees were created as tiny seedlings, or that the fish in the sea were all created as minnows, and the cattle as though they had just been born. It is reasonable to expect that every living thing, whether man, fish, bird, beast, or plant was created fully grown and would have appeared to have been many years old to someone living today. Oil and mineral deposits that one would think would take millions of years to develop could also have been part of the original creation. Likewise, the universe could have been created with a built-in time factor from the very first moment when God spoke it into existence. The Creator does not have to use a "big bang" or billions of years to let the stars and galaxies form themselves. In fact, it would be unreasonable to expect Him to do so. Creation is the very antithesis of evolution, whether of planets or man. Yet the critics of creation imagine that God would have had to develop the universe in this inefficient and time-consuming manner. It is not reasonable to think so.

CONVERTS TO ATHEISM

The landscape is littered with the wreckage of many who once considered themselves to be staunch Christians and then turned from the faith. For many, a major factor was apparent proof for evolution that finally freed them from what they had long suspected was a cruel hoax. These are the "bright spots," the successes that give atheistic evolutionists the hope that they are winning their battle. Kenneth Nahigian, one of these trophies of atheism who considers himself lucky to have escaped the "delusion of Christianity" writes:

> I had always loved science. To learn [that] evolution was all wrong, a fraud promulgated by evil secular humanist scientists, shocked me. It turned my world on its head. . . . I had to surrender most of what I thought I knew of geology . . . astronomy . . . genetics. . . . Now doubting, I sought sources and references for many things the creationists had told me. What did I find [but] misquotes, out-of-context quotes, half-truths and plain deception. . . .

Slowly it dawned that almost all creation science "research" consisted of combing science books and journals for quotes and factoids that can be pulled out of context and used to support the Genesis story . . . the way a drunk man uses a lamp post—for support, not illumination. . . .

When I told my Christian friends about this, they didn't care . . . salvation was important, not science. I wondered why Christianity must depend on falsehoods and deception to save souls. . . . What else were they not telling me? . . . Apologists trumpet stories of unbelievers who converted to Christianity . . . but we rarely hear of those who convert the other way [such as] Dr. Charles Templeton . . . Billy Graham's best friend and original preaching partner.

The guilt that haunted me, the suffocating self-doubt . . . chill terror in the sleepless night, died slowly. . . . Looking back it was inevitable. . . . Now the fear is a memory. Smiles come more easily . . . the sun shines, breath is sweet, love still gives me wings—and life is as beautiful and meaningless as a flower.[7]

With these tragic words, his "testimony" ends. The outstanding feature of his deliverance from God was the "liberating realization that everything, including life itself, is meaningless." And yet he says it is "beautiful." So, of course, beauty also is meaningless. Then, by equal logic, so is this lengthy treatise that he wrote against Christ and those who often misrepresent Him.

Undeniably, Nahigian must have had a compelling purpose for investing the time and effort it took to write his story. He wants to deliver "Christians" from what he now sincerely believes is a fraud. If there is no God, however, and everything is meaningless, why did he bother? In spite of his boast of freedom, he is still a haunted man— haunted by the inescapable conviction, no matter how deeply buried, that there is a meaning to life and death after all, which atheism cannot abolish. It may take time to admit this, but he cannot escape the fear that his new faith may be as wrong as he now thinks the last one was.

"ACADEMIC FREEDOM"—UNLESS UNWILLING
TO TOADY UP TO EVOLUTIONISTS

Ever since they took control of the schools following the Scopes fraudulent trial, evolutionists have jealously defended their territory from all who would question their theories. Evolution must not be challenged at all, which is, in itself, a violation of the very heart of scientific inquiry. Those who dare to do so are not welcome in public education, even in universities where academic freedom should prevail. As we noted in chapter 4, Dean Kenyon was the co-author of *Biochemical Predestination* (New York: McGraw-Hill), adopted widely as a graduate textbook and looked upon for years as the major book on the chemical origin of life on Earth. After years of effort in the laboratory, he had to concede that the models he had proposed could not be made to work.

Eventually, realizing that life could arise only under the direction of a supreme intelligence, Kenyon became a believer in and proponent of Intelligent Design. He still taught the evolutionary view but threw in Intelligent Design as something to be given careful consideration. That was too much for the university administration, and Kenyon was removed in the spring of 1993 from teaching introductory biology. He appealed to the Academic Freedom Committee at the university, which reviewed his case and ruled that he had been denied academic freedom and due process. In that ruling, the Committee cited the university's own guidelines to "permit and encourage vigorous dialogue, even controversy [and that] students in all academic disciplines should be exposed to effective presentations of a broad range of perspectives in their area of study."[8]

Kenyon seemed to have all the credentials for teaching both sides of the issue. He had a Ph.D. in biophysics from Stanford University and had completed post-doctoral work at UC Berkeley, Oxford, and NASA. Nevertheless, the administration refused to reinstate Kenyon. He appealed to the American Association of University Professors. They, too, ruled that Kenyon's right to academic freedom had been violated as well as his right to due process. Again the administration refused to reinstate Kenyon on the grounds that "introductory biology students are too young and naïve" to understand the intelligent design side of the argument.

National attention was created by an article in *The Wall Street Journal*, which pointed to the ironic fact that "Unlike Scopes, the teacher was forbidden to teach his course not because he taught evolutionary theory (which he did) but because he offered a critical assessment of it. . . ."[9] The author of that article earned his Ph.D. in the History and Philosophy of Science from Cambridge University and is director and Senior Fellow of the Center for Science and Culture at the Discovery Institute, Seattle, Washington.

WASTING TIME ON A CLOSED ISSUE

Evolutionists, in their critiques of "spontaneous generation," attempt to show that the calculations by creationists of mathematical probability are seriously flawed. They claim that it is not correct to use the number of molecules in even the smallest protein to calculate probabilities because, allegedly, the first protein molecule didn't spring into existence in a final form. They suggest that it gradually developed from simple chemicals to polymers, to replicating polymers to hypercycle, to protobiont, and to bacteria. The evolutionists are clearly the ones with the flawed thinking.

Not only is there no proof that any protein developed in such a way, but it wouldn't matter whether it did or not. It makes no difference in how many stages and over how long a period of time it took for the molecules that form a protein to come together. It still happened by chance and without any intelligent direction, according to the evolutionist. The end product is what must be accounted for—and there are far too many molecules for them ever to have been assembled by chance in the incredibly intricate working relationships of any known protein.

They also object that in their calculations, creationists fail to factor in natural selection. Allegedly, over a period of time, this would reduce the odds, though they can't tell us why or how much. Once again their objection is not valid. It is an oxymoron to speak of "natural selection" playing some alleged role in the "survival of the fittest" of chemicals and mere molecules. Chemical reactions are chemical reactions, and that is all they are.

Nothing is yet alive during this hypothetical process of constructing a protein molecule. When does life show itself? All of the chemical molecules needed for a cell to function can be present without *any* sign of life. No one can tell what it takes to spark this pile of chemicals to begin functioning as a living unit. Isn't it dishonest to write scholarly treatises about evolution while failing to admit that we don't know what life is?

It is further alleged that the creationists' calculations revealing the impossibility of life arising by chance are worthless because, in spite of the denial of intelligent direction, life did not arise by "chance" after all but through "the very chemical processes which underlie the development of life."[10]

In spite of the complete ignorance of what life is, the evolutionist claims that life is a natural result of "the ordering effect" innate within amino acids. Yet, amino acids are not alive. Furthermore, the protein will have an important role to play in relation to many other proteins and the functioning of the body of which it will be a part.

EVOLUTIONISTS FIGHT BACK AGAINST STATISTICAL IMPOSSIBILITY

There are many roadblocks preventing any rational defense of evolution. Consider, for example, the clotting of blood. This is a very complex mechanism that must be exactly right, or a) The subject could bleed to death before clotting could intervene; or b) If clotting were not perfectly controlled from the very beginning, the blood would not flow at all, bringing death to the subject. There are many such systems in the bodies of every living entity that are essential to survival. How did they develop? One of the clearest objections to evolution involves the immune system. Walt Brown reminds us of the well-known fact that:

> Each immune system can recognize invading bacteria, viruses, and toxins. Each system can quickly mobilize the best defenders to search out and destroy these invaders. Each system has a memory and learns from every attack.
>
> If the many instructions that direct an animal's or plant's immune system had not been preprogrammed in the organism's genetic system when it first appeared on earth, the first of thousands of potential infections would have killed the organism. This would have nullified any rare genetic improvements that might have accumulated. In other words, the large amount of genetic information governing the immune system could not have accumulated in a slow, evolutionary sense. Obviously, for each organism to have survived, all this information must have been there from the beginning.[11]

When it comes to defending evolution, its supporters have several magic wands they wave, and "presto," objections suddenly vanish. Or do they? Of course, one of these wands is the oft-cited "billions of years." Another is the claim that the odds against cells or species arising by chance cannot be calculated mathematically because of "natural selection." This supposedly would cut the odds dramatically by shortening the number of trials needed because a favorable chance hit would be retained and, step-by-step, the process would continue.

Volumes have been written either to criticize the calculations by creationists of the mathematical odds of life developing by chance or to defend such theses. The thousands of words spent in arguing this thesis from either side are just so much wasted effort. Are creationists pursuing arguments that are completely beside the point? The law of biogenesis, which no scientist has yet refuted nor have any examples been given to contradict it, slams the door on anything to the contrary. No arguments are needed to defend gravity or Boyle's law of gasses or any other established law of science. The law of biogenesis is as firmly established as any other scientific law. So what is the point of speculating about it?

Ernst Boris Chain, Nobelist in medicine for his work with penicillin, says: "The principle of [divine] purpose . . . stares the biologist in the face wherever he looks. . . . [T]he probability for such an event as the origin of DNA molecules to have occurred by sheer chance is just too small to be seriously considered. . . ."[12]

The evolutionist argues that even if the chance of certain molecules coming together in the right arrangement for life is, for example, one in one hundred quadrillion, quadrillion, quadrillion, quadrillion, etc., the combination *could theoretically* occur much sooner—even on the first attempt. That argument shows a misunderstanding of the mathematics of probability. The law of biogenesis has declared unequivocally that the chance of life arising spontaneously is *zero*! Nothing can change that law. The pretense of calculating odds measuring the possibility of life appearing spontaneously and without cause out of lifeless matter is therefore a futile effort.

Wouldn't it be foolish to object to Euclid's Theorem or Fourier's law of heat conduction? Claiming that there must be exceptions to the law of biogenesis is equally ludicrous. And what could be the motive for trying to undermine a long-established scientific law? There is only one reason. The law of biogenesis undermines the very foundations of atheism and evolution.

BUILDING ON A FANTASY FOUNDATION

Atheist Richard Carrier claims that the most compelling evidence for evolution "lies in the very chemical processes which underlie the development of life." Isn't the evolutionist building on a foundation that he hasn't laid? "Chemical processes which underlie the development of life"? Isn't it a bit premature to refer in such an authoritative way to life-producing processes when no one knows what life is? Have these processes ever been observed in nature or produced in the laboratory? Carrier sounds so sure of this "evidence" that we are curious to know what it is. If scientists know the chemical processes that produce life, why haven't they used them to do so? It seems, from all evidence, that we really need a "creator" to bring life into existence.

Lies don't die easily. With amazing persistence, Carrier continues:

> The very reason that life is composed of amino-acid chains is the fact that amino-acids naturally generate all of the ordering effects needed to create life in the first place. Ilya Prigogine won a Nobel Prize in 1977 for . . . demonstrating . . . that certain chemical systems, called "dissipative structures," naturally (i.e., as a necessary and inevitable product of chemical and physical laws) *increase* rather than decrease their complexity without violating the Law of Entropy. . . .[13]

Prigogine's Nobel Prize had nothing to do with the law of biogenesis. He did not receive that prize for discovering the secret to creating life. An even bigger prize would have to be created for that award, but it has not and never will be awarded to anyone living on this planet. God, in the act of creation, already has preempted any other claim to turning death into life.

WHAT ABOUT THE ANTHROPIC PRINCIPLE?

Furthermore, the entire universe bears the stamp of its Creator. A number of scientists have pointed out the fact that the universe has so many delicately balanced characteristics that it could only have been created *specifically* for life—indeed, specifically for man. This fact has been given the name "Anthropic Principle," defined by Patrick Glynn this way: "The seemingly arbitrary and unrelated constants in physics have one strange thing in common—these are precisely the values you need if you want to have a universe capable of producing life."[14] The universe gives the appearance that it was *designed* to support life on earth.

A large number of scientists with impressive credentials (among them many Nobel Prize winners) have given their endorsement to the Anthropic Principle. A succinct definition of this principle was given by John Wheeler, an American: "A life-giving factor lies at the centre of the whole machinery and design of the world." Wheeler coined the term "black hole" in 1967. Other endorsers include Niels Bohr (Nobel Prize in Physics, 1922) and Enrico Fermi (Italian physicist, noted for his work on the development of the first nuclear reactor, winner of the Nobel Prize in Physics in 1938, and considered one of the top scientists of the twentieth century), et al.

The Anthropic Principle was first suggested in a 1973 paper by astrophysicist and cosmologist Brandon Carter from Cambridge University. Simply put, the Anthropic Principle is an attempt to explain the observed fact that the fundamental constants of physics and chemistry are just right, or fine-tuned, to allow the universe and life as we know it to exist. These factors include the following:

> Gravity is roughly 10^{39} times weaker than electromagnetism. If gravity had been 10^{33} times weaker than electromagnetism, "stars would be a billion times less massive and would burn a million times faster."
>
> The nuclear weak force is 10^{28} times the strength of gravity. Had the weak force been slightly weaker, all the hydrogen in the universe would have been turned to helium (making water impossible, for example).
>
> A stronger nuclear strong force (by as little as 2 percent) would have prevented the formation of protons—yielding a universe without atoms. Decreasing it by 5 percent would have given us a universe without stars.
>
> If the difference in mass between a proton and a neutron were not exactly as it is—roughly twice the mass of an electron—then all neutrons would have become protons or vice versa. Say good-bye to chemistry as we know it—and to life.

The very nature of water—so vital to life—is something of a mystery (a point noticed by one of the forerunners of anthropic reasoning in the nineteenth century, Harvard biologist Lawrence Henderson). Unique amongst the molecules, water is lighter in its solid than liquid form: Ice floats. If it did not, the oceans would freeze from the bottom up and earth would now be covered with solid ice. This property in turn is traceable to the unique properties of the hydrogen atom.

The synthesis of carbon—the vital core of all organic molecules—on a significant scale involves what scientists view as an astonishing coincidence in the ratio of the strong force to electromagnetism. This ratio makes it possible for carbon-12 to reach an excited state of exactly 7.65 MeV at the temperature typical of the centre of stars, which creates a resonance involving helium-4, beryllium-8, and carbon-12—allowing the necessary binding to take place during a tiny window of opportunity 10-17 seconds long.[15]

What is the origin of life? Science only knows for sure that it cannot arise spontaneously. There is a law stating this irrefutable and unchangeable fact, the law of biogenesis: Life comes only from life. No clearer declaration could be made that life cannot possibly arise spontaneously. End of discussion.

The God of the Old Testament is arguably the most unpleasant character in all fiction: jealous and proud of it; a petty, unjust, unforgiving control-freak; a vindictive, bloodthirsty ethnic cleanser; a misogynistic, homophobic, racist, infanticidal, genocidal, filicidal, pestilential, megalomaniacal, sadomasochistic, capriciously malevolent bully.

—RICHARD DAWKINS

The kindly God who lovingly fashioned each and every one of us and sprinkled the sky with shining stars for our delight—that God is, like Santa Claus, a myth of childhood, not anything [that] a sane, undeluded adult could literally believe in. That God must either be turned into a symbol for something less concrete or abandoned altogether.

—DANIEL DENNETT, *DARWIN'S DANGEROUS IDEA*
(NEW YORK: SIMON & SCHUSTER PAPERBACKS, 1995), 18

We are grappling with a classic "chicken and egg" dilemma. Nucleic acids are required to make proteins, whereas proteins are needed to make nucleic acids and also to allow them to direct the process of protein manufacture itself. . . . The emergence of the geneprotein link, an absolutely vital stage on the way up from lifeless atoms to ourselves, is still shrouded in almost complete mystery.

—ANDREW SCOTT, "UPDATE ON GENESIS,"
NEW SCIENTIST, VOL. 106 (MAY 2, 1985), 31-32

Science offers us an explanation of how complexity (the difficult) arose out of simplicity (the easy). The hypothesis of God offers no worthwhile explanation for anything, for it simply postulates what we are trying to explain.

—RICHARD DAWKINS

Altogether a typical cell contains about ten million million atoms. Suppose we choose to build an exact replica to a scale one thousand million times that of the cell so that each atom of the model would be the size of a tennis ball. Constructing such a model at a rate of one atom per minute, it would take fifty million years to finish, and the object we would end up with would be [a] giant factory . . . some twenty kilometers in diameter, with a volume thousands of times that of the Great Pyramid.

—MICHAEL DENTON, *EVOLUTION: A THEORY IN CRISIS*
(LONDON: BURNETT BOOKS, LTD., 1985), 329-30

Precious little in the way of biochemical evolution could have happened on the Earth. It is easy to show that the two thousand or so enzymes that span the whole of life could not have evolved on the Earth. If one counts the number of trial assemblies of amino acids that are needed to give rise to the enzymes, the probability of their discovery by random shufflings turns out to be less than 1 in $10^{40,000}$ [power].

—SIR FRED HOYLE AND CHANDRA WICKRAMASINGHE,
"WHERE MICROBES BOLDLY WENT," *NEW SCIENTIST*, VOL. 91 (AUGUST 13, 1991), 415

SIXTEEN

THE EMPEROR HAS NO CLOTHES

It has not escaped the notice of logicians that omniscient and omnipotent are mutually incompatible. If God is omniscient, he must already know how he is going to intervene to change the course of history using his omnipotence. But that means he can't change his mind about his intervention, which means he is not omnipotent.[1]

—Richard Dawkins

DAWKINS THINKS HE HAS ACHIEVED a clever way of doing away with God, but it won't work. His polemic assumes that God makes mistakes and therefore *must* change His mind, but the God of the Bible says, "I am the Lord, I change not." In fact, variations of what Dawkins says have been long-time favorites of atheists. It's like the question that's asked of elementary philosophy students, "What happens when an irresistible force meets an immovable object?" Obviously, by very definition, they both can't exist at the same time. It's similar to the often heard challenge: "If God is not powerful enough to stop all evil and suffering, then he's too weak to be God; and if he could stop all evil but doesn't, then he's a monster. Either way, he's unworthy of our trust or worship." The argument, of course, is badly flawed because it ignores mankind's power of choice and blames God for man's choices.

We cannot excuse ourselves from that which is our responsibility. Selfishness cannot be blamed on selfish genes, no matter how influential Dawkins claims they are in our lives. Suppose a criminal tries to escape the penalty of the law by pleading with the judge, "It's not my fault, my selfish genes made me do it!" Or how about his lawyer declaring, "It's not my client's fault, he's simply the product of millions of years of evolution and natural selection!" Or how about this one, "Dawkins and Collins say that chimps are our closest relatives; surely you wouldn't find a chimp guilty of a crime."

Dawkins tells us that everything we are, including our thoughts, is simply what our "selfish genes" have made us—and they neither know nor care anything about us. We exist merely as vehicles whereby they do their selfish work and that keeps natural selection going, all without purpose or meaning. He admits that "a human society based simply on the gene's law of universal ruthless selfishness would be a very nasty society in which to live . . . if you wish, as I do, to build a society in which individuals cooperate generously and unselfishly towards a common good, you can expect little help from biological nature."[2] Isn't that statement sufficient proof that the theory of evolution is false? If I am the product of "natural selection," how could I have desires and act in a manner that opposes the very process that made me what I am? Why would I object to this theory? How could such thoughts even arise?

As further evidence of the warped thinking produced by atheism, Crick tells us that we are just bags of molecules and that what we imagine to be serious desires, fears, affections, as well as our highest moral and ethical thoughts are really delusions, without any significance whatsoever. We must ask, then, what gives our thoughts such composition, continuity, and consistency that we are deceived into thinking they have meaning? Is this just one more delusion manufactured by our genes in order to prolong a meaningless survival? The only answer the atheist has is, "Why, yes, of course!"

Is it our selfish genes, this "bag of molecules," that also gives us the innate conviction to reject such nonsense that denies the entire history of mankind? Does our continuing in the delusion that our government, universities, libraries, charitable organizations, etc., are meaningful somehow assist in our survival? And if this is so, wouldn't we all *naturally* know it? Doesn't the very fact that so many atheists bother to pursue research and write books in order to *persuade* us of this hypothesis prove that it isn't true?

UNCERTAINTY PILED UPON UNCERTAINTY

In Dawkins's book, *The God Delusion*, he quotes his friend and fellow atheist author, Jerry Coyne: "Why is God considered an explanation for anything? It's not. It's a failure to explain, a shrug of the shoulders, an 'I dunno' dressed up in spirituality and ritual. If someone credits something to God . . . they're attributing it to an unreachable, unknowable, sky-fairy. Ask for an explanation of where that bloke [God] came from, and odds are you'll get a vague, pseudo-philosophical reply about always having existed or being outside nature. Which, of course, explains nothing."[3]

Talk about explaining nothing! Books by evolutionists supposedly explaining the evolutionary process over millions of years that brought forth man are sprinkled with so many words expressing their uncertainty that Dawkins's quote of Jerry Coyne is almost laughable. In the seven closing pages of Coyne's book, *Why Evolution Is True*, in which he is supposed to sum up his highly acclaimed arguments, his words repeatedly betray confusion. For example, in the climax of his book, pages 227-33, we find the following phrases expressing his doubts: "might be," "could be a way of," "could represent," "assuming that"; "very likely to have evolved by selection"; "the parallels strongly imply"; "it takes some mental contortions to try to explain *every* facet of human sexuality by evolution"; "the use of symbolic language is likely a genetic adaptation, with aspects of syntax and grammar somehow coded in our brains. . . . "

He sums it all up with this statement:

> Finally, there is a very large category of behaviors sometimes seen as adaptations, but about whose evolution we know virtually nothing. This includes many of the most human universals, including moral codes, religion, and music. There is no end of theories (and books) about how such features may have evolved. Some modern thinkers have constructed elaborate scenarios about how our sense of morality and many moral tenets might be the products of natural selection working on the inherited mind-set of a social primate. . . . But in the end these ideas come down to untested—and probably untestable—speculations. It's almost impossible to reconstruct how these features evolved (or even if they *are* evolved genetic traits). . . .
>
> Yes, certain parts of our behavior may be genetically encoded, instilled by natural selection in our savannah-dwelling ancestors. But the genes aren't destiny. . . . The world still teems with selfishness, immorality, and injustice. But look elsewhere and you'll also find innumerable acts of kindness and altruism. There may be elements of both behaviors that come from our evolutionary heritage, but these acts are largely matters of choice, not of genes. . . . We make symphonies, poems, and books to fulfill our aesthetic passions and emotional needs. No other species has accomplished anything remotely similar. . . .
>
> We are the one creature to whom natural selection has bequeathed a brain complex enough to comprehend the laws that govern the universe. And we should be proud that we are the only species that has figured out how we came to be.

Coyne is groping for answers to traits that are clearly peculiar to humans. These traits are a few among the many that define our human-ness. What could have been the purpose for evolution and natural selection to develop these characteristics? What part could they possibly play in our survival? Moreover, why should we be proud of them?

So this is the climax of one of the most recent books written to prove that evolution is true. Ironically, it does the opposite. These ethical and moral capacities reveal a vast chasm that separates mankind from all other living creatures, including those that evolutionists tout as our "closest ancestors," such as Lucy and the recently discovered Ardi. Furthermore, where could such attitudes be located in the fossils of skeletons, even if they were complete from skull to toes? Where, indeed, could such defining human qualities be found even in the DNA? And why is it that the evolutionists and atheists from Darwin to Dawkins never once mention what seems to be so important?

Dawkins even speculates that "many of our human ailments, from lower back pain to hernias . . . our susceptibility to sinus infections, result directly from the fact that we now walk upright with a body that was shaped over hundreds of millions of years to walk on all fours."[4] Results *directly from*? And Dawkins can trace this back hundreds of millions of years? Is he overstating his case, or does he really know this? If this is true, why did natural selection cause man to walk upright, and why hasn't evolution eliminated this harmful posture long ago? Again, as is most often the case with what Dawkins pronounces with great confidence and authority, no substantiation is offered. This is merely one scientist's opinion.

Hitchens often indicts God with cruelty for punishing the wicked, especially for continuing the sentence after death.[5] Evolutionists don't seem concerned with the cruelty of natural selection, which slaughters left and right, leaving rotting corpses and eventually fossils all over the earth from its own failures. Why so many mistakes along this upward route, and why did this have to cost the lives of so many creatures along the way? Furthermore, if we are the ultimate product of evolution, why do we have such a concern for endangered species?

Dawkins loses credibility by attacking the most vulnerable and easiest-to-refute creationists, such as The Watchtower Bible and Tract Society, more commonly known as Jehovah's Witnesses. Most Christians consider the Witnesses to be a cult far removed from biblical Christianity. The book from which he quotes has 11 million copies in print, making it seem like a worthy target. They are not sold, however, but given away, with probably a low percentage of them ever read by anyone other than Witnesses.

Richard Dawkins thinks he has a clever argument when he says, "An atheist is just somebody who feels about Yahweh the way any decent Christian feels about Thor or Baal or the Golden Calf. As I've said before, we are ALL atheists about most of the gods that humanity has ever believed in. Some of us just go one god further."

Everyone acknowledges that there is no proof that God does *not* exist. Dawkins counters that there is no proof that Thor or Zeus or the "flying spaghetti monster" don't exist. Of course, the fact that one cannot "prove" that something or someone doesn't exist does not mean that they *do* exist. We know that Thor and Zeus were only two among a multitude of mythical gods. The Hindus have 330 million of them, some of their likenesses "made in China." Only the most ignorant and superstitious Hindus would believe that the idol itself is a god. Instead, they would say it "represents" Brahman, the one god over all.

There are numerous proofs for the existence of the God of the Bible, and we will provide some of them later. He identifies Himself in many ways, but especially as "the God of Israel," which He is called 203 times. He is also called "the God of Abraham, the God of Isaac, and the God of Jacob" 12 times. He has linked Himself with Israel to the extent that if that tiny beleaguered and much maligned nation ceases to exist, then so would the God of the Bible.

As we've seen, Dawkins, to his credit, is honest enough to admit quite openly that a belief in evolution necessarily leads to atheism. Many of his less forthright colleagues who attempt to deny this self-evident fact (as well as many liberal Christians who believe in evolution) are unhappy with him for "rocking the boat"[6] by that admission. In fact, he has not only "rocked the boat" but has sunk it.

Standing firmly for his Christian faith (in spite of his denial of it by his equal faith in evolution), Francis Collins writes: "The major and inescapable flaw of Dawkins's claim that science demands atheism is that it goes beyond the evidence. If God is outside nature, then science can neither prove nor disprove His existence. Atheism itself must therefore be considered a form of blind faith, in that it adopts a belief system that cannot be defended on the basis of pure reason."[7]

Dawkins has driven his theory into a dead end of contradiction from which there is no escape. We have given ample space to point out some of the inconsistencies and contradictions inherent in evolution and natural selection. One of the most obvious, however, is the question of why man, who is supposedly Earth's crowning achievement of natural selection, should be so at odds with nature. There is a growing environmental movement that is trying to push man into what Carl Rogers was among the first to advocate: "a comfortable relationship to nature, a responsible kinship." He found the very thought of "the conquest of nature . . . abhorrent."[8]

Undeniably, however, "nature" is not so constituted as to offer a benign and dependable kinship. It is absurd to speak of living in a "comfortable relationship" in the path of rivers of lava flowing from an erupting volcano, or of a hurricane or a tsunami. Although acknowledging that much "progress" has been abusive of nature, we dare not repudiate all that man has accomplished in what honesty must admit has been a battle with nature.

Rogers expressed an odd sentiment, considering the elementary fact that nearly every modern advance of science is unnatural, and many inventions (and most of modern civilization) have arisen from man's continual struggle for survival in the face of nature. The fact that man can reason about nature is the first stage in the proof that man is not the product of natural processes. And it is this unnatural act of reason opposing nature that brought under control a host of formerly fatal diseases (such as polio, tuberculosis, malaria, etc.), raised the survival rate of infants, and steadily increased the average life expectancy. Medical science is far from perfect, but it is the repeated unnatural act of taking out an appendix, or transplanting a heart, kidney, or liver, or removing tumors, that has saved millions of lives. Nor can even one of these unnatural abilities be attributed to natural selection or any evolutionary development.

It may be considered simplistic by atheists, but the truth is that the rejection of God is the cause of all of the unsolved problems faced by science. One need not speculate about whether the law of biogenesis applies only to the complex forms of life such as exist today, like flies, eggs, and simple proteins.

Having named a number of contemporary evolutionists who he claims were also devout Christians, Stephen Jay Gould declared: "Science can work only with naturalistic explanations; it can neither affirm nor deny other types of actors (like God) in other spheres (the moral realm, for example)."

AN UNSCIENTIFIC BELIEF
THAT PERSISTS AMONG SCIENTISTS

Pushing God out of His universe as not even worthy of consideration, many, if not most, of today's scientists embrace the Big Bang and evolution as the source of every living species, claiming that life began on Earth by chance. The next feasible conclusion would be that life also happened by chance on millions of other planets.

Hence the avid search for ETIs that most assuredly do not and cannot exist. As we have seen, scientism persists in the belief that life began by spontaneous generation. Even though scientists know this is impossible, die-hard materialists nevertheless cling to this belief as though their lives depended upon it. Actually, their livelihoods do depend upon it, because those who profess a belief in intelligent design suffer the disapproval of their colleagues, face job discrimination, and find it difficult to gain a hearing for their ideas in the scientific and academic world. This was not always the case, but it is today—one of the consequences of the wide acceptance of Darwin's theory of evolution.

So, having begun by chance in who-could-imagine how many places in the universe, according to atheistic materialists, life evolved into its present forms through "natural selection" over billions of years.

Though God is denied because of an unwillingness to admit Him into the equation by the inner circle, a preponderance of scientific evidence thoroughly debunks the belief that physical intelligent life could exist anywhere in the cosmos except by a creative act of God.

The delusion that life could occur by chance is much like the dream of exploring space. As we showed in the early chapters of this book, the distances in interstellar space are too great for man, even at the speed of light (if that were possible), ever to explore even a minute fraction of the cosmos. Likewise, the astronomical numbers of atoms and molecules and the interrelationships between them in all living things make it impossible for even the smallest unit of life (an individual cell) to be constructed by chance. Much less could the trillions of cells in the human body all come into existence and be joined together in the required intricate relationships through the unconscious and blind evolutionary process.

Every scientist knows that the mathematical impossibility of the component parts of even a single cell ever coming together by chance is thoroughly established. The facts are undeniable. Yet the mathematical impossibility is suppressed by the atheistic scientific establishment in its attempt to escape accountability to the Creator. Indeed, they have ridiculed and attempted to debunk creationists' proofs. Their arguments against the mathematics, and the creationist response, have been dealt with elsewhere in this book.

As previously noted, Linus Pauling, the only unshared two-time Nobel laureate, said that a single cell is more complex than New York City. Mathematically, not even one cell (the smallest living unit) could come into existence by chance. We need only turn to mathematics, the queen of the sciences, to find absolute proof that even the simplest cell is far too complex to be formed by accident or by any natural process except as directed by DNA. Hence, there had to be a designer and creator.

Dawkins admits that natural selection, for unknown reasons, has left us "with every species looking uncannily as though it had been designed." He also acknowledges that to deny a designer goes against the common instinct of the entire human race. These are two very puzzling facts if there is no designer after all and natural selection has made us what we are.

Dawkins's pat response, which is echoed by other atheists, is to declare, "Indeed, design is not a real alternative at all because it raises an even bigger problem than it solves: who designed the designer?"[9] This is a senseless question. The Designer, by very definition, was not designed.

Evolutionists reject our mathematical computations by claiming that the math doesn't take "natural selection" into consideration. In fact, this theory that weeds out the weak as only the strongest survive has nothing to do with the origin of life. Nor was any "natural selection" involved in the development of the parts of the cell before they were all joined together in the incredibly complex relationships that make up the whole. Furthermore, as we shall see, "natural selection" would destroy the parts not only of the cell but of the body as well before they were fully integrated into the whole, because, prior to that time, far from contributing to survival, they would be detrimental.

THE MATHEMATICS OF PROBABILITY CANNOT BE ESCAPED

It is mathematically impossible that the right atoms and molecules could come together in the correct order to build a cell, but the impossibility is of an even higher order for the instructions imprinted on the DNA to arise by any natural process, such as evolution or natural selection. These instructions for building and operating amazing chemical machinery are written out in a language that is encoded and that only certain protein molecules can read. Indeed, because it follows their directions, the instructions on the DNA cannot be in process but must be already in place as the cell is being constructed. There is no way that this could happen over millions or billions or trillions of years by "natural selection," even for a single cell—and the human brain has trillions of cells, each of which involves thousands of molecules doing different functions. The human body has about 100 trillion cells all fitted together into one perfect form, intricately related and functioning in unison.

Imagine the odds for assembling by chance the DNA in the nucleus of the cell with information greater than is contained in an entire set of encyclopedias! And that is just the nucleus, not the entire cell. Yet the prevailing view of the scientific establishment is that chance produced the first cell! Of course, that is the only choice one has when God is rejected. Such is the costly irrational path down which atheism leads.

THE MATHEMATICS IS IRREFUTABLE

There are many other reasons than the law of biogenesis why life could never result from chance. We must consider a few more if we are to rationally explore whether or not life could accidentally arise on other planets. We need not even consider fossils and adaptations, which are beside the point. When one examines life at its molecular level, there are simply too many molecules that must be strung together in even the simplest life forms for them ever to have united by chance in the proper order to create even the smallest cell. Astronomer-mathematician Sir Fred Hoyle complained about scientists who still won't admit the undeniable:

> I don't know how long it is going to be before astronomers generally recognize that the combinatorial arrangement of not even one among the many thousands of biopolymers on which life depends would have been arrived at by natural processes here on Earth. . . . [Atheists] advocate the belief that tucked away in nature, outside of normal physics, there is a law which performs miracles (provided the miracles are in the aid of biology). This curious situation sits oddly on a profession that for long has been dedicated to coming up with logical explanations of biblical miracles.[10]

Furthermore, all of the physical ingredients of a living cell or organism could be artificially thrown together, but that would not produce life. We do not know what life is or how it arises except by a living organism reproducing itself. The law of biogenesis continually mocks the theory of evolution.

The origin of life is only one of many mysteries for which science has no answer. But for our purposes, we will ignore that question along with the law of biogenesis and further consider the mathematical impossibility of putting the component parts of one cell together by chance—let alone an organ such as an eye or the brain, much less the entire body. The human brain contains over a hundred trillion electrical connections—more than all the electrical connections in all the electrical appliances in the world. To imagine that only this organ came about through a series of undirected mutations (most of them harmful) over millions of years is patently absurd.

Physicist and information theorist, Professor Hubert P. Yockey, who has studied the application of information theory to problems in biology, says that "the origin of life is unsolvable as a scientific problem." He worked under Robert Oppenheimer at the University of California, Berkeley, and also on the Manhattan Project. In his opinion, "The origin of life by chance in a primeval soup is impossible [by the laws of probability]. . . . A practical person must conclude that life didn't happen by chance."[11]

The atheists/evolutionists counter, "Of course, it isn't by chance! Natural selection doesn't work by chance!" We're not talking about natural selection, however, which can only work upon living things. The truth is that we don't know what life is or how it began. The only "explanation" that atheists have to fall back on is the great god "Chance." And this emperor has no clothes.

A single cell has millions of molecules, and thus the odds that any cell could be formed by chance are zero; even body members with their relatively small numbers of parts still compute to zero possibility of coming together by chance. For example, consider the number of bones (206) in the average adult skeleton. The probability that the skeletal structure of the body could come together without intelligent direction (which evolutionists acknowledge natural selection does not provide) is one chance in 1 followed by 388 zeros—trillions of times greater than impossible.[12] And that is without considering the impossibility of the millions of cells making up the separate parts of the skeleton first coming into existence by chance and being formed into these skeletal portions.

MATHEMATICAL IMPOSSIBILITY PILED UPON IMPOSSIBILITY

We have seen that the cosmic distances are far too great for man to explore the universe or contact other life "out there" even if it existed. Likewise, the numbers of atoms and molecules in living things are far too great for life to have occurred by chance. Let us consider some further examples.

The estimated number of atoms in the universe is usually stated as 1 with 80 zeroes after it. To tilt everything heavily in favor of life by chance, let's allow 1 billion (1 with 12 zeroes after it) as the average number of inter-atomic interactions per second per atom, and 30 billion years as an upper limit for the age of the earth. Let's also generously allow every inter-atomic reaction to produce a unique molecule. Under these impossibly favorable conditions, we arrive at 1 with 110 zeroes after it as the maximum number of unique molecules that could ever have existed in the universe's theoretical 30-billion year history. Let's also ignore the fact that only amino acids with left-handed symmetry appear in proteins that make up living things, and let us assume a relatively short protein consisting of a chain of only 200 amino acids.

John R. Baumgardner has calculated the odds of random molecular interactions putting together the right combination of amino acids to produce this small protein molecule. Assuming the above and that 999 of a minimal set of 1,000 protein molecules have already been matched,

Baumgardner calculates the mathematical likelihood of matching onto this string the one remaining molecule needed as follows:

> Let us restrict our considerations to the specific set of 20 amino acids found in living systems and ignore the hundred or so that are not [and] merely focus on . . . obtaining a suitable sequence of amino acids that yields a 3D protein structure with some minimal degree of essential functionality. Various theoretical and experimental evidence indicates that about half of the amino sites must be specified exactly.
>
> For a relatively short protein consisting of a chain of 200 amino acids, the number of random trials needed for the likelihood of hitting a useful sequence is then in the order of 20^{100} or about 10^{130}. *This is a hundred billion billion times the upper bound we computed for the total number of molecules ever to exist in the history of the cosmos!!* No random process could ever hope to find even one such protein structure, much less the full set of roughly 1000 needed in the simplest forms of life. It is therefore sheer irrationality . . . to believe random chemical interactions could ever identify a viable set of functional proteins out of the truly staggering number of candidate possibilities.
>
> In the face of such stunningly unfavorable odds, how could any scientist with any sense of honesty appeal to chance interactions as the explanation for the complexity we observe in living systems? To do so, with conscious awareness of these numbers, in my opinion, represents a serous breach of scientific integrity. This line of argument applies, of course, not only to the issue of biogenesis but also to the issue of how a new gene/protein might arise in any sort of macroevolutionary process.[13]

Baumgardner has challenged his fellow scientists where he works to find a flaw in his reasoning and mathematics, and none has been able to do so. But this is only the beginning of the impossible odds, which multiply astronomically when we consider the coded algorithms stored in DNA. Baumgardner goes on to argue:

> The simplest bacteria have genomes consisting of roughly a million codons . . . or genetic words . . . of three letters from the four-letter genetic alphabet. Do coded algorithms a million words in length arise spontaneously by any known naturalistic process. . . ? What we presently understand from thermodynamics and information theory argues persuasively that they do not and cannot!
>
> Language involves a symbolic code, a vocabulary, and a set of grammatical rules to relay or record thought. Many of us spend most of our waking hours generating, processing, or disseminating linguistic data . . . language structures are clear manifestations of non-material reality . . . independent of its material carrier. . . . Einstein pointed to the nature and origin of symbolic information as one of the profound questions about the world as we know it. He could identify no means by which matter could bestow meaning to symbols . . . symbolic information, or language, represents a category of reality distinct from matter and energy. Linguists . . . speak of this gap between matter and meaning-bearing symbol sets as the "Einstein gulf." Today . . . there is no debate that linguistic information is objectively real. . . . Its reality is qualitatively different from the matter/energy substrate on which the linguistic information rides [i.e., sound waves, electronics, paper and ink, etc.]
>
> From whence, then, does linguistic information originate? In our human experience we immediately connect the language we create and process with our minds. But what is the ultimate nature of the human mind? If something as real as linguistic information has existence independent of matter and energy, from causal considerations it is not unreasonable to suspect that an entity capable of originating linguistic information is also ultimately non-material in its essential nature.[14]

A DIGITALLY CODED DATA BASE?

What is this "digitally coded data base" in the nucleus of the cell, greater in information content than the *Encyclopedia Britannica*, to which Dawkins refers? Darwin never conceived of anything like that! He wouldn't have understood the terminology. Dawkins is referring to DNA (deoxyribonucleic acid), the existence and function of which no one in Darwin's day even imagined. It was not until 1953 that Francis H. Crick and James D. Watson jointly discovered the function of this huge molecule and proved that it was the universal storage medium for the information to form and operate all living systems (for which they shared a Nobel Prize together with Maurice Wilkins).

This double-stranded helical molecular chain of linearly linked pairs of nucleotides has written on it in a code (that only certain proteins can decode) the genetic information for the construction and operation of every cell in the entire body. There are 5,375 nucleotides of DNA in an extremely small bacterial virus (*theta-x-174*). There are about 3 million nucleotides in a single-cell bacteria, and over 3 billion in the DNA of every cell in a mammal's body, strung together by chemical bonds, each of which must be in precisely the correct sequence. It is irrational to imagine that this incredible organization was formed into its mind-boggling precision by chance. Yet evolutionists cling to this theory and defend it against the mathematical impossibilities of chance being the explanation.

If the intelligent information in a mere pinhead's size of DNA were written out on paper in words, it would create a stack of books 500 times as high as the distance from the earth to the moon. Our computers can't handle that amount of information as efficiently as can DNA. And this all came about by chance? To espouse that theory, one has to be incurably opposed to belief in God! And why? What is so objectionable about the idea of God creating life?

Furthermore, DNA is designed to replicate itself exactly. That fact alone rules out evolution. Built into the DNA mechanism are many editing safeguards to be certain that nothing changes in the wording. As has been often said by scientists, "The very existence of the DNA-coded language stalls evolution at the first hurdle."[15]

For evolution to occur from the simple to the complex, and to create new species, there would have to be an input of additional information. But the very structure of DNA would block any such attempt to alter its precise information content. And what would be the source of this information? These ingenious written instructions could come only from an intelligence with a conceptual and organizational ability beyond human comprehension.

Life comes only from living things, and living things can pass their life along to the next generation only by exactly replicating themselves. New species are ruled out by the very way DNA works. As the Bible says, God created every living thing, from grass and plants to animals and man, to reproduce itself "after his [its] kind."[16] It would take a horrible foul-up in the DNA to do otherwise—and the DNA is programmed to prevent errors, so that even small ones are very rare.

FOLLY WORTHY ONLY OF FOOLS

The only basis for a change would be the very rare glitches in the process, the vast majority of which would be detrimental or benign and not an improvement. Certainly, errors could not be the means of creating a new species. Since the DNA provides instructions for optimal performance, any mistake in transmission could never improve its function to cause upward evolution. It could only worsen it. Darwinian evolution provides no basis for creating new genetic information and adding it to the DNA. "Natural selection" can only work with the genetic information already within the system, losing some, but never producing anything new.

What have been called "mutations," as noted above, represent errors in transmitting the DNA from mother to child. These cause fluctuations in genes already present, not anything that could lead to a new species because no new genetic information has been created.

That such errors do occur from time to time is an accepted fact by both creationists and evolutionists. No matter what kinds of errors may be introduced, however, DNA can clearly accomplish only what has been programmed into it; it could never create a new species. Dr. Stephen Grocott, who holds four patents and has published more than thirty research papers, put it very simply:

> Please note that when speaking of evolution, I am talking of the appearance of new (not rearranged) genetic information leading to greater and greater complexity of genetic information. . . . I am not speaking of natural selection, which leads to a reduction in genetic information. . . . Creationists, of course, have not the slightest problem with natural selection . . . the theory of natural selection was described by creation-believing scientists long before Darwin boarded the *Beagle*.[17]

When one sees or hears information, no matter by what medium it is expressed (radio, TV, DVD, audiotape, book, carvings on a tree, or scratchings on the ground), one knows that it was placed there by an intelligent and purposeful agent. Information conveys meaning, and meaning cannot arise from anything but an intelligence. No force of nature could produce meaning. As noted previously, Einstein pointed out that matter cannot arrange itself into information. That requires an intelligence.

The information contained on the DNA is far more ingenious than we could ever create, even with our best computers. To deny that it could only have been conceived of and placed there by an infinite intelligence (i.e., God), and to insist that it came about by Dawkins's blind watchmaker, is both unscientific and irrational.

The psalmist declared, "The fool hath said in his heart, There is no God." When a scientist declares that the universe began with a "big bang," which sterilized it completely, admits that spontaneous generation from nonliving matter is impossible, and then insists that life must have begun by spontaneous generation anyway because he refuses to believe in God—if that man is not a fool, then who is?

THE SHRINKING TIME SCALE

When faced with proof that life couldn't possibly occur by chance, the evolutionist falls back upon the supposed billions of years he believes the earth has been here. His confident appraisal is that, given enough time, anything could develop by chance. It is rather humorous how the evidence, however, continues to shrink the evolutionary timetable.

For many years, Carlsbad Caverns in New Mexico were touted as proof of the ancient age of the earth. Fifty years ago, a sign above the entrance declared that the caverns were at least 260 million years old, based upon the estimated time it would take for stalactites and stalagmites to form in the limestone. In 1988, the sign was reduced to 7-10 million years, then later to 2 million years. Recently, the sign was removed entirely. It has been observed that stalactites can grow several inches a month in mines and under bridges and subway platforms.

The fish, *coelacanth*, was thought to have been extinct for 70 million years. Prior to 1938, any rock formation containing the fossil of this fish was dated by evolutionists as at least 70 million years old. Then, wonder of wonders, in 1938, this long "extinct" fish was caught in the Indian Ocean. Since then, hundreds have been landed by fishermen—and evolutionists lost another of their ancient bulwarks. As more discoveries are made, the millions and billions of years so essential to this bankrupt theory continue to erode.

THE UNIQUENESS OF OUR UNIVERSE AND PLANET

Another one of the compelling reasons for believing that we are alone in the universe is the uniqueness of the home we inhabit, this earth. We have seen that all the theories put forth to explain the structure of the universe cannot make it fit the Big Bang theory. We can't even find a cohesive explanation for our own solar system. According to the theories, this earth should not be at all what it is. Supposedly,

Earth was torn off from the sun, but that doesn't fit the earth at all.
Fred Hoyle put it like this:

> First we see that material torn from the Sun would not
> be at all suitable for the formation of the planets as we
> know them. Its composition would be hopelessly wrong.
> [Furthermore] it is the Sun that is normal and the Earth
> that is the freak. The interstellar gas and most of the stars are
> composed of material like the Sun, not like the Earth. You
> must understand that, cosmically speaking, the room you
> are now sitting in is made of the wrong stuff. You, yourself,
> are a rarity. You are a cosmic collector's piece.[18]

By normal observation and expectations, we humans are freaks
and our earth shouldn't exist. All attempts at natural explanations fail
us in the end. Harold Jeffreys pointed out that science has yet to find
a satisfactory explanation for the earth and solar system: "To sum it
up, I think that all suggested accounts of the origin of the solar system
are subject to serious objections. The conclusion in the present state
of the subject would be that the system cannot exist."[19] In 1972, Carl
Sagan and George H. Mullen first proposed that the early earth had
lots of heat-trapping methane and ammonia [because] life could not
have evolved without those gases. . . . [A]t the time of Sagan's death
(1996) he was still trying to resolve these problems."[20]

THE PRANCING STEED
HAS BUCKED THE ATHEISTS OFF

It is astonishing how much time and effort atheists expend fighting a
God who they say doesn't exist. Dawkins and his colleagues sincerely
believe they are fighting a great delusion that has somehow taken
hold on the vast majority of mankind, including about 92 percent of
Americans, according to the latest polls. That fact in itself demands
attention.

What is the evolutionary source (the only source of anything that atheists will acknowledge) of this "God delusion"? How does it aid the survival of the race so that "natural selection" has maintained it so consistently throughout the entire history of man? And if this "delusion" is indeed a beneficial factor in the survival of the race (the only explanation atheists can muster), why would atheists try to destroy it? Does it matter so much to their egos that something they reject so adamantly is held firmly by the vast majority and by nature itself, and cannot be shaken loose in spite of threats by tyrants and diligent effort?

After all, if everything, including the "God delusion," is simply the result of random motions of atoms that began with a huge explosion and is therefore meaningless, who cares what people believe? There is no truth, nothing is right or wrong, and it will all be gone in the death of the universe anyway. So why concern oneself with this delusion—or with any other—and isn't that all there is, anyway, just delusion? So why be so upset over the "God delusion"?

One would think that the vast majority of rational beings could not be consistently deceived century after century into believing in a nonexistent "God." Yet, this is the case, if atheism is true. Moreover, this delusion is incredibly persistent and plays no favorites. The wealthy and poor, educated and ignorant, civilized sophisticates and savages in the jungle, all are smitten with the same delusion and refuse to be delivered.

The Soviets spent 70 years trying by every possible means, from control of schools, media, and every facet of life, to persecution, imprisonment, brainwashing, and death, to stamp out "faith." History would report their total failure. Mao failed in China, as did Marxism. Castro's Cuba is one of the few remaining communist regimes, yet belief in God persists, as well as belief in and worship of Satan. No amount of threats and persecution has ever succeeded anywhere in wiping out a firm belief in the existence of God. That is a remarkable fact that begs an explanation. Even the usually liberal media seem critical of the New Atheists:

Atheism is in trouble. You can tell because its most eloquent spokesmen are receiving icily critical reviews in the very mainstream press that Christians often dismiss for liberal bias. Take, for example, the reviews of Richard Dawkins's book *The God Delusion* that appeared in *The New York Times*, the *London Review of Books*, and *Harper's*. No one would mistake those journals for members of the Evangelical Press Association, but the *Times* reviewer, science and philosophy writer Jim Holt, upbraided Dawkins for not fully appreciating the intellectual force of classical arguments for God, especially in light of the more sophisticated versions presented by today's theistic philosophers: "Shirking the intellectual hard work," Holt wrote, "Dawkins prefers to move on to parodic 'proofs' that he has found on the internet. . . ." In the *London Review of Books*, Terry Eagleton complained that Dawkins reduces complex social problems to simplistic narratives in which religion is the villain.[21]

Dawkins hopes to succeed where Marx, Lenin, Mao, Pol Pot, and so many other tyrants have failed in spite of the totalitarian system they imposed on their citizens. We won't question at the moment why atheism and totalitarianism go hand-in-hand and are so comfortable in partnership with one another. That fact—and it is an established fact of thousands of years—seems to corroborate the declaration in the Bible that "where the Spirit of the Lord is, there is liberty."[22]

The United States, which has been a bastion of liberty in the world since its beginning, appeals to "almighty God" in its constitution and through its founding fathers dozens of times. From the very beginning, Congress has been opened with prayer, and faith in God is repeatedly found in the speeches of senators and congressmen. On its money and on its monuments in Washington, D.C., are found the words, "In God We Trust."

Those words are hated equally by murderous and oppressive despots and atheists. We are not offering this fact as proof of anything at the moment, but it seems to be more than coincidence. This belief and especially its moral consequences, are increasingly being denied by America's leaders and, regretfully, by our current president. Thankfully, moral failures, whether by athletes, political leaders, or religious leaders, seem not to be acceptable to the majority. Perhaps, more people than we thought are awakening to the fact that the emperor has no clothes.

When I think of all the harm the Bible has done, I despair of ever writing anything to equal it.

—OSCAR WILDE

Faith is the great cop-out, the great excuse to evade the need to think and evaluate evidence. Faith is belief in spite of, even perhaps because of, the lack of evidence.

—RICHARD DAWKINS

When one person suffers from a delusion, it is called insanity. When many people suffer from a delusion, it is called religion.

—ROBERT PIRSIG, AUTHOR OF ZEN AND THE ART OF MOTORCYCLE MAINTENANCE

I regard monotheism as the greatest disaster ever to befall the human race. I see no good in Judaism, Christianity, or Islam—good people, yes, but any religion based on a single . . . frenzied and virulent god is not as useful to the human race as, say, Confucianism, which is not a religion but an ethical and educational system.

—GORE VIDAL

It is absolutely safe to say that if you meet somebody who claims not to believe in evolution, that person is ignorant, stupid, or insane (or wicked, but I'd rather not consider that).

—RICHARD DAWKINS, "IGNORANCE IS NO CRIME," FREE INQUIRY MAGAZINE, VOL. 21, NO.3

But man himself and his behavior are an emergent product of purely fortuitous mutations and evolution by natural selection acting upon them. Nonpurposive natural selection has produced purposive human behavior.

—HUDSON HOAGLAND, "SCIENCE AND THE NEW HUMANISM," SCIENCE, VOL. 143 (JANUARY 10, 1964), 113

Many scientists would rather cling to Darwin's theory, in whatever baroque form, than face the implications of its demise. Darwin's scientific detractors, moreover, are generally reticent about taking their objections public for fear of being labeled "creationist." So the newspaper-reading public has not been let in on what the British scientific journal Nature recently called "the sharp dissent and frequently acrimonious debate" over evolutionary theory, while the armies of biology teachers, science writers, and public television wildlife hosts carry on as though there were no problem with Darwin at all.

—GEORGE SIM JOHNSTON, "THE GENESIS CONTROVERSY," CRISIS (MAY 1989), 12

SEVENTEEN

MISUNDERSTANDINGS AND FALSE CHARGES

W E HAVE ALREADY POINTED OUT that who or what a man may be is not defined by molecular or skeletal structure or by DNA. This is where Francis Collins (who believes in God), as well as the Leakeys, Cricks, Hitchenses, and a host of haters of God have wandered off together into a trackless wilderness of rebellion led by the will-o'-the-wisp of "belief in God must be stamped out at all cost!"

Certainly, I would never presume to contradict Collins on anything about DNA. We have the right, however, to challenge his interpretations of the facts when they go against the very Christian faith he claims to hold. He finds what seem to be a number of either very odd coincidences or indications of relatedness between man and some extremely strange "evolutionary ancestors," including mice. Instead of taking these as evidence that there must be something wrong with his interpretation of DNA, he uses them to strengthen his faith in the religion of evolution—and evolution is unquestionably a religious faith.

Let's probe further. What is this "common ancestor" of men and mice to which Collins refers? He doesn't tell us. What fossil evidence does he have? Again, he doesn't tell us because there is none.

Furthermore, this idea that we are closely related to mice is somewhat offensive. It is too fantastic to be taken seriously.

What could drive this aberration of logic except a passionate desire to prove there is no God? This is where atheism is leading society, but human wisdom screams loudly in protest: "Stop! No matter what impressive scientific credentials Dawkins and Collins and the rest of them may have, and even if 10,000 scientists serenade us with the same siren song, we refuse to follow them down this path that leads to the destruction of human values and the denial of everything that makes our species absolutely unique!"

SINCERELY MISTAKEN—OR INTENTIONALLY MISLEADING?

When it comes to informing the public about the doctrines of biblical Christianity, most atheists are, perhaps knowingly, ill informed. Dawkins delivers misinformation for the credulous, laced with venomous denunciations. His and other atheists' inexcusable ignorance about biblical Christianity would be laughable were it not so tragic because of the multitudes they lead astray. Here is only a small but typical example:

> I have described atonement, the central doctrine of Christianity, as vicious, sado-masochistic, and repellent. We should also dismiss it as barking mad for its ubiquitous familiarity which has dulled our objectivity. If God wanted to forgive our sins, why not just forgive them, without having himself tortured and executed in payment—thereby, incidentally, condemning remote future generations of Jews to pogroms and persecutions as "Christ-killers. . . ."[1]
>
> But now, the sado-masochism—God incarnated himself as a man, Jesus, in order that he should be tortured and executed in *atonement* for the hereditary sin of Adam. Ever since Paul expounded this repellent doctrine, Jesus has been worshipped as the *redeemer* for all our sins. Not just

the past sin of Adam: *future* sins as well, whether future people decided to commit them or not![2]

The lack of understanding is appalling! We have no intention of defending anything except *biblical* Christianity, and that is in short supply. If it does not come directly from the Bible, it is simply not Christianity. Everyone is free to make up any religion that suits their fancy. In doing that, however, one is not free to call it *Islam* if it does not adhere to the Qur'an and the example set by Muhammad. It is only common sense that one does not look for the truth about Christianity to *The Passover Plot* or *The Da Vinci Code,* or even *The Passion of the Christ,* in spite of the fact that hundreds of thousands of evangelicals loved it, and thousands of evangelical pastors recommended it to their flocks. There are more popular movies and novels misrepresenting Christ than we could possibly mention. But let's take *The Passion of the Christ* as an example, because so many evangelical pastors praised it as "so true to the Bible." In fact, it was not. Let me offer a quick critique of the major scenes in the film, as I observed them at one of the early showings.

THE PASSION OF THE CHRIST

Jesus is seen praying in the Garden of Gethsemane. Satan appears to him as a woman in a monk's robe and cowl, whispering temptations to him. This is not in the Bible. It never happened. A huge snake (another depiction of Satan) comes slithering up to Christ, and Jesus stomps on its head, killing it. Again, the Bible records no such scene. After they have scourged Christ's back to a bloody pulp, with Mary Magdalene and Mary, the mother of Jesus, observing this horror, Pilate's wife brings a handful of linens to the two Marys, and they use them to wipe up Christ's blood. It did not happen, and it is not in the Bible. Jesus, in chains, is knocked over a bridge by the soldiers. Dangling there, he confronts Judas, who is cowering beneath the bridge. It didn't happen and is not in the Bible.

On the Via Dolorosa, carrying his cross toward Calvary, Jesus falls under its weight, and "Saint" Veronica gives him her veil to wipe his bloody face. As Jesus staggers on, Veronica is seen off to the side of the procession, displaying her veil, which now bears the image of the face of "Jesus" impressed upon it. This image was supposedly the first icon and the pattern for others. With Christ on the cross and a thief on either side, a huge raven flies up and plucks out the eye of one of the thieves.

Nothing of what I've just described that was portrayed so powerfully in the movie is recorded in the Bible *because it never happened*. Much of this drama comes from the visions of a mystic nun. These scenes, of course, were obviously chosen by Mel Gibson and portrayed in the film strictly for their dramatic effect on the audience, not to convey truth. How could thousands of evangelical pastors praise this misrepresentation of the crucifixion as biblical?

But this is not the worst of it. None of the four gospels gives even a hint of the brutality of the scourging that *The Passion* portrays. The Bible simply says, "When Pilate saw that he could prevail nothing . . . he took water, and washed [his] hands before the multitude, saying, I am innocent of the blood of this just person: see ye [to it]. Then answered all the people, and said, His blood [be] on us, and on our children. . . . When he had scourged Jesus, he delivered [him] to be crucified. Then the soldiers of the governor took Jesus into the common hall, and gathered unto him the whole band [of soldiers]. And they stripped him, and put on him a scarlet robe. And when they had platted a crown of thorns, they put [it] upon his head, and a reed in his right hand: and they bowed the knee before him, and mocked him, saying, Hail, King of the Jews! And they spit upon him, and took the reed, and smote him on the head. And after that they had mocked him, they took the robe off from him, and put his own raiment on him, and led him away to crucify [him]" (Matthew 27, Mark 15, Luke 23, John 18 and 19).

Why this overdoing of the scourging? This is a Roman Catholic film, as Mel Gibson, the author/director, and James Caviezel, who portrayed Christ (both devout Catholics), would be only too happy to acknowledge. Catholicism's emphasis is on the *physical* suffering of Christ; it knows nothing of the moral and spiritual suffering, such as that presented in Isaiah 53:6,10: "The LORD hath laid on him the iniquity of us all. . . . It pleased the LORD to bruise him; he hath put him to grief: when thou shalt make his soul an offering for sin. . . ."

There is nothing in the film reflecting the biblical account. Tragically, this popular film gives an altogether false impression. How could Roman soldiers, cursing and mocking and scourging Him, execute upon Christ the righteous judgment He endured for the sins of the world? He did not accomplish this expiation by enduring the suffering with which the soldiers afflicted Him. That is what *men* did to Him. Far from paying for our sins, that would only add to mankind's guilt. A major reason for the misunderstanding is the phrase, "with his stripes we are healed."[3] This is a mistranslation. The word that Isaiah uses in the Hebrew is singular, "*stripe*," referring to the one blow from the Father, who "laid on him the iniquity of us all."

Hebrews 2:9 declares that Christ "tasted death for every man." The eternal "death" He endured for every person who ever lived or would ever live had to include what all Christ-rejecters will eternally suffer in what the Bible calls the Lake of Fire. Wicked, Christ-hating Roman soldiers could not inflict God's holy wrath against sin upon Christ. Only the Father could lay our sins upon Him.

Christopher Hitchens and his fellow atheists declare it to be unjust for Christ, the innocent one, to suffer the eternal punishment that we, the guilty, deserve. When one reads the Bible carefully, from Genesis to Revelation, an understanding begins to emerge. God had pronounced a penalty upon Adam and Eve and all of their descendants. He could not "just forgive," as Hitchens and Dawkins insist He could have done, any more than a judge sitting on the bench in one of our courts could "just forgive" the guilty one standing before him. The judge, whether God or man, is bound by the law. He cannot override it, as much as he may desire to do so.

The eternal penalty had to be paid in full for every person who ever lived or would ever live. Christ, being "God manifest in flesh," was the only one who could pay that penalty for all mankind. Only a perfectly sinless person could die for the sins of others. But no one is without sin, and the penalty of eternal judgment is upon every person. To pay that penalty is why Christ died for the sins of the world.

SOME ESSENTIAL CLARIFICATION

There are millions of people who call themselves "Christians" but whose "Christianity" in no way even comes close to the teachings of the Old Testament prophets, who foretold the coming of Christ, or of Christ himself and his apostles. Dawkins is anything but a Christian, though raised as a "Christian," and is as far as one could get from that early profession of faith, which he long ago renounced. In his futile attempts to discredit the Bible, he has nothing to say that other critics haven't already said.

Misrepresentations abound in bestselling books, DVDs, plays, and even in sermons, commentaries such as *The Renovaré Spiritual Formation Bible*, and false "Bible translations," such as *The Message*. The number of these is legion, and we could not possibly deal with them all.

Suffice it to say that Dawkins has no other source of information than accusations, which have already been discredited, so why does he mention them? One can only assume that repeating these false charges is the best criticism he can muster. The accusations against the Bible by the rest of the Four Horsemen are no better. For example, the very title of Sam Harris's book, *Letter to a Christian Nation*, is a dead giveaway. Anyone who knows the Bible or has an inkling of what true Christianity is knows that there is no such political entity as a "Christian nation." The very fact that Harris would give this title to a critique of Christianity exposes his ignorance on this subject.

Dawkins is even more ignorant than Harris. An ignorance that is further exposed in the following statement:

I have already mentioned the long list of non-canonical gospels. A manuscript *purporting to be the lost Gospel of Judas* has recently been translated and has received publicity in consequence. The *circumstances of its discovery are disputed* but it *seems to have turned up* in Egypt sometime in the 1970s or 60s. It is in Coptic script on 62 pages of papyrus carbon-dated to around AD 300. . . . *Whoever the author was* [it] makes the case that Judas betrayed Jesus only because *Jesus asked him to play that role.* It was all part of the *plan to get Jesus crucified so that he could redeem mankind.* Obnoxious as that doctrine is, it seems to compound the unpleasantness, and Judas has been vilified ever since.[4] [Italics added]

This is an unverified report. It is fiction. Apparently, Dawkins is well aware of this fact, so why should he even mention it? The fact that the above document somehow "turned up" more than a thousand years after the crucifixion, without any other corroboration, makes it worthless on that account alone. Furthermore, it makes no sense. So Jesus wants to get crucified. Why? He's going to have to rise from the dead, which, if he is not God is impossible; and if he is merely a man, he will be exposed as a fraud at the end of three days when he is still in the grave. If that were the case, why were Christ's disciples convinced of His resurrection? How could Christianity gather such momentum so quickly if it was all based upon a pretended resurrection, which would be easily exposed as a lie?

Furthermore, notice the italicized phrases: "*purporting to be. . . circumstances . . . are disputed . . . seems to have turned up . . . Whoever the author was,* etc." These statements clearly show that Dawkins is willing to pass along rumors and false reports in his attempt to discredit the Bible. That is not so easily done, however. The Bible has been under attack from every angle for nineteen centuries, and no one has been able to honestly discredit it.

434 MISUNDERSTANDINGS AND FALSE CHARGES

PERVERSITY, MISUNDERSTANDING,
AND IGNORANCE

Why do I accuse Dawkins and his atheist colleagues of perversity? The Bible has been under microscopic scrutiny for centuries. Eminent historians, archaeologists, legal experts, and scientists who have spent years examining the Bible from every angle have written scores of volumes giving the evidence for why they declare it to be God's infallible and holy Word. This does not prove that the Bible is true, but it shows the naked prejudice of atheists such as Dawkins and Hitchens, who, far from offering insights, instead trot out the unsubstantiated beliefs of discredited critics and even cults that no knowledgeable, biblical Christian would take seriously.

Dawkins generously offers to let the "older folks" continue in their delusion, if that makes them feel better:

> Let me not labour the point. I've probably said enough to convince at least my older readers that an atheistic world-view provides no justification for cutting the Bible and other sacred books out of our education. And of course we can retain a sentimental loyalty to the cultural and literary traditions of, say, Judaism, Anglicanism, or Islam, and even participate in religious rituals such as marriages and funerals without buying into the supernatural beliefs that historically went along with those traditions. We can give up the belief in God without losing touch with a treasured heritage.[5]

Understandably, Dawkins, who doesn't believe in anything outside of matter and atheism, can afford to be very generous with allowing "fools" to continue their meaningless rituals. He seems unaware of the existence and influence of Christians who actually believe that the Bible is *true* and would never base their worship of Christ upon worthless statements representing nothing but tradition. To them, it is an insult to propose taking the bread and wine of communion, for example, without believing in the One whose life, sacrificial death for the sins of the world, resurrection, and return are memorialized in that act. Dawkins is insulting all true biblical Christians in expecting them to go through meaningless ceremonies honoring a Christ who supposedly never existed. True Christians are not as credulous as that, but millions of those who claim to be Christians, including their pastors and seminary professors who openly admit that they don't really believe the Bible, apparently are.

Sadly, for many such Christian leaders, what they do is merely a job. A secular columnist, with no love for Christianity, writes derisively:

> Here are the exact words said to me by the senior minister of a Presbyterian Church of 1,500 members. "Just play the game . . . just say the sweet things they want to hear, don't upset anyone with biblical and religious scholarship. Look at this beautiful church building I've got, plus all the perks, free golf and country club memberships, big salary."
>
> I said to him, "Jack, you're pathetic, you're a wimp. You're the problem."[6]

By God's grace, Christian leaders like this pastor are the exception and not the rule. Critics, however, are naturally quick to judge everyone who claims to be a Christian by the many hypocrites, such as the pastor portrayed here.

The elementary misunderstandings atheists have about the God of the Bible, whom they ridicule and reject, would fill this entire volume. Richard Dawkins in particular, although I don't understand why, is offended when we say that we don't believe in the God he doesn't believe in—but it's true. Atheists seem unconcerned that they completely misunderstand and misrepresent the God revealed in the Bible, nor are they willing to be corrected but persist with their false charges and ridicule based upon complete misunderstandings. That is an unconscionable attitude. The warped views of God, which atheists promote, are then used to support their ridicule of God and of theists.

Christopher Hitchens is too intelligent not to know what he is doing. His recital of false accusations begins on page 1 of his book,

God Is Not Great. There he describes God as "the unknowable and ineffable creator who—presumably—opted to make me this way."[7] What a convenient way to blame his warped thinking about "religion" on the God he doesn't believe in yet to whom he was introduced as a child by a woman teacher whom he apparently still admires. In the "compulsory and enforced by the state"[8] religious training, that dear lady must have taught the young Christopher at least some Bible verses that clearly refute his current false accusations.

As a young boy, he surely must have learned from her that a major theme of the Old Testament is the "God of Israel's"[9] revelation of Himself to His people. She almost certainly had him memorize Jeremiah 29:13, where God declares, "And ye shall seek me, and find me, when ye shall search for me with all your heart." Surely, he was also at least acquainted with Christ's prayer to His Father, in which He declares, "And this is life eternal, that they might know thee the only true God, and Jesus Christ, whom thou hast sent."[10] Several hundred verses scattered throughout the Bible reiterate God's revelation of Himself and His desire that all mankind might know Him.

How can we explain this blatantly false accusation in the first paragraph of Hitchens's book? We are reluctant to charge him with deliberately lying, but this gross error not only sets the tone for the tome, but others like it are found throughout. In fact, Christopher has vehemently repeated this false accusation (one of his favorites) in so many debates that he has probably come to believe it.

Most atheists fall prey to the childish error of equating Christianity with "religion." From the subtitle of his book to the last false accusation, Hitchens uses the word "religion" scores of times, seemingly without ever recognizing that biblical Christianity is not a religion.

THE BATTLE IS NOT "RELIGION VS. SCIENCE"

Imagining that their battle is against religion, the New Atheists, who claim to speak for science, betray a further ignorance. They are apparently unaware that true believers in the God of the Bible do not follow a *religion*. They follow the Bible as their sole authority, confident without the slightest doubt (based upon infallible proof) that the Bible is true in all it says.

The New Atheists, led by Dawkins, know almost nothing about the Bible. They would be shocked to learn that it is not a religious book. The phrase, "religious faith," is not found once in all its pages, the word "religion" appears only five times, and the word "religious" twice. All but one of these seven times is critical of "religion." Furthermore, in the few times it mentions religion, the Bible never means what atheists imagine when they use that word. This is only one example of the many ways in which these enemies of God reveal their bias and biblical illiteracy.

Those who attack the Bible should have, at the very least, an elementary understanding of it. Instead, we find inexcusable ignorance fueling reckless accusations. Dawkins and the rest of the "Four Horsemen" make the same mistake. Whatever they say about "religion" is irrelevant to biblical Christianity. I have no intention of defending religion of any kind. Inexplicably, they never attack biblical Christianity specifically, perhaps because they don't even understand it. So, as far as any biblical Christian is concerned, atheists are tilting at windmills. Of course they do attack the Bible but in the process betray the fact that their misapprehensions are of gargantuan proportions.

Hitchens claims that he hasn't found a Christian leader who really believes in the resurrection as a historic event, and that a common excuse is "religion might not be true, but never mind that, since it can be relied upon for comfort." Speaking personally, I have been an evangelical Christian for nearly 70 years, have preached in churches all over the U.S. and the world and have *never* met *even one biblical* Christian who would make such a statement. In fact, Hitchens has publicly debated several Christians who have told him very clearly that they believe literally in the Bible, the miracles it describes, and in Christ's resurrection, as historic events. Hitchens is exaggerating at best (which is one of his common failings) and not being truthful at worst.

WHAT ABOUT THE RESURRECTION?

What do biblical Christians—*all of them*—believe about the resurrection? The Bible repeatedly declares that it is the heart and foundation of the gospel of Jesus Christ. Paul argues in detail, "If Christ be not risen, then is our preaching vain, and your faith is also vain. Yea, and we are found false witnesses of God; because we have testified of God that he raised up Christ: whom he raised not up, if so be that the dead rise not . . . and if Christ be not raised, your faith is vain. . . . If in this life only we have hope in Christ, we are of all men most miserable."[11]

It is believed that all of the original apostles (except perhaps John) were martyred, some horribly tortured, testifying to what they claimed were the *facts* concerning the life, death, and resurrection of Jesus. Each of these men could have bought his release by denying these facts—"He never healed thousands of people with every imaginable disease, never raised the dead, never fed thousands with a few loaves and a handful of fish. The whole thing was a myth we made up; we stole his body and secretly buried it—just free me and I'll tell you the whole truth!" But none of them did! Even Robert G. Ingersoll, one of America's most famous (or infamous, in the view of many) agnostics of the nineteenth century, acknowledged that "no man is fool enough to die for what he knows is a lie—an irrefutable fact that adds great weight to the apostles' testimony."

Far from giving us a reasoned disproof of the resurrection, Hitchens is content to mock, as though no one of any intelligence ever believed this "myth." Though the opinions of others don't constitute proof, many minds, at least the equal of and certainly greater authorities on evidence than Hitchens, having carefully examined the evidence, have declared the story of the resurrection of Christ to be factual history. For example, Lord Lyndhurst, one of the greatest legal minds in British history, declared: "I know pretty well what evidence is; and I tell you, such evidence as that for the Resurrection has never broken down yet."[12]

The errors that Hitchens makes in his critique of the Bible are too many to cite in their entirety. Many of his criticisms are hopelessly (or perhaps deliberately) vague. For example: "the divine will was made known by direct contact with randomly selected human beings . . . hugely discrepant prophets or mediums [by] revelations, many of them hopelessly inconsistent. . . ." One can hardly respond to such charges, since the "randomly selected . . . discrepant prophets or mediums" and their "hopelessly inconsistent" revelations are neither identified nor specifically critiqued.

Even a minimal understanding of the Bible will reveal that not one of the prophets was "randomly selected." Furthermore, the Bible was revealed through 40 different prophets, most of whom never met or read the others' writings, yet their declarations constitute a consistent progressive revelation of the same major themes of presenting one unfolding truth from Genesis to Revelation. In fact, there are literally *hundreds* of Old Testament prophecies, which are specific in their details.

Hitchens rather venomously declares that "just like the Old Testament, the 'New' one is also a work of crude carpentry, hammered together long after its purported events, and full of improvised attempts to make things come out right." He gives us no examples, no evidence, but quotes a supposed expert whose statements suffer from the same deficiency. Nevertheless, Hitchens writes, ". . . H. L. Mencken irrefutably says in his *Treatise on the Gods*:

> The simple fact is that the New Testament, as we know it, is a helter skelter accumulation of more or less discordant documents, some of them probably of respectable origin but others palpably apocryphal, and that most of them . . . show unmistakable signs of having been tampered with.[13]

One hardly knows how to respond to such a bundle of misinformation. One would like to believe that Hitchens is not just deliberately lying. On the other hand, how could a man who claims to know so much and who poses as an expert on the Bible include so many lies about it without doing so deliberately? In fact, after reading the many false accusations made by Hitchens, we cannot escape the impression that he cites them knowingly and willingly.

For example, in a chapter titled "Religion's Corrupt Beginnings," Hitchens uses as illustrations to debunk what he calls "religion" some of the most obvious examples that could be found, among them: the indulgences sold by the Roman Catholic Church, not only in the Middle Ages but also today in a different way; Mormonism's meticulous genealogical work, so that members can trace their ancestors all the way back to Adam, who can then be baptized by proxy, and unless this is done, the person doing the genealogical work cannot be saved; he wastes time going into great detail in describing the well-known errors of Joseph Smith and his Mormon followers as though they were part of mainstream Christianity.[14] There is a great volume of documentation by Christians going back decades exposing the errors and even fraud of Mormonism.

Hitchens, like other leading atheists, refers to "religion" scores of times but never takes note of any distinctions, as though all religions were the same. In trying to destroy "religion," none of the New Atheists ever recognize the distinctiveness of *biblical* Christianity compared with other forms (Catholic, Mormon, liberals of all sorts, etc.) that do not take the Bible as their sole authority.

In attacking "religion," Hitchens even uses the South Pacific cargo cults as an example. During World War II, having seen military planes suddenly coming from the sky to earth, and unloading vast amounts of cargo, some natives built a religion of rituals aimed at attracting the gods to come back from the sky and to share the cargo with them. Hitchens treats this bizarre cult as though it were representative of all religions.[15] He is too intelligent for this to be an honest mistake. It can only be a reflection of a mind driven by a venomous hatred of God.

He even cites the child evangelist, Marjoe, and the movie made about him, as though this constituted a valid criticism of Christianity. Hitchens does explain that Marjoe was a deliberate fraud, yet he uses him to debunk Christianity. In fact, Marjoe had long ago been exposed by Christians themselves, so what is Hitchens's point?[16]

Even so, atheists persist in attacking Christianity through religion. Nobel laureate Steven Weinberg recently said, "The world needs to wake up from the long nightmare of religion. . . . Anything we scientists can do to weaken the hold of religion should be done, and may in fact be our greatest contribution to civilization."[17] In a similar vein, Richard Dawkins, declares: "I am utterly fed up with the respect we have been brainwashed into bestowing on religion."[18] These atheists think they are including biblical Christianity in the term "religion" or "religious faith." In fact, as we have already explained, Christianity is neither.

NOTHING BUT A PACK OF LIES?

If the foregoing charges are legitimate, the entire Bible should be dismissed as fraudulent, since it all hangs together. The New Testament does not stand alone. It is founded upon, and much of it came as a fulfillment of, the Old Testament prophecies. Let's take some examples of what Mencken is actually saying and what Hitchens is vengefully passing along.

If there is one particle of truth in the critics' vicious accusations, then neither Paul nor the other apostles wrote the epistles attributed to them. They must instead have been the work of lying imposters who claimed to be Paul. The same would be true for all of the other epistles. Consider, for example, the words of Peter: "We have not followed cunningly devised fables . . . but were eyewitnesses of his majesty."[19] Are Peter's words a fraud, inserted by someone writing centuries later?

The claim that the New Testament is "based on the reports of 'eyewitnesses'" is dismissed by Hitchens as "patently fraudulent"[20] Anyone who carefully reads the New Testament accounts of the life, death, and resurrection of Christ immediately recognizes that Hitchens is badly misinformed. Without any doubt, we have the testimony of bona fide eyewitnesses through the events recorded in Matthew, Mark, Luke, and John.

One of Hitchens's most serious accusations is that the New Testament (particularly the gospels) is not historical, even though it claims to be. He is merely repeating the misinformation that is still being given out by those who do not know the facts. Hitchens can hardly be looked up to as an authority on biblical history. We can certainly dismiss what he says without fear of contradiction or missing anything of importance.

Like the other Four Horsemen, Richard Dawkins, in what he imagines to be a legitimate exposé of the Bible, relies, in fact, upon false information from fellow critics who are just as biased and ill informed as he is:

> Nobody knows who the four evangelists were but they almost certainly never met Jesus personally. Much of what they wrote was in no sense an honest attempt at history but was simply rehashed from the Old Testament, because the gospel-makers were devoutly convinced that the life of Jesus must fulfill Old Testament prophecies. It is even possible to mount a serious, *though not widely supported,* historical case that Jesus never lived at all, as has been done by, among others, Professor G. A. Wells of the University of London in a number of books, including *Did Jesus Exist?*"[21] [Emphasis added]

How does Wells become such an authority in Dawkins's eyes? How does he know that the four evangelists "almost certainly never met Jesus personally"? He is accusing them of deliberately lying. That's a serious charge. What evidence do either Wells or Dawkins, his apparent disciple, have for these outrageous statements? We need evidence, but it is not forthcoming.

How does Dawkins, seemingly accepting as true whatever Wells says, know that what the apostles were writing was "in no sense an honest attempt at history"? How does he know that Matthew, Mark, Luke, and John were deliberately and dishonestly pretending to give an eyewitness account of what they had never seen or heard and knew was a lie? How can Wells or Dawkins know the innermost thoughts and motives of men who were writing 1,900 years ago and whom nei-ther Wells nor Dawkins ever met? Apparently, Dawkins trusts Wells implicitly, but on what basis could Wells contradict eyewitnesses when, in fact, he was born 1,900 years too late? Where did he get his information? He certainly was no eyewitness.

Wells, whom Dawkins relies upon heavily, has neither new evidence nor new arguments. Instead, his book is simply a rehash of the "higher criticism," which began in the 1800s in Germany. This is largely alleged textual analysis, which purportedly debunks authorship, accuracy, etc. Relying on once popular but long since discredited arguments, Wells accuses Paul and all of the other New Testament authors of being liars when they claimed to have firsthand knowledge of the facts. Yet this is a primary source of the criticism Dawkins makes of the Bible.

We have previously quoted some of the world's greatest experts on evidence, both historical and from the standpoint of legality. Among them were Professor Simon Greenleaf, co-founder of Harvard's grad-uate school of law, in his day the foremost expert on legal evidence; Lord Caldecote, Lord Chief Justice of England; Thomas Arnold, Regius Professor of Modern History at Oxford, and others, who pro-nounced on the basis of their examination of the evidence the validity of the testimony of the gospels in all they say. The supposed experts, whom Dawkins, Wells, and other critics that the Four Horsemen quote, are exposed as liars at worst and as poor scholars at best.

Furthermore, other arguments Dawkins throws into the mix are even more pitiful. For example, he offers once again the following:

> The designer himself (/herself/itself) immediately raises the bigger problem of his own origin. Any entity capable of intelligently designing something as improbable as [the flower] a Dutchman's Pipe (or a universe) would have to be even more improbable than a Dutchman's Pipe (*Aristolochia Trilobata*), all of whose parts seem elegantly designed to trap insects, cover them with pollen, and send them on their way to another Dutchman's Pipe.[22]

We have already debunked this worn-out, oft-repeated pseudo-argument of "who designed the designer," apparently one of Dawkins's favorites. To reiterate: God, by very definition, is without beginning and end. He doesn't need a designer to design Him, a thought so ridiculous that it is hardly worth discussing.

WHY IS THERE EVIL?

Atheists persist in attempting to prove that God does not exist by asking ridiculous questions. For example, one atheist website poses the oft-repeated puzzle: "If god is all powerful, then god is responsible for all the evil in the world. If humankind has free will, then God is not all-powerful." In fact, that does not follow. The implication is that an "all-powerful God" could stop all evil.

In the Bible, evil is associated with the power of choice and could not exist apart from it. Only beings capable of choice can have moral responsibility, and this very power of choice makes evil not only possible but inevitable. It is a foregone conclusion that creatures who, though made "in the image of God,"[23] are less than God (as any creation of God must be) will think thoughts and practice deeds that reflect their rebellion and not the intent of their creator.

That being the case, why would God give mankind this exceedingly dangerous ability to choose? Why would God, who is only good, allow evil of any kind or of even the smallest degree in His universe? The answer, of course, is obvious: God wanted to have a meaningful and loving relationship with mankind, beginning with Adam and Eve. Without the ability to choose to love or to hate, to say yes or to say no, it would be impossible for mankind to receive God's love and to love Him in return, for real love must come from the heart. Nor could there be genuine praise and worship unless it were voluntary.

It would hardly be glorifying to God for robots, who cannot choose to say or do otherwise, to continually sing His praises. For such beings to be programmed to say repeatedly "I love you" would be meaningless. The love and praise of God must come from beings who have the choice of not loving and praising but even of hating and denigrating Him, beings whose hearts have been captured by His love and who genuinely love Him in return. That is why, if Islam, through threats of terrorism and death, could force the entire world to submit to Allah—or if Communism through similar threats and force could take over the world today—it would not be a victory for either totalitarian system. Rather, such a world conquest would be the greatest defeat, for it would have failed to win the love and loyalty of its alleged "converts."

Of course, while giving man the power of choice made love possible, it also opened the door to all manner of evil. It is by our own personal choice that we think evil thoughts and do wicked deeds. God did not cause Lucifer, or any angels, or any of us to do evil. That tragedy came about by our individual volition. We choose to satisfy our own selfish desires rather than to glorify God, and thus we come short of His glory and demonstrate ourselves to be sinners.

How wonderful, then, that in His love and wisdom God was able to pay the penalty for our sins and thus to forgive us and make it possible for us to be in His presence, loving and praising Him from our hearts eternally! And surely His love has captured our hearts and created in us a love that is real and eternal. As 1 John 4:19 says, "We love him because he first loved us." That can only be said meaningfully by beings who are also capable of choosing *not* to love.[24]

The Bible likens the church (which is composed of all true believers) to Christ's bride. It even tells us that there will be a wedding in heaven, where Christ and His bride will be "married" for eternity, in inseparable union: "Let us be glad and rejoice, and give honour to him: for the marriage of the Lamb is come, and his wife hath made herself ready. And to her was granted that she should be arrayed in fine linen, clean and white: for the fine linen is the righteousness of saints. And he saith unto me, Write, Blessed are they which are called unto the marriage supper of the Lamb."[25]

(Israel) has reached the end of its function and will soon disappear off the geographical domain.

—PRESIDENT AHMADINEJAD, CITED IN JEFFREY GOLDBERG,
"QUESTIONS ABOUT AHMADINEJAD'S FAMOUS QUOTE," *THE ATLANTIC* (APRIL 3, 2009)

In the context of what he euphemistically called the "situation between Israelis, Palestinians and Arabs," Mr. Obama said he looked forward to the day ". . . when Jerusalem is a secure and lasting home for Jews and Christians and Muslims, and a place for all of the children of Abraham to mingle peacefully together as in the story of Isra, when Moses, Jesus and Muhammad (peace be upon them) joined in prayer."

—PRESIDENT BARACK OBAMA, CITED IN FRANK J. GAFFNEY JR.,
"AMERICA'S FIRST MUSLIM PRESIDENT?" *THE WASHINGTON TIMES* (JUNE 9, 2009)

Behold, I will make Jerusalem a cup of trembling unto all the people round about, when they shall be in the siege both against Judah [and] against Jerusalem. And in that day will I make Jerusalem a burdensome stone for all people: all that burden themselves with it shall be cut in pieces, though all the people of the earth be gathered together against it.

—ZECHARIAH 12:2-3

Scientists, like others, sometimes tell deliberate lies because they believe that small lies can serve big truths.

—RICHARD C. LEWONTIN, "THE INFERIORITY COMPLEX,"
REVIEW OF *THE MISMEASURE OF MAN*, BY STEPHEN J. GOULD,
NEW YORK REVIEW OF BOOKS (OCTOBER 22, 1981)

The picture so often painted of Christians huddling together on an ever narrower strip of beach while the incoming tide of "Science" mounts higher and higher, corresponds to nothing in my own experience. That grand myth . . . is not for me a hostile novelty breaking in on my traditional beliefs. On the contrary, that cosmology is what I started from. Deepening mistrust and final abandonment of it long preceded my conversion to Christianity. Long before I believed Theology to be true I had already decided that the popular scientific picture at any rate was false. One absolutely central inconsistency ruins it. . . . The whole picture professes to depend on inferences from observed facts. Unless inference is valid, the whole picture disappears. Unless we can be sure that reality in the remotest nebula or the remotest part obeys the thought-laws of the human scientist here and now in his laboratory—in other words unless Reason is an absolute—all is in ruins. Yet those who ask me to believe this world picture also ask me to believe that Reason is simply the unforeseen and unintended by-product of mindless matter at one stage of its endless and aimless becoming. Here is flat contradiction. They ask me at the same moment to accept a conclusion and to discredit the only testimony on which that conclusion can be based.

—C. S. LEWIS, "IS THEOLOGY POETRY?" *OXFORD SOCRATIC CLUB DIGEST* (1944)

EIGHTEEN

THE OVERLOOKED, IRREFUTABLE PROOF

WE HAVE TRIED TO BE FAIR in our citing of much scientific evidence refuting atheism, materialism, and evolution. These three fit hand-in-glove with one another and really constitute a rival religion to theism. We have shown that in spite of much effort on the part of their loyal adherents, they still lack convincing scientific evidence and must be taken by faith.

Arguments of a purely scientific nature could continue, but these alone would still leave the two sides far apart and with differences unresolved. There can be no argument, however, with clearly stated biblical prophecies or with the history recording their fulfillment.

Atheists know that they must destroy the Bible, and they have been attempting to do so for many years. Biblical Christianity, with the virgin birth, sinless life, death on a Roman cross, and resurrection of Jesus of Nazareth, the Messiah of Israel and the world, must be proved to be contrived fables. Together, in the final analysis, these attempts to discredit the biblical testimony are a rival religion—they must also be taken by faith.

Richard Dawkins calls the resurrection of Jesus Christ "petty, parochial, trivial, unworthy of the universe."[1] This statement makes him not only "anti-God" but "anti-Christ." The death, burial, and resurrection of Jesus are foundational to biblical Christianity. As did Carl Sagan, Dawkins (along with his fellow "Four Horsemen" and many other atheists) literally hates God but reveres the cosmos that he denies God created. Instead, atheists insist that it came about through a giant explosion of something called energy (though no one knows its origin or cause), leaving in its wake a chaos of gasses. The gasses that came out of this mysterious explosion somehow gathered themselves together into clumps, which, over an unknown number of billions of years, developed by chance into the cosmos that we are still trying to fathom today. What is energy and why does it exist? In spite of diligent effort and brilliant discoveries, scientists have found no answers to this or the many other "why" questions, to some of which we have already referred.

THE BATTLE FOR TRUTH HEATS UP

Declaring that theists don't know the meaning of "theory" when they attempt to demean evolution by calling it "only a theory," Christopher Hitchens says a theory is successful "if it survives the introduction of hitherto unknown facts. And it becomes an accepted theory if it can make accurate predictions about things or events that have not yet been discovered, or that have not yet occurred."[2] Evolution fails on both of these counts.

Sam Harris repeatedly betrays his monumental ignorance of the Bible and biblical Christianity while pretending superior knowledge of both. He also displays a perverse refusal to admit the vast differences between the many religions. Apparently, he sees no difference between Islam's firm declaration that there is only one true god and Hinduism's embrace of more than 300 million. Addressing Christians, he says, "CONSIDER: every devout Muslim has the same reasons for being a Muslim that you have for being a Christian."[3] He couldn't be more wrong. The reasons a Christian has for believing in Jesus Christ and all that the Bible says about Him are as different from a Muslim's reasons for believing in Allah and Muhammad as day is from night. We just mentioned the resurrection and the fact that no leader of any religion rose from the dead except Jesus Christ. The Qur'an denies the death and resurrection, plus almost everything else foundational to Christianity. Yet Hitchens and most atheists treat all "religions" as if there were only petty differences among them.

As we have already noted, the God of the Bible is called "the God of Israel" more than 200 times. Not once is He called the God of the Germans or the French or the Spanish or the Arabs or the Muslims, although He gave His Son to die for all mankind. The Bible was inspired through 40 different prophets over a period of 1,600 years. We have their names and sayings and historical documents in support of each. They were from different times in history and widely different cultures. In stark contrast, Muhammad claimed to be the *sole prophet* of Allah, who allegedly inspired him *alone* to write the Qur'an. The claim that Muhammad is the sole prophet is an integral part of Islam, including the confession that every Muslim must make and every convert declare. In contrast, every prophet inspired to write the Bible has 39 other witnesses to what each one of them declares. We have only Muhammad's word that he alone was inspired by the Prophet Elijah through the angel Gabriel to write the Qur'an. This one fact alone separates Christianity from Islam and from every religion in the world.

The Christian has archaeological, historical, and scientific proof for the Bible. Where else in the world's religious literature is such proof offered? The Bible, the God of the Bible, and Jesus Christ as the Messiah are proved irrefutably by *hundreds* of prophecies.

Nothing comparable is found anywhere else. Certainly atheism can offer no proof for its religious faith. Yet Harris mistakenly declares that Christians and Muslims have the same reasons for what they separately believe. It simply isn't true. This is only one example of the disinformation Harris foists upon his unsuspecting following and to bolster his own faith in atheism.

Hitchens and the rest of atheism's "Four Horsemen" condemn "religion" because many religious people are zealous in their attempts to make converts. With the broad brush he typically wields, Hitchens declares that religion "*must* seek to interfere with the lives of nonbelievers, or heretics, or adherents of other faiths."[4] Isn't this the very same reason why atheists write books and spread their "gospel"? As we have shown, Richard Dawkins declares: "The *atheist movement* has no choice but to aggressively spread the good news. *Evangelism* [to convert the world to atheism] is a moral imperative."[5]

When I was an undergraduate math major at UCLA nearly 60 years ago, I read everything I could find that the atheists, skeptics, and critics had written against God, Jesus, and the Bible. The more I read, the more it strengthened my faith and confidence because the critics' arguments were devoid of substance. One would think that in all the time that has elapsed since then, their rebuttals of the Bible would have improved. In fact, the same worn-out arguments are still in vogue, such as the denial of the prophecy that the Messiah would be born of a virgin. Here is the most maligned of those prophecies in the Old Testament: "Therefore the Lord himself shall give you a sign; Behold, a virgin [*almah*] shall conceive, and bear a son, and shall call his name Immanuel."[6] Sam Harris comments:

> Unfortunately for the fanciers of Mary's virginity, the Hebrew word *alma* (for which *parthenos* [Greek for virgin] is an erroneous translation [in the Septuagint]) simply means "young woman," without any implication of virginity. It seems all but certain that the Christian dogma of the virgin birth, and much of the church's resulting anxiety about sex, was the result of a mistranslation from the Hebrew. . . .

It would appear that Western civilization has endured two millennia of consecrated sexual neurosis simply because Matthew and Luke could not read Hebrew. For the Jews . . . the dogma of the virgin birth has served as a perennial justification for their persecution, because it has been one of the principal pieces of "evidence" demonstrating the divinity of Jesus.[7]

First, let's correct a few of Harris's most obvious errors. There is a vast host of Christians today (and there has been throughout history) who believe in the virgin birth and the divinity of Christ but would never persecute a Jew. In fact, they have a special love for Jews as God's chosen people and as Christ's brethren. The persecution came from the Roman Catholic Church because of its unbiblical teaching that the Church had replaced Israel as the people of God and that the Jews deserved to be hated because they had crucified Christ. Nor is the Christian belief in the virgin birth "one of the principal pieces of 'evidence' demonstrating the divinity of Jesus." Harris simply doesn't understand the Bible, though he may have read it, and that makes his ideas about Christianity not only mistaken but inexcusably ridiculous. Equally ridiculous is the idea that these two disciples, Matthew, a Jew, and Luke (though a Greek, an educated physician), both living in Israel, couldn't read Hebrew. How does Harris know this?

Harris reiterates this argument elsewhere,[8] as do other atheists. The skeptics have directed their attack against the virgin birth by focusing on Isaiah 7:14. Let's examine not only this prophecy but the many others that teach a virgin birth. Yes, *almah* means a young, *unmarried* maiden. Though not true today in Israel, in Isaiah's time an unmarried maiden was sure to be a virgin. Nor would it be a sign from God for a woman who was not a virgin to bear a child. Further, Immanuel means "God is with us." Israel was sinking deeper into apostasy, and God's judgment upon her had been pronounced by many prophets, including Isaiah, from his first chapter onward.

Therefore, this name could not have meant that God was with

Israel to bless her but that the child would be God himself, born in Israel. Could any other child be called "God is with us"? And how could such a child enter the world except by a virgin birth? The only other use of this word is found two chapters later, when Israel is called, "thy land, O Immanuel."[9] So God's land, the land of Israel, belonged to this child named Immanuel. But this is only one of numerous prophecies in the Bible, all of which corroborate one another.

THE VALUE OF BIBLICAL PROPHECY

The Bible is about 28 percent prophecy. Its major subjects are Israel and the Messiah. Biblical prophecy has four primary purposes: 1) To prove irrefutably the existence of the Creator and that He is "the God of Israel"; 2) To identify Israel beyond any doubt as the chosen people to whom that disputed land in the Middle East was given by God for "an everlasting possession,"[10] and thus belongs to them today; 3) To prove that the Bible is the Creator's Word to mankind (there are no such prophecies in the Qur'an, Hindu Vedas, Baghavad Gita, Ramayana, sayings of Buddha, or Confucius, et al.), and 4) To identify the Messiah beyond dispute so that Israel would know who He was when He came. The fulfillment, without fail, of so many specific biblical prophecies given centuries and even thousands of years in advance proves all of these points for those willing to face the facts.

Later in Isaiah, the prophet presents a clearer prophecy concerning the "child" previously spoken of: "For unto us a child is born . . . a son is given: and the government shall be upon his shoulder: and his name shall be called Wonderful, Counselor, The mighty God, the everlasting Father, the Prince of Peace. Of the increase of his government and peace there shall be no end, upon the throne of David . . . even for ever."[11] This can refer only to the promised Messiah, who (as many other biblical prophecies foretell) will reign on David's throne in endless peace. The declaration is also unmistakable that this babe is God's Son[12] and yet is God himself come to earth as a man. God is His Father, yet He himself is called both God and Father. Certainly, this one is Immanuel—and only a virgin could have the honor to be His mother. The rabbis picked up stones to kill Him when Jesus said, "I and my Father are one,"[13] but His claim agreed with the Hebrew prophets.

What about this claim to be the one and only son of God? Jews in particular reject this term, claiming that it is found only in the New Testament's record that when the angel Gabriel announced to Mary, an astonished young virgin, that she would bear a son, she was told that "He . . . shall be called the son of the Highest. . . ."

The prophet Micah declares where this amazing babe, the "son of David" and heir to his throne would be born: in Bethlehem, the city of David. The prophecy that He "shall be ruler in Israel" once again identifies this one as the coming Messiah. At the same time, Micah reiterates the fact that Israel's Messiah could only be God himself because He existed eternally before being born of a virgin into this world:

> But thou, Bethlehem Ephratah, though thou be little among the thousands of Judah, yet out of thee shall he come forth unto me that shall be ruler in Israel; whose goings forth have been from of old, from everlasting.[14]

These are not the only prophecies declaring that the Messiah would be God, virgin-born into this world. Similar prophecies come from many different biblical prophets who never knew one another and who lived at various times in history and were part of diverse cultures. The critics never present the entire scope of biblical statements concerning the virgin birth of the Messiah. The atheists hammer away at Isaiah 7:14, but that Scripture is only one of many prophecies, which all speak with one voice.

BETRAYING THEIR IGNORANCE AND BIAS

Many of the atheist critics claim to be former Christians. One can only wonder what kind of "Christians" they were to have had such ignorance of the Bible while pretending to know it so well. Take Gary Lenaire, for example, who "spent 15 years in the church . . . released nine contemporary Christian music albums, was nominated for six Gospel Music Awards . . . preached the gospel . . . around the world [and] served as a voluntary Chaplain for the Military Department."[15] He writes in *An Infidel Manifesto*:

> Biblical prophecy is perhaps the most powerful tool for religious delusion. . . . Look at any so-called prophesies [*sic*] in scripture: the wording is so general that you could attach almost any event and say "look, this is a fulfilled prophecy!" That is exactly why there are thousands of people today saying that they are witnessing prophecies being fulfilled in our generation. . . . Most of the so-called prophecies were never intended . . . as prophetical in the first place . . . the words are so general you could make them to mean almost anything. Take a look at them without the dogma of your local preacher.[16]

Lenaire the atheist poses as an expert on Bible prophecy. Instead of an accurate analysis, however, he offers little more than inexcusable ignorance and criticism based upon prejudice. Notice that he says, "*any* so-called prophecies." Although some prophecies are, by their very nature, difficult to understand, there are *hundreds* that are unmistakably clear and have been fulfilled to the letter. Many others are still in process of fulfillment. "So general you could make them to mean almost anything"? On the contrary, they are so specific that Lenaire's arguments would not merit a response were they not influencing so many to turn from God and His Word.

The existence of Israel today in the face of a long-standing, publicly sworn determination by more than a billion Muslims to destroy her and all Jews worldwide is an undeniable fulfillment of repeated and very clear Bible prophecies that God would preserve Israel for a thousand generations (i.e., forever). Opinions vary on the length of a generation—from 40 to 100 years. Even by the shortest estimates, thousands of years remain before God's guarantee runs out.

Atheism can be proved true very simply: just destroy Israel and exterminate the Jews. Many have tried, but none have succeeded—and no one ever will. The latest to announce repeatedly to the world that he will annihilate Israel is Iran's President Ahmadinajad, who apparently is not afraid to fight the God of Israel and prove the biblical prophecies wrong:

> Thus saith the LORD, which giveth the sun for a light by day, and the ordinances of the moon and of the stars by night, which divideth the sea when the waves thereof roar . . . if those ordinances depart from before me, saith the LORD, then the seed of Israel shall cease from being a nation. . . .[17]

The repeated promise by the God of the Bible to preserve the Jews and Israel stands as an embarrassing challenge to the entire Islamic world that has been attempting to destroy Israel for centuries. It is a challenge to atheists as well. Let the "Four Horsemen" lead the charge with their armies. The God of the Bible has backed Dawkins, Dennett, Harris, and Hitchens into a corner from which they cannot escape. I challenge them to do so if they can. Sometimes God has severely punished His people through their enemies, but this is *His* hand in judgment, and woe to anyone who takes this judgment into their own hands. Israel has come to the very brink of perishing under God's judgment numerous times. Consider the following: "But Hazael king of Syria oppressed Israel all the days of Jehoahaz. And the LORD was gracious unto them, and had compassion on them, and had respect unto them, because of his covenant with Abraham, Isaac, and Jacob, and would not destroy them, neither cast he them from his presence as yet."[18]

With the threat by the pope of burning him at the stake, Luther bravely declared, "I stand captive to the Word of God. I can do no other." Atheists likewise stand captive to the Word of God—not because they love God or believe His Word but because they passionately hate Him. A way of escape through faith in Christ is offered to atheists, but they refuse to accept it. One day, Christ's warning will haunt them, "The words that I have spoken will condemn you in that day."[19]

We will give many other prophecies that are precise and that have been or are in our day being unmistakably fulfilled. Any honest reader will be forced by his conscience to concede that these prophecies (which are merely a sampling of hundreds in the Bible) could come only from the one true God, speaking His infallible Word to mankind.

THE CONSISTENTLY MISSING ELEMENT

As one reads through countless books and reams of scientific articles, all trying to formulate an acceptable cosmology, it becomes more and more apparent that scientists are never going to agree because, as Jastrow and others admit, creation was unobserved, and the secret behind the existence of the cosmos is beyond human grasp. One is struck by a simple fact. In the struggle to make sense out of conflicting data, one possibility is overlooked: God did create the universe. Acceptance of that fact, for which the evidence is overwhelming, would, in one stroke, eliminate nearly all controversy.

The God of the Bible creates by words. The Bible declares in plain language that the underlying reality that brought the universe into existence is a personal being who creates by speaking matter into existence out of nothing: "God *said*, Let there be light, and there was light. . . . God *said*, Let us make man in our image and in our likeness . . . so God created man in his image. . . ," etc.[20]

Hitchens loves to say that there is no evidence that the Exodus from Egypt ever happened. What kind of evidence does he demand—footprints, ashes from campfires, etc., 3,500 years after the fact? The

Israelis at that time were nomads on a trek to the Promised Land—a journey that was extended to 40 years in judgment for their repeated rebellion on the way. They lived in tents, not houses and cities. One can't even trace the movements of desert nomads from a mere two or three hundred years ago.

Such physical evidence, however, is not needed to establish the Exodus. The Jewish Passover is all the proof one needs. The argument is simple and ironclad. Whenever there is an event that was witnessed by a multitude of people and was immediately memorialized by some national observance, we have absolute proof that it actually occurred. The Passover is such an event.

The God of Israel was executing His judgments upon the gods and people of Egypt for their abuse of the Hebrews as slaves. The Israelites had endured 400 years of cruelty, from which God finally set them free. As a warning, He graciously demonstrated His power to the Egyptians through nine plagues that were obviously supernatural, so they knew they were dealing with the only true God and that His threats were not empty. The tenth and final plague was the most severe. A way of deliverance was offered, both to the Israelites and to the Egyptians: a lamb, which represented the Lamb of God (a description often applied to Christ) who would die for the sins of the world,[21] must be slain and its blood sprinkled upon the doorposts and lintel of every home. The "destroying angel" would *pass over* every household that followed the instructions. In the households of any who refused to obey, the firstborn would be slain by an angel. This event is annually memorialized by killing a lamb, sprinkling its blood, roasting and eating it, annually.[22]

Pharaoh did not believe, refused to obey, and his household was not spared—from the lowliest slave up to the family of Pharaoh himself. Until this point, none of the other plagues had moved Pharaoh's hardened heart. This plague, however, proved to be the dénouement for the Egyptians. There would be no further extension of grace from the God of Israel. Because the destroying angel would pass over the households that had followed the instructions and were under the protection of the blood of the lamb, the memorial that occurred annually on the anniversary of this event was called "The Passover."

Why couldn't it just be a made-up tale passed along through so many succeeding generations that it came to be treated (no one remembers when) as though it actually happened? In fact, something like the Passover couldn't possibly be "made up." Why not? For any memorial, there must have been a time when it began to be observed. Suppose there never was an actual event memorialized in July fourth celebrations. Someone had just gotten the bright idea, "We should have a special celebration in memory of the day that America got its independence from Britain," when in fact, we were still a colony of Britain. There would immediately be objections: "But we never got our independence!" The reply comes, "Let's just pretend and let's start a tradition, and by the time we've been doing this for several hundred years, everybody will think it really happened. We'll say, 'We've been celebrating the fourth of July every year since 1776!'" Wouldn't the reaction be, "But we never did this before—not last year or the year before that or the year before that. . . ."

No matter when someone tried to initiate *any* tradition, the reaction would always be the same: "But we didn't do it last year!" So the celebration would be stopped in its tracks. The fact that it did start and has been going on every year since is, in itself, proof that it must really have happened.

God made this wise provision so that the Israelites would never forget this event. He instructed Moses to tell the people, "And it shall come to pass, when your children shall say unto you, What mean ye by this service? That ye shall say, It is the sacrifice of the LORD's Passover, who passed over the houses of the children of Israel in Egypt, when he smote the Egyptians, and delivered our houses." In the Passover we have the memorial of an event that happened to "the seed" of Abraham that was to inherit the land. This never happened to the Germans or Australians or to the Arabs but only to the Jews. There can be no question concerning the identity of the chosen people who inherit the land. If these facts offend the Arabs/Muslims, then their argument is not with me but with the Bible and the historic facts. The Bible cannot be changed, nor can history, though many try to do so and cover their tracks. Carried over from the days of Soviet dictatorships, the joke is still repeated in Russia today: "Russia is the only country with an unpredictable history." Not so with Israel!

Tragically, many who call themselves Christians do so on what can only be described as "blind faith," with little understanding of the evidence that God has given them for true faith. This is the very "faith" that Dawkins, Hitchens, and the other leaders in the atheist movement think is all that believers have to rely upon. In fact, these critics claim that some "Christians" even boast that this is the faith God demands. This is false; the Bible is filled with more than sufficient evidence. We have already quoted what God says, "Come now, and let us *reason* together." The Apostle John explains why he gave us a record of many of the miracles of Jesus that he had witnessed: "But these are written, that ye might believe that Jesus is the Christ, the Son of God; and that believing ye might have life through his name."[23]

Although Francis Collins, in *The Language of God*, talks of coming to faith in God, there is not one reference to the foremost proof that God himself offers for His existence: Bible prophecy. There is no reference in the index to Israel, whose history and existence today are the major proof for the existence of God. There are, however, five references to Islam, about which his knowledge is either woefully lacking or badly skewed. He presents Islam as a nonviolent religion that has been sullied by fanatics. This, in spite of the fact that the Qur'an has more than 100 verses advocating violence, including murder, to force Islam on the entire world and contradicts Christianity (of which Collins claims to be an adherent) in its foundational doctrines, even denying Christ's deity and death on the Cross and His resurrection. He even declares that "the prophet Muhammad never himself used violence in responding to persecutors."[24] The truth is that Muhammad avenged himself on those who disagreed with him. He began his career with the murder of more than 25 such persons, mostly poets and, after the fact, received a "revelation," allegedly from Allah, that justified the murders, declaring that all poets were inspired of the devil.[25] He attacked caravans and villages, leading to the slaughter (usually beheading) of those who would not adopt Islam, including hundreds who surrendered to him under promise of safe conduct and were nevertheless beheaded. This occurred at the Jewish town, Yathrib (now known as Medina), and elsewhere.

Collins seemingly accepts miracles in the Bible, yet he also accepts on an equal footing Muhammad's alleged reception of the Qur'an from Allah through the messenger angel Gabriel and Muhammad's unwitnessed ascension to heaven and hell as miraculous.[26] Either Collins is ignorant of these facts, or they don't concern him in the least. In either case, one can only wonder what kind of Christian Collins became at his conversion.

THE PAGANIZATION OF THE WORLD OF SCIENCE AND ACADEMIA

Many scientists refer to "God" in their writings. That reference can be misleading. What they, in fact, usually mean is not the personal God of the Bible but some universal, creative force. Even Einstein talked about God, as do Stephen Hawking and others. They are not talking about the God of biblical Christianity, who proved His existence by prophesying what would happen far in advance. Einstein made it clear that he did not believe in a personal God who answers prayers. Paul Davies, an engaging and popular writer who has the ability to simplify scientific theories and express complex concepts in layman's terms, even wrote a book titled *The Mind of God*, but he remains an atheist.

The god to whom Davies and his humanist colleagues refer is a "creative force" innate in nature. Could a force write detailed instructions in DNA for how to construct and operate every cell? Could an impersonal force create personal beings who can decode and read the language on the DNA molecule? As Nancy Pearcey argues, "Modern genetics seems to be telling us that life is a grand narrative told by the divine Word (John 1:1)—that there is an Author for the text of life."[27]

Of course, the god of humanist scientists is the god of the pagans, who worship the forces of nature. All those who reject the God of the Bible yet claim to believe in a force that is behind evolution are worshipers of the creation rather than the Creator—a practice that the Bible condemns as idolatry and upon which it blames all immorality.[28] As we have noted, this was the religion of Carl Sagan, and it still is of many of today's scientists. Sagan declared that "any efforts to safeguard and cherish the environment need to be infused with a vision of the *sacred*."[29]

To Sagan, the entire cosmos was sacred. This neo-paganism, which hides behind a mask of presumed scientific approval, is sponsored at the highest levels of government. Addressing the 1992 Earth Summit in Rio de Janeiro, the United Nation's Secretary-General Boutros Boutros-Ghali called the world back to the worship of nature in order to rescue the earth from ecological disaster:

> To the ancients, the Nile was a god to be venerated, as was the Rhine, an infinite source of European myths, or the Amazonian forest, the mother of forests. Throughout the world, nature was the abode of the divinities that gave the forest, the desert, or the mountains a personality which commanded worship and respect. The Earth had a soul. To find that soul again, to give it new life, that is the essence of Rio.[30]

Unquestionably, there are those at the highest levels of both governments and academia worldwide who find comfort in worshiping nature. Georgetown University political science professor Victor Ferkiss approvingly declares that ecological concern "starts with the premise that the Universe is God."[31] James Lovelock, atmospheric chemist, inventor, and environmental theorist, named the earth's biosphere Gaia, calling it a "complex, self-regulating, living 'being.'"[32] There are so many pagans in the U.S. Armed Forces that they have their own chaplains and are allowed to practice their religious ceremonies. Of course, most pagans would never admit to worshiping Satan or demons.

The Bible, however, makes the claim that behind every idol or pagan representation of "a sacred force" is at least a demon if not Satan himself.[33] In a number of places, what C. S. Lewis writes takes on prophetic meaning. A case in point is found in *The Screwtape Letters* (a fictional account of a 1942 letter from a chief demon, Screwtape, to one of his underlings, Wormwood), in which the necessity of hiding Satan's existence from mankind is explained:

> We are really faced with a cruel dilemma. When the humans disbelieve in our existence we lose all the pleasing results of direct terrorism and we make no magicians. On the other hand, when they believe in us, we cannot make them materialists and sceptics. At least, not yet. I have great hopes that we shall learn in due time how to emotionalise and mythologise their science to such an extent that what is, in effect, belief in us, (though not under that name) will creep in while the human mind remains closed to belief in the Enemy. The "Life Force", the worship of sex, and some aspects of Psychoanalysis, may here prove useful. If once we can produce our perfect work—the Materialist Magician, the man, not using, but veritably worshipping, what he vaguely calls "Forces" while denying the existence of "spirits"—then the end of the war will be in sight. But in the meantime we must obey our orders. I do not think you will have much difficulty in keeping the patient in the dark. The fact that "devils" are predominantly comic figures in the modern imagination will help you. If any faint suspicion of your existence begins to arise in his mind, suggest to him a picture of something in red tights, and persuade him that since he cannot believe in that (it is an old textbook method of confusing them) he therefore cannot believe in you.[34]

When one reads the lengthy arguments on both sides of the atheist/evolutionist controversy, the complex mathematical formulas, the endless speculation, one thing is missing: the proofs that the Bible provides through prophecy. Even those who refer to the Bible and who really believe it is the only authority fail to give the awesome proofs it provides that it is, indeed, the Word of the one true God. The greatest proof is not in the design so evident throughout the universe, although the Bible does refer to that as evidence of God's existence.

PROPHECY: THE GREAT PROOF

The major proof offered by the Bible that it is God's Word is found in hundreds of prophecies precisely foretelling what will occur centuries and even thousands of years in advance. We quoted Gary Lenaire saying that most of the prophecies were "so general you could make them to mean almost anything." Not so! Biblical prophecies are in fact so specific that no one can argue with their meaning.

In Joel 3:2 (circa 800 BC) God declared that the day was coming when all nations would divide the land of Israel: "I will also gather all nations . . . and will plead with them [punish them] for my people and [for] my heritage Israel, whom they have scattered among the nations, and parted my land."

Throughout its entire 3,000-plus-year history, the land of Israel had never been divided. It has been conquered by various nations, but even when the Turks held it as part of their Ottoman Empire for 400 years, they did not divide it. A conqueror keeps the land he has conquered intact for himself. This division of Israel has happened only in our day. Britain, which had been placed in charge of "Palestine" in the wake of World War I by the conquering allied forces, had been given the mandate by the League of Nations to see that this land should become a refuge for Jews, who had been scattered everywhere.

Instead of keeping it for Jews, Britain gave about 75 percent of it to the Arab Muslims as a favor in exchange for oil. In 1947, the United Nations, through Resolution 181 and in fulfillment of Joel 3:2, formalized this thievery and breach of trust. Israel received 13 percent of what they had been promised, a sliver of land that was indefensible. The Arabs were not happy, wanted all, and attacked, vowing to push Israel into the Mediterranean. The Israelis fought back, of course, and this is now history. These various divisions of the land of Israel by Britain and the UN were clearly in fulfillment of Joel 3:2—"they parted my land."

The God of Israel had warned in advance that He would avenge Himself upon the nations for dividing His land. In self-defense, Israel recaptured some of this land in a series of wars after being attacked by Muslim nations, which were following Allah's edict through Muhammad that the Jews must be annihilated. Long before Islam's advent, Israel's prophets had foretold the destruction of Jerusalem, the scattering of Jews to all nations, the hatred and persecution that would follow them in every place to which they would flee, and their ultimate return to the land God had promised to them.

PROPHECIES BY JESUS

Jesus himself made a number of prophecies while He was on Earth before His crucifixion, resurrection, and ascension. Like other Hebrew prophets, He foretold the scattering of Jews all over the world, and the Great Tribulation. In Luke 21:24, there is a remarkable and very specific prophecy: "Jerusalem shall be trodden down of the Gentiles, until the times of the Gentiles be fulfilled."

This "treading down" of Jerusalem by Gentiles has been going on for centuries. Jesus foretells the coming climax. Again, the exis-tence of the United Nations plays a key role. An integral part of UN Resolution 181 was the declaration that Jerusalem would be a *corpus separatum*, never part of Israel and never under the control of Jews.

Jesus foretold that Jerusalem and its Temple would be destroyed, and so it happened in AD 70. That could have been a lucky guess, say the critics. There are specific details to this prophecy, however, that cannot be explained away. Concerning Jerusalem and the Temple, Jesus said:

"For the days shall come . . . that thine enemies . . . shall lay thee even with the ground . . . and they shall not leave in thee one stone upon another . . . that shall not be thrown down. . . ."[35] These prophecies that the Temple and the entire city of Jerusalem would be "[laid] even with the ground," seemed almost unbelievable. What Josephus the Jewish historian, who witnessed the destruction of Jerusalem, records can only be in fulfillment of Christ's warning:

> The Jews were accustomed to hide their gold and other valuables in the walls of their homes. The Temple itself was also the treasury in the Jewish nation. When the fires consumed the whole of the Temple and City, the gold melted and descended into the cracks and crevices of the stone foundations. In order to recover this melted gold, the Tenth Legion had the Jewish captives uproot every stone of the Temple and the whole of the City. So much gold was discovered in this fashion, that the price of the metal in the Roman Empire went down half of its pre-war value.[36]

Consider the following from the prophet Zechariah: "Behold, I will make Jerusalem a cup of trembling unto *all the people round about,* when they shall be *in the siege both against Judah [and] against Jerusalem.* And in that day will I make Jerusalem a burdensome stone for all people: all that burden themselves with it shall be cut in pieces, though *all the people of the earth* be gathered together against it."[37]

Two groups are distinguished by the prophet: 1) *"all the people round about Judah and Jerusalem."* They will be fearful (will tremble in fear, because Israel will prove to be too strong and will defeat them in every war they fight against her, a reality that has continued from 1948 until today), and 2) *"all the people of the earth."*

These two groups are identified by two separate prophecies. To the first group, Jerusalem will be "a cup of trembling;" to the second group, "a burdensome stone." The first group is further identified as being united together "in a siege" against Judah and Jerusalem, the second group as "gathered together" against her. In fact, the first group of nations had never been united but had fought one another for centuries. What united them in this siege and continues to unite them in their goal of destroying Israel? It is the Islamic conquest, which began shortly after Muhammad's death and was continued by his successors. It spread from Spain through India to the very door of China, in its bloody imposition of the Islamic religion.

Not only was Israel divided (something that had never occurred before) by Britain's violation of the trust committed to it by the League of Nations in 1922, but, in fulfillment of Zechariah 12:2, all the nations round about Israel were united by Islam against her to destroy her even before her birth in 1948.

For all nations to be united in a common cause against Israel, there would have to be an organization of "all nations." It is no coincidence that the United Nations has come into existence just in time to be the means of fulfilling this prophecy. Again, this prophecy could never have been fulfilled in the past but only after the United Nations was formed. This 2,500-year-old prophecy is both specific in its details and perfect in its accuracy.

ANTI-SEMITISM

It's an indisputable fact of history that there is a universal obsessive hatred of Jews and Israel. According to the Bible, there are two reasons for this all-pervasive anti-Semitism. First of all, the Jews, as God's chosen people, are under His judgment for their rebellion against Him and the rejection of their Messiah.[38] Second, anti-Semitism is inspired of Satan—a being whose existence many "educated" people deny, as C. S. Lewis, in a sense, foretold. The reason for denying Satan's existence is obvious.

It was foretold that the Savior of the world would be of the "seed of Abraham."[39] His first son was Ishmael, from whom the Arabs claim descent and thus a seemingly legitimate title to the land that God had promised to Abraham and to his descendants. Abraham's first son was born to Hagar, his wife Sarah's maid; his second son was Isaac who was born to him by Sarah and from whom the Jews came. When

Abraham, with his wife Sarah and her maid Hagar, arrived in the "promised land," no such place as Palestine existed. It was the land of Canaan, and both Ishmael and Isaac were born there. A group of Arabs now living in part of the Promised Land claim that it all belongs to them because they are descended from "the original Palestinians." They also claim that Jews are "occupying" what is rightfully the Arabs' land because they descended from Ishmael, Abraham's firstborn son.

Ishmael's mother, Hagar, was an Egyptian and his father, Abraham, was a Chaldean. Both Arabs and Jews are descended from Abraham, but for either of them to claim descent from "the original Palestinians" would simply be false. Which of these rival groups of people, both descended from Abraham and now quarreling over this land, has the legitimate claim? The land into which God brought Abraham some 4,000 years ago, which He promised by everlasting covenant to him and to his heirs, and in which he and that part of his descendants through Isaac and Jacob lived for centuries, was not a nonexistent place called "Palestine." It was the historic land of Canaan.

In Genesis 15:5, God tells Abraham: "Look now toward heaven, and tell the stars, if thou be able to number them: and he said unto him, So shall *thy seed* be." This "*seed*" is further identified in verse 13. They will be "afflicted" by the Egyptians for 400 years. That never happened to the Arabs or any other nationality. Verse 18: "Unto thy seed have I given this land." It identifies the land specifically: from the River of Egypt (the Nile) to the River Euphrates, etc. The land was then called "Canaan." The people who lived there were Canaanites, not "Palestinians." No such people existed at that time.

THE REMARKABLE PROPHECY OF ANTI-SEMITISM

Asserting descent from the "original Palestinians," Arab refugees claim the entire land as theirs. The Jews, they insist, are unlawfully occupying their hereditary land and must leave.

On October 11, 1949, Egyptian Minister of Foreign Affairs, Muhammad Saleh el-Din, declared that "the Arabs intend that they [refugees] shall return as masters. . . . The Arab people will not be embarrassed to declare: 'We shall not be satisfied except by the final obliteration of Israel.'" Yet the world blames Israel for not making peace with such enemies!

Around AD 132, the Romans, who had decimated Jerusalem in AD 70, began to rebuild it for the Roman Emperor Hadrian. They began construction of a temple to Jupiter on Temple Mount at the site of the ancient Jewish temples. Understandably, there was an uprising of the Jews to prevent such desecration. It was led by Simon Bar Kochba, who many at that time considered to be the Messiah.

At first, the revolt was remarkably successful. The Romans, however, eventually destroyed nearly 1,000 villages, killed about 500,000 Jews, and sold thousands into slavery. When the revolt was finally crushed in AD 135, the Roman conquerors angrily renamed the land of Israel, *Provincia Syria-Palestina,* after Israel's ancient enemies, the Philistines. From that time forward, all those living there were known as "Palestinians."

Who lived there? Jews, of course! Chase them out and they return to the land God gave to their fathers. At that time, Arabs hadn't even dreamed that "Palestine" was their land, nor were they identifiable as a national people. That ambition would not take hold for another 500 years until the advent of Islam—and even then, Arabs would not call themselves Palestinians.

To the British Peel Commission in 1937, a local Arab leader testified, "There is no such country as Palestine. 'Palestine' is a term the Zionists invented. . . . " Professor Philip Hitti, Arab historian, testified to an Anglo-American Committee of inquiry in 1946, "There is no such thing as Palestine in history—absolutely not!"[40] As late as the 1950s, Arabs refused to be called Palestinians and declared that if there were such a people, they were Jews. To the UN Security Council on May 31, 1956, Ahmed Shukairy declared, "It is common knowledge that Palestine is nothing but southern Syria." Eight years later, in 1964,

Shukairy became the founding chairman of the Palestine Liberation Organization and coined the infamous slogan, "[W]e'll drive the Jews into the sea." Like Yasser Arafat, he was born in Cairo. The Palestine Liberation Organization was not founded by "Palestinians."

In World War II, Britain had a volunteer brigade known as "The Palestinian Brigade." It was made up entirely of Jews. The Arabs were fighting on Hitler's side. There was the Palestinian Symphony Orchestra (a Jewish orchestra) and the *Palestinian Post* (a Jewish newspaper). Of course, Jews had been called "Palestinians" for 1,600 years.

THE MYTH OF PALESTINE AND "PALESTINIANS"

Today's Arab "Palestinians" are close relatives of the Arabs living in neighboring countries, from which most of them—or their immediate ancestors—came. Arabs claim to be descended from Ishmael, Abraham's first son, and insist, therefore, that they are the legitimate heirs to the land God gave to Abraham. They do have much Ishmaelite blood in them, but there is no direct genealogy tracing today's Arabs back to Ishmael. They are a mixed nomadic race. The genealogy of the Jews, on the other hand, is carefully recorded in the Bible.

We've already seen that Isaac was the son of promise. Even if the Arabs were 100 percent Ishmaelites, they would still not be descended from the land's original inhabitants. God promised the land to Abraham before Ishmael was born. It already had many inhabitants. So how could Arab descendants of Ishmael (born to immigrants centuries after Canaan had been settled) be, at the same time, descendants of the "original inhabitants" of the Promised Land? Impossible!

It would not be until the seventh century AD, through the Islamic jihad invasions, that Arabs would come in any significant numbers into the land of Israel, which by that time was erroneously called Palestine.

Yet the world accepts these fantasies as the basis of a settlement they intend to impose upon Israel, whose legitimate ancestral claims to the land go back 4,000 years! If "Palestine" is so important to the Arabs, why is it not mentioned *once* in their holy book, the Qur'an? The word is used four times in the Bible but never refers either to the land of Canaan or to Israel. The Hebrew word from which it is translated is *pelensheth.* It referred to a small region also known as Philistia, the land of the *Pelishtee,* or Philistines. Philistia was in the same location but a bit larger than the Gaza Strip of today, named after the Philistine city of Gaza. This is the true history, of which the Qur'an knows nothing.

The Philistines were not a Semitic people like the Arabs but had invaded Canaan by sea from across the Mediterranean and occupied that particular area before the Israelites arrived. They were not the "original inhabitants of the land" but displaced certain Canaanites, just as they were themselves eventually displaced by Israel. Arab "Palestinians" (who are Semites) living there today can claim neither ethnic, linguistic, nor historical relationship to the Philistines, nor can they justify calling themselves Palestinians.

Jerusalem was established as the capital of Israel by King David 3,000 years ago. It is not mentioned once in the Qur'an. Even when Muslim empires controlled all of the Middle East, Jerusalem was largely neglected. In the late 1800s, out of a population in Jerusalem of about 40,000, most were Jews, the rest Christians of various shades, and only a few were Arabs.

Nor is there any reference to Jerusalem in the Palestine National Covenant of 1964. It was a complete turnabout when the Muslim world began to insist that the West Bank, the Gaza Strip, and Jerusalem itself had always belonged to "Palestinians" (i.e., themselves). The Islamic terrorist organization Hizballah (Party of Allah), headquartered in Syria, displays the Dome of the Rock on its promotional materials to inflame its followers against Israel. Arafat declared that "Al-Quds [Jerusalem] is in the innermost of our feeling, the feeling of our people and the feeling of all Arabs, Muslims, and Christians in the world."[41] Not surprisingly, he left out the Jews, to whom Jerusalem means more than to anyone. President Obama, when recently in Cairo, in order to be politically correct with all of the inhabitants of the Middle East except the Israelis, stated that he

> . . . looked forward to the day . . . when Jerusalem is a secure and lasting home for Jews and Christians and Muslims, and a place for all of the children of Abraham to mingle peacefully together as in the story of Isra, when Moses, Jesus and Muhammad (peace be upon them) joined in prayer.[42]

The current Muslim attempt to claim Jerusalem as an Islamic holy city would shock Muslims from past centuries. It is simply one more ploy in the propaganda campaign to oust Israel. World hatred of the Jews and of Israel is fulfillment of Bible prophecy. That hatred will likely gather momentum until Israelis are desperate enough to cry out as one voice for the Messiah to rescue them—and He will do so, as the Bible foretells.

History has shown that wherever anti-Semitism has gone unchecked, the persecution of others has been present or not far behind. Defeating anti-Semitism must be a cause of great importance not only for Jews, but for all people who value humanity and justice. . . .

—U.S. DEPARTMENT OF STATE,
CONTEMPORARY GLOBAL ANTI-SEMITISM REPORT (MARCH 13, 2008)

Worst of all, Darwinism opened the door to racists who wanted to apply the principle of natural selection to better mankind. Darwin's theory in biology, transferred to Germany and nurtured by Ernst Haeckel, inspired an ideology that led eventually to the rise of the Nazis.

—KENNETH J. HSÜ, "DARWIN'S THREE MISTAKES,"
GEOLOGY, VOL. 14 (JUNE 1986), 534

During these two years I was led to think much about religion. . . . But I had gradually come, by this time, to see that the Old Testament, from its manifestly false history of the world . . . was not more to be trusted than the sacred books of the Hindus, or the beliefs of any barbarian.

—CHARLES DARWIN, "AUTOBIOGRAPHY," REPRINTED IN *THE VOYAGE OF CHARLES DARWIN*, EDITED BY CHRISTOPHER RAWLINGS (BBC, 1978), "A SCIENTIST'S THOUGHTS ON RELIGION," *NEW SCIENTIST*, VOL. 104 (DECEMBER 20/27, 1984), 75

I could show fight on natural selection having done and doing more for the progress of civilization than you seem inclined to admit. . . . The more civilized so-called Caucasian races have beaten the Turkish hollow in the struggle for existence. Looking to the world at no very distant date, what an endless number of the lower races will have been eliminated by the higher civilized races throughout the world.

—CHARLES DARWIN, LIFE AND LETTERS, I, LETTER TO W. GRAHAM,
JULY 3, 1881, P. 316, CITED IN *DARWIN AND THE DARWINIAN REVOLUTION*,
BY GERTRUDE HIMMELFARB (LONDON: CHATTO & WINDUS, 1959), 343

The Jews are the most worthless of all men. They are lecherous, greedy, rapacious. They are perfidious murderers of Christ. They worship the Devil. Their religion is a sickness. The Jews are the odious assassins of Christ and for killing God there is no expiation possible, no indulgence or pardon. Christians may never cease vengeance, and the Jew must live in servitude forever. God always hated the Jews. It is essential that all Christians hate them.

—ST. JOHN CHRYSOSTOM, *ORATIONS AGAINST THE JEWS*, WRITTEN IN THE YEAR 379

NINETEEN

THE ROLE OF ISRAEL AND OF CHRIST AS FURTHER PROOF

ONE OF HISTORY'S most inexplicable phenomena has been virulent anti-Semitism. It seems irrational that these particular people should be marked out in this way. The worldwide dispersion and slaughter of the Jews is another undeniable fulfillment of prophecy: "And the LORD shall scatter thee among all people, from the one end of the earth even unto the other; . . . And thou shalt become an astonishment, a proverb, and a byword, among all nations whither the LORD shall lead thee.[1] God also declares:

> And I will . . . deliver them to be removed to all the kingdoms of the earth, to be a curse, and an astonishment, and an hissing, and a reproach, among all the nations whither I have driven them.[2]

A Jewish friend of mine puts it like this: "Why do I speak with a Brooklyn accent and love bagels and lox? Because God has scattered us Jews to every part of the world."

The worst, however, that Israel, including Jews worldwide, has ever seen is yet to come. This is called "the time of Jacob's trouble." The prophecy continues:

> . . . but he shall be saved out of it . . . though I make a full end of all nations whither I have scattered thee, yet will I not make a full end of thee: but I will correct thee in measure, and will not leave thee altogether unpunished.[3]

God issues a warning to the entire world: "Hear the word of the Lord, O ye nations . . . He that scattered Israel will gather him, and keep him as a shepherd doth his flock."[4] In other words, although Israel is under God's judgment at this time, she is also under his protection, and woe to all who seek to harm her. They will find they are fighting against God—the God of Israel—and the consequences will be severe.

Hitler had identified 11 million Jews in eastern and western Europe and was determined to exterminate every one, to the last man, woman, and child. Why should this be? An even larger question, however, looms before us, and that is the hatred of Israel. Although the outward expressions of anti-Semitism in general seem to have largely subsided in much of the world, its corollary, animosity toward Israel, is growing and raises even larger questions because it threatens world peace. Many ethnic or religious groups have been traditional enemies of one another. Their clashes can sometimes turn violent. This happens in isolated parts of the world, but rarely does this animosity threaten world peace. Anti-Semitism, however, is the exception. It also presents a larger puzzle. Hiding behind it is hatred for Israel.

Why should this tiny nation attract the eyes of the entire world? Everyone seems to realize that the peace of the world depends upon the peace of Israel. It can hardly be denied that if the problems in the

Middle East are not peacefully resolved, there will be no peace for the world. How this all works out could bring about World War III and a much-feared nuclear holocaust. Iran has been working on nuclear weapons and delivery systems in spite of its denials. Israel cannot allow that process to continue until Iran becomes capable of making good on her threats. She cannot wait for the UN to discuss this matter endlessly and vote on it. She's well able to silence Iran's threats and will act decisively when she deems it appropriate.

Of course, if Israel suddenly and violently wipes out Iran's nuclear threat, she will be condemned by the entire world. Israel cannot apologize or back down. She can only act in her own defense and cannot wait for anyone to help or allow anyone to hinder her. What lies ahead in the Middle East will only be according to God's will. We do know that biblical prophecies must be fulfilled and that many of them assure Israel of God's protection.

When the Messiah defeated Satan's designs against mankind by paying the penalty for the sins of the world, the battle had not yet come to an end. Israel still exists and that is why she must be destroyed. To destroy Israel is Satan's last hope. If that could be accomplished, as we've already noted, the "God of Israel" would be destroyed as well. Part of God's promise to Abraham was, "In thee shall all nations of the earth be blessed." This could only be through the Messiah, who, according to the prophet Isaiah, when He came the first time would be "despised and rejected of men, a man of sorrows, and acquainted with grief."[5] Isaiah goes on to say that the Messiah would be "cut off out of the land of the living [die]" for the sins of the world and would rise again. The second coming of the Messiah after His death, burial, and resurrection is also foretold. He will return at the battle of Armageddon when Jerusalem is surrounded and all the nations of the world have come to fulfill the "final solution" that Hitler dreamed of—the destruction of all the Jews. That is when Israel will be in such desperation that she will cry out to the Messiah to rescue her, and He will respond and destroy all those nations that come against her.

GOD HAS TIED HIS INTEGRITY
TO ISRAEL AND THE MESSIAH

God promised that the Messiah, who would redeem mankind from Satan's power and sin's penalty, would be a virgin-born Jew[6] who would reign forever on King David's throne in Jerusalem. Consequently, to defeat God, Satan had to bring about the annihilation of the Jews. Anti-Semitism, the satanically inspired persecution and slaughter of Jews like no other people all through history, was foretold in the Bible.[7] Satan's only hope to escape eternal doom was to destroy those whom God chose "to be a special people unto himself, above all people that are upon the face of the earth."[8] From that moment on, Satan watched for opportunities to prevent the birth of the Messiah. His problem was that he did not know who the mother would be. She would be a virgin Jewess of the tribe of Judah and in the lineage of David, but how to identify her further was difficult. He watched and waited.

Had Satan been able to destroy the Jews before the birth of the Messiah (or at any time thereafter), he would have defeated God. For promising a Messiah who never came, God would have been proved to be a liar and would have lost any moral ground for punishing Satan.

The Bible records Satan's many attempts to frustrate God's purposes concerning the Messiah, even before His birth. We can mention only a few of these. While the Jews were slaves in Egypt, Pharaoh commanded the Hebrew midwives to destroy all male babies that were born, but they "feared God" and disobeyed this edict.[9] Years later, so that she could continue his reign as queen, Athaliah, upon the death of her son Ahaziah, king of Judah, sought to destroy all of the male children who could have carried on the Messianic succession. One of these children, however, was taken by Ahaziah's sister and given to Jehoiada, the priest, who hid him in the "house of God [for] six years." At that time, with the priest beside him and loyal warriors for his protection, Joash was presented to Israel and accepted as their new king. Once again, Satan's schemes were thwarted.

Moving on, we come to Haman, close advisor to Emperor Ahasuerus. Haman persuaded Ahasuerus to issue an edict that all Jews in his empire (which stretched from India to Ethiopia) should be killed on an appointed day. God had placed Esther, a beautiful Jewess, among his wives. She identified herself at last as a Jew and pleaded for her people. The laws of the Medes and Persians could not be revoked, but Ahasuerus issued another edict allowing the Jews, on that same day, to defend themselves. This they did and destroyed their enemies. Once again, the Messianic line was preserved.[10]

The birth of Jesus was marked by a "star in the East," as prophecies foretold.[11] Magi followed this star. When it led them into Israel, they apparently stopped watching the star and assumed that Jerusalem must be where the King of the Jews had been born. Entering Jerusalem and asking, "Where is he that is born King of the Jews?" they were taken to King Herod, who was highly alarmed by their mission. He asked the Hebrew scribes to consult their Scriptures, and they found that He would be born in Bethlehem.[12] Herod asked them how long they'd been following the star and also instructed them to tell him where the babe was as soon as they found him so that he, too, could "come and worship him." "Being warned of God in a dream that they should not return to Herod, they departed into their own country another way."[13] Seeing that he was mocked by the magi, Herod commanded soldiers to kill all the male babies two years old and younger. In the meantime, Joseph and Mary had been warned in a dream to flee to Egypt with Jesus, where they remained until the death of Herod and then returned to Israel.[14] Satan, who at last knew the identity of the Messiah as a two-year-old babe (now living with his parents in Nazareth), plotted to find another way to kill Him.

Satan is not all knowing, as some imagine. He is a self-deluded egomaniac. He knows what the Scriptures say, but their meaning is a mystery to him. It seems likely that he actually believes that he will triumph. Why not? He offers all the sensual pleasures—but Christ demands of His followers denial of self and warns them of persecution and possibly death at the hands of those who hate Him. As someone once said, "Lord, you've asked us to follow You, but how can we do it? Your footsteps led to the Cross." Of course, Satan knew Psalm 22 and other scriptures prophesying the crucifixion. At one point, he inspired Peter to attempt to keep Christ from going to the Cross.[15] Later, he inspired Judas to plot Christ's crucifixion.[16] When Jesus died, Satan must have gloated in triumph. At last, his conspiracy had come to a most successful conclusion! Little did Satan know that he himself would be defeated forever by Christ's death, burial, and resurrection.

The coming of the Messiah, descended from David via a virgin mother, had first been prophesied by God himself to Adam and Eve. As we have already noted, speaking to the serpent (a depiction that Satan loves and that has inspired his worship all over the world in the form of serpents), God, foretelling the virgin birth of the Messiah, said, "And I will put enmity between thee and the woman, and between thy seed and her seed; it shall bruise thy head [a mortal wound], and thou shalt bruise his heel."[17]

The Bible declares that the Messiah came and defeated Satan by "tast[ing] death for every man"[18] and bearing "our sins in his own body on the tree."[19] This is expressed beautifully in an old hymn:

> In weakness like defeat, He won the victor's crown;
>   Trod all our foes beneath His feet by being trodden down.
>
> He Satan's power laid low. Made sin, He sin o'erthrew.
>   Bowed to the grave, destroyed it so,
>
> And death, by dying, slew.

That victory did not end the battle between God and His archenemy for the hearts, minds, and eternal destiny of mankind. A fierce battle continues to rage—and Israel is still at its center. The Bible contains hundreds of prophecies that, although God would severely punish Israel for her sins, He would preserve a remnant and bring the scattered Jews back into their own land.

Here we confront another remarkable prophecy whose fulfillment in our day cannot be denied:

> Therefore, behold, the days come, saith the LORD, that it
> shall no more be said, The LORD liveth, that brought up the
> children of Israel out of the land of Egypt; But, The LORD
> liveth, that brought up the children of Israel from the land
> of the north, and from all the lands whither he had driven
> them: and I will bring them again into their land that I gave
> unto their fathers.[20]

Satan could still escape his eternal doom if he could wipe out Israel.
That fact provides the only rational explanation for the Muslims' irrational obsession with destroying that tiny nation. It also stands as
continuing evidence that Satan is a reality, not a myth.

FURTHER TESTIMONY FROM HISTORY

Rome's destruction of Jerusalem in AD 70 (1.2 million killed) was
followed in AD 135 with the destruction of 985 towns and the death
of 580,000. The situation eased under some Caesars, worsened under
others. Constantine (280-337) briefly granted Judaism equal status
with other religions—but after becoming a "Christian," he oppressed
the Jews. Succeeding Roman emperors continued the persecution.

The popes, successors to the Roman emperors, persisted in the
oppression. Inspired by Pope Urban II (1096), Crusaders murdered Jews all along their route and the taking of the Holy Land.
Church Councils, such as Vienna (1311), Zamora (1313), and Basel
(1431-33) strengthened anti-Semitism as official Roman Catholic
doctrine. More than 100 anti-Semitic Church documents were published between the sixth and twentieth centuries. During the Roman
Catholic Church-dominated Middle Ages, Jews were driven out of
nearly every European nation including England. Somehow, they
clung to life, confined to ghettos. Islam's founder, Muhammad (570-
632), killed every Jew in Arabia except for the few who escaped. In
North African and Middle Eastern countries, following the Muslim
conquest in the seventh century, the Jews were brutalized, massacred,
and their homes pillaged.

As the Romans had done with Jerusalem in AD 135, any city designated a "holy city of Islam," such as Kairouan in Tunisia in the thirteenth century, was made Jew-free. What Islam modeled was repeated in Nazi Germany in the last century, as one village or city after another was declared *Juden frei*.

In the German elections of May 1928, the Nazi party, aided by Vatican funds given to Hitler by Cardinal Eugenio Pacelli (who later became Pope Pius XII), gained its first twelve seats in the Reichstag. On January 1, 1930, Hitler's Stormtroopers killed eight Jews, the first victims of the Nazi era. "Jews were molested in public places, and synagogue services were constantly interrupted. . . ."[21] In the 1930 elections, with Hitler's "Brownshirts" intimidating voters, the Nazi seats rose from 12 to 107.

On January 30, 1933, a political compromise made Hitler, then 43, Germany's Chancellor. He swiftly established a Nazi dictatorship, with no dissent allowed. *Mein Kampf* had promised an end to the Jews, who were now beaten in the streets, their stores looted, then boycotted.

The reaction outside Germany was brief and muted. Mass rallies were held in New York's Madison Square Garden, Paris's Trocadero, and London's Queen's Hall to protest Germany's growing anti-Jewish pogroms. But an uncaring world turned a blind eye to the Holocaust, which still haunts all who have a conscience.

By 1934, the campaign to create "Jew-free" villages was spreading. Jews were driven out of all professions and education. In the growing terrorism, Stormtroopers would enter a village, smash and loot Jewish shops, trample the Torah in the synagogue, and assault and kill Jews in the streets. Frightened and bewildered Jews fled to neighboring towns, only to be expelled again—and eventually taken to extermination camps.

For centuries, Jews had been fleeing Europe to return to their ancient land. There, in the 1920s and '30s, funded by the Nazis and aided by the British "peace-keepers," anti-Jewish riots were led by Haj Amin al-Husseini, British-appointed Grand Mufti of Jerusalem, terrorist, friend and admirer of Hitler and Himmler, and Yasser Arafat's great uncle, mentor, and model. The Mufti, to whom Hitler on Nov. 21, 1941, promised "a solution for the Jewish problem" similar to what he was pursuing in Germany, was "personally responsible for the concentration camp slaughter of hundreds of thousands of Jews. . . ."[22]

During World War II, Haj Amin fled to Berlin, from which place he broadcast, "Arabs rise as one man and slaughter the Jews wherever you find them. This pleases Allah. . . ." Jews fought on the side of the Allies; the Arabs joined Hitler. As a reward, he promised to exterminate the Jews in their countries, as he was doing in Europe. In February 1945, when Allied victory was certain, Egypt, Saudi Arabia, Syria, and Lebanon declared war on Germany—an act required before March 1, 1945, by any country that desired to join the newly organized United Nations.

On Nov. 29, 1947, after 6 million Jews had perished, a briefly conscience-stricken UN, in Res. 181, gave surviving Jews 13 percent of the ancient land of Israel, misnamed "Palestine," *all of which* the League of Nations, in the Mandate for Palestine, July 24, 1922, recognizing its "historical connection [to] the Jewish people," had allotted for their national homeland and was to have been administered by Britain under the Balfour Declaration. Unhappy with being given the remaining 87 percent of what the League of Nations admitted belonged to the Jews (and demanding it all), "employing outside forces and arms from Arab states as distant as Iraq," Arabs rioted, plundered, and murdered Jews, encouraged by the British, who were hoping for an excuse to abandon their mandate to establish the Jewish homeland. Britain's betrayal of the Jews, beginning in the 1920s in favor of the oil-rich Arabs, brought about the end of its empire, "on which the sun had never set"—another fulfillment of God's warning, "I will curse him that curseth thee."[23]

As we read the history, which has been recounted in so many sources, it is difficult to reject the obvious fact that this incredible, widespread hatred and slaughter of Jews was a precise fulfillment of what the Bible had foretold.

THE SCOURGE OF ISLAM

Something worse than Nazism was rising—an Arab religion called Islam, which centuries before had forcefully conquered most of the known world. This time, its monopoly of oil was its major weapon. When Israel declared its independence in May 1948, it was instantly attacked by the regular armies of six Muslim nations, whose leaders publicly vowed to annihilate every Jew. Azzam Pasha, Secretary-General of the Arab League, promised, "This will be a war of extermination. . . ."[24] "Palestine," like Arabia, was to be made Jew-free.

Muslim leaders, both political and religious, more openly than Hitler, repeatedly called for the extermination of Jews. Islam requires this extermination before its "Last Day" resurrection can occur. On November 23, 1937, Saudi Arabia's King Ibn Saud said, "for a Muslim to kill a Jew . . . ensures him an immediate entry into Heaven. . . ." PLO leader Farouk Kaddoumi vowed, "This Zionist ghetto of Israel must be destroyed." Palestinians marching in support of Saddam Hussein's invasion of Kuwait chanted, "Saddam, you hero, attack Israel with chemical weapons."[25]

An Arabic translation of *Mein Kampf* remains a bestseller today in Palestinian Authority territory. Textbooks in Syria lead pupils to the "inevitable conclusion . . . that all Jews must be annihilated."[26] Calls for annihilation of Jews still resound throughout the Muslim world, such as the Friday sermon in Gaza's Zayed bin Sultan Aal Nahyan mosque, October 14, 2000, by Ahmad Abu-Halabia: "The Jews . . . must be butchered. . . . Have no mercy . . . kill them . . . and those Americans who . . . established Israel here, in the beating heart of the Arab world. . . ." Sheikh Ibrahim Mahdi vowed in a sermon on Palestinian television, June 8, 2001, "Allah willing . . . Israel will be erased . . . the United States will be erased . . . Britain will be erased. . . . Blessings to whoever put a belt of explosives on his body or on his sons' and plunged into the midst of the Jews. . . ."

Incredibly, Zionism (the belief that Jews have a right to their national homeland) was condemned as racism by UN General Assembly Res. 3379 on November 10, 1975. Sixteen long years later

(December 16, 1991) that vote was reversed over Muslim protests. Yet Zionism is still a capital crime in Iraq.

Few, whether Jews or their enemies, acknowledge that the Middle East conflict involves the "last days" reestablishment of God's chosen people in the land that He promised to them. Today's events were foretold in biblical prophecies that, beyond dispute, validate the Bible as God's Word. As prophesied, Israel has become what President Eisenhower called "the most strategically important area in the world."

When it became a nation once again in 1948, about 800,000 Jews (nearly double the number of original "Palestinian" refugees) fled to Israel from the horror, including the murder of thousands, that they had long endured in Muslim countries. Oddly, under all the emphasis that is given to the "Palestinian" refugees and their plight, one never hears a word about the even larger number of Jewish refugees who fled from Muslim countries. Israel never persecutes the Arabs living within her boundaries but instead gives them full citizenship voting rights. Some are even members of the Knesset. Such treatment for Jews in Muslim countries would be unthinkable.

Here is the tally documenting the numbers of forgotten Jewish refugees who fled from various countries beginning in 1948—and the few who are left today: Algeria 140,000 then, 75 now; Egypt 75,000 then, 200 now; Iraq 150,000 then, 100 now; Lebanon 20,000 then, 50 now; Libya 38,000 then, none remain; Morocco 265,000 then, 5,800 now; Syria 30,000 then, 150 now; Tunisia 105,000 then, 1,500 now; Yemen and Aden 63,000 then, 150 now; etc. Following the Six-day War (1967), the UN Security Council determined to investigate the treatment of Jews in Arab countries. Syria, Iraq, and Egypt, however, refused to allow the entrance of the investigative commission.

We now look back with disbelief and shame upon the Nazi era and the barbaric determination to exterminate a race. In contrast, the Islamic world looks back with approval. Their only regret today is that Hitler didn't finish his intended annihilation of the Jews. As Egyptian newspaper columnist Ahmad Ragab wrote, "Thanks to Hitler, blessed memory. . . . Although we do have a complaint . . . his revenge on [the Jews] was not enough."[27]

At the same time, much of the Muslim world denies the Holocaust. As University of Gaza history lecturer Dr. Issam Sissalem declared: ". . . they are all lies . . . no Dachau, no Auschwitz! . . . the holocaust was against our people. . . ."[28] There is no denying the fact that Islamic hatred and persecution of Jews in their countries continues to this day. The lone exception is Saudi Arabia. Why are no Jews persecuted there? No Jew is allowed to set foot within its borders!

NUCLEAR GIANTS BUT MORAL MIDGETS

The history that we have recounted and the horror of the world we live in, which supposedly is the result of natural selection and evolutionary processes that are leading man ever higher, would seem unbelievable had the Bible not foretold, in many places, "evil men and seducers shall wax worse and worse, deceiving and being deceived."[29] Yet sociologists, psychologists, and social scientists, et al., persist in the optimistic declaration that humans are becoming more and more enlightened and that a bright future lies ahead for mankind. Why should this be?

"God created man in his own image,"[30] with the capacity to choose whether to love and obey Him or to rebel. God desires our willing and loving obedience, but love cannot be forced. Liberty to choose is essential for love. Seeking to win man's heart, God pleads, "Come now, and let us reason together."[31] Over and over, God says, in many ways, to mankind, "I love you." Still, the rebellion of "enlightened" man continues. One day, the horror of what that means will come crashing in upon Earth's rebels. Psalm 2 expresses it like this:

> Why do the heathen rage and the people imagine a vain thing? The kings of the earth set themselves and take counsel together against the LORD and against his anointed, saying, Let us break their bands asunder and cast their cords from us. He that sitteth in the heavens shall laugh. The LORD shall have them in derision.

The last two sentences quoted contain the most frightening words one finds in the Bible. Obviously, this is not an amicable laugh. It is a precursor to judgment. Yet that judgment has been delayed by God's grace. How long? We do not know, but certainly His patience is being sorely tried.

In contrast to the love and freedom God offers, Satan enslaves mankind with lies. "Whoever commits sin is the servant of sin."[32] Tyrants enslave their fellows. The worst offense of the Caesars, the popes, the Muhammads, Hitlers, Pol Pots, Kim Jong-ils, and all who still follow their example is not the enslavement of flesh and blood but the tyrannical attempt to conquer the human soul and spirit. There is no reasoning with tyrants.

A few years ago, my wife and I were in Canada, where I was speaking at a conference. Returning to our hotel room, we turned on the television to see what the news of the day might be. Instead, we caught an interview of a Canadian who had been working in Saudi Arabia, arrested under a false accusation, and horribly tortured. He was eventually released through diplomatic channels. What he said has been indelibly imprinted in my memory:

> I learned two lessons. 1) No matter how strong you may think you are, the torturers can make you hurt so much that you will confess to anything. To stop the torment, you would confess to killing your mother, or even that you killed God. 2) I also learned that they *cannot make you believe it*!

Such examples of the horror of Islam (which claims to be peaceful and offers freedom to all) could be multiplied, but one more should suffice. A graphic description of what continues to occur in Saudi Arabia is given by one of its recent almost-victims:

> Remember those bizarre, wooden "confessions," haltingly delivered by scared-looking men on Saudi television? One of those came from me. If I looked petrified, it may have been because I'd been dragged to prison, threatened,

sleep-deprived, and beaten so severely that I almost died of a heart attack.

In a numb state of shock, I would have confessed to anything. As it was, I said I'd committed a series of laughably impossible "turf war" crimes that never even existed. The farce continued. I was subjected to two perfunctory, completely scripted trials at which I was told to plead guilty and beg for mercy. I was sentenced to death, tried again twice, without being in the courtroom at all, and again sentenced to death by beheading.

This, remember, is what happened just a handful of years ago in a justice system in an influential Middle Eastern country that enjoys excellent diplomatic relations with most of the world's countries, including Britain. It was only this time last year, for example, that we were rolling out the red carpet for King Abdullah's state visit. . . . At the time of my ordeal, there was much talk of "diplomatic efforts" to secure our release. This was mostly UK government spin— they had to put it about that they were trying hard to get us out. Yes, they will have exerted pressure on the Riyadh authorities, but I later learnt that I and my fellow detainees had been released because of a "prisoner exchange" involving five Saudis being held by the U.S. at Guantanamo Bay.

Finally, released in August 2003, after 864 days of solitary confinement, torture, and dehumanizing terror, I harbor no delusions about what saved me: my passport. There was no apology, no official pardon, just a perfunctory granting of "clemency" and immediate expulsion from the country. An accident had preserved me and eventually my release became a political expediency.[33]

Saudi Arabia, Islam's Holy Land, has accomplished what Nazi Germany aimed for: a Jew-free country. In obedience to Islam's founding prophet, Muhammad, no Jew is allowed in Saudi Arabia, and only Muslims can be citizens.

There is not one Muslim country today where basic God-given liberties are enjoyed. Saudi Arabia abstained from the International Declaration of Human Rights adopted on December 10, 1948, by the UN. Instead, an Islamic Declaration of Human Rights was adopted by Muslim nations on September 19, 1981. The "rights" it offers are all according to Shari'a (Islamic Law exactly as the Taliban practice it).

In contrast, the Bible says, "Where the spirit of the Lord is, there is liberty." That is why on our coins is written "In God We Trust," and the Declaration of Independence guarantees to every citizen, in the name of that God, the right to "Life, Liberty, and the Pursuit of Happiness."

Terrorism is not "fanaticism." *It is Islam.* Muhammad said, "Whoever relinquishes his faith, kill him." Upon Muhammad's death (poisoned by the widow of a man he had murdered), thousands of Arabs attempted to abandon Islam into which they had been forced by the sword. In the "Wars of Apostasy," tens of thousands of former Muslims, all Arabs, were killed in bringing Arabia back under Islam. For years there has been an ongoing holocaust in Muslim countries. More than 2 million non-Muslims, mostly Christians, have been killed in Indonesia, Nigeria, Sudan, and elsewhere, with hundreds of churches destroyed.

As we have noted, whether the rest of the world likes it or not, the Jews are God's chosen people. That fact carries not only blessings and privileges but also responsibilities—and penalties for disobedience. Israel has experienced both God's blessing and judgment in the past. Both testify to the integrity of God and His Word. Israel remains in His hands and under His protection today, even while she is at the same time experiencing His discipline. God must fulfill His Word concerning judgment—as well as the prophesied full restoration and eternal blessing—for the remnant that survives Armageddon. Woe to those who oppose God's promises to Israel.

PROPHECIES BY AND ABOUT JESUS

"For the days shall come upon thee, that thine enemies shall . . . compass thee round . . . and shall lay thee even with the ground, and thy children within thee . . . because thou knewest not the time of thy visitation."[34] And so it was that in AD 70 this prophecy was fulfilled when the Roman armies destroyed Jerusalem, killing 1.2 million Jews and selling thousands into slavery. Hear Paul's indictment in his first recorded sermon:

> For they that dwell at Jerusalem, and their rulers, because they knew him not, nor yet the voices of the prophets which are read every sabbath day, they have fulfilled them in condemning him. . . . Beware therefore, lest that come upon you, which is spoken of in the prophets; Behold, ye despisers, and wonder, and perish: for I work a work in your days, a work which ye shall in no wise believe. . . .[35]

The crucifixion of the Messiah was prophesied centuries before that torturous means of execution was even known on Earth. Nor is crucifixion officially practiced any more—another reason why it is too late for the Messiah's first coming. Those who follow Antichrist as the Messiah will have to deliberately ignore the obvious fact that he was never crucified nor did he rise from the dead. King David foretold Christ's crucifixion:

> [All] my bones are out of joint . . . they pierced my hands and my feet. . . . They part my garments among them, and cast lots upon my vesture. . . . All the ends of the world shall remember and turn unto the LORD. . . .[36]

How many candidates meet the prophetic criteria and thus qualify as Messiah? There are literally no competitors with Jesus of Nazareth! Because the leaders of the Jews were looking for a way to kill Him, He had been avoiding Jerusalem. There are too many prophecies to cite them all. The rabbis wanted to take Him as soon as possible and stone Him, but crowds had gathered for the Passover, causing those who sought to kill Him to agree among themselves: "Not on the feast [day], lest there be an uproar among the people."[37] For the prophecies to be fulfilled, however, He had to be on the cross at the same time the lambs were being slain for the Passover. Thus Jesus, the Lamb of God, who died for the sins of the world, rode into Jerusalem on the very day that the lamb was annually taken out of the flock for that year's Passover, to be kept under observation for four days to make certain that it was a perfect specimen. Only then would it be killed, to be eaten at the Passover. Jesus was hailed as the Messiah by the crowds that lined the road as He came from the Mount of Olives into Jerusalem, where He spent four days teaching in the Temple under observation by the people. Inexplicably, it would seem, those who had hailed Him suddenly turned against Him. As Pilate presented Him to them as the King of the Jews, now scourged and crowned with thorns, a cry arose from the assembled throng: "Away with him! Crucify him!"[38]

It was foretold that Messiah's crucifiers would do to Him what was never done, and would not do to Him what was always done in crucifixion. The major purpose of crucifixion was to exact a slow torture upon the victim. Only when he had suffered long enough would his legs be broken to prevent him from supporting himself, and, unable to breathe, he would die. He would never be prematurely killed by thrusting a spear into his side, for that would end the intended agony.

But Scripture said of the Passover lamb, a type of the Messiah, "neither shall ye break a bone thereof."[39] David prophesied of the Messiah, "He [God] keepeth all his bones: not one of them is broken."[40] There was no need to break his legs. Christ was already dead, a fact that Pilate found unbelievable.[41] Jesus had said, "No man taketh it [my life] from me, but I lay it down of myself. I have power to lay it down, and I have power to take it again."[42]

The Hebrew word in David's prophecy quoted above, "They pierced my hands and my feet," is *aryeh*, descriptive of what occurs in crucifixion. Referring to His Second Coming to rescue Israel at Armageddon, however, Yahweh, the God of Israel, declares: "And they shall look upon me whom they have pierced."[43] The Hebrew word here is *dawkar*, appropriate for the piercing of a spear. John records, "But one of the soldiers with a spear pierced his side, and . . . he [John] that saw it bare record . . . that ye might believe."[44]

Why did the soldier use the spear? Perhaps he acted in angry frustration that they had been denied the satisfaction of watching this man's full agony. Crucified with Him, the thieves were still alive, but He was dead already. He had not died from weakness but had shouted in triumph, "*It is finished!*" i.e., the payment for our sins. The Greek word He used was *tetelestai*. It meant "Paid in full" and, in those days, was marked on invoices and promissory notes when full payment had been made: "And when Jesus had cried with a loud voice, he said, Father, into thy hands I commend my spirit: and having said thus, he gave up the ghost."[45]

These prophecies and the biblical record of their fulfillment are unacceptable to most Jews and non-Jews alike. Muslims reject them because they are specifically denied in the Qur'an: "They slew him not nor crucified, but it appeared so unto them . . . they slew him not for certain. But Allah took him up unto Himself."[46] Evangelical Christians reject the Qur'an's contradiction of the Bible and accept what the Bible says because it is backed by numerous prophecies and eyewitness accounts of their fulfillment and irrefutable evidence that, according to some of the greatest legal experts in history, would constitute proof in any court of law today.

THE CRUX OF THE CONFLICT

At the very heart of the gospel of Jesus Christ, and proving it to be true, are the numerous prophecies concerning Israel, her land, and her Messiah. Christ's genealogy, first advent, Second Coming, and future reign on Earth are intertwined with Israel. Muslims cannot accept the forgiveness offered by the true God, because the Qur'an denies that

Jesus died for the sins of the world and was resurrected. Moreover, at the very heart of Islam is a determination to destroy Israel, which, if it could be accomplished, would prove the Bible false, including its promise of the Messiah.

In further contrast, Muhammad's successors fought among themselves, killed one another, and spread Islam by the sword. But Christ's disciples all died at the hands of others as true martyrs, who did not take the life of a single person with them. They died not only as martyrs, out of devotion to Christ, but as witnesses to the life, miracles, sinless character, death, and resurrection of Christ. No one is fool enough to die for what he knows is a lie. The fact that none of the disciples bought his freedom by promising his would-be executioners that he would expose the miracles and resurrection as lies is proof of the validity of their testimony—testimony that stands as irrefutable proof today.

Neither Islam nor any other religion has even one such witness to its validity. Christianity is opposed not only by Islam but by all of the world's religions, including atheism. Whether or not to believe the testimony of prophecy and eyewitnesses is a choice that every person may freely make. From the evidence we have given, there is only one rational choice.

GOD'S INTEGRITY IS AT STAKE

The everlasting covenant by which God gave Israel the Promised Land calls for David's heir, the promised Messiah, to rule an eternal kingdom on his reestablished throne over the twelve tribes of Israel and the entire world from Jerusalem.[47] Nor is it any less clear that this One, as we have seen, must be "The mighty God, The everlasting Father," if He is to be "The Prince of Peace" and reign forever over the world from David's throne.[48] That fact, however, is unpalatable to Jews and Gentiles alike, who want the Messiah to be a good man who sets an example for us to follow but surely not God come as a man through a virgin birth, much less that the depths of man's sin will be revealed in his crucifying the Creator. The Qur'an, while admitting that Jesus was without sin, specifically denies that He is either God or the Son of God.

In spite of Israel's rejection of her Messiah and the years of unbelief and rebellion against Him, God will not go back on His Word to Abraham, Isaac, and Jacob. Christians who deny that the Jews are still the people of God or that they have any special significance are denying God's Word. Those who deny God's promises of the full and final restoration of Israel to her land are denying to God the glory that is His in keeping His Word to Abraham, Isaac, and Israel. Did He not say, "I AM. . . . The LORD God of your fathers, the God of Abraham, the God of Isaac, and the God of Jacob . . . this is my name for ever, and this is my memorial unto all generations"?[49] That memorial would be worse than meaningless—it would mock the God of Israel—if Israel did not continue to exist and finally be fully restored.

The nations of the world are openly defying what God has plainly and repeatedly declared in His Word concerning the land that He gave to Israel by an everlasting covenant. In rejecting Israel, they are rejecting the Messiah and the salvation that He alone could bring and that God offers to all who will believe on Him. They will bear the consequences of this defiance.

Why has a book that has been involved mainly with science and with arguments against atheism on the basis of the scientific evidence turned at the last to Bible prophecy? This discussion could go on almost endlessly, with both sides still at odds. We have turned to prophecy because science has nothing to say about it and certainly cannot refute it. The fulfillment of prophecy, on the other hand, is one proof for the existence of God that cannot be denied by anyone, including the greatest scientists and the staunchest of atheists.

Every good gift and every perfect gift is from above, and cometh down from the Father of lights, with whom is no variableness, neither shadow of turning" (James 1:17). The word "turning" is from the Greek trope. *When combined with the Greek for "in" (that is,* en*), it becomes* entrope, *which means in the Greek "confusion" or "shame." We get our English word "entropy" from this source, which literally means "inturning." In science, any system which "turns in" on itself, without drawing on external sources of energy or information (in other words, a "closed system") will experience an increase of entropy, or disorganization. This is, so far as all evidence goes a universal principle of science, and seems to reflect God's curse on "the whole creation" (Romans 8:22). That is, all things are being conserved in quantity by God, but they are deteriorating in quality, running down toward physical chaos and biological death. But God Himself, who imposed these laws on His creation, is not bound by them. There is not even a "shadow of turning" with Him.*

—HENRY M. MORRIS, *THE NEW DEFENDER'S STUDY BIBLE*
(NASHVILLE, TN: WORLD PUBLISHING, INC., 2006), 1923

We are surrounded by endless forms, most beautiful and most wonderful, and it is no accident, but the direct consequence of evolution by non-random natural selection—the only game in town, the greatest show on Earth.

—RICHARD DAWKINS, *THE GREATEST SHOW ON EARTH*
(NEW YORK: FREE PRESS, 2009), 426

Here is a riddle: how is your religion like a swimming pool? And there is the answer: it is what is known as an attractive nuisance. The doctrine of attractive nuisance is the principle that people who maintain on their property a dangerous condition that is likely to attract children are under a duty to post a warning or to take stronger affirmative action to protect children from danger of that attraction.

—DANIEL DENNETT, *BREAKING THE SPELL* (NEW YORK: VIKING, 2006), 298-99

The only position that leaves me with no cognitive dissonance is atheism. It is not a creed. Death is certain, replacing both the siren-song of Paradise and the dread of Hell. Life on this earth, with all its mystery and beauty and pain, is then to be lived far more intensely: we stumble and get up, we are sad, confident, insecure, feel loneliness and joy and love. There is nothing more; but I want nothing more.

—CHRISTOPHER HITCHENS, *THE PORTABLE ATHEIST* (DACAPO PRESS, 2007), 480

Man's derived supremacy over the earth; man's power of articulate speech; man's gift of reason; man's free-will and responsibility . . . —all are equally and utterly irreconcilable with the degrading notion of the brute origin of him who was created in the image of God. . . .

—SAMUEL WILBERFORCE, BISHOP OF OXFORD (1860)

TWENTY

WHAT IF. . . ?
WHAT THEN?

R ICHARD DAWKINS asks the question, "Who will say with confidence that sexual abuse is more permanently damaging to children than threatening them with the eternal and unquenchable fires of hell?"

If this life on Earth is all there is, then Dawkins raises a legitimate question. I can never forget the words of a nuclear physicist who, as a young atheist, scoffed at his grandmother's warnings about hell. His friends were impressed with the good cheer he spread at his cocktail parties and often asked him about his psychiatrist. In fact, he was dying inside and was contemplating suicide but was kept from the deed by the disturbing thought, what if Grandma is right and when you find yourself in hell you can't get back? Through faith in Jesus, whom he came to believe had died for his sins and had risen from the dead, the former atheist found a new kind of joy. At one last visit, he told his psychiatrist, "I don't need you. You need me!"

John Lennox, in his concluding remarks in the debate with Richard Dawkins, affirmed his belief in the Resurrection of Jesus:

Atheism, ladies and gentlemen, is not only false—it contains no message that deals with the central problem of human rebellion against God. History is littered with attempts to build a godless utopia, each one of them based, as the Book of Genesis suggests they would be, on a denial that God has ever spoken, or even that He exists. And I would remind you that the world which Richard Dawkins wishes to bring us to is no paradise except for the few. It denies the existence of good and evil, it even denies justice. But . . . our hearts cry out for justice. And centuries ago, the Apostle Paul spoke to the philosophers of Athens and pointed out that there would be a day in which God would judge the world by the Man that He had appointed, Jesus Christ, and that He'd given assurance to *all* people by raising Him from the dead. And the resurrection of Jesus Christ—a miracle, something supernatural—for me constitutes the central evidence upon which I base my faith, not only that atheism is a delusion but that justice is *real*. And our sense of morality does not mock us. Because if there is no resurrection, if there is nothing after death, in the end, the terrorists and the fanatics have got away with it.

This elicited a response from Richard Dawkins:

Yes, well, that concluding bit rather gives the game away, doesn't it? All that stuff about science and physics and the complications of physics and things, what it really comes down to is the resurrection of Jesus. And there's a fundamental incompatibility between the sort of sophisticated scientist, which we hear part of the time from John Lennox, and it's impressive and we are interested in the argument about multiverses and things. And then, having produced some sort of a case for a kind of deistic god, perhaps, some god— the Great Physicist, who adjusted the laws and constants of the universe—that's all very grand and wonderful, and then suddenly we come down to the resurrection of Jesus. It's so petty, it's so trivial, it's so local, it's so earthbound, it's so unworthy of the universe.[1]

It is amazing how their hatred of God seems to unhinge atheists. Typical is another statement from Dawkins: "As ever, the theist answer [i.e., "in the beginning God created"] is deeply unsatisfying because it leaves the existence of God unexplained."[2]

Isn't this the pot calling the kettle black? In fact, what Dawkins and other atheists believe leaves *everything* unexplained. For a start, let these "brights" explain the origin of the energy of which everything is made and which supposedly first revealed its existence with a huge explosion that began everything we now see and know. Let them tell us what energy itself is.

Let them explain why they continually disregard the law of biogenesis, which uncompromisingly declares that life *comes only from life*. As we have seen in the millions of words they have written, they leave unanswered the questions that really matter: *what are life, death, truth, purpose, meaning, an atom, an electron, gravity, love, hope, joy, etc.? What was man's origin and what is his destiny?* By the same standard that they apply to us, atheism is "deeply unsatisfying" because, in denying God, it leaves an entire universe unexplained. It is a pitiful response for Dawkins to repeat, "We're working on that."

The atheist tries desperately to make his belief more respectable by giving it an important part even in ethics. Einstein should have stuck to his science. Having stated that science and religion have nothing in common and professing the "wisdom of Solomon," he declared:

> A man's ethical behavior should be based effectually on sympathy, education, and social ties; no religious basis is necessary. Man would indeed be in a poor way if he had to be restrained by fear of punishment and hope of reward after death.[3]

Such idealism may sound brave until one thinks about it carefully. That is when humanism's house of cards collapses. What Einstein intended as a defense of humanity turns out to be a blanket condemnation of it. Is it not true that without police, crime would run even more rampant than it does now? Are all of those who occupy prisons today exceptions to this marvelous race of humans that Einstein, in effect, claims do not need any restraint at all? Policemen, judges, and parole officers would find Einstein's idealism simply ludicrous, betraying a very skewed understanding of human nature and behavior.

Wasn't Germany, at the time, the most scientifically advanced and sophisticated country in the world, yet out of it came Nazism and the Holocaust? America is probably, at the moment, the most advanced country when it comes to technology and science, particularly in the areas of space exploration and military weaponry, except for Israel. China has a way to go to catch us. But what has our technology gotten us? We have the highest crime rates in the world, the largest prison population, etc.[4]

It takes only one word to reduce humanism's proud structure to a heap of ruins: "Why?" As Stephen Hawking asks, in some bewilderment, "Why does the universe go to all the bother of existing?" Why are we here? Why is there war? Why is something right and something else wrong, and why do human beings have a conscience? Indeed, *why*?

When atheists present us with valid answers to these questions, then we may have some reason for taking them seriously. Until then, we will have to accept the clear declaration found twice in the Bible: "The fool hath said in his heart, There is no God."[5]

What do these "fools" who call themselves "brights" say? Sounding like Hitchens, Mark Twain boasted: "I do not fear death, in view of the fact that I had been dead for billions and billions of years before I was born, and had not suffered the slightest inconvenience from it."[6] Twain was a clever humorist, but it is not likely that a person who has been told by a doctor that he has 60 days to live would spend that short time watching the funniest shows on TV. Twain had a rude awakening when he died and found that the Bible was right after all: "It is appointed unto men once to die, [and] after this the judgment."[7]

One could hardly believe that this was anything but one of Twain's typical "smart aleck" remarks. It wouldn't provide any comfort to a dying person who still had his full faculties. Mark Twain certainly had not been "dead for billions and billions of years before [he] was born." Of *course* he hadn't suffered before he was born. He hadn't even existed. The fact that the body to which his friends had said their fond farewells has probably been consumed by now after nearly 100 years in the grave does not relieve the anguish of soul and spirit and the torment of a guilt-stricken conscience that he suffers eternally—and with no place to hide from the face of the resurrected Jesus, whose eyes Scripture says are "like a flame of fire."

The following statement by Christ is not a parable. The rich man that He mentions must be a real person, and certainly the beggar, Lazarus, whose name is given, must be a historic person as well. We may therefore conclude that hell is literally being described by Christ:

> There was a certain rich man, which was clothed in purple and fine linen, and fared sumptuously every day: and there was a certain beggar named Lazarus, which was laid at his gate, full of sores. And desiring to be fed with the crumbs which fell from the rich man's table: moreover the dogs came and licked his sores. And it came to pass, that the beggar died, and was carried by the angels into Abraham's bosom: the rich man also died, and was buried; and in hell he lift up his eyes, being in torments, and seeth Abraham afar off, and Lazarus in his bosom.
>
> And he cried and said, Father Abraham, have mercy on me, and send Lazarus, that he may dip the tip of his finger in water, and cool my tongue; for I am tormented in this flame.
>
> But Abraham said, Son, remember that thou in thy lifetime receivest thy good things, and likewise Lazarus evil things: but now he is comforted, and thou art tormented. And beside all this, between us and you there is a great gulf fixed: so that they which would pass from hence to you cannot; neither can they pass to us, which would come from thence.

> Then he said, I pray thee therefore, father, that thou wouldst send him to my father's house: for I have five brethren; that he may testify unto them lest they also come into this place of torment.
>
> Abraham saith unto him, They have Moses and the prophets: let them hear them.
>
> And he said, Nay, father Abraham: but if one went unto them from the dead, they will repent.
>
> And he said unto him, If they hear not Moses and the prophets, neither will they be persuaded, though one rose from the dead.[8]

There are no physical bodies in hell, even though the "rich man," who perhaps had been there for a long time, longed for just a drop of physical water to assuage what he thought was physical thirst and begged to have it placed on his "tongue." In fact, his tongue and every other part of his body were rotting in the grave.

As he had sought during his lifetime to satisfy his spiritual hunger and thirst with physical pleasures—fine clothes, entertainment, and gourmet food—the rich man apparently still suffered from a similar delusion in hell. He imagined that his pain was physical, when in fact it was a far greater anguish of soul.

A misconception of hell has probably turned many people away from God. A God that tortures people in physical flames (though this is the popular image that most hold in their minds) is a delusion inspired by Satan.

We do not know how long it takes the damned after arriving in hell to recognize that the unbearable, burning pain they are experiencing is the torment of a guilt-ridden conscience under the piercing gaze of Christ's eyes that burn like unquenchable fire[9] and from which there is no escape.

Christopher Hitchens claims that if hell exists, there can be no free will because the pressure to "believe in God, or else" could be likened to a threat to torture and kill someone unless that person agreed to a certain belief. How can explaining the simple facts be a threat?

Is a doctor threatening his patient by forthrightly explaining that he has a terminal disease, gives him six months to live, but then offers a new miracle medication that will in fact cure him? Is the doctor to blame if the patient refuses the cure? Is God to blame, as Hitchens implies, when those to whom He extends the offer of the eternal remedy through the death, burial, and resurrection of Jesus, refuse to accept it?

UNBELIEF IN THE CHURCH

Among Satan's most deadly lies that have probably caused more people to reject belief in God than any others reasons are (as C. S. Lewis's Screwtape explained to Wormwood) the related theories of psychoanalysis and organic evolution, which have effectively mythologized science. Psychologists study and treat man like an animal, and evolution tells him, as Dawkins triumphantly declares, "You *are* an animal!"

Another of the foundational delusions is the belief that scientists are infallible and that anything declared to be "scientific" must therefore be true. Scientists are in fact little boys and girls, "grown up" but still carrying, to their dying day, prejudices, misinformation, and ignorance.

To make religion "scientific" was one of Satan's masterstrokes of pure genius. Out of that brilliance came the mind science cults: "Christian Science," "Religious Science," "Science of Mind," and a host of other delusions, with their many mind-over-matter offspring.

Oprah Winfrey has been one of the most successful recent promoters worldwide of such vain hopes: "You can be what you want to be, have what you want to have, achieve what you want to achieve," by repeating affirmations and by use of visualization. It takes very little thought to see that this belief is pure hokum. Suppose that a warehouseman, truck driver, secretary in training, and in-house legal counsel of XYZ corporation, having been trained by an Oprah Winfrey expert on how to get what one wants, all aspire to become corporate president, while the president is using the same techniques to keep his position. What will happen? Irresolvable clashes of egos will prevail everywhere that these courses are being taught, practiced, and seriously believed.

EVOLUTION JOINS THE CHURCH

In May 1982, honoring the 100th anniversary of the death of Richard Dawkins's most admired hero, Charles Darwin, there was a gathering of scientists at the Vatican's Pontifical Academy of Sciences. Most non-Catholics were surprised when Pope John Paul II, in a paper he read to the Academy, October 23, 1996, once again spoke in favor of evolution. Actually, he only reiterated Catholicism's official position of many years. In part, the pope said:

> In his Encyclical *Humani generis* (1950), my predecessor Pius XII had already stated that there was no opposition between evolution and the doctrine of the faith about man. Pius XII stressed this essential point: if the human body takes its origin from pre-existent living matter, the spiritual soul is immediately created by God. . . . The exegete and the theologian must keep informed about . . . the natural sciences . . . truth cannot contradict truth. . . .
>
> The theory of evolution . . . has been progressively accepted by researchers, following a series of discoveries in various fields of knowledge. The convergence . . . of the results of work that was conducted independently is in itself a significant argument in favor of this theory.[10]

Here we have open defiance of the many statements in the Bible that clearly contradict evolution. It is impossible to reconcile the creation account described in Genesis with the evolutionary belief promoted by the popes, who claim that after descending from a long line of anthropoid-like creatures, Adam and Eve received from God the infusion of a human soul and spirit. Such an evolutionary process, leaving billions of fossils as a result of billions of years of "natural selection," defies the biblical declaration that death came only after Adam's sin.[11]

February of 2009 marked the 150th anniversary of the publication of Darwin's first book, *On the Origin of Species*, which, as we've already pointed out, oddly enough doesn't give the origin of even one species. Nor has any atheist/evolutionist been able to do so since. It was also the year of his 200th birthday. There were celebrations of "Darwin Day" throughout the world.

As we have, on almost every page of this book, attempted to follow logic, we must do so here as well. Of course, we don't expect atheists and agnostics and outright skeptics (not to mention Muslims or Hindus et al.) to believe the Bible. We have already presented, however, and are attempting to further present, what ought to be more than sufficient proof that the Bible is, in fact, infallible, whether it speaks to science or faith or morals.

The skeptics will argue that the writers of Scripture didn't have access to all of the materials produced by "experts" that we have today. They were too poorly educated to realize that *all* of Scripture couldn't be inspired and that it's up to us to decide which parts are and which aren't. Nor is much of the Bible, according to the critics, to be taken literally, especially when it speaks of the universe being created in six 24-hour days. "Science," though it contains many contradictions, is to be trusted rather than God—as though the Creator doesn't know His universe better than any creature.

The above "scientific" view, however, contains some serious and innate problems. Logically, if we can't trust *every word* of the Bible, then there is no infallible authority to guide us, and we ourselves become the final judges of what we are to believe and do—poor counsel for guilty sinners standing before the Supreme Judge of the universe. As the old saying goes, "The man who represents himself in court has a fool for a client." We earthlings are right in harmony with the beginning of Israel's rebellion against God and her apostasy, which is only worse today: "Every man did that which was right in his own eyes."[12]

Jesus believed the entire Old Testament and often referred to it.[13]

If these new "Christians scholars" are right, then such ignorance on Christ's part would prove that He could not have been the Son of God, Messiah and Savior of the world, and thus could not have paid the infinite penalty for the sins of all mankind, as the Bible claims. We have lost the foundational creation account and with it the infal-libility of God's Word—the source of the Christian faith, including Christology. We are left to flounder in uncertainty, waiting for groping scientists to tell us how the universe really came into existence—and maybe even a new way of salvation.

Atoms do not think, nor does the universe that is made of them. While this author cannot agree with Erwin Schrödinger's Vedantic philosophy, Schrödinger makes a good case for the necessity of con-sciousness not being part of the physical universe nor arising out of it. He argues that it would be unreasonable for thoughts and mind to have risen out of the physical universe only after it came into exis-tence because that would mean that the magnificent act of creation would "all have been a performance to empty stalls." He adds:

> But a world, existing for many millions of years without any mind being aware of it, contemplating it, is it anything at all. . . ? Most painful is the absolute silence of all our scientific investigations toward our questions concerning the meaning and scope of the whole display. . . . The show that is going on obviously acquires a meaning only with regard to the mind that contemplates it. But what science tells us about this relationship is patently absurd: as if mind had only been produced by that very display that it is now watching and would pass away with it when the sun finally cools down and the earth has been turned into a desert of ice and snow.[14]

Philosopher-historian Herbert Schlossberg pointed out: "What mod-ern man cannot know through the senses, he feels safe in dismissing from further consideration. One of the first and most notable casualties of this reasoning is the idea of purpose. The senses are silent on such topics."[15]

DESCENT INTO MEANINGLESSNESS

It is right here that the scientific establishment, dominated today by atheists, fails us completely. Science can offer no solace in the face of life's most important questions. It has theories but no ultimate answers to give because the true nature of reality eludes material analysis, as Sir James Jeans pointed out long ago. Lee Smolin, a theoretical physicist, founding member and research scientist at the Perimeter Institute for Theoretical Physics in Waterloo, Canada, has said: "When a child asks, 'What is the world?' we literally have nothing to tell her."[16] And science never will.

Is there nowhere else to look, no one else to ask? Does it matter? The fact that the "why" questions persist indicates that it really does matter very much to most people. Atheists avoid this inevitable question because the only rationally possible answer would upset their entire apple cart.

As Nobel Laureate Sir Peter Medawar advises young scientists, "There is no quicker way for a scientist to bring discredit upon himself and upon his profession than roundly to declare . . . that science knows, or soon will know, the answer to all questions worth asking, and that questions which do not admit a scientific answer . . . only simpletons ask. . . . [That's exactly what Dawkins states and promises!] The existence of a limit to science is made clear by its inability to answer childlike elementary questions to do with . . . 'How did everything begin? What are we all here for? What is the point of living?'"[17] As Lennox says, "There is clearly no inconsistency involved in being a passionately committed scientist at the highest level while . . . recognizing that science cannot answer . . . some of the deepest questions that human beings can ask."[18]

In defensive protection of their impotence, atheists resent anyone asking *why*, claiming that it is a meaningless and illegitimate question. Of course, that is true in the uncaused universe they insist upon—a universe that by their own definition has no reason for existing, and thus no legitimacy, as Hawking implies. Common sense, however, logically demands that there must be a *reason* for everything—and science can't provide it for *anything* that it has so laboriously studied for centuries. The scientific establishment diligently pursues its quest for ever-increasing knowledge about the material nature of the universe with seemingly no concern at all for the most basic questions, while at the same time running as fast as it can from the inescapable: *why* is it here?

And there is a reason why materialistic science fails us at this crucial point. It cannot answer the truly important questions precisely because it claims that nothing but matter exists, and matter can offer no *reason* for its own existence. The question *Why?* cannot be addressed to the universe but only to its Creator. There is no reasoning with nature, no understanding or sympathy there. Materialistic science, therefore, which is wholly given to probing, examining, and analyzing the physical universe (which it must claim created itself and is all that exists), can offer no answers to the important questions that trouble every thinking person who seriously faces the issues of life and death.

Here we have another compelling reason (yes, *reason*) for rejecting atheistic materialism. It cannot help us in life's most difficult moments: when we face the death of a loved one or our own impending demise and we ask ourselves why we are here and where we go next. Without an all-powerful and all-knowing Creator, there are no *reasons* for anything. The only "comfort" the atheist can offer at that moment is, "You had no purpose for being here; your life is without any ultimate meaning in this vast universe, which itself is dying a slow death that will put its final stamp of meaninglessness on everything and everyone that ever was."

Yet we are rational beings, with the logical and pressing desire for understanding innate within us. And atheistic, materialistic science is speechless when we ask *Quo vadis*—where are you going?

DANGER OF SCIENTIFIC MATERIALISM
APPLIED TO MAN

Amazingly, the truth that Schrödinger spoke has been largely ignored by most of the scientific establishment through its commitment to materialism. In the early and mid-1900s, the great hope of science was that the laws of physics and chemistry, when applied to the brain, would explain human personality and behavior. That would allow psychiatrists to retune the physical brain much like an auto mechanic tunes engines. There was even talk that political and military leaders ought to be under the control of psychologists, who would give them periodic tests along with appropriate drugs and therapy to eliminate aggressiveness.

Supposedly, as science learned more about that three pounds of grey matter inside the skull that consumes about 20 percent of the body's energy, all inappropriate behavior would in time be eliminated, including crime, unhappiness, and even wars. The world would become a symphony of kindness, pleasure, and fulfillment. The Eden that science refused to believe had been originally created by God and destroyed by man would now be *recreated by man*!

And how would this happen? Naturally, the new god "science" would provide the answer, leading the way to paradise. Since the brain is allegedly just a mass of matter produced by the Big Bang and the thoughts emanating from it are all meaningless carryovers from that giant explosion, it could be treated with drugs that could change one's mood from aggression, depression, or despair to a sense of well-being and even euphoria. After all, such moods are merely the product of neural activity in the brain (from a materialist's view) and ultimately meaningless, so all one would need would be to adjust the brain through appropriate drugs to achieve a brief sense of well-being.

At least one psychiatrist, however, a leading expert in this field, has warned that although a psychiatrist's patients "believe or hope that they are relying on seemingly objective science, in reality they are placing their faith in drug company marketing . . . one of the most successful public relations campaigns in history . . . and so are their doctors."[19]

"Science" is not immune from error; and when a scientific theory is wrong, the theories built upon it compound the original delusion. Scientists are fallible people prone to the same human frailties as others, from pride to stubbornness to selfishness, greed, and a reluctance to admit when one is wrong. Nowhere is that susceptibility to error more dangerous than when it involves understanding and dealing with human behavior—and especially when attributing personality, thoughts, and motives to the physical organ known as the brain. This is scientific materialism at its most dangerous level—and much of the public has gullibly accepted it as established scientific fact:

> Regardless of their religion or philosophy, many educated and informed people have come to believe that psychiatry and psychiatric drugs provide the best last resort for themselves when in psychological distress . . . indeed . . . the *first* resort. It appears that we have replaced reliance on God, other people, and ourselves with reliance on medical doctors and psychiatric drugs. The ultimate source of guidance and inspiration is . . . biopsychiatry with its narrow view of human nature.
>
> This view of ourselves is a most astonishing one. . . . Our emotional and spiritual problems . . . are declared to be biological and genetic in origin. . . ."Psychiatric disorders" [are] best treated by specialists who prescribe psychoactive drugs. As a result, many educated Americans take it for granted that "science" and "research" have shown that emotional upsets or "behavior problems" have biological and genetic causes and require psychiatric drugs.[20]

CONFUSION IN THE WORLD
OF NATURAL SELECTION

"Natural selection is the only workable explanation for the beautiful and compelling illusion of 'design' that pervades every living body and every organ. Knowledge of evolution may not be strictly useful in everyday commerce. You can live some sort of life and die without ever hearing the name of Darwin. But if, before you die, you want to understand why you lived in the first place, Darwinism is the one subject that you must study."[21]

This statement in a book by the late theoretical evolutionary biologist and geneticist John Maynard Smith is nothing less than astonishing. Richard Dawkins, who wrote the above Foreword, claims that natural selection has created a "compelling illusion of 'design' that pervades" the universe. As we have previously asked, if natural selection were true, why would it create an "illusion" that undermines the whole theory of evolution? And, on top of that, why would natural selection, at the same time, design the human brain to reject this illusion? We know that John Maynard Smith, Richard Dawkins, and many of their fellow evolutionists are confused, but this is an intriguing idea—that the process of natural selection is itself confused in overseeing the alleged evolution of man.

What would be an appropriate epitaph on Richard Dawkins's tombstone? Several possibilities come to mind: "Here lies a man who dedicated his life to the purpose of proving that life has no purpose because there is no God." Will the final line add, "Unfortunately, he failed to produce an ironclad proof of his thesis"? Or will it say, "He died a hero to all mankind, having become the first to accomplish the worthy goal of proving to everyone's satisfaction that life has no goal"? Which will it be?

Will it even matter? As we have seen, this is the necessary conclusion to which materialism leads. Clearly, atoms and molecules have no concept of purpose and meaning—and if that is all we are, then we have no purpose or meaning either. It is worth quoting Francis Crick again to see the hopelessness and worthlessness of this philosophy:

> "You," your joys and your sorrows, your memories and your ambitions, your sense of personal identity and free will, are in fact no more than the behavior of a vast assembly of nerve cells and their associated molecules.[22]

Dawkins claims to have lived a very happy and fulfilling life. He often says that he feels very lucky to be alive, to have been one of the few gene containers whose genes won the natural selection lottery, since most of them die along the way. We have also quoted him saying that there is no significant difference between a man and a garden slug.

In describing the wonders of nature, atheists find themselves unable to avoid using terms that imply an all-knowing and all-powerful Creator. Dawkins claims to have a great admiration and appreciation for the marvels of life. As we have quoted earlier, he declared: "When you were first conceived you were just a single cell, endowed with one master copy of the architect's plans."[23] He would surely have avoided using such a word were there any better way to say it! Obviously, he knew of no other appropriate word.

Yet Dawkins denies the existence of the only "architect" who possibly could conceive these detailed instructions for building every nano-chemical machine in every cell, and supervise from start to finish (as architects do) this incredible construction project, the end of which is about 100 trillion living cells, all perfectly fitted together to become one unique human body. To conceive these plans and to supervise them from the very beginning until a complete body is formed in the womb is infinitely beyond the capabilities of the most brilliant team of scientists and computers that could be assembled today.

Remember, Dawkins admits that it could take *centuries* for scientists to understand the process:

> Proteins not only constitute much of the physical fabric of the body; they also exert sensitive control over all the chemical processes inside the cell, selectively turning them on and off at precise times and in precise places. *Exactly how this eventually leads to the development of a baby is a story which it will take decades, perhaps centuries, for embryologists to work out.*[24]

Only the infinite Creator would be capable of this feat, yet atheists deny His existence. Clinging to materialism as their only hope of denying the Creator, atheists search year after year for some key to human behavior in the anatomy of the brain. They are beating a dead horse. There is no location in the brain where the most important parts of what makes a man can be found: the hopes, ambitions, determination, goals, artistic ability, aesthetics, scientific genius, etc.

A major problem that the materialist tries to sweep under the carpet is the fact that in spite of the herculean effort in the lab to explain human behavior by the brain alone, in the real world of daily human experience, common sense will not allow the ordinary person to countenance the theory that he doesn't have his own opinions and doesn't by his own initiative make real decisions. And still the atheist slogs on through life with the single-minded purpose of proving that life *has* no purpose.

Why would proving that God does not exist, if it could be proven, make the atheist happy? The only one who could impart meaning to life would be a personal Creator. To prove there was no meaning in life would be tantamount to proving that God, who alone could impart such meaning, either does not exist or does not care.

Is there evidence justifying rejection of God as the supreme Architect? No, there is none. No one has been able to produce proof that God does not exist. Is there evidence for His existence? Indeed there is. As we have proved throughout this book, such evidence is overwhelming. The evidence from DNA alone is irrefutable. It is self-evident, as Einstein declared, that matter cannot arrange itself into information. Whatever the form in which it appears, information can come only from an intelligent source. Period!

Clearly, the intelligence behind DNA could only be described as infinite. Then why the irrational rejection of the God to whom all the evidence so clearly points? It is not for scientific reasons but because atheists would both lose credibility if they admitted the obvious and would face ultimate justice after they died.

These atheists claim to be on the side of nature. Then why do they reject what seems to have been the intuition of almost the entire human race from the beginning of time right up to the present? Dawkins mourns in hopeless despair the agonizing death of his god

Darwin, "It is almost as if the human brain were specifically designed to misunderstand Darwinism, and to find it hard to believe." Then why cling to this bankrupt theory that is so contrary to what evolutionists think has made us? And how can this be, when everything we think, say, and do was supposedly produced by evolution?

Richard Dawkins cheerfully insists, "Flowers and elephants are 'for' the same thing as everything else in the living kingdoms, for spreading Duplicate Me programs written in DNA language. Flowers are for spreading copies of instructions for making more flowers. Elephants are for spreading copies of instructions for making more elephants."[25] And Dawkins delights to declare that none of them has any purpose or meaning.

"I regard it as an enormous privilege to be alive . . . especially at the beginning of the twenty-first century, to be a scientist and therefore to be in a position to understand something of the mystery of existence . . . why we exist. I think that religious explanations are now petty and parochial. The understanding we can get from science of all those deep questions that religion once aspired to explain are now better, more grandly, and in a more beautiful and elegant fashion, explained by science."[26]

"*Why we exist*"? But Dawkins vociferously denies that there is any meaning. Certainly matter, if that's all we are (as he claims), knows nothing of meaning or purpose.

WHAT ABOUT DEATH?

Science is unable to explain what life is or how it began. Given the above facts, it is not surprising that scientists cannot explain what death is. Why does this living body, retaining its chemical composition and the order seen in all living things, suddenly die? We can understand this in terms of a mortal wound or fatal disease or some other visible cause, but when the body retains all of the chemicals that seemingly contained life and suddenly loses that invisible spark that no one can explain, we cannot help but ask *why*?

Unquestionably, God, who gives us the life we think we possess, must be the one who takes it away. What we thought belonged to us was only lent to us by our Creator for whatever brief time He decided to grant it. Why does life inevitably come to an end? Medical science cannot answer this question. Where shall we turn but to God himself?

The Christian, who believes that the Bible is God's Word because of the many proofs it gives us, looks to the Bible for answers. The Bible declares that at death, "Then shall the dust return to the earth as it was: and the spirit shall return unto God who gave it."[27]

Here again, as always, we have the biblical rejection of materialism in the clearest terms. There is a difference between matter and spirit that cannot be denied. This understanding, of course, has broad repercussions leading to the realization that *brain* and *mind* are not the same. Nobelist Sir John Eccles titles one of his most intriguing books *The Wonder of Being Human: Our Brain and Our Mind.*

As Sir Arthur Eddington reminds us: "There is a clear distinction between natural law, which *must* be obeyed, and moral law, which *ought to* be obeyed. *Ought* takes us outside of physics and chemistry." Only the materialists who deny the existence of anything but matter reject this vital differentiation but cannot rationally or scientifically support their objection.

Whether or not one objects to the existence of God, nowhere do we find a better explanation of life and death than in the Bible. The God of the Bible explained in solemn terms to Adam and Eve that the penalty for sin is death, which is eternal separation from Him. Isn't that rather harsh? The couple was driven from the garden paradise by their Creator for the seemingly minor infraction of eating some fruit. How could that be worthy of eternal punishment?

Human beings, whether atheist or Christian, have a careless view of sin, looking at the act alone and denying, or at least forgetting, against whom the act was committed. The sin of Adam and Eve was not merely eating the forbidden fruit. It was deliberate defiance of and rebellion against the One who had created them and the entire universe. From mankind's viewpoint, David's sins of adultery, murder, and lying were far more reprehensible. But David knew what sin was: "Against thee, thee only, have I sinned, and done this evil in thy sight."[28]

It may seem noble or magnanimous to accept an apology from someone who we are convinced has wronged us. The natural reaction is to hold a grudge. Many people feel they have a right to hold a grudge against God because they think He has wronged them in some way. But what about recognizing our obligation to our Creator and asking His forgiveness for our rebellion against Him? We have committed high treason against the Lord of the Universe. Why should He forgive us? From the Cross, Christ prayed to His Father for those who had hated, mocked, scourged, and crucified Him, "Father, forgive them for they know not what they do."[29] Jesus said that if we will not forgive others, how can we dare to ask God to forgive us?

HIGH TREASON AGAINST THE CREATOR

However else and in whatever way we attempt to define sin, at its heart, sin is deliberate treason, open and defiant rebellion, against the Creator and Ruler of the universe. We need to remember this fact. We cannot minimize our rebellion. Most Christians who, when convicted by conscience, fall on their faces and confess their sins are not really confessing the horror of what they've done. It is not enough to repent of the deed. We must confess also that, no matter how trivial we think the act was, we have repeated Adam and Eve's treason *against the Lord God*. The Christian should understand that without this admission, deeply felt as a conviction in one's heart, the confession is incomplete, and, one can almost say, really empty.

The atheist, of course, ridicules the very thought of God, in whom he does not believe and to whom he feels no obligation. As a consequence, there is no sin and no guilt, because there is no one to whom his atheism will allow him to be accountable. We are not arguing whether God exists, but we are pointing out what the issues are and the clear distinctions that are made in the Bible. Here is the only sensible explanation both for life and death.

Sam Harris has apparently studied the Bible, but with very superficial understanding. He says that to follow the Bible, "We must . . . stone people to death for heresy, adultery, homosexuality, working on the Sabbath, worshipping graven images, practicing sorcery, and a wide variety of other imaginary crimes."[30] Three things he fails to understand: 1) The seriousness of rebelling against God, who created the universe, who makes the rules, and who must enforce them; 2) The fact (which many a parent or probation board discovers too late) that to allow the culprit merely to mutter, "I'm sorry!" and go free only encourages further rebellion; and 3) After showing both Israel[31] and the church[32] at their beginnings that rebellion warrants death, God did not continue to enforce that physical penalty immediately in this life—or no one would have survived!

Sir James Jeans often repeated his famous statement, "God is a mathematician, and the universe begins to look more like a great thought than a great machine." Elaborating further, he wrote:

> Mind no longer appears as an accidental intruder into the realm of matter; we are beginning to suspect that we ought to hail it as the creator and governor of matter—not, of course, our individual minds . . . [but] the mind of some Eternal Spirit.[33]

Jeans did not elaborate upon the logical consequences of what he declared, but they are inescapable.

ARE HUMANS JUST SOPHISTICATED ROBOTS?

Though behaviorist psychologists such as B. F. Skinner tried for years to convince themselves and others that man is a stimulus-response robot without the power to genuinely make choices—to love or hate, to do good or evil, to be kind or vicious—few scientists (and even few psychologists) retain that opinion today. Apparently, one person who still may is William H. (Bill) Gates, III, founder of Microsoft and the richest entrepreneur in the world, now worth about 40-50 billion dollars. For years, Gates has believed "that we'll someday be able to replicate intelligence and emotions in a machine, but he admits that the joy of raising daughter Jennifer [and now her brother and sister as well] 'goes beyond analytic description.'"[34]

Bill and Melinda Gates now have three children: Jennifer Katherine (1996), Rory John (1999), and Phoebe Adele (2002). We hope that Bill has finally realized that Jennifer, Rory, and Phoebe are not at all like any machine, because they were made by God in His image. Nor will any artificial intelligence, designed by Bill Gates or any other computer genius, ever be able to take the place of human beings.

The rebellion that began in the Garden of Eden becomes ever more sophisticated, ingenious, and "scientific." For decades, man has been attempting—unsuccessfully—to "create life." The latest effort is to create "artificial intelligence." If the robot can apparently think and talk and reason and give human-like responses in a conversation, then today's belief is *what does it matter whether it is real or artificial?* These are terms that we can't even define. So let's forget reality and go with pretense. A machine that can pretend to be alive and pretend to converse with us—why shouldn't that be enough? Well, it's all that science is going to get from its creations! I don't believe that your average human being could ever be satisfied with mere make-believe. We would be back to the ancient fables that were entertaining but that no one took seriously.

Gates would never imagine that a robot with artificial intelligence could spontaneously come into existence. It seems equally irrational that the creator of these robots, having programmed them with the ability to think for themselves and even to choose to rebel against their creator, would stand by and helplessly watch as his brilliantly constructed machines destroyed themselves and all he had created.

We are simply uncovering the reasons why God gave man the power of choice. He was not satisfied with having robots, nor would any rational human being be satisfied with such a companion. God made man in His image, "in the image of God created he him, male and female created he them."[35] He made a woman to be man's companion and intended that they should share genuine love with one another—not just as animals do, but something far beyond that. A union of love, if it is to have any meaning, must have moral and spiritual dimensions and consequences. The highest ambition of some married couples is to have children, and some couples have achieved ten or twelve or even more. If that is the ultimate goal of human life, then rabbits do it far more effectively than we, and microbes exceed all other living things. Scientists are hoping to create artificial life and the ultimate achievement, a "sex slave," through whom men could satisfy their basest desires. This was never God's intention, nor would any man who lives up to the image in which God created him desire a robot for a wife.

SCIENCE CAN NEVER BE OUR SAVIOR

Sadly, looking to science for the ultimate answers that all men seek has undermined the faith of multitudes even within evangelical circles. Science has become a substitute for God, credited with infallibility and omniscience. Theistic evolution (the belief that evolution is the way man was created by the God of the Bible) has taken over many, if not most, denominational seminaries. The result has been the rejection of God's Word in favor of pseudo-translations that actually contradict and undermine what God has said. One of the most blasphemous examples is found in *The Renovaré Spiritual Formation Bible*. It regards Genesis 1-11 as pagan mythology, slightly modified to give it a monotheistic flavor—certainly not inspired of God through Moses.[36] Yet this abomination is endorsed by more than fifty pastors and "biblical scholars."

This is no light matter. If the Genesis account of creation isn't reliable, then how can we trust any other part of the Bible? If the Bible is wrong about the origin of man, how can we trust what it says about man's destiny? If the Bible is wrong about how sin entered into the world, then how can we trust its solution for sin? Moreover, Christ must therefore not be God and capable of saving us but a mere man who foolishly took the story of Adam and Eve literally because He lacked the insights of modern science. Though many Christians don't seem to understand, atheists have long known the consequences of denying the historicity of Adam and Eve:

> Destroy Adam and Eve and original sin, and in the rubble you will find the sorry remains of the Son of God and take away the meaning of his death.[37]

The evidence from nature for God as Creator begins in the ingenious structure of the atom. Dawkins says he doesn't know much about chemistry.[38] It is a pity that he doesn't, because a basic understanding of the periodic table of the elements should be all that is needed to convince any honest seeker of the existence of God the Creator. Shall we give the credit to the mindless Big Bang for holding together in the center of the atom the neutrons and protons that ought to repel one another in a giant explosion? Or for keeping the electrons in their distinctive orbits, whirling about and magically changing one element to another by adding to or subtracting from their number?

THE "RIGHT TO MURDER" MOVEMENT

The newest delusion of this genre is the "scientific explanation" of love. We have quoted great scientists declaring that science cannot answer life's deepest questions. But now, *voilá*! the genius of science-gone-mad has at last "proved" that "True love can last a lifetime." How do they know? Brain scans have revealed this alleged fact. Husband and wife who have been married, for no matter how long or short a time, can once again be glad at heart with confidence. They now have the support not only of one another, but science is on their side. Isn't that wonderful?

As for this sentimental silliness of using a heart as a symbol on Valentine's Day, how unscientific can one get! For centuries, novels, poems, operas, etc., have referred to love as a "matter of the heart," and lovers surely know what that means. Now, at last, thanks to the religion of science, we realize that the entire human race has been dead wrong all the time! It's really all in the head and selfish genes— and don't forget to give due credit to a huge explosion that started this human adventure off with an appropriate "Bang."

One of the worst consequences of looking to science for answers to life's ultimate questions has been the devaluation of human life. It is no exaggeration to say that Darwinism has led to the killing of untold millions of human beings. To highlight just a few examples: eugenics (philosophical Darwinism) inspired Margaret Sanger to found Planned Parenthood and the pro-abortion movement. *Parenthood?*

Eugenics helped Hitler to convince an entire country to follow him in his attempt to wipe out the "inferior" Jews, not to mention the toll in blood it took to stop him. These days, Peter Singer, a Princeton professor of bioethics, advocates that parents be allowed to dispatch their imperfect infants up to 30 days after birth. The misguided "right to die" movement is rapidly becoming the "right to kill" movement, as we witnessed severely disabled (but not dying) Terri Schiavo starved to death by court order, with the approval of a large portion of the country. Meanwhile, more than a million babies continue to be aborted every year from wombs that ought to be the safest haven of protection for the fetus. None of these horrors could have occurred in a culture that understood each human life to be a unique creation of God, stamped with His image—much less one that followed the teaching and example of Jesus Christ.

As we have seen, numerous scientists (like Einstein) are willing to acknowledge some "force" behind creation but categorically reject a personal God. Not so Eddington, who wrote: "[Concerning] the question of a personal God . . . there is a tendency to substitute such terms as 'omnipotent force' or even a 'fourth dimension' [though] unsuitable for the scientist to whom the words 'force' and 'dimension' convey something entirely precise and defined."[39]

For Eddington, as for Einstein, religion and science could not be mixed: "I am wholly opposed to any . . . proposal to base religion on scientific discovery . . . for here reasoning fails us altogether. Reasoning . . . cannot start without premises. . . . We can and must believe that we have an inner sense of values which guides us . . . otherwise we cannot start on our survey even of the physical world. Consciousness alone can determine the validity of its convictions."

Eddington has also said,

> In the case of our human friends we take their existence for granted, not caring whether it is proven or not. . . . I think that it is something of the same kind of security we should seek in our relationship with God. The most flawless proof of the existence of God is no substitute for it; and if we have a relationship the most convincing disproof is turned harmlessly aside. If I may say it with reverence, the soul and God laugh together over [atheism's] odd conclusion.[41]
>
> We want an assurance that the soul in reaching out to the unseen world is not following an illusion. . . . We do not want a religion that deceives us for our own good.[42]
>
> [Even] a very shallow materialist . . . connives at an attitude towards knowledge which does not treat it as something secreted in the brain by the operation of unbreakable laws of nature. It is to be judged in relation to its truth or untruth. . . .[43]
>
> Dismiss the idea that natural law may swallow up religion; it cannot even tackle the multiplication table singlehanded.[44]
>
> I think that those who would wish to take cognizance of nothing but the measurements of the scientific world made by our sense organs are shirking one of the most immediate facts of experience, namely that consciousness is not wholly, nor even primarily a device for receiving sense-impressions . . . in practice a more transcendental outlook is almost universally admitted.[45]

Study of the scientific world cannot prescribe the orientation of something which is excluded from the scientific world.[46]

We have traveled far from the standpoint which identifies the real with the concrete. . . . Time must be admitted to be real, although no one could attribute to it a concrete nature.[47]

There are many things that the one true God, the God of the Bible (in spite of being Almighty and Sovereign), *cannot do.* Anyone who takes the time to think this through will be able to list a number of these impossibilities. Among other things, God cannot sin, He cannot make a mistake, He cannot lust, and He cannot lie or deceive. Though many are the complaints against God, He cannot act unjustly or unfairly. He cannot contradict Himself, He cannot force anyone to love Him, and He cannot violate His own justice.

Bertrand Russell wrote: "All the labor of the ages, all the devotion, all the inspiration, all the noonday brightness of human genius are destined to extinction in the death of the solar system."[48]

It could not be said more clearly that one day nothing will be left of the proud structures man has built on earth. Not a trace will be left of any of man's greatest accomplishments (including Russell's works), which, after all, according to his own philosophy, were meaningless anyway. That being the case, can there be any ultimate meaning to our existence? And if there isn't, can we learn to live happily with that knowledge? What is "happily"? Science knows nothing of such emotions.

A CHOICE TO MAKE

"God is love" (1 John 4:8), but He is also just. Love cannot condone rebellion against the Creator. Only because the Messiah paid the penalty in full can God justly forgive anyone. In denying that Jesus is God and that He died for our sins, the world rejects man's only hope.

The real issue is whether or not the Bible is God's infallible Word.

If it isn't, then nothing has any meaning, the universe happened by chance, and all mankind, along with it, is headed for oblivion. One day, it will all be as though it had never been, and nothing we have said or done will have been of any significance. But if the Bible is the Word of the Creator of this universe (we have sufficiently proved that to be true through a multitude of prophecies fulfilled concerning Israel and the Messiah), then the United Nations, United States, European Union, Russia, and the entire world are all heading for God's judgment.

If one denies that the God of the Bible exists—the One who has proved Himself with hundreds of prophecies fulfilled—then indeed there is no hope. If the God of Abraham, Isaac, and Jacob is not the true God, we are left without purpose or meaning to life. To deny that God chose a man named Abraham through whom He would bring mankind back to Himself; to deny the true history of this chosen people and the land given to them, to which the Messiah came as prophesied and to which He will return to rule the world; to deny the hundreds of prophecies fulfilled in Jesus Christ alone—is to deny the only hope for mankind.

The choice is open to all—but it must be a free choice. The true God does not coerce anyone. The purpose of this volume is simply to present the facts so that the reader will have an intelligent basis for making a vital choice for eternity.

THE HAUNTING QUESTION: WHAT THEN?

The hope of many is that after a life of hard work and perhaps some "good luck," at last comes the well-deserved reward of retirement. And what then? Sooner or later death comes, of course, and hopefully a quiet grave at the worst. Was Hitler right, after all, that the "final solution" is to destroy the Jews and that the way of escape from the consequences of what he wrought was in suicide? Is the atheist right that death ends it all? Such is the promise that Christopher Hitchens gives his fans as he joins with atheism's Four Horsemen in one last charge into oblivion: "You didn't know anything before you were born and you won't know anything after you die." Freud's consoling words were, "The goal of all life is death," but psychology provides no answer to the haunting question, "What then?" Nor did Shakespeare, though he expressed the dilemma eloquently in the words of Hamlet in his soliloquy:

> *To die; to sleep;*
> *No more; and by a sleep to say we end*
> *The heartache and the thousand natural shocks*
> *That flesh is heir to. 'tis a consummation*
> *Devoutly to be wish'd. To die; to sleep;*
> *To sleep? Perchance to dream. Ay, there's the rub;*
> *For in that sleep of death what dreams may come*
> *When we have shuffled off this mortal coil,*
> *Must give us pause. . . .*
> *For who would bear the whips and scorns of time,*
> *But that the dread of something after death,*
> *The undiscover'd country from whose bourn*
> *No traveler returns, puzzles the will*
> *And makes us rather bear those ills we have*
> *Than fly to others that we know not of?*
> *Thus conscience doth make cowards of us all.*

King Solomon, the son of David, king over Israel in Jerusalem, wrote:

> Vanity of vanities, all is vanity. What profit hath a man of all his labour which he taketh under the sun? One generation passeth away, and another generation cometh: but the earth abideth for ever.[49]
>
> Boast not thyself of tomorrow; for thou knowest not what a day may bring forth.[50]

Everyone knows the familiar truism, "Two things are certain: death and taxes." Is that really true? In his eighth century BC *The Iliad*, Homer solemnly declared: "Death in ten thousand shapes hangs ever over our heads, and no man can elude him." He gave us no answer to the solemn question: What then?

The universal instinct persists that death, though it comes as regularly as birth, is an alien intruder that ought not to be and robs us of that to which it has no right. Although we know it is inescapable, nevertheless it seems an unbearable injustice that death should have the last word to say about life.

No matter how brave the resignation we muster, something within us rises up in anger and cries out in helpless protest whenever death snatches from us what we struggle to retain. Though death has been taking its toll regularly since the beginning of time, something still seems horribly wrong—not only that a baby but that the elderly as well should become, as Milton expressed it in *Paradise Lost*, "Food for so foule a Monster."

Struggling for words to express our grief, we find it inexpressible. Of Juliet, Lady Capulet lamented, "Death lies on her like an untimely frost upon the sweetest flower of the field." Untimely or not, the solemn fact remains that our time on this earth, no matter how prolonged, is at most very brief. Death is often unexpected and always comes too soon. Thomas Carlyle said it well: "One life—a little gleam of time between two eternities."

To be ready for life's one certainty, i.e., its earthly end, should surely be our priority. Yes, God's creative grandeur extended even to its finale, when life, recreated in resurrection splendor, was to be the triumphant culmination of the Creator's plan. May each of our readers choose well as they travel that "little gleam of time between two eternities."

NOTES

ONE

1. Jeremy Manier, "Scientists Are Split on Whether Lunar Base Is Too Ambitious," *Chicago Tribune*, January 7, 2007, http://www.redorbit.com/news/space/791549/ scientists_are_split_on_whether _lunar_base_is_too_ ambitious/index.html.

2. Ibid.

3. Mortimer J. Adler, *The Difference of Man, and the Difference It Makes* (New York: Fordham University Press, 1967).

4. Richard Dawkins, *The Selfish Gene,* 30th Anniversary ed. (New York: Oxford University Press, 2006), 1.

5. Stephen Hawking, *A Brief History of Time: From the Big Bang to Black Holes* (New York: Bantam Books, 1988), 190.

6. Erwin Schrödinger, cited in *Quantum Questions*, ed. Ken Wilber (Boston: New Science Library, 1984), 81, 83.

7. Dawkins, *Selfish Gene*, 1.

8. John Lennox, *God's Undertaker: Has Science Buried God?* (Oxford: Lion Hudson, 2007), 40-41.

9. Robert L. Trivers, Foreword to Dawkins, *Selfish Gene.*

10. John C. Sanford, *Genetic Entropy: The Mystery of the Genome*, (Lima, NY: Elam, 2005), 116-17.

11. Dawkins, *Selfish Gene*, 2.

12. "Mankind must colonise other planets to survive, says Hawking," *Mail Online*, December 1, 2006, http://www.dailymail.co.uk/sciencetech/article-419573/ Mankind-colonise-planets-survive-says-Hawking.html;jsessionid= 68E159A86C3F26E3AD61F227C599DA80.

13. *U.S. News & World Report*, Dec. 23, 1991. See also http://www.leaderu.com/real/ ri9501/bigbang2.html.

14. Wernher von Braun, "My Faith—A space-age scientist tells why he must believe in God," *American Weekly*, February 10, 1963.

15. Richard Dawkins, *The God Delusion* (Boston: Houghton Mifflin, 2006), 117-18.

16. Alicia Chang, "Online astronomers seek out new worlds," *USA Today.com*, January 15, 2007, http://www.usatoday.com/tech/science/space/2007-01-15-amateur -astronomers_x.htm.

17. Wayne Spencer, "Revelations in the Solar System," *Creation* 19 (3): 26-29, June 1997, http://www.answersingenesis.org/creation/v19/i3/solar.asp.

18. *NASA Facts*, "Origins Program," Jet Propulsion Laboratory, California Institute of Technology, Pasadena, CA, February 1997, http://www.jpl.nasa.gov/news/ fact_sheets/origins.pdf.

19. Richard A. Kerr, "The Solar System's New Diversity," *Science*, Vol. 265, September 2, 1994, 1360.

20. http://richarddawkins.net/quotes.

21. Von Braun, "My Faith."

22. Richard Dawkins/John Lennox, *The God Delusion Debate*, Birmingham, AL, 2007.

23. David Waters, "First Communion on the Moon," *Washington Post*, July 20, 2009, http://newsweek.washingtonpost.com/onfaith/undergod/2009/07/first _communion_on_the_moon.html?hpid=talkbox1.

TWO

1. "Dawkins, Darwin's Dangerous Disciple," Interview with Frank Miele, http:// tabish.freeshell.org/dawkint.html.

2. Francis Crick, *The Astonishing Hypothesis: The Scientific Search for the Soul* (New York: Simon & Schuster, 1994), 3.

3. Carl Sagan, cited in Dawkins, *God Delusion*, 47.

4. Dawkins, *God Delusion*, 366.

5. Richard Dawkins, video, *The Root of All Evil? Part 2: The Virus of Faith*, http:// evomech5.blogspot.com/2006/10/richard-dawkins-root-of-all-evil-virus.html.

6. 1 Corinthians 15:32.

7. Adler, *Difference*.

8. Dawkins, video *Root of All Evil*.

9. Richard Dawkins, "An Atheist's Call to Arms," at TED (Technology, Entertainment, Design) conference, February 2002, http://www.youtube.com/ watch?v=VxGMqKCcN6A.

10. Isaiah 14:14.

11. Romans 2:14-15.

12. Dawkins, *God Delusion*, 68.

13. Dawkins/Lennox Debate, 2007.

14. http://www.highbeam.com/doc/1G1-193898952.html; Rama Singh, "Evolution is a fact, not just a theory," *The Hamilton Spectator,* February 18, 2009, http://www.thespec.com/article/515412; Nancy Sherer, "Evolution is the fact...how it works is the theory," *The Evolution Primer* (Salmon River, 2004), http://salmonriver.com/lightscience/evolution2.html; et al.

15. "A Scientific Dissent from Darwinism," www.discovery.org.

16. Frank Newport, "Third of Americans Say Evidence Has Supported Darwin's Evolution Theory," *Gallup.com*, November 19, 2004, http://www.gallup.com/poll/14107/third-americans-say-evidence-has-supported-darwins-evolution-theory.aspx.

17. James Owen, "Evolution Less Accepted in U.S. Than Other Western Countries, Study Finds," *nationalgeographic.com*, August 10, 2006, http://news.nationalgeographic.com/news/2006/08/060810-evolution.html.

18. Dawkins, "Atheist's Call to Arms."

19. Ibid.

20. Richard Dawkins, *The Blind Watchmaker: Why the Evidence of Evolution Reveals a Universe Without Design* (New York: W. W. Norton, 1996), 10.

21. Albert Einstein, 1954, from *Albert Einstein: The Human Side*, ed. Helen Dukas and Banesh Hoffman (Princeton University Press, 1981).

22. Dawkins, *Selfish Gene.*

23. Colin Patterson, in a letter to Luther D. Sunderland, 4/10/79, quoted in Luther D. Sunderland, *Darwin's Enigma: Ebbing the Tide of Naturalism* (San Diego: Master Books, 1988), 89.

24. Richard Lewontin, "Billions and Billions of Demons," *New York Review*, January 9, 1997, 31.

25. http://www.richarddawkins.net/quotes#41.

26. Romans 1:21-23.

27. *Science Digest*, November 1981, 39.

28. Carl Sagan, *Cosmos* (Random House, 1980), 243.

THREE

1. Michael D. Lemonick and Andrea Dorfman, "Ardi Is a New Piece for the Evolution Puzzle," *Time*, October 1, 2009.

2. Stephen Jay Gould, "Evolution's Erratic Pace," *Natural History* 86, May 1977, 14.

3. Trivers, in Dawkins, *Selfish Gene*, xix.

4. http://www.richarddawkins.net/quotes#42.

5. Dawkins, *God Delusion*, 163.

6. Dawkins, *Selfish Gene,* 22-23.

7. James H. Marden, "How Insects Learned to Fly," *The Sciences*, November-December, 1995.

8. Richard Dawkins, *Climbing Mount Improbable* (New York: W. W. Norton, 1996), 113-14.

9. Dawkins, *Watchmaker*, 4.

10. Ibid., Preface, xviii.

11. Ibid., 29.

12. Richard Dawkins, *A Devil's Chaplain: Reflections on Hope, Lies, Science, and Love* (New York: W. W. Norton, 2003) 10.

13. *New Scientist*, September 17, 2005, 33.

14. Richard Dawkins, in John Maynard Smith, *The Theory of Evolution*, Foreword, (2000), xvi, http://bevets.com/equotesd3.htm.

15. Dawkins, *God Delusion*, 123.

16. Dawkins, *Devil's Chaplain*, 248.

17. Dawkins, *Selfish Gene*, 192-93.

18. Ibid., 24.

19. Richard Dawkins, "Why Darwin Matters," *guardian.co.uk*, February 9, 2008, http://www.guardian.co.uk/science/2008/feb/09/darwin.dawkins1.

20. George Wald, "The Origin of Life," *Scientific American*, Vol. 190, August 1954, 46.

21. Dawkins, *Selfish Gene*, 24.

22. Dawkins, "Why Darwin Matters."

23. Dawkins, *God Delusion*, 73.

24. Ibid., 114.

25. Dawkins, *Watchmaker*, Preface, xviii.

FOUR

1. George Wald, "A Generation in Search of a Future," March 4, 1969 at an antiwar teach-in at MIT.

2. Dawkins, *Mount Improbable*, 326.

3. Francis Collins, *The Language of God: A Scientist Presents Evidence for Belief* (New York: Free Press, 2006), 136-39.

4. Ibid.

5. Ibid., 137.

6. Ibid., 104.

7. Dawkins, *Selfish Gene*, 22.

8. Christopher Hitchens, in his debate with Rabbi Shmuley Boteach (disciple of now deceased Lubavitch leader, Rabbi Menachem Mendel Schneerson), January 30, 2008.

9. Stephen Jay Gould, "Nonoverlapping Magisteria," *Natural History* 106, March 1997, 16-22.

10. Albert Einstein, cited in *Quantum Questions*, ed. Ken Wilber, 5.

11. Victor Aksiuchitz, "Theomachy of Leninism," *Pravoslavie.ru*, December 30, 2003, http://www.pravoslavie.ru/enarticles/031230131852.

12. Dawkins/Lennox Debate, 2007.

13. C. S. Lewis, *They Asked for a Paper: Papers and Addresses* (London: Geoffrey Bles,1962).

14. Genesis 2:7.

15. Genesis 3:19.

16. Genesis 2:19.

17. Genesis 2:7.

18. A. S. Eddington, *Science and the Unseen World* (New York: Macmillan, 1929), 49.

19. Ibid., 53-54.

20. Ibid., 57-58.

21. Robert Roy Britt, "Big Bang Theory Warmed by Ancient Heat Discovery," *Space.com*, December 20, 2000, http://www.space.com/scienceastronomy/astronomy/space_heat_001220.htm.

22. Paul Davies and John Gribbon, *The Matter Myth* (New York: Simon & Schuster, 1992), 14.

23. Ibid., 13.

24. Dawkins, *Selfish Gene*, 13.

25. Dawkins/Lennox Debate, 2007.

26. Massimo Pigliucci "Where do we come from?: a humbling look at the biology of life's origin," *Skeptical Inquirer*, September/October 1999.

27. Ibid.

28. Brig Klyce, "The Second Law of Thermodynamics," *Cosmic Ancestry*, http://www.panspermia.org/seconlaw.htm.

29. Dawkins, *Watchmaker*, 1.

30. Dawkins, *Selfish Gene*, 23.

31. Mark I. Vuletic, "Frequently Encountered Criticisms in Evolution vs. Creationism," November 19, 1997, http://www.holysmoke.org/cretins/refute.htm.

32. Robert Jastrow, *Los Angeles Times*, June 25, 1978, Part VI, 1, 6.

33. *Arizona Daily Sun*, Flagstaff, AZ, July 17, 1997, 6, "Letters to the Editor."

34. Mary Long, "Visions of a New Faith," *Science Digest*, November 1981, 39.

35. Colin Patterson, from transcript of 1981 presentation, "Can You Tell Me Anything About Evolution?" available at http://www.arn.org/arnproducts/audios/c010.htm, Item #C010.

36. Richard Carrier, from *The Argument from Biogenesis: Probabilities against a Natural Origin of Life*, addendum B: Are the Odds Against the Origin of Life Too Great to Accept?, November 2004, http://www.infidels.org/library/modern/richard_carrier/addendaB.html.

37. Max Planck, "The Mystery of Our Being," in *Quantum Questions*, ed. Wilber, 153.

38. George Wald, "The Cosmology of Life and Mind," Los Alamos Fellows Colloquium, 1988.

39. Lewontin, "Billions."

40. Collins, *Language*, 164.

41. J.W.N. Sullivan, *The Limitations of Science*, (New York: Viking Press, 1933), 94.

42. Pigliucci, "Where?"

43. Ibid.

44. Michael Bumbulis, "Christianity and the Birth of Science," Lambert Dolphin's Library, November 24, 1996, http://www.ldolphin.org/bumbulis/.

45. Ibid.

46. Ibid.

47. *U.S. News & World Report*, Dec. 23, 1991. See also http://www.leaderu.com/real/ri9501/bigbang2.html.

48. Signed affidavit presented to the court in Edwards v. Aguillard, United States District Court, E 11-12.

49. Dan Cray, "God vs. Science," *Time*, November 5, 2006, reprinted as "God vs. science: Can religion stand up to the test?" *CNN.com*, November 5, 2006, http://www.cnn.com/2006/US/11/05/cover.story/index.html?eref=rss_topstories.

50. Charles Colson, "The Nobel Scientists: What They Say About God," *Breakpoint.org*, October 13, 2000, http:/www.breakpoint.org/commentaries/3463-the-nobel-scientists.

51. Crick, *Astonishing*, 265-68.

52. Dawkins, *Selfish Gene*, 322.

53. Lewontin, "Billions."

FIVE

1. Dawkins, *Watchmaker*, 337.

2. Friedrich Engels, cited in Lennox, *God's Undertaker*, 66.

3. Hawking, *Brief History*, 46, cited in Lennox, *God's Undertaker*, 66.

4. A. S. Eddington, "The End of the World from the Standpoint of Mathematical Physics," *Nature*, 127 (1931), 450, cited in Lennox, *God's Undertaker*, 66.

5. Lennox, *God's Undertaker*, 66.

6. Dawkins/Lennox Debate, 2007.

7. Dawkins, *God Delusion*, 137.

8. A. S. Eddington, *The Nature of the Physical World* (New York: Macmillan, 1929), 282.

9. Sir James Jeans, *The Mysterious Universe* (Cambridge: Cambridge University Press, 1931), 111.

10. Karl Popper, *Unended Quest* (Glasgow: Fontana, 1976), 151.

11. Lennox, *God's Undertaker*, 71.

12. Dawkins/Lennox Debate, 2007.

13. Willis W. Harman & Elisabet Sahtouris, *Biology Revisioned* (Berkeley, California: North Atlantic Books, 1998), xv, 2, 3, 39-40, 64, 75, 102-3, 111, 113, 114, 116, 121, 136, 225.

14. Christopher Hitchens, *God Is Not Great: How Religion Poisons Everything* (New York: Hachette Book Group USA, 2007), index.

15. Kenneth R. Miller, *Finding Darwin's God: A Scientist's Search for Common Ground Between God and Evolution* (New York: Harper Perennial, 1999), 48-53.

16. Ibid., 54-55.

17. Hebrews 11:3.

18. John M. Cimbala, essay in *In Six Days: Why Fifty Scientists Choose to Believe in Creation*, ed. John F. Ashton (Sydney: New Holland, 1999), 184-85.

19. Charles Templeton, *Farewell to God* (Toronto: McClelland & Stewart, 1996), 4-5.

20. Ibid., 6.

21. Ibid., 7.

22. Ibid., 11-12.

23. Exodus 3:14.

24. Genesis 2:4.

25. Acts 17:24-30.

26. Gary Wolf, "The Church of the Non-Believers," *Wired*, November 2006, 182-93.

27. Sanford, *Genetic Entropy*, 151.

28. Simon Greenleaf, *The Testimony of the Evangelists* (Grand Rapids, MI: Kregel, 1995).

29. http://www.dissentfromdarwin.org/links.php.

30. BBC Interview with Richard Dawkins, "Richard Dawkins on Richard Dawkins," February 14, 2009, http://news.bbc.co.uk/go/pr/fr/-/2/hi/science/nature/7885670.stm.

31. Wolf, "Church of Non-Believers," 182-93.

32. 1 Timothy 6:20.

33. Wolf, "Church of Non-Believers," 186.

34. Robert Jastrow, *God and the Astronomers* (New York: W. W. Norton, 1992), 107.

35. *The Renovaré Spiritual Formation Bible*, New Revised Standard Version, ed. Richard J. Foster (San Francisco: HarperSanFrancisco, 2005), 13-15.

36. Isaiah 36:6.

37. "Message from Professor Robert Jastrow," (Board of Directors), *Truth Journal*, updated July 14, 2002, http://www.leaderu.com/truth/1truth18b.html.

38. Pigliucci, "Where?"

39. Ibid.

40. Ibid.

41. Stephen Hawking, "The Edge of Spacetime," an essay in *The New Physics*, ed. Paul Davies (Cambridge University Press, 2000), 68-69.

42. Romans 8:2.

43. Collins, *Language*, 89-91.

44. Genesis 1:27; 2:7.

45. Collins, *Language*, 90.

46. J.B.S. Haldane, *Possible Worlds* (London: Chatto & Windus, 1927), 209.

47. Charles Darwin, "From His Autobiography," http://skeptically.org/thinkersonreligion/id17.html.

48. C. S. Lewis, *God In the Dock* (Grand Rapids, MI: Eerdmans, 1970), 52-53.

49. James Perloff, *Tornado in a Junkyard: The Relentless Myth of Darwinism* (Arlington, MA: Refuge Books, 2000), 274.

SIX

1. Jonathan Sarfati, *Refuting Compromise* (Green Forest, AR: Master Books, 2004), 164.

2. C. S. Lewis addressing the Oxford Socratic Club in 1943.

3. Massimo Pigliucci, *Denying Evolution: Creationism, Scientism, and the Nature of Science* (Sunderland, MA: Sinauer Associates, 2002), 209.

4. Dawkins, *Selfish Gene*, 22.

5. Sanford, *Genetic Entropy*, V.

6. Ibid., 16.

7. Ibid., 17-18.

8. Collins, *Language*, 132.

9. Ibid., 131.

10. Ibid., 132.

11. Genesis 1:3.

12. Genesis 1:26-27.

13. Patterson, letter to Sunderland, quoted in Sunderland, *Darwin's Enigma*, 89.

14. Stephen Jay Gould, "Evolution's Erratic Pace," *Natural History*, Vol. 86, May 1977, 12, 14.

15. Stephen Jay Gould, "Is a New and General Theory of Evolution Emerging?" *Paleobiology*, Vol. 6, No. 1, 1980, p. 127.

16. Perry Marshall, "If You Can Read This, I Can Prove God Exists: Language, Information, and Naturalism vs. Intelligent Design," http://www.cosmic fingerprints.com/ifyoucanreadthis1.htm, Perry Marshall's talk at Willow Creek Truthquest, South Barrington, Illinois, June 3, 2005.

17. Ibid.

18. Ibid.

19. Dawkins, *Devil's Chaplain*, 91-103.

20. Dawkins, *Watchmaker*, 164.

21. Royal Truman, "The Problem of Information for the Theory of Evolution: Has Dawkins really solved it?" *True Origin Archive*, 1999, http://www.trueorigin.org/dawkinfo.asp.

22. Theodore Roszak, *Unfinished Animal* (Harper and Row, 1975), 101-2.

23. Francis Darwin, ed., *Life and Letters of Charles Darwin*, vol. 1 (New York: D. Appleton, 1887), 282; cited in Miller, *Darwin's God*, 287.

24. Quoted by Charles Colson in "The Nobel Scientists," http://www.breakpoint.org/commentaries/3463-the-nobel-scientists.

25. Phillip E. Johnson, *Defeating Darwinism by Opening Minds* (Downers Grove, IL: InterVarsity Press, 1997), 81-82.

26. Ibid., 70.

27. Albert Einstein, cited in an essay by John R. Baumgardner in *In Six Days*, 211.

28. Baumgardner, *In Six Days*, 211.

29. Jerry R. Bergman, essay in *In Six Days*, 17-20.

30. Edmund R. Leach, "Men, Bishops and Apes," *Nature* 293, September 3, 1981, 20.

31. Steven M. Stanley, *Macroevolution: Pattern and Process* (San Francisco: W. H. Freeman, 1979), 39.

32. Nils Heribert-Nilsson, *Synthetische Artbildung* (*The Synthetic Origin of Species*) (1953), 1212.

33. Charles Darwin, *The Life and Letters of Charles Darwin*, Vol 2., ed. Francis Darwin (New York: D. Appleton and Co., 1899), 66-67.

34. Riccardo Levi-Setti, *Trilobites*, 2nd edition (Chicago: University of Chicago Press, 1993), 29-74; cited in Walt Brown, *In the Beginning: Compelling Evidence for Creation and the Flood*, Eighth ed., (Phoenix, AZ: Center for Scientific Creation, 2008), 54.

35. Stephen Jay Gould, "The Return of Hopeful Monsters," *Natural History* 86, June/July 1977, 24.

36. Stephen Jay Gould, "The Ediacaran Experiment," *Natural History*, February 1984, 22-23.

37. Robert Lee Hotz, "A Lens into Nature's Gifts: A Starfish Grows Tiny Crystals that far Outperform Synthetic Optics Yielding a Design Breakthrough," *Los Angeles Times*, November 12, 2001, http://articles.latimes.com/2001/nov/12/news/mn -3365.

38. Gertrude Himmelfarb, *Darwin and the Darwinian Revolution* (Garden City, NY: Doubleday, 1959), 320-21.

39. Charles Darwin, *The Origin of Species* (1872; reprint, New York: Random House, 1993), 227.

40. Perloff, *Tornado*, 25.

41. Genesis 1:4, 10, 12, 18, 21, 25, 31.

SEVEN

1. Richard Dawkins, *The Big Question: Why Are We Here?* http://www.livevideo .com/video/9230F15FCF8942449FE109E91C99F47A/richard-dawkins-the -big-question-why-are-we-here-.aspx.

2. Psalm 8:4.

3. John 4:24.

4. Psalm 8 deals profoundly with this most important question.

5. John 19:5.

6. Matthew 16:26.

7. 1 John 2:17.

8. Ecclesiastes 12:1.

9. Dawkins, *Selfish Gene*, 1.

10. Cicero, *On the Nature of the Gods*, trans. Horace McGregor (Harmondsworth, England: Penguin Books, 1972), 144-45.

11. Reported by Clive Cookson, "Scientists Who Glimpsed 'God,'" *Financial Times*, April 29, 1995, 20.

12. Dawkins/Lennox Debate, 2007.

13. See statement by Schrödinger in chapter 13, p. 361.

14. Dawkins, *Selfish Gene*, 22-23.

15. Richard Dawkins, *The Greatest Show on Earth* (New York: Free Press, 2009), 214-15.

16. Hawking, *Brief History*, 190.

17. Jastrow, http://www.leaderu.com/truth/1truth18b.html.

18. Dawkins, *God Delusion*, 58.

19. Ibid.

20. Margaret Geller, cited in Michael D. Lemonick, "Big Bang Under Fire," *Time*, September 2, 1991.

21. Pigliucci, "Where?"

22. Daniel C. Dennett, *Darwin's Dangerous Idea: Evolution and the Meaning of Life* (New York: Simon & Schuster, 1995), 25.

23. Ibid., 520.

24. Jim Holt, *Wall Street Journal*, praising Daniel Dennett on the back cover of *Darwin's Dangerous Idea*.

25. Dennett, *Dangerous*, 62-63.

26. Ibid., 62.

27. The idea that life on earth can be explained by postulating an infinite number of universes, and out of all of those, surely chance would allow one to have life on it, and, of course, that turned out to be Earth.

28. Dennis Scania, cited in "The Fine Tuning of the Universe," Rabbi Mordechai Steinman, *SimpletoRemember.com*, http://www.simpletoremember.com/articles/a/creatorfacts/.

29. Richard Swinburne, *Evolution*, 2nd ed. (London: Natural History Museum, 1999), 120.

30. The principle states that "Entities should not be multiplied unnecessarily." Many scientists have adopted or reinvented Occam's Razor, as in Leibniz's "identity of observables," and Isaac Newton stated the rule: "We are to admit no more causes of natural things than such as are both true and sufficient to explain their appearances." The most useful statement of the principle for scientists is "when you have two competing theories that make exactly the same predictions, the simpler one is the better." — http://math.ucr.edu/home/baez/physics/General/occam.html.

31. Cited in Lennox, *God's Undertaker*, 73.

32. Steven Weinberg, cited in "Fine Tuning."

33. Ibid.

34. Ibid.

35. Roger Penrose, cited in "Fine Tuning."

36. Hawking, *Brief History*, 131.

37. Pigliucci, "Where?"

38. Ibid.

39. E. O. Wilson, *On Human Nature* (Cambridge, MA: Harvard University Press, 1978), 192.

40. Deuteronomy 6:5.

41. Mark 7:6.

42. Genesis 1:31.

43. Dawkins, *Selfish Gene*, 14-15.

44. Ibid., 15.

45. Romans 1:21-25.

46. Peter R. Breggin, M.D. and David Cohen, Ph.D., *Your Drug May Be Your Problem: How and Why to Stop Taking Psychiatric Medications* (Cambridge, MA: Perseus, 1999), 10.

47. Ibid., 35.

48. Ibid., 41.

EIGHT

1. Richard Dawkins, "Lecture from 'The Nullifidian,'" *RichardDawkins.net*, May 11, 2006, http://richarddawkins.net/articles/89.

2. Richard Carrier, *Sense and Goodness Without God: A Defense of Metaphysical Naturalism* (Bloomington, IN: AuthorHouse, 2005), 74.

3. Bergman, *In Six Days*, 15-21.

4. Dawkins, *God Delusion*, 361.

5. Pierre Teilhard de Chardin, *How I Believe* (Harper Collins, 1969).

6. Paul Davies, *The Edge of Infinity* (New York: Simon & Schuster, 1981), 161.

7. Lemonick, "Big Bang Under Fire."

8. Ron Cowen, "Starlight Casts Doubt on Big Bang Details," *Science News*, Vol. 140, Sep. 7, 1991, 151.

9. Hannés Alfven, cited in Eric J. Lerner, "The Big Bang Never Happened," *Discover* 9 (June 1988), 78.

10. Malcolm Longair. "The new astrophysics," essay in *New Physics*, ed. Davies, 201.

11. Chris Isham, "Quantum Gravity," essay in *New Physics*, ed. Davies, 92-93.

12. "The Electric Universe," October 29, 2006, http://www.holoscience.com/news.php?article=d4fsrk24.

13. Ibid.

14. Ben Patrusky, "Why is the Cosmos 'Lumpy'?" *Science*, June 1981, 96.

15. Ibid.

16. Eric J. Lerner, "The Big Bang Never Happened," http://www.spaceandmotion
    .com/cosmology/lerner-big-bang-never-happened.htm.

17. James Trefil, *The Dark Side of the Universe* (New York: Charles Scribner's Sons,
    1988), 3.

18. Fred Hoyle, "The Big Bang Under Attack," *Science Digest*, May 1984, 84.

19. Ivars Peterson, "Seeding the Universe," cited in Brown, *Beginning*.

20. William R. Corliss, *Stars, Galaxies, Cosmos: A Catalog of Astronomical Anomalies*
    (Glen Arm, MD: Sourcebook Project, 1987), 177.

21. Collins, *Language*, 89.

22. Brown, *Beginning*, 88.

23. Robert Matthews, "Spoiling a Universal 'Fudge Factor,'" *Science*, Vol 265, August
    5, 1994, 740-41.

24. Michael Denton, *Evolution: A Theory in Crisis* (Chevy Chase, MD: Adler & Adler,
    1986), 342.

25. Keith H. Wanser, essay in *In Six Days*, 93.

26. Sarfati, *Refuting*, 160.

27. *New Scientist*, 157 (2120): 26-30 (February 7, 1998).

28. Professor J. Richard Bond, cited in Dennis Overbye, "In the beginning . . . ,"
    NYTimes.com, July 23, 2002.

29. Charles J. Lada and Frank H. Shu, "The Formation of Sunlike Stars," *Science*, Vol.
    248, May 4, 1990, 564.

30. *Creation*, September-November, 1997, 42-44.

31. Sarfati, *Refuting*, 166-67.

32. "Deepest Infrared View of the Universe: VLT Images Progenitors of Today's Large
    Galaxies," http://www.eso.org/public/news/eso0234/.

33. Trefil, *Dark Side*, 3, 55.

34. Sarfati, *Refuting*, 163.

35. Roy C. Martin, Jr., *Astronomy on Trial: A Devastating and Complete Repudiation of
    the Big Bang Fiasco* (New York: University Press of America, 1999), xv.

36. Brown, *Beginning*, 89.

37. "Bedeviling Devil's Advocate Cosmology," *Chandra Chronicles*, updated March 27,
    2008, http://chandra.harvard.edu/chronicle/0306/devil/.

38. "Scientists Examine 'Dark Energy' of Antigravity," *New York Times*, November 16,
    2006.

39. Sarfati, *Refuting*, 169.

40. Ibid.

41. "The Big Bang Never Happened," report on Pavis Workshop, First Crisis in
    Cosmology Conference, CCC-I, Monçao, Portugal, June 23-25, 2005, http://
    bigbangneverhappened.org/p17.htm.

42. "Electric Universe," http://www.holoscience.com/news.php?article=d4fsrk24.

43. Hawking, *Brief History*, 191.

44. Stephen Hawking, *Black Holes and Baby Universes and Other Essays* (New York: BantamBooks, 1994), 159.

NINE

1. Dawkins, *Selfish Gene*, 22.

2. Albert Einstein, "Remarks on Bertrand Russell's Theory of Knowledge," in *The Philosophy of Bertrand Russell*, P. A. Schilpp, ed. (Tudor Publications, 1944), 290; J. W. Oller, Jr., *Language and Experience: Classic Pragmatism* (University Press of America, 1989), 25.

3. Collins, *Language*, 124-25.

4. Wallace Ravven, "Antenna on Cell Surface Is Key to Development and Disease," *New York Times*, May 19, 2009.

5. Collins, *Language*, 125.

6. Sanford, *Genetic Entropy*, 28.

7. Thomas Jefferson, cited in Dawkins, *God Delusion*, 42.

8. Oller, *Classic Pragmatism*, 25.

9. Andrew McIntosh, essay in *In Six Days*, 144-46.

10. Collins, *Language*, 123-24.

11. President Bill Clinton, cited in Nancy Pearcey, "Copying the Human Script: Genome Project Raises Hopes, Fears," *World*, July 8, 2000.

12. Richard Dawkins, "Genetics: Why Prince Charles Is So Wrong," Checkbiotech .org, January 28, 2003.

13. Antony Flew, *There Is A God: How the World's Most Notorious Atheist Changed His Mind* (New York: HarperOne, 2007), 75.

14. Richard Carrier Blogs, November 6, 2007, http://richardcarrier.blogspot .com/2007/11/antony-flew-bogus-book.html.

15. Dawkins, *Selfish Gene*, 23.

16. Collins, *Language*, 81-82.

17. Dawkins, *God Delusion*, 19.

18. Ibid.

19. Sanford, *Genetic Entropy*, 124.

20. Crick, *Astonishing*, 81.

21. Dawkins, *Watchmaker*, 4.

22. Dawkins, *God Delusion*, 73.

23. Dawkins, *Selfish Gene*, 13.

24. Ibid., 50.

25. Dawkins, *Watchmaker*, 27.

26. Ecclesiastes 11:5 (977 BC).

27. Dennett, *Dangerous*, 20.

28. http://www.dissentfromdarwin.org.

29. Nancy M. Darrall, essay in *In Six Days*, 174.

30. Lee Spetner, *Not by Chance: Shattering the Modern Theory of Evolution* (New York: Judaica Press, 1997).

31. Sarfati, *Refuting*, 228.

32. Gerald A. Kerkut, *Implications of Evolution* (Oxford: Pergamon Press, 1960), 157.

33. James S. Allan, essay in *In Six Days*, 114-19.

34. Dennett, *Dangerous*, 42-43.

35. Stephen Grocott, essay in *In Six Days*, 135-36.

36. Timothy G. Standish, essay in *In Six Days*, 103.

37. Dennett, *Dangerous*, 21, 23.

TEN

1. Dawkins/Lennox Debate, 2007; Richard Dawkins, Steve Jones, and Lewis Wolport: Public Debate on Complexity vs. Evolution.

2. Dawkins, *Watchmaker*, Preface, xviii.

3. Dawkins, *God Delusion*, 137.

4. Ibid., 137-39.

5. Ibid., 137.

6. Baumgardner, *In Six Days*, 207-8.

7. Genesis 1:31.

8. Dawkins/Lennox Debate, 2007.

9. Dawkins, *God Delusion*, 46.

10. Ibid., 51, 113, etc.

11. Denis Brian, *Einstein: A Life* (New York: Wiley, 1996), 186.

12. Albert Einstein, cited in Dawkins, *God Delusion*.

13. Sanford, *Genetic Entropy*, 3-4.

14. Collins, *Language*, 99.

15. Ibid., 135.

16. Ibid., 100.

17. Ibid., 102-3.

18. Ibid., 104.

19. Ker C. Thomson, essay in *In Six Days*, 199-200.

20. Sanford, *Genetic Entropy*, 143-44.

21. "What's the Difference Between Mice and Men?" *ScienceDaily.com*, November 14, 2006, http://www.sciencedaily.com/releases/2006/11/061113180424.htm.

22. Collins, *Language*, 133.

23. Ibid., 132-33.

24. Ibid., 132.

25. John F. Stover, *History of the Baltimore and Ohio Railroad* (West Lafayette, IN: Purdue University Press, 1987, ISBN 0-911198-81-4), 59–60. The message was sent from the Old Supreme Court Chambers in the capitol in Washington, D.C. to the Old Mt. Clare Depot in Baltimore. This message was chosen by Annie Ellsworth of Lafayette, IN, later Mrs. Roswell-Smith (Roswell, NM, was named after her husband), the daughter of Patent Commissioner Henry Leavitt Ellsworth.

26. Dawkins, *Watchmaker*, 107-8.

27. Ibid., 107-10.

28. Lord Adrian, guest editorial, "The brain as physics," *Science Journal*, vol. 3, no. 5, May 1967, 3.

29. Cited by Chauncey D. Leake, "Perspectives in Adaptation: Historical Background" in *Handbook of Physiology* (Washington, D.C.: American Physiological Society. 1964), 5-6.

30. Lewontin, "Billions."

31. John Gliedman, "Scientists in Search of the Soul," *Science Digest*, July 1982, 78.

32. Wilder Penfield, cited in Herbert Benson, M.D., with William Proctor, *Your Maximum Mind* (Random House, 1987), 46.

ELEVEN

1. Dawkins, "Nullifidian," http://richarddawkins.net/articles/89.

2. Press release: "Free Dawkins DVD for all secondary schools to celebrate Darwin 200," July 8, 2009, http://www.politics.co.uk/opinion-formers/press-releases/education/free-dawkins-dvd-for-all-secondary-schools-to-celebrate-darwin-200-$1309876$365873.htm.

   * In fact, this DVD has already been distributed as promised. Richard Dawkins also has his own YouTube channel with the capability of presenting full-length episodes of his "Growing Up in the Universe" series, at no cost to the viewer.

3. Colin Patterson, cited in Stephen Jones, "Evolutionism and Creationism" November 5, 1981, 1.

4. Dr. Gary Parker, *Creation: Facts of Life* (Green Forest, AR: MasterBooks, 2007), 134.

5. Dawkins, *Watchmaker*, 337.

6. Collins, *Language*, 136-37.

7. Ibid., 137.

8. Ibid., 104.

9. Eric McLamb, "Earth's Beginnings: The Origin of Life,"*Ecology.com*, updated April 4, 2008, http://ecology.com/features/originsoflife/index.html.

10. Elizabeth Anne Viau, "The Evolution of Plants," http://www.world-builders.org/lessons/less/les8/Vles8r.html.

11. *The Columbia Electronic Encyclopedia*, 2007, Columbia University Press; http://www.infoplease.com/ce6/sci/A0857622.html.

12. Dawkins DVD series, *Growing Up in the Universe*.

13. "Candidates' Evolution Stand Stirs Heat," *ArcaMax.com*, May 14, 2007, http://www.arcamax.com/religiousnews/s-192706-112005.

14. Tom Ashbrook, Interview with Christopher Hitchens, May 11, 2007, http://www.onpointradio.org/2007/05/christopher-hitchens-on-religion.

TWELVE

1. "Galaxy has 'billions of Earths,'" *BBC News*, http://news.bbc.co.uk/2/hi/science/nature/7891132.stm.

2. Hitchens, *Not Great*, 84.

3. Cited in Dean Keith Simonton, *Origins of Genius* (Oxford: Oxford University Press, 1999), 134.

4. Dawkins, *God Delusion*, 157.

5. Albert Einstein, cited in Baumgardner, *In Six Days*, 211.

6. Oller, *Classic Pragmatism*, 25.

7. Martin Roberts, "Spanish parliament to extend rights to apes," *reuters.com*, June 25, 2008, http://www.reuters.com/article/scienceNews/idUSL256586320080625.

8. Collins, *Language*, 141.

9. Genesis 1:3, 6, 9, 11, 14, 20, 24, 26; Psalm 139:14, Hebrews 11:3a, etc.

10. Romans 5:12.

11. George Gaylord Simpson, *Tempo and Mode in Evolution* (New York: Columbia University Press, 1944), 107, cited in Brown, *Beginning*.

12. Brown, *Beginning*, 63.

13. Dr. Niles Eldredge, "Missing, Believed Nonexistent," cited in Brown, *Beginning*.

14. Collins, *Language*, 88.

15. Hawking, *Brief History*, 174.

16. John 1:3.

17. John 1:4.

18. Brown, *In the Beginning*, 29.

19. Romans 1:20-23.

20. http://www.wasdarwinright.com/adapt&mutate-f.htm.

21. Collins, *Language*, 18.

22. Ibid., 106-7.

23. Ibid., 81-82.

24. Lynn Barton, "Why intelligent design will change everything," *WND.com*, March 25, 2006, http://www.wnd.com/news/article.asp?ARTICLE_ID=49431.

25. Paul Davies, "How we could create life," *guardian.co.uk*, December 11, 2002, http://www.guardian.co.uk/education/2002/dec/11/highereducation.uk.

26. John 1:3-4.

27. Collins, *Language*, 104.

28. Ibid., 112-16.

29. "Scientists: True love can last a lifetime," *CNNhealth.com*, January 4, 2009, http://www.cnn.com/2009/HEALTH/01/04/true.love.found/index.html.

30. Matthew 22:35-40.

31. George Wald, MIT speech, 3/4/69 at an antiwar teach-in at MIT, "A Generation in Search of a Future."

THIRTEEN

1. Alister McGrath/Christopher Hitchens Debate, 2007.

2. Dawkins, *God Delusion*, 137.

3. John 4:24.

4. Steven Weinberg, *New York Times*, April 20, 1999.

5. Dawkins/Lennox Debate, 2007.

6. Sir John Eccles and Daniel N. Robinson, *The Wonder of Being Human: Our Brain and Our Mind* (Boston, MA: New Science Library, 1985), 71.

7. (AP) "24 Air Force Academy Cadets Admit Cheating on a Test," *FoxNews.com*, February 16, 2007, http://www.foxnews.com/story/0,2933,252341,00.html.

8. John 15:13.

9. Austin Bogues, "Parents Receive Medal of Honor for Soldier Killed in Iraq," *New York Times*, June 3, 2008, http://www.nytimes.com/2008/06/03/washington/02cnd-medal.html?ref=us.

10. Dawkins/Lennox Debate, 2007.

11. Dawkins, *Selfish Gene*, 193.

12. Eccles/Robinson, *Wonder*, 33.

13. Eccles, cited in : "Genesis of Eden, Fractal Neurodynamics and Quantum Chaos: Resolving the Mind-Brain Paradox Through Novel Biophysics," http://www.dhushara.com/book/paps/consc/brcons1.htm.

14. Penfield, cited in Benson/Proctor, *Maximum Mind*, 46.

15. Dawkins, *Selfish Gene*, 24.

16. Douglas Futuyma, "Natural Selection: How Evolution Works," *actionbioscience* *.org*, December 2004, http://www.actionbioscience.org/evolution/futuyma .html#fullbio.
17. Dawkins/Lennox Debate, 2007.
18. John 1:3.
19. Luke 12:15.
20. Dawkins/Lennox Debate, 2007.
21. Ibid.
22. Schrödinger, cited in *Quantum Questions*, ed. Wilber, 81, 83.
23. Michael Polanyi, *The Tacit Dimension* (New York: Anchor, 1967), 37; cited by Lawrence LeShan, *The Science of the Paranormal: The Last Frontier* (Wellingborough, U.K.: Aquarian Press, 1987), 80.
24. Eddington, *Unseen World*, 55.
25. Ecclesiastes 8:15; 1 Corinthians 15:32.
26. "B. F. Skinner, Behavioral Psychologist," http://www.sntp.net/behaviorism/ skinner.htm.

FOURTEEN

1. "A Conversation With Jonas Salk," *Psychology Today*, March 1983, 56.
2. Gould, "Magisteria."
3. C. S. Lewis, *The Oxford Socratic Club*, 1944, pp. 154-65.
4. Eccles/Robinson, *Wonder*, 43.
5. Charlie Butts, "APA revises 'gay gene' theory," *OneNewsNow.com*, May 14, 2009, http://www.onenewsnow.com/Culture/Default.aspx?id=528376; "Answers to Your Questions For a Better Understanding of Sexual Orientation & Homosexuality," p. 2, (downloadable report available at http://www.apa.org/topics/sorientation .html).
6. Sam Harris, *Letter to a Christian Nation* (New York: Alfred Knopf, 2006), viii.
7. Ibid., 24.
8. Ibid., 23-24.
9. Ibid., 24.
10. John Thomas Scopes, *World's Greatest Court Trial* (Cincinnati: National Book Co., 1925), 178-79, 182.
11. Harris, *Letter*, 24.
12. Ibid., 14-19.
13. Collins, *Language*, 20.
14. Ibid., 21.
15. Dwight D. Eisenhower, cited in Peter Berger, *Facing Up to Modernity: Excursions in Society, Politics, and Religion* (New York: Basic Books, 1977), 155.
16. From the Qur'an, Surahs 2:132; 4:157-58; 20:8,14,96; 21:107; and from the Hadith, Ishaq:324.

17. John 14:6.
18. Nancey Murphy, "Phillip Johnson on Trial: A Critique of His Critique of Darwin," *Perspectives on Science and Christian Faith* 45, no 1 (1993): 33.
19. Wolf, "Church of Non-Believers," 186.
20. Michael D. Lemonick, "What Makes Us Different?" *Time*, reprinted at *CNN.com*, October 1, 2006, http://www.time.com/time/magazine/article/0,9171,1541283-8,00.html.
21. Werner von Braun, cited in Henry M. Morris, *Men of Science—Men of God* (El Cajon, CA: Master Books, 1988), 85.

FIFTEEN

1. Dawkins, *God Delusion*, 73.
2. Stephen Jay Gould, "Impeaching a Self-Appointed Judge," *Scientific American* 267 (1992), 118-21.
3. Ecclesiastes 1:7.
4. Fritjof Capra, *The Web of Life* (New York: Anchor Books, 1996), 228.
5. Rebecca L. Cann et al., "Mitochondrial DNA and Human Evolution," *Nature*, Vol 325, 1 January 1987, 31-36; Ann Gibbons, "Calibrating the Mitochondrial Clock," *Science*, Vol 279, 2 January 1998, 29; cited in Brown, *Beginning*, 319-20.
6. Brown, *Beginning*, 322.
7. Kenneth Nahigian, "How I Walked Away," http://www.infidels.org/library/modern/testimonials/nahigian.html.
8. John Myers, "A Scopes Trial in Reverse," updated June 14, 2004, http://www.leaderu.com/real/ri9401/scopes.html.
9. Steve Meyer, "Danger: Indoctrination—A Scopes Trial for the '90s," *Wall Street Journal*, December 6, 1993.
10. Richard Carrier, "Bad Science, Worse Philosophy: The Quackery and Logic Chopping of David Foster's The Philosophical Scientists (2000)—Misrepresenting Darwinism," *Infidels.org*, http://www.infidels.org/library/modern/richard_carrier/foster8.html.
11. http://www.creationscience.com/onlinebook/LifeSciences45.html; Brown, *Beginning*, 19.
12. Ernst Boris Chain, cited by Charles Colson in "BreakPoint Commentaries," "Health & Science: The Nobel Scientists," http://www.bpnews.net/printerfriendly.asp?ID=6691.
13. http://www.infidels.org/library/modern/richard_carrier/foster8.html.
14. Patrick Glynn, *God the Evidence: The Reconciliation of Faith and Reason in a Postsecular World* (New York: Three Rivers Press, 1999), 22.
15. Ibid., 29-30.

SIXTEEN

1.   Dawkins, *God Delusion*, 77-78.

2.   Dawkins, *Selfish Gene*, 3.

3.   Jerry Coyne, cited in Dawkins, *God Delusion*, 134, fn 65.

4.   Dawkins, *God Delusion*, 134.

5.   Hitchens, *Not Great*, 233.

6.   Dawkins/Lennox Debate, 2007.

7.   Collins, *Language*, 165.

8.   *Life Times: Forum for a New Age*, Number 3, 48.

9.   Dawkins, *God Delusion*, 121.

10. Fred Hoyle, "The Big Bang in Astronomy," *New Scientist*, Vol 92, November 19, 1981, 526.

11. Hubert P. Yockey, *Information Theory and Molecular Biology* (Cambridge: Cambridge University Press, 1992), 257.

12. Bergman, *In Six Days*, 25, 26.

13. Baumgardner, *In Six Days,* 207-9.

14. Ibid., 210-11.

15. McIntosh, *In Six Days*, 146.

16. Genesis 1:11, 12, 21, 24, 25.

17. Grocott, *In Six Days*, 134.

18. Fred Hoyle, "The Nature of the Universe," Part IV, *Harper's*, March 1951, 65.

19. Harold Jeffreys, *The Earth: Its Origin, History, and Physical Constitution*, 6th ed. (Cambridge: Cambridge University Press, 1976), 387.

20. Brown, *Beginning*, 84.

21. Editorial, "The New Intolerance," *Christianity Today*, February 2007, http:// www.christianitytoday.com/ct/2007/february/17.24.html.

22. 2 Corinthians 3:17.

SEVENTEEN

1.   Dawkins, *God Delusion*, 253.

2.   Ibid., 252.

3.   Isaiah 53:5.

4.   Dawkins, *God Delusion*, 252.

5.   Ibid., 344.

6.   *The Chieftain* (Pueblo, CO, July 22, 1995), 4B.

7. Hitchens, *Not Great*, 1.

8. Ibid., 2.

9. The God of the Bible is 203 times identified as "the God of Israel," as the listing in any concordance reveals.

10. John 17:3.

11. 1 Corinthians 15:14-19.

12. Frank Morison, *Who Moved the Stone?* (Downer's Grove, IL: InterVarsity Press, 1969), 9–10.

13. Hitchens, *Not Great*, 110.

14. Ibid., 161-68.

15. Ibid., 155-58.

16. Ibid.,160.

17. Cited in Lennox, *God's Undertaker*, 8.

18. Beyond Belief Symposium: Science, Religion, Reason and Survival, Salk Institute, La Jolla, CA, November 5-7, 2006; http://goliath.ecnext.com/coms2/gi_0199 -6922273/Believing-in-God.html.

19. 2 Peter 1:16.

20. Hitchens, *Not Great*, 111.

21. Dawkins, *God Delusion*, 96-97.

22. Ibid., 120.

23. Genesis 1:26-27.

24. Excerpt taken from *In Defense of the Faith*, by Dave Hunt (Bend, OR: The Berean Call, 2009).

25. Revelation 19:7-9.

EIGHTEEN

1. Dawkins/Lennox Debate, 2007.

2. Hitchens, *Not Great*, 85.

3. Harris, *Letter*, 6.

4. Hitchens, *Not Great*, 17.

5. Wolf, "Church of Non-Believers."

6. Isaiah 7:14.

7. Sam Harrris, *The End of Faith: Religion, Terror, and the Future of Reason* (New York: W. W. Norton, 2004), 95.

8. Ibid., 58.

9. Isaiah 8:8.

10. Genesis 13:15, 17:8; 1 Chronicles 16:15-18, and many other places.

11. Isaiah 9:6-7.

12. For further references in the Hebrew Scriptures to the Son of God see Psalm 2:7, 12; Proverbs 30:4, etc.

13. John 10:30.

14. Micah 5:2.

15. Gary Lenaire, *An Infidel Manifesto: Why Sincere Believers Lose Faith* (Baltimore, MD: PublishAmerica, 2006), back cover.

16. Ibid., 120-21.

17. Jeremiah 31:35-36.

18. 2 Kings 13:22-23.

19. John 12:48; Prov 1:24-31.

20. Genesis 1.

21. Exodus 12:3-7; John 1:29.

22. Exodus 12:14: "And this day shall be unto you for a memorial; and ye shall keep it a feast to the LORD throughout your generations; ye shall keep it a feast by an ordinance for ever."

23. John 20:31.

24. Collins, *Language*, 41.

25. Surah 26:221-27; Dave Hunt, *Judgment Day* (Bend, OR: The Berean Call, 2005).

26. Collins, *Language*, 48.

27. Nancy Pearcey, *Total Truth: Liberating Christianity from Its Cultural Captivity* (Wheaton, IL: Crossway Books, 2005), 201.

28. Romans 1 and 2.

29. The Moscow Plan of Action of the Global Forum on Environment and Development for Human Survival, January 1990 (final draft), 12.

30. Cited in *Ground Zero* (C.T. Communications, Box 612, Gladstone, MB R0J 0T0, Canada, Oct./Nov., 1996), 8.

31. Mary B. W. Tabor for *New York Times News Service*, "Publishers spread wings with spiritual books, reap benefits," in *Daily Astorian*, August 11, 1995, 9A.

32. Andrew Heywood, *Political Ideologies* (New York: Macmillan, 2003).

33. 1 Corinthians 10:20: But I [say], that the things which the Gentiles sacrifice, they sacrifice to devils, and not to God: and I would not that ye should have fellowship with devils." Also Isaiah 44:19, 20.

34. C. S. Lewis, *The Screwtape Letters* (New York: Macmillan, 1976) 45-46.

35. Luke 19:43-44; Matthew 24:2.

36. Flavius Josephus, *The Complete Works of Josephus: "The Wars of the Jews,"* Book VI, chapter V, 2; Book VI, Chapter VI, 1.

37. Zechariah 12:2, 3.

38. Deuteronomy 28:15-68; 29:24-28; 30:17-20, etc.

39. For more information, see Genesis 12:3; 2 Samuel 7:8-16; Isaiah 9:6-7; Micah 5:2, etc.

40. Philip Hitti, cited in Eliyahu Tal, *Whose Jerusalem?* (Tel Aviv: International Forum for a United Jerusalem, 1994), 93.

41. *Jerusalem Post*, August 29, 2000.

42. Frank J. Gaffney Jr., "America's first Muslim president?" *Washington Times*, June 9, 2009.

NINETEEN

1. Deuteronomy 28:37, 64.

2. Jeremiah 29:18.

3. Jeremiah 30:7, 11.

4. Jeremiah 31:10.

5. Isaiah 53:3.

6. Genesis 3:15; 12:3; Isaiah 7:14; 9:6, etc.

7. Deuteronomy 28:37; Jeremiah 29:17-19, etc.

8. Deuteronomy 7:6.

9. Exodus 1:15-20.

10. The Book of Esther.

11. Numbers 24:17.

12. Micah 5:2.

13. Matthew 2:12.

14. Matthew 2:13-15.

15. Matthew 16:23.

16. John 13:27.

17. Genesis 3:15.

18. Hebrews 2:9.

19. 1 Peter 2:24.

20. Jeremiah 16:14-15.

21. Martin Gilbert, *The Holocaust* (Henry Holt, 1985), 29-30.

22. Cited in Joan Peters, *From Time Immemorial* (New York: J KAP, 1984), 363.

23. Genesis 12:3.

24. Interview on BBC, May 15, 1948.

25. Associated Press, August 12, 1990.

26. Meyrav Wurmser, *The Schools of Ba'athism: A Study of Syrian Textbooks* (MEMRI, 2000), iii.

27. *Al-Akhbar* (Egypt), April 18, 2001.

28. PA TV Broadcast, 11/29/00.

29. 2 Timothy 3:13.

30. Genesis 1:26, 27.

31. Isaiah 1:18.

32. John 8:34.

33. William Sampson, "How I survived chop chop square," *guardian.co.uk*, October 14, 2008, http://www.guardian.co.uk/commentisfree/2008/oct/14/saudiarabia -humanrights.

34. Luke 19:43-44.

35. Acts 13:27, 40-41.

36. Psalm 22:14-18, 27.

37. Matthew 26:5; Mark 14:2.

38. Mark 15:13, 14; Luke 23:21; John 19:6, 15.

39. Exodus 12:46.

40. Psalm 34:20.

41. Mark 15:44.

42. John 10:18.

43. Zechariah 12:10.

44. John 19:34-35.

45. Luke 23:46.

46. Surah 4:157-58.

47. 2 Samuel 7:4-17.

48. Isaiah 9:6-7.

49. Exodus 3:14-15.

TWENTY

1. Dawkins/Lennox Debate, 2007.

2. Dawkins, *God Delusion*, 143.

3. http://richarddawkins.net/quotes, #68.

4. "Basic Facts About the Criminal Justice System," Political Research Associates, May 2005, http://www.defendingjustice.org/pdfs/factsheets/7-Fact%20Sheet%20 -%20Basic%20Facts.pdf.

5. Psalm 14:1; 53:1.

6. http://richarddawkins.net/quotes, #83.

7. Hebrews 9:27.

8. Luke 16:19-31.

9. Revelation 1:14-17.

10. Pope John Paul II, "Message to Pontifical Academy of Sciences," *L'Osservatore Romano* (30 Oct. 1996), 3, 7.

11. Romans 5:12.

12. Judges 21:25.

13. Luke 24:25-27, 44; John 5:39, etc.

14. Erwin Schrödinger, *What Is Life?* (Cambridge: Cambridge University Press, 1967), 136-38.

15. Herbert Schlossberg, "Reenchanting the World," *Chronicles*, April 1987, 26.

16. Lee Smolin, cited in Dennis Overbye, "Physics awaits new options as Standard Model idles," *Symmetry*, vol 03, issue 06, August 06.

17. Peter Medawar, *Advice to a Young Scientist* (London: Harper and Row, 1979), 31; also Peter Medawar, *The Limits of Science* (Oxford: Oxford University Press, 1984), 66.

18. Lennox, *God's Undertaker*, 41.

19. Breggin/Cohen, *Your Drug*, 4.

20. Ibid., 3-4.

21. Richard Dawkins, Foreword to *The Theory of Evolution* by John Maynard Smith (2000), xvi.

22. Crick, *Astonishing*, 3.

23. Dawkins, *Selfish Gene*, 23.

24. Ibid.

25. Dawkins, *Mount Improbable*, 272.

26. Dawkins/Lennox Debate, 2007.

27. Ecclesiastes 12:7.

28. Psalm 51:4.

29. Luke 23:34.

30. Harris, *Letter*, 8.

31. The stoning at God's command of a man for gathering sticks on the Sabbath, Numbers 15:32-36.

32. For example, the sudden death of Ananias and Sapphira for lying to God, Acts 5:1-11.

33. Jeans, *Mysterious*, 147-58.

34. *Time*, January 13, 1997, 57.

35. Genesis 1:26.

36. *Renovaré Bible*, ed. Foster, 14-15.

37. *American Atheist* (1978), 19 as cited in *Christian News*, November 11, 1996, 15.

38. Dawkins/Lennox Debate, 2007.

39. Eddington, *Unseen World*, 81.

40. Ibid., 72-74.

41. Ibid., 70.

42. Ibid., 68.

43. Ibid., 60-61.

44. Ibid., 58.

45. Ibid., 44.

46. Ibid., 43.

47. Ibid., 33.

48. Bertrand Russell, "A Free Man's Worship," from the 1929 U.S. edition (pp. 46-57) of *Mysticism and Logic* (London, 1918), http://www.positiveatheism.org/hist/russell1.htm.

49. Ecclesiastes 1:1-4.

50. Proverbs 27:1.

SELECTED
BIBLIOGRAPHY

Adler, Mortimer J. *The Difference of Man and the Difference It Makes*. New York: Fordham University Press, 1967.

Allan, James S. Untitled essay in *In Six Days: Why Fifty Scientists Choose to Believe in Creation*, edited by John F. Ashton. Sydney: New Holland, 1999.

Ashton, John F., with Michael Westicott. *The Big Argument: Does God Exist?* Green Forest, AR: Master Books, 2005.

———, ed. *In Six Days: Why Fifty Scientists Choose to Believe in Creation*. Sydney: New Holland, 1999.

———, ed. *On the Seventh Day: Forty Scientists and Academics Explain Why They Believe in God*. Green Forest, AR: Master Books, 2002.

Baumgardner, John R. Untitled essay in *In Six Days: Why Fifty Scientists Choose to Believe in Creation*, edited by John F. Ashton. Sydney: New Holland, 1999.

Beauregard, Mario and Denyse O' Leary. *The Spiritual Brain: A Neuroscientist's Case for the Existence of the Soul*. New York: HarperCollins, 2007.

Behe, Michael J. *Darwin's Black Box*. New York: Free Press, 1996.

———. *The Edge of Evolution: The Search for the Limits of Darwinism*. New York: Free Press, 2007.

Bergman, Jerry R. Untitled essay in *In Six Days: Why Fifty Scientists Choose to Believe in Creation*, edited by John F. Ashton. Sydney: New Holland, 1999.

Boslough, John. *Stephen Hawking's Universe*. New York: Avon Books, 1985.

Breggin, Peter R., M.D. and David Cohen, Ph.D. *Your Drug May Be Your Problem: How and Why to Stop Taking Psychiatric Medications*. Cambridge, MA: Perseus, 1999.

Brian, Denis. *Einstein: A Life*. New York: Wiley, 1996.

Brown, Walt. *In the Beginning*, 8th ed. Phoenix, AZ: Center for Scientific Creation, 2008.

Capra, Fritjof. *The Web of Life*. New York: Anchor Books, 1996.

Carrier, Richard. *Sense and Goodness Without God: A Defense of Metaphysical Naturalism*. Bloomington, IN: AuthorHouse, 2005.

Cimbala, John M. Untitled essay in *In Six Days: Why Fifty Scientists Choose to Believe in Creation*, edited by John F. Ashton. Sydney: New Holland, 1999.

Collins, Francis. *The Language of God: A Scientist Presents Evidence for Belief*. New York: Free Press, 2006.

Comte-Sponville, André. *The Little Book of Atheist Spirituality*. New York: Viking Press, 2006.

Corliss, William R., ed. *Stars, Galaxies, Cosmos: A Catalog of Astronomical Anomalies*. Glen Arm, MD: Sourcebook Project, 1987.

Coyne, Jerry A. *Why Evolution Is True*. New York: Viking Press, 2009.

Crick, Francis. *The Astonishing Hypothesis: The Scientific Search for the Soul*. New York: Simon & Schuster, 1994.

Darrall, Nancy M. Untitled essay in *In Six Days: Why Fifty Scientists Choose to Believe in Creation*, edited by John F. Ashton. Sydney: New Holland, 1999.

Darwin, Charles. *The Origin of Species*. New York: Gramercy Books, 1979.

Davies, Paul. *The Edge of Infinity*. New York: Simon & Schuster, 1981.

———. *The Mind of God: The Scientific Basis for a Rational World*. New York: Simon & Schuster, 1993.

Davies, Paul and John Gribbin. *The Matter Myth: Dramatic Discoveries That Challenge Our Understanding of Physical Reality*. New York: Simon & Schuster, 1992.

Dawkins, Richard. *A Devil's Chaplain: Reflections on Hope, Lies, Science, and Love*. New York: Mariner Books, 2004.

———. *The Ancestor's Tale: A Pilgrimage to the Dawn of Evolution*. New York: Mariner Books, 2004.

———. *The Blind Watchmaker: Why the Evidence of Evolution Reveals a Universe Without Design*. New York: W. W. Norton, 1996.

———. *Climbing Mount Improbable*. New York: W. W. Norton, 1996.

———. *The Extended Phenotype: The Long Reach of the Gene*. Oxford: Oxford University Press, 1982.

———. Foreword to the Canto ed. *In The Theory of Evolution*, by John Maynard Smith, xvi. Cambridge: Cambridge University Press, 1993.

———. *The God Delusion*. Boston: Houghton Mifflin, 2006.

———. *The Greatest Show on Earth*. New York: Free Press, 2009.

———. *The Oxford Book of Modern Science Writing*. Oxford: Oxford University Press, 2008.

———. *The Selfish Gene*, 30th Anniversary ed. Oxford: Oxford University Press, 2006.

———. *Unweaving the Rainbow: Science, Delusion and the Appetite for Wonder*. Boston: Houghton Mifflin, 1998.

Dennett, Daniel C. *Breaking the Spell: Religion as a Natural Phenomenon*. New York: Viking Press, 2006.

———. *Consciousness Explained*. New York: Back Bay Books, 1991.

———. *Darwin's Dangerous Idea: Evolution and the Meanings of Life*. New York: Simon & Schuster, 1995.

Denton, Michael. *Evolution: A Theory in Crisis?* Chevy Chase, MD: Adler & Adler, 1986.

Dolphin, Lambert T. *Jesus, Lord of Time and Space*. Green Forest, AR: New Leaf Press, 1988.

D'Souza, Dinesh. *What's So Great About Christianity?* Washington, D.C.: Regnery, 2007.

Eccles, Sir John, and Daniel N. Robinson. *The Wonder of Being Human: Our Brain and Our Mind*. Boston, MA: New Science Library, 1985.

Eddington, A. S. *Science and the Unseen World*. New York: Macmillan, 1929. (Facsimile ed. by Kessinger Publishing.)

Ehrman, Bart D. *God's Problem: How the Bible Fails to Answer Our Most Important Question—Why We Suffer*. New York: HarperOne, 2008.

Flew, Antony, with Roy Varghese. *There Is a God: How the World's Most Notorious Atheist Changed His Mind*. New York: HarperOne, 2007.

Foster, Richard J., ed. *The Renovaré Spiritual Formation Bible*. New Revised Standard Version. San Francisco: HarperSanFrancisco, 2005.

Futuyma, Douglas J. *Science on Trial*. New York: Pantheon Books, 1982.

Gilbert, Martin. *The Holocaust*. New York: Henry Holt, 1985.

Glynn, Patrick. *God the Evidence: The Reconciliation of Faith and Reason in a Postsecular World*. New York: Three Rivers Press, 1999.

Gould, Stephen Jay. *Wonderful Life*. New York: W. W. Norton, 1989.

Greenleaf, Simon. *Testimony of the Evangelists: The Gospels Examined by the Rules of Evidence*. Grand Rapids, MI: Kregel, 1995.

Grocott, Stephen. Untitled essay in *In Six Days: Why Fifty Scientists Choose to Believe in Creation*, edited by John F. Ashton. Sydney: New Holland, 1999.

Haldane, J.B.S. *Possible Worlds*. London: Chatto & Windus, 1927.

Harman, Willis W., and Elisabet Sahtouris. *Biology Revisioned*. Berkeley, CA: North Atlantic Books, 1998.

Harris, Sam. *The End of Faith: Religion, Terror, and the Future of Reason*. New York: W. W. Norton, 2004.

———. *Letter to a Christian Nation*. New York: Alfred Knopf, 2006.

Hawking, Stephen. *A Brief History of Time: From the Big Bang to Black Holes*. New York: Bantam Books, 1988.

————. *Black Holes and Baby Universes and Other Essays.* New York: Bantam Books, 1994.

Heribert-Nilsson, Nils. *Synthetische Artbildung* (Synthetic Speciation). 1953.

Himmelfarb, Gertrude. *Darwin and the Darwinian Revolution.* Garden City, NY: Doubleday, 1959.

Hitchens, Christopher. *God is Not Great: How Religion Poisons Everything.* New York: Hachette Group, USA, 2007.

Humphreys, D. Russell. *Starlight and Time: Solving the Puzzle of Distant Starlight in a Young Universe.* Green Forest, AR: Master Books, 1994.

Hunt, Dave. *In Defense of the Faith.* Bend, OR: The Berean Call, 2009.

————. *Judgment Day! Islam, Israel, and the Nations,* 3rd ed. Bend, OR: The Berean Call, 2006.

————. *Occult Invasion.* Eugene, OR: Harvest House, 2004.

Hunt, Dave, and T. A. McMahon. *America, the Sorcerer's New Apprentice.* Eugene, OR: Harvest House, 1988.

Jastrow, Robert. *God and the Astronomers.* New York: W. W. Norton, 1992.

Jeans, Sir James. *The Mysterious Universe.* Cambridge: Cambridge University Press, 1931.

Jeffreys, Harold. *The Earth: Its Origin, History, and Physical Constitution,* 6th ed. Cambridge: Cambridge University Press, 1976.

Johnson, Phillip E. *Defeating Darwinism by Opening Minds.* Downers Grove, IL: InterVarsity Press, 1997.

————. *Reason in the Balance: The Case Against Naturalism in Science, Law & Education.* Downers Grove, IL: InterVarsity Press, 1998.

Kerkut, Gerald A. *Implications of Evolution.* Oxford: Pergamon Press, 1960.

Lenaire, Gary. *An Infidel Manifesto: Why Sincere Believers Lose Faith.* Baltimore, MD: PublishAmerica, 2006.

Lennox, John C. *God's Undertaker: Has Science Buried God?* Oxford: Lion Hudson, 2007.

LeShan, Lawrence. *The Science of the Paranormal.* Wellingborough, UK: Aquarian Press, 1987.

Lewis, C. S. *God in the Dock.* Grand Rapids, MI: William B. Eerdmans, 1970.

————. *Mere Christianity.* New York: Macmillan, 1952.

————. *The Screwtape Letters.* New York: Macmillan, 1976.

————. *They Asked for a Paper: Papers and Addresses.* London: Geoffrey Bles, 1962.

Martin, Roy C., Jr. *Astronomy On Trial: A Devastating and Complete Repudiation of the Big Bang Fiasco.* New York: University Press of America, 1999.

McGrath, Alister. *Dawkins' God: Genes, Memes, and the Meaning of Life.* Maldon, MA: Blackwell, 2005.

McIntosh, Andrew. Untitled essay in *In Six Days: Why Fifty Scientists Choose to Believe in Creation*, edited by John F. Ashton. Sydney: New Holland, 1999.

Medawar, Peter. *Advice to a Young Scientist*. London: Harper and Row, 1979.

———. *The Limits of Science*. Oxford: Oxford University Press, 1984.

Miller, Kenneth R. *Finding Darwin's God: A Scientist's Search for Common Ground Between God and Evolution*. New York: Harper Perennial, 1999.

Mills, David. *Atheist Universe: The Thinking Person's Answer to Christian Fundamentalism*. Berkeley, CA: Ulysses Press, 2006.

Morison, Frank. *Who Moved the Stone?* Downer's Grove, IL: InterVarsity Press, 1969.

Morris, Henry M. *Men of Science—Men of God*. El Cajon, CA: Master Books, 1988.

———. *That Their Words May Be Used Against Them*. Green Forest, AR: Master Books, 1997.

Oller, J. R., Jr. *Language and Experience: Classic Pragmatism*. University Press of America, 1989.

Paley, William. *Natural Theology: Evidences of the Existence and Attributes of the Deity*. Lincoln Rembrandt. (A facsimile reproduction of the 12th ed.)

Parker, Gary E. *Creation: Facts of Life*. Green Forest, AR: Master Books, 2007.

Patterson, Colin. *Evolution*. London: Routledge & Kegan Paul, 1978.

———. Transcript of Colin Patterson's Presentation at the American Museum of Natural History, New York City, November 5, 1981. Paul A. Nelson, ed. Colorado Springs, CO: Access Research Network, 2000. www.arn.org.

Pearcey, Nancy. *Total Truth: Liberating Christianity From Its Cultural Captivity*. Wheaton, IL: Crossway Books, 2005.

Perloff, James. *Tornado in a Junkyard: The Relentless Myth of Darwinism*. Arlington, MA: Refuge Books, 2000.

Peters, Joan. *From Time Immemorial*. New York: J KAP, 2000.

Pigliucci, Massimo. *Denying Evolution: Creationism, Scientism, and the Nature of Science*. Sunderland, MA: Sinauer Associates, 2002.

Pigliucci, Massimo, and Jonathan Kaplan. *Making Sense of Evolution: The Conceptual Foundations of Evolutionary Biology*. Chicago: University of Chicago Press, 2006.

Planck, Max. "The Mystery of Our Being." In *Quantum Questions*, edited by Ken Wilber. Boston: New Science Library, 1984.

Polanyi, Michael. *Personal Knowledge: Towards a Post-Critical Philosophy*. Chicago: University of Chicago Press, 1974.

Reppert, Victor. *C. S. Lewis's Dangerous Idea: In Defense of the Argument from Reason*. Downers Grove, IL: InterVarsity Press, 2003.

Robertson, David. *The Dawkins Letters: Challenging Atheist Myth*. Fearn, UK: Christian Focus Publications, 2007.

Roszak, Theodore. *Unfinished Animal.* Harper and Row, 1975.

Sagan, Carl. *Cosmos.* New York: Random House, 1980.

Sanford, John C. *Genetic Entropy: The Mystery of the Genome.* Lima, NY: Elim, 2005.

Sarfati, Jonathan. *Refuting Compromise.* Green Forest, AR: Master Books, 2004.

Sartre, Jean-Paul. *Nausea.* Trans. Lloyd Alexander. New York: Directions, 1964.

Schrödinger, Erwin. *What Is Life?* Cambridge: Cambridge University Press, 1967.

Smolin, Lee. *The Life of the Cosmos.* New York: Oxford University Press, 1997.

Smoot, George, and Keay Davidson. *Wrinkles in Time: The Imprint of Creation.* London: Little, Brown, 1993.

Spetner, Lee. *Not by Chance: Shattering the Modern Theory of Evolution.* New York: The Judaica Press, 1997.

Standish, Timothy G. Untitled essay in *In Six Days: Why Fifty Scientists Choose to Believe in Creation,* edited by John F. Ashton. Sydney: New Holland, 1999.

Stanley, Steven M. *Macroevolution: Pattern and Process.* San Francisco: W. H. Freeman, 1979.

Stenger, Victor J. *The Comprehensible Cosmos: Where Do the Laws of Physics Come From?* Amherst, NY: Prometheus Books, 2006.

———. *God, the Failed Hypothesis: How Science Shows That God Does Not Exist.* Amherst, NY: Prometheus Books, 2008.

———. *Has Science Found God? The Latest Results in the Search for Purpose in the Universe.* Amherst, NY: Prometheus Books, 2003.

———. *Not By Design: The Origin of the Universe.* Amherst, NY: Prometheus Books, 1988.

Sullivan, J.W.N. *The Limitations of Science.* New York: Viking Press, 1933.

Sunderland, Luther. *Darwin's Enigma: Ebbing the Tide of Naturalism.* Green Forest AR: Master Books, 1998.

Swinburne, Richard. *Evolution,* 2nd ed. London: Natural History Museum, 1999.

Teilhard de Chardin, Pierre. *How I Believe.* New York: HarperCollins, 1969.

Templeton, Charles. *Farewell to God: My Reasons for Rejecting the Christian Faith.* Toronto: McClelland & Stewart, 1996.

Thomson, Ker C. Untitled essay in *In Six Days: Why Fifty Scientists Choose to Believe in Creation,* edited by John F. Ashton. Sydney: New Holland, 1999.

Tinbergen, Nikolaas. *The Study of Instinct.* New York: Oxford University Press, 1974.

Trefil, James. *The Dark Side of the Universe.* New York: Charles Scribner's Sons, 1988.

Wanser, Keith H. Untitled essay in *In Six Days: Why Fifty Scientists Choose to Believe in Creation,* edited by John F. Ashton. Sydney: New Holland, 1999.

Wells, George Albert. *Did Jesus Exist?* Amherst, NY: Prometheus Books, 1987.

Wilber, Ken, ed. *Quantum Questions: Mystical Writings of the World's Great Physicists.* Boston: New Science Library, 1984.

Wilder-Smith, A. E. *Man's Origin, Man's Destiny: A Critical Survey of the Principles of Evolution and Christianity.* Minneapolis, MN: Bethany House, 1968.

Wilson, E. O. *On Human Nature.* Cambridge, MA: Harvard University Press, 1978.

Yockey, Hubert P. *Information Theory and Molecular Biology.* Cambridge: Cambridge University Press, 1992.

INDEX

C

HITCHENS, CHRISTOPHER—

Christian leaders don't believe in resurrection, claims, 437

confuses Catholicism with Christianity, 440

critique of the Bible, 50, 439, 441-42, 456-57

death ends all, according to, 45-46, 196, 495, 499-501, 522-23

definition of "theory," 448

description of God, 194, 363, 436

Four Horsemen of New Atheists, one of, 41-42, 49, 348, 442, 450, 455, 522

"God-bashing book," 9, 343

God Is Not Great: How Religion Poisons Everything, 93, 136, 147, 436

hatred of God, 93, 194, 363, 407, 427, 435-36, 438-39, 500-501

Hitchens Challenge, the, 49-51, 316

relegates all religions to the same treatment, 436, 440-41, 449-50

religion is manmade, coercive, incoherent, according to, 316, 348, 500-501

science explains everything, according to, 93, 137, 321, 363

unjust for innocent Christ to pay penalty for guilty, according to, 431

HITLER, ADOLF—

anti-Semitic, 474-81, 483, 522

Arabs on his side, 469, 482-83

eugenicist, 519

Germany, 24, 364

Harris's assessment of, 378

Holocaust, the, 474, 480, 484, 498, 519

Mein Kampf, 482

not a victim of his genes, 372

suicide, 196, 522

HOYLE, SIR FRED—

30, 133, 166, 190, 211, 234, 386, 402, 413, 422

HUCKABEE, GOV. MIKE—

315-16

HUMANISM—

10, 271, 276, 318, 344, 428, 497-98

HUMAN LIFE—

atheists' confusion regarding, 26, 202, 359, 519

atheists equate with animal life, 276

God-given, 358-59, 519

value of, 23, 519

HUXLEY, ALDOUS—

"Confessions of a Professed Atheist," 276

HUXLEY, JULIAN—

41, 85

HUXLEY, THOMAS—

207-8

I

"ILLUSION OF DESIGN"—

See under design

J

N

NAHIGIAN, KENNETH—
392-93

NASA—

NATURAL SELECTION—

U